Diaspora and Zionism in Jewish American Literature

Brandeis Series in American Jewish History, Culture, and Life

Jonathan D. Sarna, Editor

Sylvia Barack Fishman, Associate Editor

Leon A. Jick, 1992
The Americanization of the Synagogue, 1820–1870

Sylvia Barack Fishman, editor, 1992
Follow My Footprints: Changing Images of Women in American Jewish Fiction

Gerald Tulchinsky, 1993
Taking Root: The Origins of the Canadian Jewish Community

Shalom Goldman, editor, 1993
Hebrew and the Bible in America: The First Two Centuries

Marshall Sklare, 1993
Observing America's Jews

Reena Sigman Friedman, 1994
These Are Our Children: Jewish Orphanages in the United States, 1880–1925

Alan Silverstein, 1994
Alternatives to Assimilation: The Response of Reform Judaism to American Culture, 1840–1930

Jack Wertheimer, editor, 1995
The American Synagogue: A Sanctuary Transformed

Sylvia Barack Fishman, 1995
A Breath of Life: Feminism in the American Jewish Community

Diane Matza, editor, 1996
Sephardic-American Voices: Two Hundred Years of a Literary Legacy

Joyce Antler, editor, 1997
Talking Back: Images of Jewish Women in American Popular Culture

Jack Wertheimer, 1997
A People Divided: Judaism in Contemporary America

Beth S. Wenger and Jeffrey Shandler, editors, 1998
Encounters with the "Holy Land": Place, Past and Future in American Jewish Culture

David Kaufman, 1998
Shul with a Pool: The "Synagogue-Center" in American Jewish History

Roberta Rosenberg Farber and Chaim I. Waxman, editors, 1999
Jews in America: A Contemporary Reader

Murray Friedman and Albert D. Chernin, editors, 1999
A Second Exodus: The American Movement to Free Soviet Jews

Stephen J. Whitfield, 1999
In Search of American Jewish Culture

Naomi W. Cohen, 1999
Jacob H. Schiff: A Study in American Jewish Leadership

Barbara Kessel, 2000
Suddenly Jewish: Jews Raised as Gentiles

Jonathan N. Barron and Eric Murphy Selinger, editors, 2000
Jewish American Poetry: Poems, Commentary, and Reflections

Steven T. Rosenthal, 2001
Irreconcilable Differences: The Waning of the American Jewish Love Affair with Israel

Pamela S. Nadell and Jonathan D. Sarna, editors, 2001
Women and American Judaism: Historical Perspectives

Annelise Orleck, with photographs by Elizabeth Cooke, 2001
The Soviet Jewish Americans

Ilana Abramovitch and Seán Galvin, editors, 2001
Jews of Brooklyn

Ranen Omer-Sherman, 2002
Diaspora and Zionism in Jewish American Literature: Lazarus, Syrkin, Reznikoff, and Roth

Diaspora and Zionism in Jewish American Literature

Lazarus, Syrkin, Reznikoff, and Roth

Ranen Omer-Sherman

Brandeis University Press
Published by University Press of New England
Hanover and London

Brandeis University Press
Published by University Press of New England, Hanover, NH 03755
© 2002 by Brandeis University Press
Printed in the United States of America
5 4 3 2 1

This book was published with the support of the Koret Foundation.

Library of Congress Cataloging-in-Publication Data

Omer-Sherman, Ranen.
    Diaspora and Zionism in Jewish American literature : Lazarus, Syrkin,
    Reznikoff, and Roth / Ranen Omer-Sherman.
        p.   cm.—(Brandeis series in American Jewish history, culture,
    and life)
        ISBN 1-58465-202-0 (pbk.)—ISBN 1-58465-201-2 (cloth)
        1. Jewish literature—History and criticism. 2. Zionism in
    literature. 3. Jewish diaspora in literature. 4. Lazarus, Emma,
    1849–1887—Criticism and interpretation. 5. Syrkin, Marie,
    1899–1989—Criticism and interpretation. 6. Reznikoff, Charles,
    1894–1976—Criticism and interpretation. 7. Roth, Philip—Criticism
    and interpretation. I. Title. II. Series.
    PN842 .O44 2002
    809'.88924—dc21   2001005972

In warm memory of Yeruham Yarden.

Palestine was a halting place,
One of many. Our kin, the Arabs
Wander over their desert. Our desert
Is the Earth. Our strength
Is that we have no land.
Nineveh and Babylon, our familiar cities,
Become dust; but we Jews have left
for Alexandria and Rome.
When the land is impoverished, as lands become,
The tree dies. Israel is not planted,
Israel is in the wind.

—CHARLES REZNIKOFF

A time must arrive when cultures will have no need of armies to maintain their
uniqueness . . . The Yiddish-speaking Jew, his fear of physical and spiritual
effacement, his desperate effort to sustain the values and the languages of his
history, his struggle for independence and his actual dependence on the good
will of others—this Jew symbolizes to me the whole human species. Man must be
both himself and an integrated part of the whole, loyal to his own home and origin
and deeply cognizant of the origin of others. He must possess both the wisdom
of doubt and the fire of faith. In a world where we are all basically strangers, the
commandment "And thou shalt love the stranger" is not just an altruistic wish
but the very core of our existence.

—ISAAC BASHEVIS SINGER

Contents

Acknowledgments

I first studied Jewish literary modernism and the Objectivist poets with Stephen Fredman, and it is a great pleasure to acknowledge my debt for his invaluable guidance, encouragement, and advice. Like most readers of Charles Reznikoff, I recognize that without Milton Hindus's early commitment to the poet's legacy, we would all be impoverished, and I thank him for his work, which has benefited so many of us. Thanks are due also to Gerry Bruns, Norman Finkelstein, Andrew Furman, Glenn Hendler, Sandra Gustafson, Anita Norich, Alicia Ostriker, and Stephen Whitfield, who read substantial portions or complete drafts of the entire work and made numerous insightful comments. For their incisive comments in the late, critical stages of revision I'm grateful to Emily Budick, Anne Dewey, and Paul Vita. Phyllis Deutsch gave me the benefit of her acumen, experience, and strong commitment to this project; without her guidance it would have been impossible to see this book through its last stages. I wish to thank the editors of *MELUS*, *Modern Jewish Studies*, and *Shofar* for permitting republication of parts of chapters 1, 3, and 4 that appeared in earlier forms that were housed in those journals. I am delighted to express my deepest appreciation to the wonderful staff of the American Jewish Archives, located at Hebrew Union College in Cincinnati, as well as for a fellowship that allowed me to spend a rewarding month of research there in the summer of 1998. The visionary and beneficent Koret Foundation helped pay for publication costs.

In a less tangible way, I am also indebted to the desert landscape and the people of the spectacular Arava desert, especially Kibbutz Yahel, where I began my own search for a sense of Jewish place and where in many ways my heart still resides. Without the early encouragement of Russ McGaughey and other members of the English faculty at Humboldt State University, I would never have set out on this journey. I owe a debt to my University of Notre Dame and University of St. Louis students who participated in my courses in Israeli, Jewish American, and Holocaust literature, for their stimulating responses to many of the ideas presented here. My mother, Betty Sherman, provided good humor and love during some of the most challenging years of my life.

Above all I thank my wife, Gilat Omer, for her intellectual companionship, patience, and numerous sacrifices. My daughter, Kesem, kept me sane during difficult times with her exuberant laughter, bravery, and wisdom. With all my love, I dedicate this book to them.

Diaspora and Zionism in Jewish American Literature

Introduction

Diasporic cultural identity teaches us that cultures are not preserved by
being protected from "mixing" but probably can only continue to exist
as a product of such mixing. Jewishness disrupts the very categories of
identity because it is not national, not genealogical, not religious, but all
of these in dialectical tension with one another. When liberal Arabs and
some Jews claim that the Jews of the Middle East are Arab Jews, we
concur and think that Zionist ideology occludes something very
significant when it seeks to obscure this point.

—Daniel and Jonathan Boyarin, *Diaspora*

I believe in the Diaspora, not only as a fact but a tenet. I'm against Israel
on technical grounds. I'm very disappointed that they decided to become
a nation in my lifetime. I believe in the Diaspora. After all, they *are* the
chosen people. Don't laugh. They really are. But once they've huddled in
one little corner of a desert, they're like anyone else: Frenchies, Italians,
temporal nationalities. Jews have one hope only—to remain a remnant in
the basement of world affairs—no, I mean something else—a splinter in
the toe of civilizations, a victim to aggravate the conscience. . . . I am only
trying to say that they aren't meant for geographies but for history. They
are not supposed to take up space but to continue in time.

—Grace Paley, "The Used-Boy Raiser"

In 1905, eight years "after Dr. Herzl formulated the program of our modern
Zionism," Josephine Lazarus, surviving sister of the poet Emma Lazarus,
sought to prove the logical continuities of her American and Zionist identities, or at least to downplay the differences between them: "In reality, Zionism, like Americanism, is an emancipation, a release from enforced limitation
and legislation: from a narrow, petty, tribal polity of life, whether social or

religious, and from old-world prejudice and caste" ("Zionism and Americanism" 267). Acknowledging the sharp resistance of the vast majority of American Jews to the Zionist platform, Josephine observed that, "Of the one hundred and fifty congregations in this land that comprise the liberal, reformed Jewish element, one hundred and forty-five, it is safe to say are anti-Zionistic both in pulpit and pew." But perhaps against expectations she then proceeded to argue that successful acculturation in America would require closing the distance between Home and Exile. Striving for the greatest gift that the American Jew can offer means not the assimilated ("modernized, occidentalized, liberalized") Judaism of the congregations but rather the authentic Oriental essence that is, she contends, the Jew's eternal nature. Ultimately the Jew belongs "more to the East than to the West." But by Zionism's syncretic consolidation of the Eastern and Western worlds—through "interdependence and interchange of gifts spiritual and material"—the prophetic visions of Amos and Jeremiah would be fulfilled. In terms that bear a striking correspondence to one of the most famous presidential speeches of the mid-century, she argues that, "Like Americanism, Zionism is the democratization of our people, wherein all are made one and equal—all nationalities and all shades of belief. . . . Zionism no longer asks, What has America to give me? But what have I to give to America in return for what she has so generously given me, and what she gives to the world?" (267) Somehow the Jew would achieve an at-homeness in America by reclaiming a distant origin, bridging the old and the new.

Nowhere is the inchoate poetics of the early American Zionist imagination more fully revealed than in these lines:

The West has never originated any great religion. It has only adapted and elaborated theologies and systems of philosophy, fitting or misfitting them to Western forms and purposes. But we Jews still carry in our hearts the divine spark—the day star of the Orient. . . . We still bear in our soul the soul of the desert—the wide, vast spaces, the great silence, the great solitude, the silent watches of the night under the calm, large stars of the East, "the flight of the alone to the Alone." (268)

As this vivid passage suggests, Josephine Lazarus's lyrical romanticism was torn between advocacy for the smooth rationalism of American democracy and for a discourse (that also had enormous appeal for Emerson and others in her day) that proclaimed the dismembered, supernatural "truth" of the Orient, the authority that only antiquity and the essentialized exotic can bestow. Carrying forward the spirit of her sister's Jewish nationalism, Josephine Lazarus avowed that the "gift that America needs" from its Jewish strangers required nothing less than a full commitment to their own immutable spirit, the mystique of the "life-spring of our race" (268). Paradoxically, it seemed that only by thoroughly "Orientalizing" the Jew could Josephine Lazarus remove the taint of European decadence and the stigma of modernity. In doing so, she articulated the eminently confusing terms of difference, territorialism, and assimilation in much the same forms that would trouble Jewish discourse into our time.

This study is devoted to introducing readers to the creative tension between personal and collective myth that has proved so rewarding for the development of Jewish American literature. In doing so I am mindful that, since Josephine Lazarus's time, a seemingly endless variety of poetic and political signifiers has been invoked to describe the experiences of dispossession and movement: border, creolization, transculturation, transnationalism, hybridity, and marginal identities. These spatial/historical paradigms are often at the crux of current cultural debates in much the way that W. E. B. Du Bois's concept of *double consciousness* would once have occupied center stage. At the top of the list ranks *diaspora* (and frequently the somewhat elusive *diasporic*), which is the focus of journals such as *Diaspora* and *Transition* as well as a wide range of academic periodicals that have devoted special issues to the theme.[1] As the editor of the journal *Diaspora* observed in its inaugural issue, "Diasporas are the exemplary communities of the transnational moment." The term has a staggering degree of resonant applications, as exile, displacement, and cultural loss continue to be the norms that most consistently underscore the human condition. According to James Clifford, "diaspora discourse is being widely appropriated. It is loose in the world, for reasons having to do with decolonization, increased immigration, global communications, and transport—a whole range of phenomena that encourage multi-locale attachments, dwelling, and traveling within and across nations" ("Diasporas" 306). A glance at the day's headlines will confirm this. But what is all too often forgotten is that, in one way or another, these conceptual permutations and mutations of diaspora can be traced to a late-nineteenth-century movement among Jewish intellectuals who sought ways to account for the Jews' persistence over the long span of centuries in a variety of lands that were not their homeland.

This dwelling elsewhere was accompanied by a divided consciousness—a messianic projection of Return in response to a present dystopia—and inevitably a marked ambivalence about actual physical return. And without succumbing to cultural chauvinism it is fair to say that Jewish writing is the best place to begin for an authentic reckoning with the literary foundations of the current multicultural preoccupation with the landscape of Diaspora. In considering the position of the contemporary Jewish writer in America, this reality is further complicated by Arnold Eisen's observation that "Jewish culture *there* [Israel] is the conversation in which competing definitions of that culture are acted out in the public sphere, in everyday life, and in the law, whereas in the United States these competing definitions are acted out largely in the *private* sphere—most visibly in books and other productions of high culture" ("In the Wilderness" 36). Hence the Jewish American writer, perhaps unjustly, has a special communal role thrust upon him or her, a condition that sometimes has acute consequences for the reception of the writer's work.

In part, the impetus for this project arose from my realization that, in spite of noteworthy efforts such as Andrew Furman's ground-breaking *Israel Through the Jewish-American Imagination* (1997), Jewish American critics have largely failed, on the whole, to come to terms with the staggering variety of literary riffs on Zionism's and Diaspora's intrinsic roles in the formation of Jewish subjectivity—a struggle of competing representations renewed and intensified in each generation. In another sense, the origins of this book emerge from my interest in the idea of America as a land of possibility that presented itself to Jews in Europe at the very moment that Zionism promoted Palestine as the avenue of redemption: Immigrant writers such as Abraham Cahan and Mary Antin left Eastern Europe for the United States in precisely the years that other Jews (fewer in number) departed for Palestine as pioneer settlers in the wave that has become known as the First Aliyah. Unlike the largely communal experience of previous generations of the Diaspora, the Jewish writers investigated here share a profound interest in the fact that their emancipation resulted from an act of *individual* expression. As Ira Katznelson observes, "emancipation for American Jews took place not by the passage of new laws or the removal of existing legal debilitations, but by crossing a great ocean. Emancipation thus was a self-generated act, individual by individual, family by family" (170). This phenomenon suggests that, besides sharing a common European origin, in the early days the new Jews of America and Palestine alike were linked by a giddy sense of fraught *potential*—a common desire to forget their origins, to break away from the inherent disabilities of the old world. In different ways, the writers presented in this study come to terms with the fact that the dynamic impulse of both groups was a rebellion against Jewish history itself—a history that seemed to connote only the exhausting tropes of exile: expulsions, inquisitions, pogroms, exclusions, powerlessness, wanderings and homelessness.

It has often been noted that the diasporic narrative imagination began with the Babylonian exile of 587 B.C.E., which generated a prayer service that replaced the materialism of the Temple sacrifices with hopes that "offerings of the lips" would "find favor" with God, like the sacrifices on the Temple Mount: "May my prayer be established as fragrant incense before You" (Psalms 141:2). From this moment on—as Torah replaced the terrain of Temple and study replaced sacrifice—language assumed increasing primacy. As hopes for worldly sovereignty and dwelling in one's land proved ephemeral, disenfranchisement opened up a vast space for the Jewish liturgical and literary imagination that still speaks to the staggering variety of global displacements and expulsions that, tragically, have become the common underpinnings of modernity and postmodernity.

The struggle of Jewish writers to express their subjectivity in this space while negotiating with the challenges of both communal identification in America and the beckoning call of Zionism has yielded a conflicted literary identity for which I do not pretend to provide a comprehensive canvas. I intentionally resist making the hubristic claims of writing a study of the "modern Jewish canon." Ruth Wisse's brilliant but flawed study by that title ignores both poetry and Sephardic literature and generally repudiates any writer whose sympathy for deterritorialization or universal justice exceeds the parameters Wisse establishes for Jewish particularity (i.e., liberalism is a dead end if not the ultimate betrayer of the Jew). Both Jewish American literature and Zionist rhetoric have evolved in vast and unwieldy ways that necessarily evoke fierce debates, not always sufficiently nuanced or productive. But I have sought ways to understand both a little better by putting them into conversation in ways that I think truly illuminate the meaning of Jewish American life as understood by some of our most probing writers and poets. This treatment is unavoidably selective rather than exhaustive, a sampling rather than a survey; we will encounter the tips of many icebergs. Nevertheless, engaging with a wide array of periods, authors, and genres, the present work does aspire to illuminate the ways in which American Jews have reexamined their position as Jewish writers in light of Zionist rhetoric and diasporic continuity.

The recent appearance of Wisse's *The Modern Jewish Canon* (2000) added a greater sense of urgency to my hopes to develop a counter-paradigm of a more expansive Jewish American canon by treating undeservedly neglected writers of both sexes. Indeed, Philip Roth is the only popular figure present. And though I am primarily interested in the Jewish American literary response to the twentieth century, I should acknowledge here that the chronological boundaries of this work are fluid. For instance, the nineteenth-century poet Emma Lazarus has emerged as a figure essential to my inquiry into twentieth-century Jewish identities. Her life and work embody the issues of self-representation as well as translation of Jewish alterity that are intrinsic to my study of the formation of contemporary Jewish American identity. Each of the figures investigated here represents the strongest literary link I could find to the ideological debates and creative uncertainties of his or her generation.

One boundary remains fixed. I have chosen to pursue here the issue of Jewish writing as part of a conversation with America. Hence, this study addresses writers whose works are composed in English, not Yiddish (the struggle of Yiddish during the ascendancy of the Zionist worldview warrants volumes) or Hebrew. Though both of these literatures contain numerous imaginative responses of their own to the themes addressed here, after establishing the foundations of Lazarus's configuration of the new Jew, my chapters proceed roughly in step with chronology. Throughout, I have tried to clarify the social and historical conditions that influenced the writers' treatment of the disparate claims of Diaspora and Zionism. Moving between the alarming daily headlines from Israel and this book, it seems to me to be a matter of greater urgency than ever before to draw attention to the Jewish writer's awareness that Zionism has not always dominated the Jewish conversation on identity and that it sometimes competed (and still does) with a number of creative alternatives. Hence, from time to time, I will juxtapose literary analysis with other discourses—cultural critiques of socialism, Jewish nonterritorial nationalism, secular humanism, postmodernism, and religious thought—all of which have had a profound influence on Jewish modernity. Like Zionism, each of these has enriched the writer's struggle to situate Jews in disparate formulations of community, history, and selfhood.

◆

Although I am certainly not the first scholar of Jewish Studies to make such an observation, it bears emphasizing that Zionism itself was a creative response to the nineteenth-century double bind that modernity imposed on European Jews, the peculiar aspects of which Max Nordau described in his speech to the First Zionist Congress:

[The] emancipated Jew in Western Europe has abandoned his specifically Jewish character, yet the nations do not accept him as part of their national communities. He flees from his Jewish fellows, because anti-Semitism has taught him . . . to be contemptuous of them, but his Gentile compatriots repulse him as he attempts to associate with them. He has lost his home in the ghetto, yet the land of his birth is denied to him as his home.[2]

Zionism grew out of the national debates that raged throughout the nineteenth century, particularly in response to the Enlightenment's challenge to the Jews to determine whether they were individuals or a nation. The terms of the Enlightenment could no longer allow for the historical ambiguity that had accompanied the Jews on their wanderings: namely, that they were both a collective entity and individuals searching for autonomy. The early Zionist imagination was fed by a perception of potential exclusions that threatened to rupture the reality of the individual's cultural, intellectual, and economic accomplishments. In other words, the Zionists could no longer tolerate the ambiguity of exile, which in some ways is also the ambiguity of Jewish secular literature. Hence, the Zionist negation of exile, *shelilat-ha-golah*, rapidly became a prominent feature of their rhetoric. It was crucial for the "nation" to overcome the blight of its primitivism by conforming to modernity's embrace of nationhood. Like other European nationalisms (Italians under Garibaldi, Poles under Kosciuszko), it invited Jews to reinvent themselves by means of a nation of their own. There is a distinct, if underexplored kinship between this political feat of self-creation and the literary imagination. Beginning with Emma Lazarus, my study explores the parallels and discontinuities between Zionist rhetoric and the writer's situatedness in his or her culture.[3] As George Steiner argues, "The 'textuality' of the Jewish condition, from the destruction of the Temple to the foundation of the modern state of Israel . . . has been seen by Zionism, as one of tragic impotence" (5). Zionism has no use for the "tensions, the dialectical relations between an unhoused at-homeness in the text," and its lust for "the territorial mystery of the native ground" represents a harsh repudiation of the meaning of Jewish culture for diasporists. From the sacrifice of Isaac to Jacob's wrestling with an angel to Job's suffering, the Hebrew scriptures are preoccupied with struggles over the agony of living in this world, rather than redemption.

Though I alone am responsible for the vision of the Jewish American and Israel nexus articulated in this book, my position continues to be much inspired by Steiner as well as by Daniel Boyarin's cogent argument that Diaspora has been the primary cultural feature of Jewish existence for "more than" two thousand years:

To emphasize the words "more than" is tantamount to declaring that Diaspora is not a condition foisted upon the Jews but a cultural practice, because the myth of the forced Diaspora requires that it begin after the destruction of the Temple, while in fact at the time of the destruction of the Temple, more Jews already lived abroad than "at home." ("Purim and the Cultural Poetics of Judaism" 189)

Like many Israeli Jews who shudder at the bloody toll exacted by the Al-Aqsa Intifada, I find myself deeply attracted to the notion of a diasporic sensibility resistant to the seductions of the state even in antiquity—a skepticism and restlessness that precedes the Jewish assimilation to the state in modernity. Boyarin's spatial/historical model of Jewish dispersal challenges at least two universalizing forms of human community that have proven detrimental to minority populations.[4] In Pauline universalist humanism, a "love" for all humanity exacts a sacrifice of total assimilation/conversion—or sometimes death. On the other hand, in autochthonous nationalism, the collective all too frequently defends its place of origin by excluding those with newer claims of belonging. I claim kin with writer Grace Paley in that my exploration of literary diasporism is inspired by the renunciation of both of these violent forms of universalism and calls for an embrace of the arts of exile, adaptation, and coexistence—a mode of exchange as well as a way of remaining apart—with Others.

Ultimately, my goal in these essays is to bring the products of Jewish American literary creativity into the kind of broad multicultural perspective the Boyarins' sociopolitical work seems to invite.[5] Accordingly, since diasporism presumes "disaggregated" cultural forms that allow for contradictory identities, my anchoring chapter explores the nineteenth-century poet Emma Lazarus's conflicted struggle to take on the daunting post-Enlightenment task of justifying the Jew to America, paying particular attention to the rhetorical role the language of ethnic nationalism performed in that effort. I am reading Lazarus's poetry in relation to a cultural schism; whereas the Jews of Western Europe and the United States, leaned toward a Judaism that was a religion without an explicitly communal identity, the Jews of Eastern Europe leaned toward a distinct notion of peoplehood. Lazarus envisioned Palestine as "a land without people" that waited to be redeemed by "a people without a land." But her outer vision of a dormant people and a dormant landscape, both caught in a kind of suspended animation, owed much to an inner matrix of American scientific, political, and Christian literary discourses centering on Palestine, rather than any tangible Jewish "identity." For Lazarus, the starting point or enduring feature of Jewish identity was *absence*, the loss of an organizing reality. Her conservative verse, conjuring up a Hebraic past that forsakes the woeful present in favor of the ideal or millennial, addresses an America that had created an identity within its own biblical narrative, with its own reference points for events described in the Bible. Lazarus's rhetorical agenda was to show that Jews too were territorially rooted, that they came from a definite landscape that might be reclaimed. In later generations the consolidation of the American Jewish community around the Zionist movement would evolve as a kind of center that long held—though its widening cracks are readily apparent—the increasingly fragmented community together, just as Lazarus intimated it would. As Henry L. Feingold remarks in *Lest Memory Cease*, by the 1930s, Zionism "became a crucial element in a new kind of civil religion for American Jews when the purely religious modality was no longer tenable . . . it is the cement that holds Jews to its corporate memory" (49).

In subsequent chapters, the differences between Jewish American writing and the European Jewish writing that preceded it will emerge as a more substantial concern because of the different political realities that each mirrored. For instance, Marie Syrkin's skeptical poetical and rhetorical gestures owe their allegiance to the European pessimism that shaped Zionism. My analysis pivots on understanding the writer's relation to the paradigms of *wandering*—whether viewed as a disabling humiliation or an enabling blessing. To clarify the nature of this cultural and literary schism, my three chapters on the intellectual lives and poetics of Marie Syrkin and Charles Reznikoff discuss the subject positions that both Zionist and diasporic discourse produce, focusing on the unique concept of history and identity that each presumes. All too often ignored by Jewish literary critics, Reznikoff is America's preeminent English language poet of Diaspora, whose works filled the intellectually influential *Menorah Journal* for three decades. By scrutinizing Reznikoff's prose and verse alongside that of his wife, Syrkin, a famous Zionist activist, prolific essayist, and poet in her own right, we can learn how lived experience pushes against the particulars of literary representation and influences the select transmission of two starkly contrasting versions of Jewish exile.

Syrkin writes in the material world of conquered space and genocide, where the Zionist narrative compels its followers, including poets, to accept one of two alternatives: Either return to history through the recovery of Place and the effective use of force—or face martyrdom. Though both poets are redactors of historical trauma, in the Objectivist poet Charles Reznikoff's competing version of Jewish reality, we will turn to explore a poetry in which Jewish subjectivity is situated in Time, not in subservient relation to place, Zion or otherwise. The formidable assemblage of Syrkin's passionate post-Holocaust ethnocentrism, set against the critical disengagement and universalism raised by Reznikoff's alternative construction of Jewish difference within a cosmopolitan community, produces a fascinating window into the choices Jewish Americans have made. In examining Syrkin's and Reznikoff's equally impassioned but ultimately divergent responses to the Holocaust, to the prospect of a distant homeland, and to the meaning of Jewish allegiance, we can map out an account of the most important contradictions embedded in Jewish American identity and surfaced by Zionism's challenge to the autonomous writer's Jewish identity in the first half of the twentieth century.

Syrkin's and Reznikoff's disparate poetics responded to a debate that struggled to define the nature of Judaism itself. In Germany as well as America, classical Reform had insisted that Judaism was a universalist creed. Others presumed that Judaism's destiny was to enact a parochial version of ethnic nationalism. For the latter group only a pro-Zionist orientation could ensure the survival of the Jewish people. It is useful to consider Syrkin's poetry in the context of a growing American Jewish consensus on the Jewish National Home, which, even before the Holocaust, began to appear as a matter of life and death. From this perspective it is crucial to explore her relation to two paradigms: the growing sense that the Holocaust could be defined as the failure of the Jewish political strategy of accommodation in the Diaspora as a whole; and the perception by Zionists of the imminent demise of American Jewry under the gentler but equally inexorable force of assimilation.

By contrast, I continue to be astounded by Reznikoff as an exemplary representative of an insufficiently understood generation of immigrant Russian Jews, and their children, who, despite fresh memories of European anti-semitism, did not thoughtlessly opt for conventional forms of assimilation that precluded solidarity with other disenfranchised groups. Reznikoff had a particularly keen awareness of the condition of African Americans, who were the subject of both his first published piece of writing and, apparently, his last project. In spite of the fact that he often seems close to constructing a universal allegory of human experience based on Jewish exile, Reznikoff avoids transforming Jewish tradition into a normative model, finding instead ways to affirm the experiences and narratives of a variety of other groups. He is always acutely aware of his own radical freedom of movement in the American city, but perhaps this is because it was the enabling factor that allowed him to observe—and think deeply about—what it meant to be perceived as an existential Other.

Such an identification provides Reznikoff not only with what might be called the long perspective vis-à-vis Jewish history but ultimately with a special openness to the experience of non-Jews. This holds true for neglected aspects of Judaism itself. I invite the reader to join me in considering Rezni-koff's entire oeuvre as a counter-history that speaks urgently to the present moment by protesting both the normative orthodox tradition (he makes frequent allusions to Spinoza and other favorite "heretical" figures, acclaiming idealists while keeping ideologies at bay) and the assimilative tendencies of Zionism. Here I must hasten to add that my reading of both Syrkin and Reznikoff has been greatly elevated by David Bleich's cogent championing of the disruptive capacity of Jewish American poetics over its canonical prose fiction (Yezierska, Bellow, Roth). Whereas the former issues a monolingual "complaint about the struggle" of its assimilationist protagonists, the latter offers us an "authentic celebration of Jewish history, values, experience, language and consciousness . . . voices that are deeper, calmer, more realistic" (179–80).

Different issues move to the forefront of my discussions of Philip Roth's novels in chapters 5 and 6. Here, sadly, the major question is whether the contemporary Jewish novelist has anything left to contribute to the definition of the self in America. It is as though Reznikoff's liberated poetic subject has ground to a halt in a malaise of assimilation. Roth's manifest failure to affirm a conventionally successful diasporic identity invites us to speculate on the reasons for that refusal or inability. Just what accounts for this novelist's radical disavowal of a hospitality quite unparalleled in Jewish history? I propose that, ironically, just as the "secular" poet Reznikoff cleaves to the manifestly theological "doctrine of the saving remnant" during the years that Jews faced physical annihilation, Roth's notoriously slippery narratives (and outrageous protagonists) contend with the insurmountable instability that follows the loss of what I suspect is an even more intrinsic Jewish tradition—the imperative of an "Amalek" in every generation. This chapter engages with several novels that offer Roth's sustained and increasingly melancholic meditations on the fate of Jewish writing (and by extension, Jewish identity) at the apparent end of history's long siege—the end of immigrant struggle and European persecutions alike. My discussion of Roth begins in chapter 5 with a discussion of his surreal juxtapositions of diasporic and Zionist identities (*The Counterlife*, *Operation Shylock*) and concludes in chapter 6 with an analysis of his idiosyncratic narration of the aftermath of the struggle between communal origins and cosmopolitan loyalties and the increasing anachronism of the pariah status, which had sustained Jewish culture (*Sabbath's Theater*, *American Pastoral*, *The Human Stain*). My modest goal here is to offer a new reading of Roth as a writer who, self-consciously poised at the end of immigrant struggle and European persecutions, is persuaded that in his lifetime a previously unimagined Jewish endgame is being played out, with unwelcome and perhaps disastrous consequences already being felt. What will become of Jewish American literature (not to mention belief and practice)—indeed, of the Jewish subject—in an entirely accommodating world? What new meanings will Diaspora accrue?

From time to time I have found it pertinent to emend my literary readings with discussions of a broad range of theorists of diaspora. In addition to the insights of Jewish American intellectuals such as Daniel and Jonathan Boyarin, the non-Jewish anthropologist James Clifford, the Black Atlantic diasporist Paul Gilroy, as well as the Palestinian intellectual Edward Said have also taught me a great deal, no doubt because each of these has readily acknowledged his creative debts to the pioneering intellectual efforts of Jewish diasporists. Taking my cue from Gilroy's *Black Atlantic: Modernity and Double Consciousness*, I hope to enhance the view that understanding how collective identities are formed in the tensions between Homeland and Diaspora is key to understanding contemporary constructions of race and ethnicity in ways that are intrinsic both to Jewish literature and to the American nation as a whole.

The debates about identity formulated by these diasporists are important to me because they speak so revealingly of past, present, and future possibilities, with implications not just for Jewish communities but for us all.[6] As Alan Shapiro argues, "in his homelessness the Jew has always been the most uncomfortable reminder of history itself, of change, of difference, to the pedigree-loving cultures he has moved among. The Jew was the first American long before America existed" (154). In wonderfully diverse ways, the texts that I have been drawn to—Lazarus's pogrom-inspired accounts of Jewish dispossession, Syrkin's poetics of witness, Reznikoff's nuanced mediation of modern homelessness and urban Others via the Jewish tradition of diaspora, and Roth's unsettling dramas of pariahs and passing—have all intimated as much.

◆

Finally, I must hasten to add that I am reading these texts through the prism of my own Israeli and American experiences. In 1975 I immigrated to Israel, served in the IDF, and for many years was a genuine convert to the Zionist notion that Jews could redeem the land and themselves by physical labor and commitment to collective life. After spending most of my early adult life on a newly established desert kibbutz where I milked cows, harvested dates, and led Jewish teenagers from around the world on desert treks, I remained long enough to witness the precipitous decline of kibbutz ideology and the general waning of the pioneer spirit throughout the country. In the seventies, it was not so unusual for starry-eyed idealists like myself to uproot ourselves and devote our lives to farming in the Negev. I am not embarrassed to confess that many of us thought we were doing it for the betterment of humanity, particularly those of us who went selflessly to a life of struggle on pioneer kibbutzim. We arrived in Israel with little conception, if any, of the Palestinians. But today, the escalating marginalization of the kibbutz experiment and the frantic charge toward materialism on the backs of foreign workers are diminishing the institution that made Israel most appealing for young Westerners. Currently, few North Americans make aliya for ideological reasons, and those who do are usually right-wing fundamentalists who go to inhabit land they would appropriate from the Palestinians, while the promise of the Negev remains unfulfilled. After thirteen years, the distance between the Zionist rhetoric that had once swayed me and the reality I lived became too painful to bear. Nonetheless, the final parting was painful, too, and in leaving both the land and a tightly knit community I felt the loss of all my ideals of organic connectedness.

In a vital sense, leaving the kibbutz was a monumental step away from the youthful confidence and ideology that had so easily remapped my own identity, toward an uncertainty that I have never resolved. From the moment I left Israel for a career as a Jewish academic in Catholic and Jesuit institutions abroad, I became aware that Jewish life is filled with exiles within exiles, a perception enhanced by reading and teaching Grace Paley in the United States, and more recently, Judah Halevi in Spain. But the seeds of this project were probably planted in the hilly villages of southern Lebanon, where as a paratrooper I discovered that the "Jewish" state was built on power, not Jewish values, and that its official rabbis were in thrall to statism. It has long seemed to me that these rabbis—in sanctifying soil above human life—are among the most assimilated Jews in our history. The literary works that have interested me ever since have been those that have helped clarify my moral understanding of the misgivings I experienced then and subsequently. So today my interest in the Jewish writer's embrace of diaspora as a condition of his or her very being owes a great debt to the powerful provocation of Reznikoff. The deeply humane vision of this appallingly neglected poet continues to inform my own questioning of the meaning of my experiences as a citizen-soldier in the kibbutz, in Lebanon, in Israel. Reznikoff's dedication to renewing prophetic Judaism's discomfort with the state hastened my own rethinking of the variety of compromises, excesses, and betrayals that have taken a toll on Jewish culture, both in America and the Jewish state.

It is my humble hope that this study, the first of its kind, will open up new conversations in literary, Diaspora, and Israel studies. Much of this book was written against the backdrop of the fatalistic cycle of revenge that every day seems to threaten a full-fledged war. This conflict is being waged between two communities, both of which eminently deserve a homeland free of violence. The Palestinians and Israelis, each rightly persuaded of their own victimhood, are suffering terribly from the violent consequences of traversing Exile and Home. Perhaps it is inevitable that my sense of loss and uncertainty in the wake of that carnage has infiltrated this study. Reflecting a desire to recover a sense of the Jewish moral imagination I undoubtedly share with many Jews in this time of crisis, these essays reveal how, since its origins, Jewish American literature has been a perpetual process of vacillation, indecision, and translation, for which the discursive space of nationalism has often been a primary catalyst.

Chapter One

"Thy People Are My People"

Emma Lazarus, Zion, and Jewish Modernity

in the 1880s

Even in America, presumably the refuge of the oppressed, public opinion has not yet reached that point where it absolves the race from the sin of the individual. Every Jew, however honorable or enlightened, has the humiliating knowledge that his security and reputation are, in a certain sense, bound up with those of the meanest rascal who belongs to his tribe, and who has it in his power to jeopardize the social status of his whole nation. ——Emma Lazarus, *The Poems of Emma Lazarus*

Introduction

There were years when it seemed that the Jewish poet Emma Lazarus (1849–1887) might enter as a full-fledged participant into the elite realm of America's Protestant literary culture.[1] By the late 1870s and 1880s, Browning, Whitman, Henry James, Emerson (the latter two among her many ardent correspondents), and many others had all praised her translations of Heine as well as her own verse that appeared in *Lippincott's* and the *Century*. But she was fated to be memorialized exclusively for "The New Colossus," her great paean to (or plea for) American largesse, and by Jewish Americans for the few years of poetry, essays, and political activity dedicated to their cause.[2] Representative of this trend, Henrietta Szold (1860–1945) would celebrate her as "the most distinguished literary figure produced by American Jewry and possibly the most eminent poet among Jews since Heine and Judah Loeb Gordon."[3] And in the mid-twentieth century a highly regarded Jewish scholar, Solomon Liptzin, helped secure her reputation, claiming that in the

15

crucial years of the late nineteenth century "only a single Jewish writer, the Sephardic poetess Emma Lazarus, succeeded in groping her way during solitary and tragic years from early ignorance and indifference to profound insight and prophetic vision. Phoenix-like, the tired heiress of Colonial Jewry arose resplendent in fresh vigor and heralded a heroic resurgence of her ancient people" (113).

Certainly as far as Jewish women of Szold's generation are concerned, Lazarus demonstrated previously unimagined ways of intervening in American public culture. Nevertheless, her achievements have been largely forgotten; among late-twentieth-century scholars, Lazarus's contribution to Jewish American history has been condescendingly noted at best. Though Lazarus played a significant proto-Zionist role, she is even ignored in major studies of American Zionism.[4] And yet to fully understand the unusual literary and polemical pedigree of American Zionism, one must begin with a careful consideration of Lazarus's assimilationist strategies, and an acknowledgment of her cultural force. By far the most influential Jewish American literary figure of the nineteenth century, Lazarus's reflections on the status of the Jew in gentile society and on the question of the Jews' return to Palestine offer a rich literary and historical context for examining later imaginative responses to the perpetually conflicted nature of Zionism in America. Moreover, if one of the earliest concerns facing the Jewish writer was the problem of how one's Jewishness might be translated from the marginal exotic into the foundation for an American identity, Emma Lazarus must surely be regarded as preeminent among those who took up this challenge.

Such a reappraisal must surely be balanced with a judicious understanding of the poet's Jewish ambivalence. Lazarus's 1871 volume of poetry, *Admetus and Other Poems*, contains no mention of Judaism and sits firmly within traditional western culture, but a volume issued a few years before her death, *Songs of a Semite* (1883), has been embraced as the birth volume of Jewish American poetry.[5] In marked contrast to the poet's earlier silence, it deals *exclusively* with Jewish identity, albeit as a dormant phenomenon situated in the past, awaiting political redemption. What accounts for this transformation? With a great deal of textual justification, Barbara R. Gitenstein argues that "only after George Eliot's 1876 *Daniel Deronda* did Lazarus become a Jewish poet."[6] Taking a cue from Gitenstein's skepticism about earlier arguments for the poet's lifelong commitment to "her people," I will go even further in challenging the notion that Lazarus's belated turn to Judaism constitutes an unqualified conversion, because it is the poet's ambivalence that remains the hallmark of her career—and links her most strongly to the

Jewish American literature of later generations. For ironically, Lazarus, like later American Zionists, drew her ideology and discursive authority from a religious tradition from which she felt radically estranged.

Previous studies have rightly highlighted this poet's success in claiming a privileged cultural position as the reanimator of a tradition and of a people in decline. More recently, feminist critics have rightly claimed Lazarus as a founding Mother of Jewish American literature, unfairly neglected because of gender. This chapter investigates a less discussed dimension of the poet's work—namely, her timely appropriations of Protestant conventions relating to the "Hebrews" and the "Holy Land," as well as Eliot's stirring advocacy of Jewish nationalism. In examining the real meaning of homeland and Diaspora for this poet, we can begin to assess the nature of the strings that tie modern Jewish American writers to Jewish communal identity as well as the true significance of the gap that separates them from it. Lazarus's self-realization, though it involves a repudiation of both Reform Judaism and the old religious rituals of the persecuted Jews arriving from eastern Europe, is marked by becoming newly conscious of what America looks like from the gaze of the Other. For someone who grew up fully assimilated, Lazarus's works exhibit a surprisingly consistent fascination and sympathy for the strangeness and "authenticity" of foreignness. Reading Lazarus as the harbinger of the modern American *ethnic* Jew (and perhaps American ethnic writing as a corpus), one witnesses the competing claims of an insider and an outsider sensibility. Encountering her lyrics today can teach us a great deal about the degree of imagination required in the journey from the humiliation of dispersal to the normative gains of both Jewish and American nationalisms.

◆

Anticipating the cultural strategies of Horace Kallen in a later generation, Lazarus embraced ethnicity, not religion, as the key to Jewish survival. Since her time, this has proven to be the most congenial way for translating the "Jew" into terms that would be palatable in the American milieu. Jewish ethnicity, if it was to have any tangible substance, would necessarily be linked to a concrete discourse of distinct origins and homelands. Hence, Lazarus's prose and lyrics must be understood in relation to the typology of nineteenth-century European nationalist movements, which were committed to physical boundaries and containment as well as her own conflation of "race" with Emersonian organicity and authenticity. The tendency to identify contemporary Jews with popular images of a distant past was made further tempting by a Christian discourse that identified Judaism not with living

Jews but, whenever possible, with a distant time and place—the Holy Land of "Bible days."

To fully understand Lazarus's crucial role in shaping an "American Zionism," it is necessary to consider the ways in which her poetry and prose corresponded to Christian America's increasing interest in Palestine in the late nineteenth century. Her works exhibit a canny awareness of (and ultimately contribute to) her age's dichotomizing tendencies, particularly in contrasting the martial Jew of antiquity to the hopelessly decadent and passive Jew of European culture. This ethos, combined with an awareness of the widely held Christian millennial dreams of a reborn Jewish nation, enabled Lazarus to create a bridge between the mystical, Christian-like Zionism of antebellum America and the practical platform of twentieth-century American Zionism. Lazarus's experience anticipates the writers dealt with in subsequent chapters of this study who, by the middle of the twentieth century, were still beleaguered by the challenge to articulate a hyphenated identity as Americans and ambivalent about what lay on either side of that hyphen. Except for the fact that later generations of poets and novelists would create speakers and characters who would explicitly state this ambivalence, her complex relation to a Jewish nationalist identity greatly resembles much of what was to follow in the twentieth-century war between the Jewish writer and the collective.

"I felt I had won for myself a place": Emerson's Authority and Jewish Literary Ambition

For honor never will be won by the cult of success or fame, by cultivation of one's own self, nor even by personal dignity. From the "disgrace" of being a Jew there is but one escape—to fight for the honor of the Jewish people as a whole. —Hannah Arendt, *The Jew as Pariah*

Two of Lazarus's great-grandfathers were already in this country at the time of the American Revolution. Until the time of her father, Moses Lazarus, generations of his family had been active within the insular social and religious sphere of Shearith Israel, the oldest Jewish congregation in the United States. These earlier Americans had barely been noticeable to the rest of society, though they had followed the Sephardic ritual, observing the laws of Kashrut and the observances prescribed by the Torah.[7] But Emma's father, a well-off sugar refiner, seems to have challenged this religious tradition by striving to integrate his family even more into the cosmopolitan life of New

York City. Like many Sephardic Jews in the nineteenth century, he chose a more assimilationist path, belonging simultaneously to Shearith Israel and to the Knickerbocker Club. In her own words, Lazarus described her house as one of liberal culture, as befitted a member of the old Jewish aristocracy of old New York: "brought up exclusively under American institutions, amid liberal influences, in a society where all differences of race and faith were fused in a refined cosmopolitanism" (*Selections* 80). Poetry was an intrinsic feature of that milieu just as it had been in the Sephardic intermingling with other cultures throughout Spain's Golden Age.

Tutored in German, French, and Italian, Lazarus also had both the appetite and leisure to become intimately familiar with the tradition of English literary verse that was still popular in American letters. In 1867, at the age of seventeen, her first book, containing her translations of Schiller, Dumas, Hugo, and Heine, was printed by her father. Until the late 1870s Lazarus borrowed most of her motifs and narratives from Greek and Germanic mythology and incidents from great periods of Hebraic and Italian culture, inspired by Greek mythology and continental Romanticism. Interestingly, a contemporary reviewer of her translations of Heine's poems and ballads, while admiring her "delicate apprehension" of the German writer's style, pointed out that the body of this work "lacked any statement by a Jew about Heine as a Jew" (Lyons 80).[8]

Her sister Josephine once remarked that Lazarus received no "positive or effective religious training" at home and that "it was only during her childhood and earliest years that she attended the synagogue," later abandoning the "prescribed rites and usages" as a relic of the remote past that had "no bearing on modern life."[9] A hint of Lazarus's alienation from religion may be traced to an exchange during the 1870s, when her family's rabbi, Gustav Gottheil, encouraged her to write verses for a new Reform prayer book. Though she would eventually contribute a few translations of medieval Jewish poetry, she told him that "the more I see of these religious poems, the more I feel that the fervor and enthusiasm requisite to their production are altogether lacking in me" (Harap 289).

Lazarus's resistance to her Jewishness seems even more striking when one considers the most common thread in critical responses by several friendly contemporaries. Interestingly, non-Jewish intellectuals strongly encouraged her to reexamine her Jewish roots. Some time after she had achieved a degree of fame, Edmund C. Stedman reproached her for exhibiting indifference to "her people": "There is a wealth of tradition you are heir to and could use as a source of inspiration." To Stedman she replied only that, though "proud of my wealth and heritage . . . Hebrew ideals do not appeal to me" (Harap 289). In roughly the same period John Burroughs also urged her to reexamine the Hebraic tradition, claiming that all the truly vital literary figures of recent decades, from Carlyle through Whitman, were measurably "Hebraic."[10] From this point on, literary representations of the Jew by contemporary non-Jewish writers would always play a consistent role in Lazarus's revisioning of Jewish identity. As an eighteen-year-old, Lazarus had already emulated the subject (as well as meter and stanzaic structure) of Henry Wadsworth Longfellow's "The Jewish Cemetery at Newport" to produce "In the Jewish Synagogue at Newport" (1867). Like Emerson, Longfellow was concerned less with coming to terms with the reality of the few Jews then living in the United States than with the transmission of a cultural idea of the faded past.

Representing the Jew as part of an exotic, vanished East, Lazarus evades the question of what a distinct Jewish presence in modern America might look like:

> Now as we gaze, in this new world of light
> Upon this relic of the days of old,
> The present vanishes, and tropic bloom
> And Eastern towns and temples we behold.

Nurtured on Byron and Shelley, the young Lazarus embraced the romantic trope of the "ruin." Ironically, though her poetry often seeks out the past for its "vitality," its heavy reliance on death imagery overshadows that intent. The Newport synagogue lyric draws more from the old Romantic awe of mortality than from a living Jewish culture. Thus her earliest poem on an ostensibly "Jewish theme" utterly withholds comment on the future viability of the Jewish people. Juxtaposing the new light of modernity with the Jewish "relic" of the fusty past, the lyric suggests no apparent synthesis. Moreover these lines might be about *any* vanished community, particularly her elegiac lines about "the funeral and the marriage, we know not which is sadder to recall" (*Selections* 32–33). Lazarus returns time after time to this sentimental, ahistorical bent, drawn to what she regards as Judaism's sublime immobility, its quaint priestly garments and Eastern relics:

> No signs of life are here; the very prayers
> Inscribed around are in a language dead;
> The light of the "perpetual lamp" is spent
> That an undying radiance was to shed.
> (*Admetus* 160)

Yet where Longfellow's speaker impassively contemplates the ruin of the Jewish nation, Lazarus hedges just a little. Though "No signs of life are here" and "the very prayers / Inscribed around are in a language dead," the final lines hint of an unexplained mystery of continuity: "the sacred shrine is holy yet." Interestingly, the identities of the poem's speakers are concealed: we are not sure if the observers of this scene are Jews (and if so, just what the poet's relation to the communal "we" might be) or merely the curious drawn to a picturesque spectacle. Yet another Longfellow work would have a lasting influence on Lazarus's Jewish poetics. From its appearance in December 1871, Longfellow's poetic five-act drama, *Judas Maccabeus*, ingratiated itself into the imagination of American Jewry, perhaps because it celebrated a martial victory of the Jews set in the mythic past. As her later works suggest, Lazarus must have been drawn to a number of poignant scenes in the work that evoke the desperation of Jews besieged by Greek culture. But most of all, Lazarus must have been struck by Jason, the high priest who had submitted to the ways of the politically dominant Greek Syrians and who poignantly announces his own downfall, near the end of the play, crying: "I am neither Jew nor Greek but stand between them both, a renegade to each in turn" (Longfellow 4:325).

◆

In spite of her fascination with Longfellow, Lazarus's fullest realization of the alienating dimensions of her heritage was abruptly initiated by another great man of American letters whom she had trusted to welcome her into the American canon. It is impossible to overestimate Lazarus's attraction to Ralph Waldo Emerson, whose approval meant far more to her than that of any rabbi. In 1868, after meeting the Transcendentalist at the home of Samuel Gray Ward, she sent a copy of her first book of poetry to him. Emerson proved an enthusiastic mentor, and the two enjoyed a warm correspondence between 1866 and the year of Emerson's death, 1882, throughout which he encouraged Lazarus to think of him as her guide: "I should like to be appointed your professor" (*Letters to Emma Lazarus* 4).

Lazarus visited him on at least two occasions, in 1876 and 1879, reverentially referring to him in her correspondence to friends as the "Sage of Concord." For years Emerson expressed enthusiasm for her poems, while coaxing her to read more widely (Marcus Antoninus, Tennyson, and Charles Wilkin's recent translation of the "Bhagvat Geeta" were among these) and making suggestions about how to improve her lyrical voice. *Admetus and Other Poems* (1871) was proudly dedicated to "my friend Ralph Waldo

Emerson," and in 1884 Lazarus wrote an affectionate sonnet on the occasion of the opening of the Concord School of Philosophy, where she names Emerson "Master and father" and refers to herself as one of his American literary "children." Reading Emerson's great poem of medieval persecution, "The Rabbi of Bacharach," apparently inspired her own poems on the subject, "Raschi in Prague" (March 25, 1880) and "Death of Raschi" (April 8), both veiled indictments of modern European persecution. After reading her epic *Admetus*, Emerson wrote "You have written a noble poem, which I cannot enough praise" (Rusk 9). The evidence of their early alliance underscores the reasons for Lazarus's deep dismay when *Parnassus* (1874), Emerson's encyclopedic volume of poetry, appeared containing none of the verses he had lavishly praised.

Profoundly hurt, Lazarus immediately wrote Emerson a letter of protest, expressing her extreme disappointment at what appeared to be a public retraction of her mentor's once "extravagant admiration":

May I not now ask which alternation I am to adopt—whether I must believe that a few years which have elapsed since you wrote me these letters have sufficed to make you reverse your opinion of my poems, or whether that opinion was even then ill-considered & expressed in stronger language than your critical judgment warranted? . . . I felt as if I had won for myself by my own efforts a place in any collection of American poets, & I find myself treated with absolute contempt in the very quarter where I had been encouraged to build my fondest hopes. (Vogel 51)

For the first time in what even today reads as a remarkably close correspondence, Emerson chose not to reply.[11] Forsaken by America's great man of letters, she was badly shaken.[12] From this point Lazarus must have intimated that she would always owe her exile from American letters not to gender but to her uncertain American identity.

Like Theodor Herzl (1860–1904), the founder of modern political Zionism, Lazarus had never questioned the natural progress of assimilation and American equality. But Emerson's snub seems to have set in motion a radical reenvisioning of her precarious position in American letters.[13] Lazarus, now thirty-three, no longer presumed that a Sephardic Jewess might join the company of the New England men who had made use of European literary traditions. Until this time her cosmopolitan correspondence had encompassed a transatlantic group of literary luminaries. Now her attention shifted to Jewish and Christian advocates of Jewish nationalism, such as Laurence Oliphant.[14] At the same time she became a startlingly productive poet. In the first fifteen years of her literary career she had produced just two books of verse, a few translations, a novel and a play, but in the monumental year of 1882 she produced nearly as much. In a striking cultural coincidence, Lazarus's marginality was made explicit to her just as the Jews of Eastern Europe unexpectedly began to make their presence felt in America.

"A curiousity, a freak, an archaeological specimen": Emma Lazarus and the Restoration of Jewish Vigor

There is no good reason not to embrace the view posed by the sibling authority of Josephine Lazarus, who argued that Emma "reclaimed" her Jewishness in 1882, for in that year Lazarus's ardent poetry responded to the unsettling phenomenon of thousands of refugees who were crowding toward the borders of Russia and onward to other countries in the West. When the first human cargo of the Jewish migration from Russia arrived in New York in August 1881, Lazarus was there to witness the grotesquely visible, nonassimilated products of *Galut*. By the fall of 1882, she began to take an activist's interest in the east-European immigrants. Besides teaching English to immigrant girls and working as a celebrity volunteer in the Hebrew Emigrant Aid Society, Lazarus often visited Ward's Island, where two hundred and fifty Jewish refugees were held, and was there the day a riot broke out in protest against inadequate food.

To understand Lazarus's dedication to Jewish nationalism, it is worth pausing to examine the immediate consequences of this dispersion. By the late nineteenth century, the Jews of eastern Europe were increasingly impoverished. Ever since the Russian state seized most of the old Kingdom of Poland at the end of the eighteenth century, east-European Jews had faced unprecedented residential restrictions and exclusions from public visibility. The Czarist government created a Pale of Settlement and, throughout the nineteenth century, expelled the Jews from border areas and villages. This was exacerbated soon after the events of March 13, 1881, when Czar Alexander II was killed by bombs thrown by Nihilists. When his son ascended the throne the following day, he immediately blamed the disaster on recent reforms, referring to the Jews. Alexander II had been the only Russian ruler to stand against nullification of the rights of the Jews; six weeks after his death the first pogroms began, devastating the Jewish community of Kiev and other districts. But the effects of powerlessness also engendered a new reality, for the Pale of Settlement rapidly became the home of an enormous Jewish population with a social and economic structure resembling, in many ways, that of a modern nation.

Whether socialist revolutionaries, Zionists, or anti-nationalists, all of the emerging Jewish political movements were forced to grapple with the demographic and social dimensions of this reality. The Jews had always seen themselves as a nation in exile during the period of the Diaspora, but now their new politics began to accommodate the idea that the Jews were a nation in reality and not merely in memory. Strikingly less assimilated and "modern" than their American counterparts, the new exiles aroused anxieties across the spectrum of the established Jewish community. Nineteenth-century Jewish Americans were vexed by the new/old risks of suddenly becoming visible to the surrounding culture.

As an uneasy observer of the Jewish involvement at the 1893 Chicago World's Fair admitted: "We have no doubt, our congresses will be among the best attended by—non-Jews. For, there is no use denying it, for many thousands and thousands of non-Jews, we are a curiousity, a freak, an *archaeological* specimen."[15] It is hardly surprising that the urban, Americanized, and comfortably established Sephardic and German Jews did not always welcome what Lazarus herself calls those who came "blinking forth from the loathsome recesses of the Jewry" of Russia and Poland in the eighties. The majority of American Jews feared that their own reputation would suffer from the popular habit of regarding all Jews as alike. As early as 1872, a popular magazine article by an assimilated German American Jew begged the public not to judge its Jews by the "ignorant . . . bigoted, and vicious" Poles and Russians who clustered around Chatham Street and East Broadway (Higham 126). In reading Lazarus's works, we must keep this cultural tension in mind.

Her first public assessment of this situation was complicated by her obligation to respond to a *Century* article by a Russian writer, Madame Zinaida Alexeievna Ragozin, who justified the Russian pogroms.[16] "Russian Jews and Gentiles, from a Russian Point of View" argues that the violence must be looked at coolly and logically, "from a historical perspective" (Jacob 112). A recent immigrant herself, Ragozin served as the advance agent for an "informed" antisemitic movement. She charged that the Jews were secretly conspiring to engross the entire wealth of her mother country; if people all over the world were turning against the Jews, it was because the Jews waged an interminable war against them. Since the parasitical Jews choked the life out of labor, commerce, and industry, Russia was justified in doing whatever was required to exclude them. Ragozin implied that just as the Jews sought to destroy the Babylonian Empire by inviting the Persians into their country 2,500 years ago, they now conspired with foreign states to destroy Russia. "The Jews are disliked, nay, hated in those parts of East Europe and Russia," she wrote, "not because they believe and pray differently, but because they are a parasitic race who, producing nothing, fasten on the produce and the land and labor and live on it, choking the life out of commerce and industry as sure as the creeper throttles the tree that holds it."[17] And why did the Jews not "manfully" defend themselves when they were attacked? Evidently, the Jews' money was more important to them than their manhood. Ragozin, author of books for juveniles that celebrated "Aryan heroes" such as Roland, contrasts the unmanly, underhanded Jew with "that compound of Grecian refinement and Teutonic manliness which we call modern culture." Obviously, Ragozin's condemnation of Jewish masculinity would require a powerful defense.

Conceding the "extremely medieval aspect" of these charges, the *Century* editor invited Lazarus to reply in the next number. In "Russian Christianity Versus Modern Judaism," her eloquent and spirited rebuttal (encompassing three essays), exhibiting both historical knowledge and exquisite irony, Lazarus "proves" the Jews' loyalty to their host nations by citing biblical injunctions that command fidelity to ruling governments. Interestingly, Lazarus was the first American writer to invoke Heinrich Heine's famous insight into the relation of Jews to their "host" country:

Was it not Heine who said: "Every country has the Jews it deserves"? Mme. Ragozin says the Jews are hated not because of different race, religion, dress, peculiar customs, etc., but because of their "servility, their abjectness, their want of manliness, their failure to stand up for themselves and resent injuries." Any one who aims at being as strictly logical as Mme. Ragozin might know that it is in vain to expect the virtues of freemen from a community of slaves.

Ragozin had insisted that she had no ill will toward well-behaved Jews: it is not the "Jews of the Bible" but the "Jews of the Talmud to whom we object." Arguing from a distinctly Enlightenment perspective, Lazarus apparently concedes Ragozin's point about the "debased" condition of the Jews in Russia. But she is quick to remind her readers that "it is the glory of America that she finds among the Israelites the purest and strongest elements of republican liberty." This statement lends itself just as easily to an effacement of Jewish identity as it does to its validation, but it was also a reminder that, since the Pilgrim founders were spiritual descendants of the biblical Hebrews, almost "crypto-Jews," the Americanization of the modern Jew was almost an organic process. In spite of her rigorous defense on this occasion, Lazarus must have had Ragozin's provocative injunction in mind (that Jews utterly suppress their indecorous religious and cultural life prior to receiving the benefit of citizenship) during the composition of many of her lyrics in this period.

Lazarus's lyrics and polemics show signs of interiorizing the essence of her adversary's charges. Crucial features of Ragozin's attack eventually became part of her own binary articulation of Jewish culture. The problem of the Jews' lost masculinity was particularly at issue.Lazarus's choice of the title "An Epistle to the Hebrews," under which many of her late essays were gathered, reveals her uncertain position in addressing this theme. The inter-textual reference to St. Paul's epistle in the New Testament hints that she too speaks from an alienated position, as an insider-outsider like Paul. Here she expresses anxiety over the pitiful condition of her east-European coreligionists: "We read of the Jews who attempted to rebuild the Temple using the trowel with one hand, while with the other they warded off the blows of the molesting enemy. Where are the warrior-mechanics of today equal to either feat?" Not only do the Jews of the present age fail to measure up to this messianic struggle, but their "body has been starved, and has become emaciated past recognition." The Jewish body is "undeniably stunted and debilitated" (*Selections* 85).[18] Calling for Jewish men to take up labor, particularly agriculture, as opposed to learning, as a means of support, Lazarus delineates them in apologetic terms as "a race of soft-handed, soft-muscled men," insisting that they return to the "avocations of our ancestors in the day when our ancestors were truly great and admirable."[19]

Lazarus's rhetorical strategy was nothing if not ambitious, as she selectively invoked sacred texts, at once to smother Ragozin's slur and to pursue her own assimilationist goals. Since this is an "insider's" address, Lazarus even invokes some familiarity with traditional Jewish legal sources: "The Talmud says: 'Get your living skinning carcasses in the street if you cannot otherwise; and do not say, I am a priest, I am a great man, this work would not fit my dignity'" (*Selections* 83). Lazarus's emphasis on manual labor as the elect path to redeem the Jewish body and provide the masses with the necessary means for participating invisibly in the demanding modern market economy predates that of more famous Zionists. In fact, nearly two decades later Max Nordau's famous paradigm of "muscle Judaism" and "coffeehouse Jews" at the Second Zionist Congress of 1898 formally distinguished between the latter, always pale and stunted, and the former "deep-chested, robust and clear-eyed."[20] In their search for "authenticity," both polemicists bow to anti-semitic stereotypes and to the notion of the Jews as parasitic interlopers in Western culture.

Lazarus soon followed the *Century* essays with the first of her ambitious lyrical attempts to supplant Old World religion with modern nationalism. "In Exile," the most triumphal poem of *Songs of a Semite*, is set within an idyllic return to a masculinized, agrarian folk life. Years before the Zionist congresses would highlight the Jews' return to the body and nature by displaying postcards and posters contrasting virile young farmers in Palestine with old and decrepit Orthodox Jews, Lazarus sought to build a new Jew with muscles. The lyric begins with a few lines from a letter written to Lazarus by a grateful Russian refugee in Texas: "now our life is one unbroken paradise. We live a true brotherly life. Every evening after supper we take a seat under the mighty oak and sing our songs" (*Poems* II, 5). In the poem's penultimate lines, Lazarus imagines the Jewish shtetl dwellers—now "herdsmen tanned . . . with limbs relaxed" in the "sun-bathed" Southern prairie—redeemed by agrarian life.

To a remarkable degree, Lazarus anticipated the utopian self-representation of the early kibbutz movement, particularly the thought of Nachman Syrkin and Ber Borochov. Intellectual luminaries of the east-European Jewish nationalist movement, Syrkin and Borochov felt that the Jewish people suffered internally from an "inverted occupational pyramid," having a "relatively small number of manual workers . . . along with a sizeable lumpenproletariat." This view held that "the Jews in the diaspora had been prevented by antisemitism from joining the ranks of the proletariat, the class of the future" (Reinharz 12). Challenging rabbinical Judaism's opposition to European romantic conventions of martial heroism, Lazarus reconfigures the Jew as thoroughly westernized (and yet bearing the truth of ancient civilization), singing of a mystic symbiosis of Hebraic exile and American democracy that would be

> Freedom to love the law that Moses brought,
>   To sing the songs of David, and to think
> The thoughts Gabirol to Spinoza taught,
>   Freedom to dig the common earth, to drink
> The universal air—for this they sought
>   Refuge o'er wave and continent, to link
> Egypt with Texas in their mystic chain,
> And truth's perpetual lamp forbid to wane.
>
>   (*Poems* II, 5)

This poem's pivotal image of the "perpetual lamp" links it to numerous other lyrical narratives by Lazarus (including *The Dance to Death*, "The Choice," "The Feast of Lights" and "Gifts") that establish the universality, or even the American values, of the essential Jewish consciousness. A later prose poem triumphantly proclaims that the sweating body of the new Jew asserts the success of his Americanization: "The herdsman of Canaan and the seed of Jerusalem's royal shepherd renew their youth amid the pastoral plains of Texas and the golden valleys of the Sierras" (*Poems* II, 64).

Lazarus's ecstatic rubric of settlement forms one of the earliest expressions of what Sidra Ezrahi delineates as "the Jewish idea of place in America, a variation on the American ethos of vastness, of expansive, imaginative spaces and the ever-deferred frontier: the ultimate, detoxified—and eventually, perhaps, self-destructing—expression of *galut*" (*Booking Passage* 29). But at the same time these lyrics seem to withhold something, as if mirroring America's own confusion in relating to itself as the new Zion while becoming increasingly interested in the rebirth of Palestine. Though the Russian Jewish family has left behind the sheltered ignorance of the shtetl to follow the rejuvenating sun to a farm in Texas, it seems likely that Lazarus was already speculating about a return to the desert expanses of Zion.

The manifold instabilities and ambivalences of her late Jewish lyrics—the unprecedented emergence of an "ethnic" voice from the site of "native" American culture—must be read carefully in the context of the alarmingly productive industry of antisemitic rhetoric in the late nineteenth century—particularly in popular representations of the Jew's body (to invoke Sander Gilman's famous phrase)—that accompanied the sudden and unprecedented Jewish immigration to the great urban and commercial centers of the United States. Interestingly, Lazarus's vision of an end to the Jewish pariah is strategically aligned with the romantic conventions embedded in Christian literary culture as she strategically echoes Gray's immensely popular eventide lyric, "Elegy Written in a Country Churchyard":

> Twilight is here, soft breezes bow the grass,
>   Day's sounds of various toil breaks slowly off.
> The yoke-freed oxen low, the patient ass
>   Dips his dry nostril in the cool, deep trough.
> Up from the prairie the tanned herdsmen pass.

The robust human figures are reminiscent of pastoral rustics. But the poem's real hook is that these "tanned herdsmen" of the pastoral lyric are "miraculously" revealed to us as a family of east-European ghetto Jews. Lazarus dwells reverently on their transformed physical health, vigor, and well-being, which have been nurtured by a new landscape, the benevolent "broad prairie." Stumbling into the new Eden, an "unbroken paradise," the new "exiles" are the very model of Lazarus's rehabilitated Jewish body:

> Strange faces theirs, wherethrough the Orient sun
> Gleams from the eye and glows athwart the skin.
> Grave lines of studious thought and purpose run
> From curl-crowned forehead to dark-bearded chin
> In fire and blood through ages on their name,
> Their seal of glory and the Gentiles' shame.
>
> (*Poems* II, 40–41)

This quintessence of manliness now exhibits a classical, almost Grecian physiognomy at home in the pastoral world of the prairie. Like Antaeus in the Greek myth, the Jew's return to the land, whether Zion or the American prairie, instantaneously restores full vigor. Lazarus transfers the Jew's fabled intellect from the stereotypical "coffee-house Jew" into a new robust body.[21] Ironically, much as did the antisemitic tradition she struggled against, Lazarus inscribed an inherent relationship between a healthy public mind and the healthy body. She wants her reader to see that the reconstructed Jew will no longer stand apart from the popular ideology in which the true citizen has a healthy body (itself a sign of mental health) that confirms his ability to be a full-scale citizen.[22]

Lazarus did not advocate "renationalization" or a total "ingathering of the exiles" in precisely the same terms as Theodore Herzl would in the 1890s. She envisioned Zion as a "secure asylum" exclusively for the oppressed east-Europeans. Nevertheless, it is stunning to note the degree to which her rhetoric is consistent with the political Zionism of later years, as her poetry replaces the link to the historical, immediate past with a utopian bond to a distant mythological past, calling upon all Jews to become farmers, masons, and carpenters like the ancients who had rebuilt and defended the Temple. Zion was to be a refuge from the pogromists and, even for the assimilated Jew who chose to remain in *Galut*, a matter of pride. This is a two-pronged struggle, which articulates a response to the prevailing antisemitic rhetoric of her age, and at the same time issues an urgent challenge to her coreligionists. For Lazarus, in the aftermath of centuries of oppression (and perhaps because of the pervasive discourse of Darwinism), the Jewish "race" had lost its pure and heroic state. The German-romantic model of culture that would soon influence Zionism's development, positing an ideal of nation-building founded on homogeneous culture, proved irresistible to the poet. This paradigm of a beleaguered inner essence yearning to burst free is commemorated in "The Banner of the Jew":

> Oh for Jerusalem's trumpet now,
> 　　To blow a blast of shattering power,
> To wake the sleepers high and low,
> 　　And rouse them to the urgent hour!
> No hand for vengeance–but to save,
> A million naked swords should wave.
>
> O deem not dead that martial fire,
> 　　Say not the mystic flame is spent!
> With Moses' law and David's lyre,
> 　　Your ancient strength remains unbent.
> Let but an Ezra rise anew,
> To lift the *Banner of the Jew!*
> 　　　　　　　　　　　　(*Selections* 36)

And yet, the essential terms of Ragozin's calumny continue to provoke Lazarus, for the poem predicates the renaissance of the Jewish "nation" on martial heroism and melodramatic identification with a mythic victory. There is little interest here in traditional Jewish literature where the God-intoxicated prophet, the teacher, and even the law-giver are redemptive archetypes. In various circumstances each of these can redeem the collective, but for Lazarus, conforming to the norms of Western culture, only a hypermasculinity suffices:

> From Mizpeh's mountain-ridge they saw
> 　　Jerusalem's empty streets, her shrine
> Laid waste where Greeks profaned the Law,
> 　　With idol and with pagan sign.
> Mourners in tattered black were there
> With ashes sprinkled on their hair.
>
> Then from the stony peak there rang
> 　　A blast to ope the graves: down poured
> The Maccabean clan, who sang
> 　　Their battle-anthem to the Lord.

Five heroes lead, and following see,
Ten thousand rush to victory!
(*Poems* II, 10–11)

Speculating on a hidden relation between her era's fascination with Darwinian views and Lazarus's contemplation of the Jewish Question, Dan Vogel argues provocatively that, above all else, her critique affirms "that Jews had survived into the nineteenth century *as a species*, not merely as vestiges of a former people; second, they had *developed* over millennia of persecution" (137, emphasis mine). Perhaps. Still, it is evident that Lazarus remained torn between portraying an unchanging nation, whose racial essence was best suited to Palestine, and an adaptive community whose creative responses to persecution showed that they were capable of marvelous transformations. For instance, in a letter to the *American Hebrew* (October 1882), she angrily accuses traditional Jewish charities of perpetuating decadence and passivity; she warns against the dangers of "ignorant . . . short-sighted philanthropy" and demands establishment of technical and industrial education that will build self-esteem and Jewish bodies (*Letters* 103). Consistently returning to this theme of reform, she often invokes the language of Darwin and Spencer, fully aware that she inhabits a world where these men are the preeminent interpreters of reality:

Mr. Spencer and Mr. Darwin, not to cite less authoritative names, have pointed out the positively maleficent effects of ignorant philanthropy, and the portentous evils of that short-sighted charity which neglects to take into account the laws of nature and of natural selection. In justice to future generations, in justice to ourselves, in justice to the objects of our sympathy, we must dispense only those gifts which strengthen the character and the mind, and we must study how best to avoid the rush of enfeebling the race by pauperization, and the artificial preservation of the vicious and the idle. (Young 60)

Lazarus vacillates over the Jews' potential for reinvention. Certainly the discourse of racial inheritance creates numerous contradictions in her account of Jewish identity. On the one hand: "A race whose spiritual and intellectual influence upon the world has been universally accounted second to none, and whose physical constitution has adapted itself to the vicissitudes of every climate, *can be whatever it will*" (*Selections* VI, 35). But elsewhere she hastens to qualify her visionary proposition: "for the mass of semi-Orientals, Kabalists and Chassidim, who constitute the vast majority of East-European Israelites, some more practical measure of reform must be devised than their transportation to a state of society utterly at variance with their time-honored customs and most sacred beliefs" (*Selections* XIV, 77).

Territorialism, always supplemented by a return to agriculture, is her Darwinian remedy for the weak Jews of eastern Europe.[23] The poet seems to find hope in the prospect of "mutation," the future possibility of "reversal" of the centuries of degradation, as well as Spencer's optimistic account of the capacity of modern societies to erase differences, as illustrated by the rapid Americanization of Irish immigrants. The proper environment would allow the natural capacity for change to take its course and any remaining problem of persecution would be resolved when Jews are no longer "an insignificant minority" among the Gentiles, but "a resolute and homogeneous nation" unto itself (*Selections* 82–83).[24] And yet once she had authorized her crusade by invoking the two great men of science, Lazarus's efforts to legitimize her "race" as a homogeneous entity meant also that she must overcome the problem of *difference*, the irrepressible visibility that marked the Jews in a hostile Gentile culture.

Lazarus and the Universal Jew

Though ostensibly marking the Jew as "Other," Lazarus's proto-Zionism must also be understood in its relation to a central principle of the European Enlightenment's universalizing discourse of rationalism, namely that, in spite of atavistic tendencies, human nature embodied an essential oneness.[25] She invoked a race "whose members are unmistakably recognized at a glance, whatever be their color, complexion, costume or language," but in her desire to eradicate difference she called for a "universal religion," repudiating "the whole rotten machinery of ritualism, feasts and fasts, sacrifices, oblations, and empty prayers" (*Selections* 98). This tendency is often apparent in Hermann Cohen's thought and other Jewish thinkers of the nineteenth century. The argument for the universality of ethical values in the Bible often provoked what Ze'ev Levy identifies as the paradoxical realization "that if the 'eternal' values of Judaism have become an integral part of western culture, there is no longer any need to link them to the particular tradition which had been their cradle" ("Tradition" 51). For Lazarus, this interiorized logic means that even though the religious tradition has nourished these values, they need no longer be situated in that tradition. Sweeping away this accumulation of "cobwebs," "rubbish," and "dust," Emma Lazarus urges the revival of a nationalist spirit that would overcome the limitations of religious insularity.

It is important to understand that when the wave of Jewish refugees began to impose itself on her awareness, Lazarus used their experience less as an affirmation of her own Judaism than as a vehicle to illuminate universal ideals of the nation-state. Like Herzl in later years, Lazarus saw the Jewish collective return to a lost sovereignty as deeply rooted in the interests of the family of nations. Accordingly, the most advanced ideals of modern Europe would be realized in the Jewish homeland once the Jews extracted themselves from the traditions of the European Diaspora. Lazarus fully recognized that the high stakes of this discussion rested on whether the Jew could possibly be accommodated to the universality of Enlightenment thought.

An earnest struggle to confirm the "universality" of the Jew's mission is evident in "The Crowing of the Red Cock," a lyric also notable for its immediacy and timeliness in denouncing the Czarist pogroms. Written shortly after her editorial for *Century*, the poem's sentimental piety accompanies a sense of mourning rather than the immediacy of a living connection:

> Where is the Hebrew's fatherland?
> The folk of Christ is sore bestead;
> The Son of Man is bruised and banned,
> Nor finds whereon to lay his head.
> His cup is gall; his meat is tears,
> His passion lasts a thousand years.
>
> Each crime that wakes in man the beast,
> Is visited upon his kind.
> The lust of mobs, the greed of priest,
> The tyranny of kings, combined
> To root his seed from earth again,
> His record is one cry of pain.
>
> *(Poems* II, 3-4)

Besides the "lachrymose" perspective that Lazarus articulates—Jewish history is *Galut*, not "Diaspora"—there is also a hint of the direction she would soon take in "The New Colossus," the fullest expression of her revival of the myth of America as a refuge for the oppressed. Portraying the enemy of the Jew as the enemy of "mankind," or rather *Americans*, singling out the tyrannical figureheads of priest and king from which America differentiates itself, deriving its national legend and universalistic sense of national identity—it is as if she erases Jewish difference. But at the same time, whenever a tension between particularity and assimilation lurks, as in the last stanza, Lazarus enigmatically suggests that the best way for the Jew to overcome antisemitism is through *forgetfulness*:

> Who singly against worlds has fought
> For what? A name he may not breathe,
> For liberty of prayer and thought.
> The angry sword he will not whet,
> His nobler task is—to forget.
>
> (*Poems* II, 3–4)

Two years later she returned to the problem, again opposing active memory and open wounds to the consolations of forgetfulness. The metaphysical meditation entitled "The Choice," first published in the *American Hebrew* and reprinted in *The American Israelite* in 1884, commemorates the recuperation of memory as an explicitly *painful* act of solidarity. One can't help thinking of the poet's own grim awakening:

> Soul, choose thy lot!
> Two paths are offered; that, in velvet-flower,
> Slopes easily to every earthly prize.
> Follow the multitude and bind thine eyes,
> Thou and thy sons' sons shall have peace with power.
> This narrow track skirts the abysmal verge,
> Here shalt thou stumble, totter, weep and bleed,
> All men shall hate and hound thee and thy seed,
> Thy portion be the wound, the stripe, the scourge.
>
> (*Poems* II, 15)

In her zeal to universalize the Jewish religion, Lazarus frequently turned to the figure of Jesus, even making reference in *Epistle to the Hebrews* to the contemporary artist Mark Antolsky, whose *Ecce Homo* portrays Jesus in ancient Hebraic dress, with Semitic features, side curls, and skullcap. Here, as in "Crowing of the Red Cock," Lazarus inaugurated a new symbolism that would attract later generations of Jewish poets.[26] Lazarus's ecumenical fantasy of universal redemption in which the crucifixion emerges as a pivotal symbol anticipates a flurry of similar treatments by early-twentieth-century Yiddishists. For instance, in Sholem Asch's story, "In a Carnival Night" (1909), a sixteenth-century papal procession that includes the beating of eight venerable Jews is disrupted when Jesus climbs down from the cross at St. Peter's Cathedral to join the martyrs below (265). Like Asch, rather than express Christian sorrow or sentimentalism, Lazarus's lyric is militant in tone.

Appropriating the Christological motifs of "wound, stripe and scourge" to convey the present suffering of living Jews is daring enough, but even more innovative is the pre-echo of a familiar trope introduced in the lines that immediately follow:

> But in thy hand I place my lamp for light,
> Thy blood shall be the witness of my Law,
> Choose now for all the ages!
>
> (*Poems* II, 15)

The "lamp for light" would eventually be magnified in her famous sonnet as the "beacon-hand" that "[g]lows world-wide welcome" and illuminates America's ever-hospitable "golden door." Significantly, years before Lazarus linked the Jewish Question to this universal trope of enlightenment, Reform rabbis in America explored similar strategies, already emphasizing Judaism's essential compatibility with the Nation, describing it as a mission with a universal message in their rhetoric. In adapting this subtle symbiosis, Lazarus confirmed her American and Jewish citizenships, anticipating the strained efforts of later Zionist Americans to forge a logical Hebraic/American identity.

Like other gifted sentimental writers, Lazarus had a knack for domesticating alien experience, for creating a sympathetic portrait of the Other. For instance, in "The Eleventh Hour" (1878), originally published in *Scribner's*, Lazarus delineates the alienation of Sergius, a young Romanian artist ("of mixed parentage") who has left his European home for the sake of "American liberty." Interestingly, though his essential foreignness is unmistakable, Sergius's ethnicity and lineage are both as indeterminate and controversial as Jay Gatsby's would be at the peak of American nativism:

The slender stock of actual information which the town possessed in regard to Azoff's history was more than counterbalanced by the variety and extravagance of the versions supplied by the "pipe of rumor, blown by surmises, jealousies, conjectures." He was a noble Polish refugee; a Russian prince in disguise; a dangerous adventurer; he was the disinherited son of a high Russian dignitary, degraded from his native rank in his own aristocratic country by his artist proclivities and bohemian associates; he was a Hungarian nobleman, whose stormy youth had already exhausted a magnificent fortune. . . . (243)

It is as though, in this Whitmanian catalogue of *possible* origins, the stranger's ethnic difference might dissolve away into a universal morass of merging or indistinct identities:

Sergius Azoff was a lucky fellow. It was little more than a year since he had landed, friendless and penniless, in New York, with a barbarous name utterly unfamiliar to American artists and critics; yet already he had taken his place as undisputed master in the instruction of his art, and as the most brilliantly gifted young painter in town. (242)

Beyond its obvious sympathy for the alien artist, who reflects a markedly Emersonian disappointment in America's failure to develop an art that will express its unique self, this narrative expresses manifest approval of the regenerative spirit of the newly arrived expatriate. Eventually, Lazarus would imagine anointing herself as the redeemer-artist who, not in spite of but *through* foreignness and an outsider status, could invigorate America. But as this early example suggests, even if "The Eleventh Hour" exhibits a struggle to authorize "otherness" as a source of national renewal, it is also true that Sergius's ethnic origins are gradually deemphasized in the narrative's celebratory announcement of the birth of the Emersonian ("all-American") artist.

Following her translations of Heine's poems about medieval persecution, she attempted two of her own—"Raschi in Prague" (March 25, 1880) and its sequel "Death of Raschi" (April 8). What is most interesting about the universalist strategies in both lyrics is Lazarus's eagerness to mask the particularity of talmudic culture. Lazarus is so anxious to ennoble the legendary martyr that he emerges as a unidimensional figure, as bland as one of her earlier Teutonic heroes:

> From his clear eye youth flamed magnificent;
> Force masked by grace, moved in his balanced frame;
> An intellectual, virile beauty reigned
> Dominant on domed brow, on fine, firm lips,
> An eagle profile cut in gilded bronze . . .
> Above all beauty of the body and brain
> Shone beauty of a soul benign with love.
>
> (*Poems* II, 26)

In this narrative, Raschi has arrived in Prague, where he is cheered by thousands, just as a pogrom is initiated by advisors to the ruling duke. Brought before the duke and bishop, the sage utters a speech that so spectacularly negates centuries of exilic history that it is reminiscent of Stowe's emancipatory "apology" for black inferiority in the postscript to *Uncle Tom's Cabin*:

> Grace for my tribe! They are what ye have made.
> If any be among them fawning, false
> Insatiable, revengeful, ignorant, mean—
> And there are many such—ask your own hearts
> What virtues ye would yield for planted hate,
> Ribald contempt, forced, menial servitude,
> Slow centuries of vengeance for a crime
> Ye never did commit?
>
> *(Poems* II, 38)

By selecting the subject of martyrdom (which would invite the sympathy of Jews and Christians alike) to represent Jewish suffering, Lazarus once again reveals a sophisticated sense of rhetorical timeliness. On May 25, 1882, she wrote to the editors of the *American Hebrew*, urging them to publish "The Dance to Death," her play of pious martyrdom "*now*, in order to arouse sympathy and to emphasize the cruelty of the injustice done to our unhappy people" (*Letters* 35). In her lyrical response to crisis, Lazarus, like a wide range of later Jewish American poets such as Karl Shapiro, Charles Reznikoff, and Jerome Rothenberg, aspired to form a powerful linkage to an ancient literary tradition whose style could glide fluidly between lamentation and assertion.

As a romantic poet, Lazarus was naturally attracted to the sagas of medieval Judaism, yet as a secular intellectual she abhorred the enduring insularity of old customs, and so she sought to encourage the immigrant Jews to transcend their physical and cultural confines by embracing the ideals of the Enlightenment. But persuading others of the Jews' "universalism" was no easy matter. Thanks to Ragozin and others, the European phrase "Jewish Problem" was rapidly inculcated into American culture. The fact that Lazarus herself refers to the "Jewish Problem" is of some historical interest. This phrase, which was already in vogue among Jews and antisemites alike, would fester as an insidious stain until the time of Hitler. Political theorists employed the term to argue that the Jews were either too capitalistic or too socialistic to assimilate properly and to share the host country's values. But for Jews like Lazarus the "problem" encompassed the Western failure to curb anti-Jewish activities and laws as well as the violent excesses in eastern Europe.

Lazarus used the phrase as the title of a remarkable *Century* essay that challenged the prevailing chauvinism of Christian historians in forceful language. In "The Jewish Problem"(1883) she struggles to disavow the notion of the Jews as "a curious relic of remote antiquity . . . petrified in the midst of advancing civilization" (*Selections* 77). There is a vehement passage in her polemic worth quoting at length:

It is assumed by Christian historians that the Jews, with their inflexible adherence to the Mosaic Code, are, as a people, a curious relic of remote antiquity, a social anachronism, so to speak, petrified in the midst of advancing civilization. This assumption is without foundation; the Jews are, on the contrary, most frequently the pioneers of progress. . . . The modern theory of socialism and humanitarianism, erroneously traced to the New Testament, has its root in the Mosaic Code. . . . [T]he very latest reforms urged by political economists, in view of the misery of the lower classes, are established by the Mosaic Code, which formulated the principle of the rights of labor, denying the right of private property in land, asserting that the corners of the field, the gleanings of the harvest belonged in [Hebraic] *justice*, not in [Christian] *charity*, to the poor and the stranger; and that man owed a duty, not only to all humanity, but even to the beast of the field, and the "ox that treads the corn." (*Selections* 77–78)

Here she is every bit the equal of the philosemite Thorstein Veblen in "The Intellectual Pre-Eminence of Jews in Modern Europe" (1919), where he extols Jewish creativity and iconoclastic thinking. For Lazarus, all truly progressive movements, up to and including Marx's scientific socialism, were based upon the original Hebraic vision. Of equal importance to her claim that the Jews were more "Christian" than their persecutors, is her insistence that Judaism "is at one with the latest doctrines of science" (77). So it seems strange that, as if in counter-argument to her prose works, the lyrical voice concretizes and sustains the Jews' relation to antiquity. The striking parallels between the embedded logic of Lazarus's proto-Zionist lyrics and the newly racist, now genuinely antisemitic, virulence of the 1880s are inescapable. Lazarus and the latter both posit the Jews' immutable characteristics. And yet in the very same essays and poetry, Lazarus manages to hail the "universal Jews" as civilization's innovators and as pioneers of progress and democracy.

◆

Generations of scholars of nascent nationalisms—from Hans Kohn to Boyd Shafer to Eric Hobsbawn—have shown that activists of nineteenth-century political movements unfailingly devoted their energies to the construction of a past, frequently an ancient past, to validate their struggle.[27] Only then could the assimilation of a diverse population be solidified as a monistic identity organized around a territorial ideology. In view of Lazarus's attraction to the ancient Hebrews, her discomfort with the modern Jewish body, her apparent acquiescence to certain antisemitic myths, her rebellion against religion, and her yearning for ancient myths and legends, she deserves to be recognized as a sort of unacknowledged literary foremother to the Zionist "Canaanite" movement ("Young Hebrews"), which notoriously distanced itself from the older generation of European Jews, seeing it as weak and rotting. For Lazarus, the final separation between the body and soul of the Jew had occurred in the year 135, a final "death-struggle" marking the "definite extinction of Israel's national and political life." She refers to Bar Kochba's leadership in the Second Revolt against Rome as embodying "in one last supreme manifestation the martial spirit of his people." Now the Jews are "a dismembered nation." Just as most national movements in the nineteenth century (and certainly Fascism in the early twentieth century) stressed bodily rejuvenation, Lazarus's proto-Zionism was driven by the virile image of ancient culture. In "The Test," the poet "brood[s] upon the Passion of Israel," conjuring up a tableau of proud prophets, poets, and princes: "These I saw . . . the monumental dead and the standard-bearers of the future," only to suffer a rude awakening: "suddenly I heard a burst of mocking laughter, and turning, I beheld the shuffling gait, the ignominious features, the sordid mask of the son of the Ghetto" (*Poems* II, 63).

It is a sign of the heightened anxiety of this period that one public Jew's "universalist" strategy would frequently provoke another to uneasily counter with an even more cautious approach. For example, Abram S. Isaacs, influential editor of *The Jewish Messenger*, reproached Lazarus: "It is unwise to advocate the impression that Jews can never be patriots, but are only Palestinians, Semites, Orientals."[28] Discerning the curious proximity of her plea for Jewish settlement in Palestine and the aims of German antisemites, Isaacs nervously observes that,

It may be strange to Miss Lazarus to learn that . . . the plan she advocates is favored by Stoecker and his followers. At the recent anti-Semitic Congress at Dresden, one of the "planks" in the platform adopted was that the Jews should emigrate from Europe and settle in Palestine. And it is perhaps the mistaken zeal of sincere friends and ardent champions at the eleventh hour, which is intensifying the mischievous and erroneous impression to which the anti-Semites give every currency, that the Jews are but Semites after all, strangers and aliens in Europe and America, patriots only in Palestine.[29]

In her contemporary's plea we see that, in Lazarus's bold articulation of practical and wholly secular goals via mythological argumentation and a romanticized antiquity, contradictions arose between what American Jews hoped to become and the destiny she prescribed for the *Ostjuden* masses.

Emma Lazarus and America's Holy Land Passion

In 1882, the seminal year of pogroms and flight, Samuel Sullivan Cox, member of the House of Representatives, returned from the Holy Land to argue that,

> in the full blaze of history, one cannot help but feel that this is especially the city of the Jews. Christians may fight for and hold its holy places: Moslems may guard from all other eyes the tombs of David and Solomon, the site of the temple on Mount Moriah may be decorated by the mosques of Omar and Aksa; but if ever there was a material object on earth closely allied with a people, it is this city of Jerusalem with the Jews. In all their desolation and wandering, was there ever a race so sensitive as to the city of its heart and devotion? All the resources, native and acquired, of this rare race, including its love of music and domestic devotion, have been called in to summarize and aggrandize the soreness of its weeping and the tearfulness of its anguish over the fate of Jerusalem and the restlessness of its exiles.[30]

These remarks were made at a time of growing confidence among a number of influential Americans that the Jew was destined to return to Palestine. This was an era in which Protestant and Jewish nostalgia for Palestine coexisted, which sometimes meant that Protestant desires for the restoration of Palestine took the form of sympathy for the Jews, and an unspoken messianism that has arguably shaped American foreign policy to this day. Earlier in the century, after hearing of Mordechai Noah's proto-Zionist ambitions, John Quincy Adams wrote him that "I really wish again in Judea an independent nation" (Feingold 1974, 197).[31] For Cox, Adams, and many others, the whole significance of Jewish continuity resided in their relation to a land they no longer inhabited or possessed.

As subsequent chapters will reveal, Jewish poets in modernity struggled to find imaginative ways of secularizing the theological notion of the "saving remnant" that was intrinsic to Jewish textual traditions. But in Lazarus's eagerness to efface the humiliating centuries between Exile and Redemption, she strategically linked her own vision to the Protestant view by adapting a prophetic posture that dismissed the past as a subterranean and dormant condition and looked toward a future of national redemption:

Through cycles of darkness the diamond sleeps in its coal-black prison
Purely incrusted in its scaly casket, the breath-tarnished pearl slumbers in
  mud and ooze
Buried in the bowels of earth, rugged and obscure, lies the ingot of gold
Long hast thou been buried, O Israel, in the bowels of earth
long hast thou slumbered beneath the overwhelming waves
long hast thou slept in the rayless house of darkness."

  ("Treasures" *Poems* II, 60)

In its strategic relation to Cox's remarks, and to other political utterances of the era that had begun to shape America's relationship to Palestine, Lazarus's advocacy of Jewish nationalism was timely. In "The World's Justice" (November 1882), one of her most scathing lyrics, the poet condemns the world's aversion to validating the Jewish nation's revival, presenting the "welcome" news of their endurance in an immensely appealing exclamatory style:

  If the sudden tidings came
    That on some far, foreign coast,
  Buried ages long from fame,
    Had been found a remnant lost
  Of that hoary race who dwelt
    By the Golden Nile divine,
  Spake the Pharaoh's tongue and knelt
    At the moon-crowned Isis' shrine—
  How at the reverend Egypt's feet,
  Pilgrims from all lands would meet!
    (*Poems* II, 16–17)

In its evocative reminder of Egypt's vanquished civilization, the lyric celebrates the phenomenal endurance of the tribe of slaves who have outlived Pharaoh. Lazarus could not have found a more receptive moment to persuade Americans that the Jews' modern exodus warranted their attention. Prior to the poet's years of activism, programs for settlement in the Holy Land had already begun to appeal to a growing number of Jews in the United States.[32] But at the same time, these programs complemented the Christologically millenarian view that posits that the return of the Jews to the Holy Land (and sometimes, but not always, their conversion) will establish God's kingdom on earth. By the time Lazarus entered the scene, a millenarian-fermented century, had produced a variety of texts looking toward the restoration of Palestine, from the intellectualized pilgrimage of Melville's

Clarel to sentimentalized travel narratives. To understand the essential relation of Lazarus's proto-Zionist poetry to her age, the commanding features of this millenarian treatment of Palestine warrant closer attention.

In two classic works on the role of myth in American cultural rhetoric, *The Puritan Origins of the American Self* (1975) and *The American Jeremiad* (1978), Sacvan Bercovitch stresses how the Puritan writers justified their undertaking in America by appropriating Hebraic topoi and Jewish messianism, thus raising America into redemptive history. Two decades earlier, Samuel H. Levine observed how the symbology of early American literary culture had been informed by "the meta-physical transference of Holy Land specifics to New World identities" (62). Both these writers illuminate how, beginning in the Colonial era, Americans sought to understand themselves in relation to the Holy Land in ways that saturated American culture and sometimes obfuscated distances of time, space, and national identity. As Bercovitch notes, one can trace this strained cultural identity to Cotton Mather's exclamation in 1690: "How Goodly are thy Tents, O *New-England*, and thy Tabernacles, O *thou American Israel!*" (Bercovitch 1978, 16). In a similar vein, Moshe Davis points out how the framers of the Declaration of Independence often referred to the Hebrew Bible, particularly the Exodus narrative—in which King George III was Pharaoh and the Atlantic Ocean was the Red Sea—as a living part of their own struggle with reality (*America and the Holy Land* 12).

Prior to the founding of the Republic, the Puritans had defined America as the New Israel and The Promised Land. Most of the dissident Protestant sects that settled in the New World preserved a robust biblical proto-Zionist strain that spatially legitimized their new identities in America.[33] At the same time, the *actual* "Holy Land" remained a dynamic feature of the American religious imagination.[34] The resulting synthesis generated a conceptualization of Palestine that

was highlighted by emphasis on the general, *the religiously poetic past or the religiously visionary and poetic future*, rather than on the present, the specific, the realistic, or the probable future. To such an extent was the Palestine of the Christological metaphor, of the "poetic," a part of American culture and the American mind, that even Emerson, Bryant, and Poe, when mentioning Palestine in their poetry, wrote of it in this fashion. (S. H. Levine 34, emphasis mine)

Lazarus was well aware of this fraught literary milieu as she faced the challenge of reclaiming the landscape and language of the Bible for the success of a new Exodus for contemporary Jews. But her poetic representations of Jewishness so successfully conformed to this past-oriented aesthetics—by situating her verse in the remote past, the ideal, the millennial—that she was never able to respond to Emerson's demand that the "American" poet abandon memory to encompass the real, the observable, the current, and the mundane.

Though Lazarus apparently hoped to sound the opening note to a nationalistic Jewish revival, she knew few Jews and avoided contact with them as individuals, even as she ministered to them as refugees. At the same time that she witnessed the degraded reality of their contemporary condition, Lazarus conjured up a consoling ideal of their past. This paradigm particularly underlies her late poetry, which strives to distract the reader's gaze from the embarrassing spectacle of the modern Jew's audacious encroachment on the American scene. For a time, ancient Israel and, less frequently, the martyrdoms of medieval Europe served as her models, until a utopian nationalism of proto-Zionism began to surface. Reluctantly at times, Lazarus responded to the unalterable fact of her Jewish identity through uneasy layers of sympathy and contempt—sympathy for the victims of pogroms and contempt for Jews who attracted the wrong sort of attention, particularly those who were stubbornly attached to Old World religion.

In her frequent affirmations of the Jewish people's ancient lineage and their explicit relation to a holy space of their own, Lazarus's brilliance as a rhetorical strategist is evident in her acute awareness of her age's dichotomizing impulse to contrast the heroic ancient Jew to the modern.[35] In "Bar Kochba," "Raschi in Prague," "The Banner of the Jew," and other poems, Lazarus's lyrical voice exults over ancient displays of martial courage and heroism. Lazarus recognized that the notion of "Zion" as the embodiment of spiritual, and occasionally political, ideals informs both American and Jewish cultures, providing a cultural designation that might make the "Jew" more palatable to the American public. Her mission to link the present to antiquity was surely given impetus by the fact that the position of "Zion" in the American imagination intensified in the mid-nineteenth century as the technology of photography and new modes of travel brought it closer to the American mind: "From tourism to political activism, from personal memoirs to large public events, from the creation of religious articles to the mass production of Palestine images, Americans fashioned new connections with the Holy Land" (Shandler and Wenger 12). In Lazarus's time, the Middle East became dramatically more accessible via steamship and railway. Soon, American perceptions of the Holy Land were shaped by increasing reports from a wide variety of Christian intrusions, including archaeologists, diplomats, missionaries, colonists, and tourists.

As Lester Vogel observes, "hundreds of popular monographs and periodical articles about the Holy Land were available to American readers, amounting to a huge storehouse of thoughts and descriptions that testified to America's deep-seated interest in the Holy Land" (4). In addition, the authors of literary works on the Holy Land included William Cullen Bryant, John Ross Browne, George William Curtis, John W. De Forest, Herman Melville, John Lloyd Stephens, Bayard Taylor, and Mark Twain.[36] This alien landscape was strangely *familiar* to Americans through attachments formed by textual traditions. As Yehoshua Ben-Arieh argues:

Exploring the Holy Land was unlike the penetration of Africa or the discovery of other unknown regions. *Here, even the unknown was somehow familiar.* The Bible, Josephus, the writings of the church fathers, Crusader chronicles—all seemed to come alive out of the dusty ruins and the forsaken landscape. To this day, archaeological discoveries in Israel have this familiar quality about them. (12, emphasis mine)

At once past-oriented and messianic, Americans renewed a collective Holy Land image as a frame of reference that could provide a receptive stage for the emergence of American Zionism, even in this arguably "pre-political" era of American relations with modern Palestine. In 1890, the American journal *The Missionary Review of the World* reported with millenary fervor that there were twice as many Jews in Palestine as the number who returned from Nebuchadnezzer's Babylonia (Plesur 62).

Not surprisingly, Lazarus recognized that the "Jew" would never be free from the impact of Christian beliefs concerning the restoration of the Holy Land. Moreover, this traditional association could work to the advantage of homeless Jews whose presence bore the stamp of an ancient spiritual heritage. The very fact that a greater number of Americans were exposed to the Holy Land meant that it was coming into sharper focus as a part of America's expansive cultural reality. It is not surprising that a national discourse of this magnitude, encompassing the vast attractions of antiquity, proved irresistible to a young poet eager to channel it into positive images of the Jews. Like prevailing sentiments about the "Holy Land," Lazarus's sympathetic poetic portrayal of invigorated Jews is also a bold attempt to escape from the problematic reality of historical circumstance into a realm of timelessness.

Lazarus was perceptive enough to recognize that the idea of the Holy Land as a place of shared spiritual heritage and cultural authority had been crucial to the struggle of Jews in earlier generations to position themselves in American society; now the urgency of this effort escalated. Instead of an unwanted relic of the past, the Jews somehow had to be seen as the key to future redemption. Above all else, Lazarus sought to convince Americans that their fascination with the appeal of the Holy Land could not be divorced from the plight of the remnant of its original inhabitants. Gradually, Protestant Americans came to see the Jews who lived among them almost exclusively in relation to Palestine. Such associations of Jews with the Holy Land of antiquity and the exotic East caused messy entanglements of religion, race, and nationality, as Jews came to be seen as racialized and immobilized relics of the ancient world. Anticipating later generations who would bolster their standing through vicarious identification with the new tough Jew of Israel, Lazarus saw that the Jews benefited from a distinguished territorial ancestry that might compete more readily with the pedigrees of other American ethnicities. Somehow, she intuited that the peculiar circumstances that had brought about the rediscovery of the land had to set the stage for the rediscovery of the people who were supposed to belong to that land. Appropriating from the typological rhetoric of Puritan culture, she struggled alone toward the first successful literary synthesis of American and Jewish identities.

Lazarus took great pains both to accommodate America's growing fascination with the East and to counter the Christian reclamation of Palestine for its own narratives. In doing so, she (not Bialik) was the first modern poet to inscribe the central features of the ideology Herzl would disseminate: that only in its own territory could Jewish existence prove tenable. Her interest and influence in regard to Jewish colonization in the Holy Land are important features of her published correspondence. In 1882–83 there was a flurry of such activity. Noteworthy in this regard is Lazarus's epistolary relationship with Edwin R. A. Seligman.[37] Seligman's keen advocacy of Jewish colonization seems particularly significant to her because it was his father, Joseph, founder of the banking firm of J. and W. Seligman and Company, who had suffered discrimination in the famous Seligman-Hilton incident in Saratoga, where he was refused rooms at the Grand Union Hotel because he was a Jew.[38] During the years from 1883 to 1885, Lazarus kept Seligman informed about her settlement activities, recounting meetings from which he was occasionally absent:

We agreed that the Re-Colonization of Palestine was the only solution possible of the Jewish Problem of Eastern Europe. And being desirous to extricate our unfortunate co-religionists from their present untenable position, we decided that the first step would be to draw up a Circular stating that "we, the undersigned" have formed an association for the purpose of promoting this project, & that we seek co-operation, aid & advice from the community, Jewish & Christian alike. (Young 202–3)

To secure the support of her non-Jewish friends, Lazarus circulated among them Laurence Oliphant's article the "Jew and the Eastern Question" and *The Land of Gilead*. Her own essay, "The Jewish Question," reveals the impact of Oliphant's territorial rhetoric, his insistence that the "racial" genius of the Jews can reach its potential only on their native soil (*Selections* 99). But Lazarus had other ideas. Anticipating the later platform of the American Zionist leadership, the poet sought to link the spirit of Hebraic messianism to American national identity.

In a brilliant rhetorical move we can see the crucial role Lazarus performed in bridging the gap between the Christian-inspired "Zionism" of the nineteenth-century and the practical political Zionism of Brandeis and Kallen. Her essay idealizing Bar Kochba's revolt against Rome, expresses a thrilling revelation: "In that little Judaic tribe, I see the spiritual fathers of those who braved exile and death for conscience's sake, to found upon the New England rocks, within the Pennsylvania woods, over this immense continent, the Republic of the West" (*Selections* 103). Here she sucessfully reclaims the typology usurped by the Puritans in the shaping of their cultural identity.

This happy confluence of American, Christian, and Hebraic identities achieves particular visiblity in a prose poem written in the year of her death, at the age of thirty-eight. "The Exodus (August 3, 1492)" artfully links the historical expulsion from Spain to redemption in the New World. The lyric opens on a scene of "dusty pilgrims" traversing a hostile landscape. No sooner does the speaker's gaze penetrate the multitude than it uncovers a "youth with Christ-like countenance," who though "his own heart is broken" manages to bring comfort to "father and brother, maiden and wife." As always, Lazarus's mediation between Christian American and Zion-based identities is a predominant feature of her lyric. Not only do the exiles exhibit Puritan-like productivity and agrarian values; their lingering biblical identity is also apparent as the lyric underscores "the grape, the olive, and the fig; the vines they planted, the corn they sowed . . . the altar, the hearth, and the grave of their fathers" (*Poems* II, 59).

With its striking focus on the expulsion from Spain, this late lyric underscores Lazarus's Sephardic awareness of her genealogical relation to exile. Issuing a prophetic call, the poem links Columbus, that "world-unveiling

Genoese"—a foundational figure in America's myth—with the nationless outcasts of Sepharad: "O bird of the air, whisper to the despairing exiles, that to-day, from the many-masted, gayly-bannered port of Palos, sails the world-unveiling Genoese, to unlock the golden gates of sunset and bequeath a Continent to Freedom!" (*Poems* II, 60). As Joseph Lyons suggests, for Lazarus, 1492 "was the stroke by which history had at once cast the Jews out from the best civilization they had known in the Diaspora and also sent forth an explorer to discover a land in which the scattered Jews might finally find a new home" (84). Thus, centuries before its founding, the United States is *already* "Zion," a haven that somehow amends all previous expulsions. This linkage is strengthened in a sonnet of the same period, "1492" (*Poems* II, 22–23), where the "two-faced year" of expulsion from the Old World (of "the children of the prophets of the Lord") yields anchorage in the New World (a "virgin world" that "smiling" says "Ho, all who weary, enter here!" [*sic*]). However, a problem remains. The unintended result of Lazarus's rhetorical subordination of the Jewish historical experience in Diaspora under the American mythic typology is that there is hardly room left for Jews as a living, distinct presence. In other words, Lazarus is still writing for a society that, though willing to embrace the attractive image of itself as asylum, is not quite sure how to accommodate difference. Yet, given most Americans' sentimental associations with the Holy Land, perhaps it was not as difficult as might be imagined for a Jewish woman in the nineteenth century to articulate her mission in ways that might attract Christians who were sympathetic to contributing toward the land's—and her people's—redemption.[39]

"The shadows of their Oriental temperament": Lazarus, *Daniel Deronda*, and "Race"

> Since I began to read and know, I have always longed for some ideal task, in which I might feel myself the heart and brain of a multitude—some social captainship, which *would come to me as a duty, and not be striven for as a personal prize.* You have raised the image of such a task for me— to bind our race together. (Emphasis mine)
>
> —George Eliot, *Daniel Deronda*

There are critics for whom Lazarus's sudden identification as a Jew amounts to an unqualified epiphany, something like a conversion experience. Clearly a confluence of personal and public events produced a shift in Lazarus's earlier indifference. Nevertheless, the poet's ambivalence toward authorizing a separate Jewish identity endured in ways that invite closer scrutiny. The scope of Lazarus's "Jewish" imagination was actually determined by her reading of an English novelist's representation of the Jewish future in Palestine.

Daniel Deronda (1876) is the most startlingly philosemitic text of the nineteenth century. George Eliot's last novel weaves a sympathetic narrative of Jewish emancipation around a Protestant eschatological vision of history. Her Sephardic hero is portrayed as a redeemer, bearing striking resemblance to Renan's 1863 portrayal of Christ.[40] The critical commonplace that Eliot's representations of Jews are "almost entirely approving," even idealizing, has persuaded generations of readers.[41] But Deborah Heller's analysis alerts us to the fact that the English novel actually expresses a profound unease about the Jews. Her nuanced observations are in fact central to my reading of the troubling dimensions of Lazarus's indebtedness to Eliot's crucial influence. Tracing the alarming stereotypes that inform much of the novel, including conventionally cunning Jewish thieves and pawnbrokers who reduce the value of everything to financial terms, Heller cites numerous offensive passages, including Eliot's loaded description of a six-year-old child eager to swap pocket knives with the novel's hero, Daniel: "His small voice was hoarse in its glibness . . . as if it belonged to an aged commercial soul, fatigued with bargaining through many generations" (Heller 37–38). In spite of such passages, the novelist's success in projecting the collectivist-romantic ideal of a Jewish national state into the main currents of Jewish political and cultural discourse cannot be overestimated. *Daniel Deronda* remains one of the indisputable influences on the doctrine that would coalesce in Herzl's *Jewish State* twenty years later.

In thinking about Heller's perspicuous analysis, it has become clear to me why the novel's obsession with unsavory aspects of Jewish particularism and their eventual resolution via a normalizing nationalism was such a powerful influence on Lazarus's thought. The sheer utopianism of the novel's Jewish plot, its Germanic ideal of organic totality, proved irresistible to other early European Zionists such as A. D. Gordon, who quoted from it in his Hebrew polemics. But apart from Lazarus, few contemporary Jews in the West expressed interest in the novel's premises. That fact in itself underscores her radical alienation from her American and English coreligionists. In sharp contrast to its reception among east-European Jews, the novel provoked severe consternation among the cosmopolitan Jewish communities of England and America. Certainly this is due in part to Eliot's relentlessly romantic dichotomizing between noble Jews and Jewesses and their shopkeeping brethren, but undoubtedly these populations were also upset by the novel's strident advocacy of Jewish separatism. When *Daniel Deronda* was written, it was the British government, not the Jewish community, that promoted Jewish settlement in Palestine as the former urgently sought to create a realm of influence in the disintegrating Ottoman Empire. Ironically, as Susan Meyer notes, these proto-Zionists were often antisemites of the "defensive" variety. For instance, Lord Ashley, "the most eminent of the proto-Zionist Evangelicals," had delivered a speech in the House of Commons in 1847 opposing Jewish emancipation and affirming Arnold's perception that "[the Jews] are voluntary strangers here and have no claim to become citizens but by conforming to our own moral law, which is the Gospel" (Meyer 749). This notion of the English Jews' essential apartness may have owed in part to the fact that, like France and Russia, which prudently secured their interests in the Ottoman empire by becoming "protectors" of the Catholic and Greek Christian communities, Britain sought to shelter an indigenous Palestinian community of its own. Thus the necessity for a British consulate in Palestine would be fully justified by extending its presence for the sake of the Jews. Conveniently, Britain's imperial ambitions were zealously supported at this time by its population of Protestant Evangelicals, whose millennialist vision looked toward the return of the Jews to the Holy Land, the requisite conversion of the latter, and the Second Coming.

But in the 1880s British and American Jews alike were still far more concerned with assimilation and securing civil rights at home. For these readers, Eliot's attempts to counter Jewish secularization by recasting the Jew as a separate race held little sway because her novel underscored the Jews' unsuitability for shouldering the burden of modernity. Lazarus would remain the notable exception in the West. As Leonard Stein observes of the English Jews in this period, "the suggestion that they were waiting to go back to Palestine could only embarrass them in their long drawn-out struggle for relief from civil disabilities" (10). I suspect that much the same would hold true in America, which is why Lazarus's impassioned jeremiads initially had more impact on American Gentiles than on Jews. The novel's influence on Lazarus's desire to heal the radical division between the ancient Hebrews and modern Jews cannot be overestimated.

We first encounter Deronda as a youth of indeterminate heritage who, adopted and raised by a wealthy British peer, struggles to discover his authentic identity. After nearly achieving happiness with the novel's Christian heroine, Gwendolen Harleth, Deronda nobly repudiates the rewards of a union that would have elevated him to the highest levels of English society.

Fleeing the taboo of marital miscegenation to pursue his destiny elsewhere, Deronda ultimately rescues a Jewish girl from suicide and discovers Mordechai in London's Jewish neighborhood, a pivotal figure whom Deronda comes to regard as a true prophet of Jewish national redemption. Throughout the novel, this revelation is surprisingly congruent with Lazarus's rhetoric. For, learning from Mordechai the true nature of the messianic Jewish destiny, Deronda too "romanticizes and idealizes the facts of Jewish history . . . measur[ing] every modern Jew as falling short of the heroic Jews of the past," as in the following passage:

> If the scenery of St Mary Axe and Whitechapel were imaginatively transported to the borders of the Rhine at the end of the eleventh century, when in the ears listening for the signals of the Messiah, the Hep! Hep! Hep! of the Crusaders came like the bay of bloodhounds; and in the presence of those devilish missionaries with sword and firebrand the crouching figure of the reviled Jew turned round erect, heroic, flashing with sublime constancy in the face of torture and death—what would the dingy shops and unbeautiful faces signify to the thrill of contemplative emotion? (431)

Like Lazarus, Deronda constantly measures the contemporary Jew—compromised by and contributing to a debased modernity—against the antiquated sublime. Invariably it is the former who is constantly found wanting. For instance, one quaint character who falls under Deronda's gaze is "the most unpoetic Jew he had ever met with in books or life: his phraseology was as little as possible like that of the Old Testament; and no shadow of a Suffering Race distinguished his vulgarity of soul." But his attraction to a more picturesque heritage hastens his determination to restore his people to a political hegemony like other people's.

Not surprisingly, Lazarus read *Daniel Deronda* with enormous enthusiasm for its "intellectually cultured, morally fervid" Jewish hero. But her attention was undoubtedly drawn to a less flamboyant feature of the novel that provides perhaps its most sternly cautionary note. Two critics have recently done much to enrich our perception of Eliot's problematic representation of Leonora Halm-Eberstein, a pivotal but often neglected character. After the death of her Orthodox father, Leonora fled an arranged marriage with her cousin to pursue a glamorous life on the stage as an actress, abandoning her son Daniel to be raised by one of her English admirers. For her callous act, Amanda Anderson describes Leonora as "a willfully cosmopolitan woman" (42). Ragussis goes even further, to suggest that she is represented as "the mother who is seen as squelching his life, in some sense murdering him" (284). It seems clear that Leonora is a surrogate for the larger question posed by "liberating" assimilation and "smothering" Jewish tradition. Like Lazarus (in the latter's early exchange with Rabbi Gottheil), Leonora's encounter with Jewish tradition results in her renouncing much of her heritage. But instead of approving Leonora's feminist disavowal of patriarchy, Eliot apparently associates her with what she calls "the more extreme dangers of modern detachment" (*Daniel Deronda* 52).

It seems worth exploring the likely effects of Eliot's incendiary representation of this culturally opportunistic character on Lazarus's changing awareness of her own ambiguous situation. Speculating on Lazarus's response to the novel's tactics, I am proposing that the poet's earlier repudiations of a fixed Jewish identity and her transatlantic forays into the world of English letters were followed by a crucial later phase—an uncanny "recognition" of herself in Eliot's portrayal of the rootless cosmopolitan. Not unlike Lazarus, Leonora is "a hypermodern subject" whose successful evasion of the inhibitions of her traditional heritage casts her adrift; her sole bond has been with "the transnational force of art" (53). In the wake of Lazarus's disillusionment with Emerson, it seems likely that the novel's language of spiritual missions and organic connections to culture produced a stirring encounter with the limitations of her own detachment from the constraints of the collective.

After years of participating in the modern, autonomous world of American poetics, she had thought to have earned her sense of belonging. But now Emerson's snub, followed by the Jewish exodus from Europe, led to a cathartic resolution, relieving what must have been an incessant crisis of identity. Consider the terms of Leonora's description of her self-emancipation: "I was to care for ever about what Israel had been; and I did not care at all. I cared for the wide world, and all that I could represent in it" (697). Then there is the moment before her death, when Deronda, as the Victorian Moses, overcomes his mother's unburdened cosmopolitanism, sternly instructing Leonora to make her peace with the legitimate claims of the past: "The effects prepared by generations are likely to triumph over a contrivance which would bend them all to the satisfaction of self" (727).

It is to this text's inscribed ethic of care and duty, specifically through Deronda's organic imagery of the deeply rooted ethnic tree, that we can trace the communal mission that would preoccupy Lazarus throughout her remaining years. Particularly if we are to fully understand Lazarus's effort to articulate a collective identity, Mordechai's appealing vision of restoration and wholeness is worth our attention. He conjures up a seductive organicism, ironically expressed in strikingly Emersonian terms: "I believe in a

growth, a passage, and a new unfolding of life whereof the seed is more perfect, more charged with the elements that are pregnant with diviner form"
(585).[42] When considering such seductive rhetoric, it hardly seems strange
that Lazarus learned from a Gentile how to recast the Jews' notorious reputation for insularity and narrowness as a virtue of national identity, in the very
mold of European and American ideals of nationhood. It was a way of no
longer thinking about her unhappy relation to American literary authority.

Eliot's positing of the need for a restoration of an "organic centre" to Jewish life rapidly became the basis for Lazarus's evolving Zionist thought, for
Zionism from its genesis required admitting that the Gentile is essentially
right about the decadent Jew of modernity. This was certainly the case in
Lazarus's response to Ragozin. In adapting Eliot's organicist nationalistic
doctrine, Lazarus anticipated Zionism's eventual subsumption of the individual into the state, as the collective enactment of racial destiny. As Mordechai
argues, fully accepting one's Judaism means to embrace a reified narrative of
nationalism: "Let us . . . choose our full heritage, claim the brotherhood of
our nation, and carry into it a new brotherhood with the nations of the Gentiles" (598). Lazarus agreed. The compelling problem was that, as a "race,"
the Jewish people suffered from a variety of losses but each of these was
invariably linked to the loss of geographical space: "When our race shall have
an organic center, a heart and brain to watch and guide and execute, the outraged Jew shall have a defense in the court of nations, as the outraged Englishman or American" (*Poems* I, 28). In uncritically accepting Eliot's romantic organicist views, and eagerly seizing on her own culture's Holy Land
identifications, Lazarus affirmed the Hegelian notion that the Jewish race displayed a recalcitrant separatist character.

There is a poignant correspondence between her need to derive meaning
from her canonical exclusion—even some sense of renewed purpose—and
the novel's subtext. Deronda, an Englishman descended from Iberian Jews,
cleaves to his oppressed people, rather than rise to his potential station in
English Protestant society. My point is that at the same time that Eliot's
Sephardic hero renounces his cosmopolitan identity and selflessly struggles
to make "them a nation again," he also recovers a *best self.* Deronda's greatest
moment of personal triumph occurs at the moment that he publicly embraces
a collective, Jewish identity. There must have been a considerable source of
identification for Lazarus in the English novel: identifying implicitly with
Deronda, she could simultaneously bid farewell to a form of cultural advantage that was apparently not hers anyway and—like the fictional Sephardi—
claim the role of liberator of her persecuted people.

Still, Lazarus would hardly have embraced what Susan Meyer insightfully exposes as the underlying agenda of *Daniel Deronda*'s proto-Zionism, "through which Eliot simultaneously expunges female impulses to transgress social boundaries and [also] expunges those who penetrate England's national boundaries" (734). Eliot's intention is to remove those "who have strayed and transgressed." And it is true that this is entirely consistent with the logic of most nineteenth-century emancipatory fiction, wherein the ethnic or racial hero seemingly fulfills his destiny by going Home and by aspiring to lead his people back to their geographical origins. Ragussis, too, notices the intolerant substrata of these "liberal" texts, finding a startling similarity in the logic of the nineteenth century's two greatest novels of "emancipation": "Isn't the ending of *Uncle Tom's Cabin* a blueprint for the ending of *Daniel Deronda?*" he asks. "Stowe's novel ends with George Harris, the African American who can pass as a white man, deciding to leave the United States to dedicate himself to the work of his oppressed race, especially in the cause of bestowing on them a national identity" (Ragussis 267). Similarly, the Jewish hero who has "passed" as a Christian Englishman departs England forever, to rekindle his own and his ancestral people's racial identity in their homeland. Eliot's ideology of containment aspires to return the Jews, in the novel's language, "safely to their own borders" and halt the insidious process of Diaspora.

For the historical irony of Eliot's vision is inescapable: at the very moment that the converted Sephardic Jew Disraeli attains leadership of Protestant England, Eliot's novel features a converted and assimilated Jew who elects to depart from England for the sake of his "authentic" community. It is true that in foregrounding the oppressions that promote this separatism, Eliot appears friendly to the Jewish cause. But at the same time the Englishwoman is in deadly earnest that all true nations must defend themselves against the subversions of alien blood: "It is a calamity to the English, as to any other great historic people, to undergo a premature fusion with immigrants of alien blood; that its distinctive national characteristics should be in danger of obliteration by the predominating qualities of foreign settlers. . . . I am all ready to unite in groaning over the threatening danger" (*Theophrastus Such* 158).

On the surface it is not readily apparent that Eliot really desires to exile the alien Jews. She wants to "improve" them and transfer "their incommodious energies into beneficent channels" (163). But this is a final solution that rids the West of Jewish otherness. After all, "Improvement" requires renationalization, a process that might be a transcendent, cleansing experience in spite of the fact that it ran counter to assimilative desires. The pre-Herzlian

Zionism that Lazarus found in the pages of this English novel is, in effect, the combined product of antisemitism, British imperial self-interest, and Evangelical dreams.

Notwithstanding the novel's seeming repudiation of a permanent Jewish Diaspora in Western culture, Eliot's interest in the political restoration of the Jews in a Palestinian commonwealth would surface as the crucial legitimizing referent of Lazarus's argument a few years after the novel's publication, in her own treatment of "The Jewish Problem" (1883):

The idea formulated by George Eliot has already sunk into the minds of many Jewish enthusiasts, and it germinates with miraculous rapidity. "The idea that I am possessed with," says Deronda, "is that of restoring a political existence to my people; making them a nation again, giving them a national centre, such as the English have, though they, too, are scattered over the face of the globe. That is a task which presents itself to me as a duty. . . . I am resolved to devote my life to it. *At the least, I may awaken a movement in other minds such as has been awakened in my own.*" Could the noble prophetess who wrote the above words have lived but till to-day to see the ever-increasing necessity of adopting her inspired counsel . . . she would have been herself astonished at the flame enkindled by her seed of fire. (*Poems* I, 27–28)

It is clear that Lazarus does not suspect even a latent antisemitism. She is all too prepared to greet Eliot as a sister-prophetess, whose vision for the beleaguered Jews is solely altruistic.[43] But in spite of her estrangement, Jewish restoration in Palestine held little promise for rewarding those, like Lazarus, for whom art or an autonomous literary existence might matter. Hence, in Lazarus's imagination it is not so much the Americanized Jew who must be banished to the place from which he has strayed but rather the visible and noxious "Talmudic" Judaism of the immigrants. Still, it is not difficult to surmise that the English novelist affords the Jewish poet what might be called a voyage of self-discovery. As in her own case, Deronda's highly cultivated cosmopolitanism inhibits his own identification with the insular confines of tradition, even as he yearns to, if not truly "belong," then at least intervene on behalf of an "authentic" community. Just as Deronda yearns for an epic contingency that will make him an "organic part" of collective life instead of the luftmensch that he is: "roaming . . . like a yearning, disembodied spirit, stirred with vague social passion, but without fixed local habitation to make fellowship real," Lazarus discovers her own fierce instincts toward peoplehood. By the early eighties a complex web of circumstances—Emerson's rejection, the pogroms, and the flow of refugees—did provide her with the motivating force.

◆

Where does this leave us? Should we conclude that, in appropriating much of Eliot's cultural logic, Lazarus's poetry succeeds only in repeating Eliot's aesthetics of expulsion on American soil? I think that this is unlikely. For at the same time that Lazarus surrenders something to Eliot's yoke of organic mystification, Eliot's narrative does not wholly persuade her, does not entirely remove the schism that had earlier existed between her and Judaism itself. In the end, it is telling that Lazarus hesitated, not as eager as Eliot to divorce the Jew from the West, not fully translating the novelist's vision into an American milieu. Whereas in *Daniel Deronda*, the possibility of reconciling the modern Jew with English society is rejected, Lazarus, who anticipates so much of what was to follow in the Zionist movement, looked toward a future America-Palestine nexus.

The poet imagined that each Jewish civilization, one embedded in the East and the other in the West, would participate in a constant interchange with their surrounding cultures. Though Eliot was a dominant cultural influence, there are signs that Lazarus struggled to advance a more radically ambivalent, less coherent account of the Jewish cultural-national entity of the future. And yet she was clearly torn between articulating a cosmopolitan, modernist conception of Judaism and adopting Eliot's tendency to relegate Judaism to the place of time-bound tradition. Like so many Jewish American writers in the twentieth century, she struggled toward what might be called a reflective distance, a cool removal from the constraints of strict cultural identification, which is the destiny prescribed by *Daniel Deronda*. Lazarus's alienation from the communal suggests the need to situate her much more carefully in the later canon of the famously skeptical Jewish American writing from which she has all too often been excluded.

In Lazarus's exposure to the enigmatic figure of Deronda, she discovered a hero who could make full use of ethnic nationalism to affirm an intellectual position similar to her own: "Our fathers themselves changed the horizon of their belief and learned of other races. But I think I can maintain my grandfather's notion of separateness with communication" (*Daniel Deronda* 792). The spirit of Deronda's intellectual orientation evokes the twentieth-century identities of the Jewish intellectuals in America who, while resisting "full submission," would crave to situate themselves in some dynamic relation with the past. Like Eliot's Deronda, Lazarus aligned herself with a notion of "heritage"—but only through the critical questioning intrinsic to cosmopolitan disengagement. As we will see in our investigation of later writers, the very fact of one's own subjectivity undermines the totalizing work of the universal. Ultimately, Lazarus's cosmopolitan imagination exceeds the English novelist's because she envisaged *two* centers of Jewish continuity: Zion and America.

"Two Divided Streams": Lazarus and Jewish American Identity

Significantly, in her very last years, when Lazarus was writing more and more self-consciously as a Jew, she was simultaneously more resolute in her *American* identity. For example, the lyric "How Long" (*Poems* I, 54), which issues a call for a "yet unheard of strain" that will celebrate America's wild prairies, plains, and mountains, situates Lazarus in an obvious way among those nineteenth-century American writers who were demanding a "native" literature liberated from British forms. And within 1881–82 there came a rapid succession of essays that addressed the requirements of a national culture. "American Literature," an Emersonian defense against the charge that America had no literary tradition of its own, was followed by "Henry Wadsworth Longfellow" and her eulogy, "Emerson's Personality," which were published just a few short months after the parochial "Russian Christianity vs. Modern Judaism."

In the end, unlike Eliot's Leonora Halm-Eberstein, Lazarus's proto-Zionism would fail to resolve her own conflicting yearnings for universalism and nationalism, cosmopolitanism and tribalism. Much like Brandeis and later generations of American Zionists, Lazarus refused to relinquish her claim on America: "There is not the slightest necessity for an American Jew, the free citizen of a republic, to rest his hopes upon the foundation of any other nationality" (*Epistle to the Hebrews* 41). This insinuates that there were two complementary, not competing, Zions. Her restoration program was simply not intended for American Jews, for "wherever we are free, we are at home" (*Selections* 72), but rather for unassimilable Others, for whose sake she struggled to establish the short-lived "Society for the Improvement and Colonization of East-European Jews."

Lazarus's literary inspiration, George Eliot's *Daniel Deronda*, measured the decadent Jew of modernity against utopian accounts of the heroic Hebrews of antiquity. Similarly, Lazarus's own lyrical treatments of the legend of Bar Kochba and other heroic Jews of antiquity strain against a culture that was saturated by negative images of them. In this regard it is worth remembering, as Sander Gilman has cogently illustrated, that the internalization of negative images can lead to anxiety or even self-hatred, but also to productive strategies of resistance. Lazarus exhibits both these behaviors in her brief career. In acknowledging this we should not underestimate the magnitude of the challenge she took up—to effectively recast the image of ghetto dwellers from the status of *pariah* to the living embodiment of America's universal ideals.

For example, nowhere is the tug-of-war between Lazarus's assimilationist desires and her group loyalty more apparent than in her ambivalent discussion of Disraeli in her essay "Was the Earl of Beaconsfield a Representative Jew?" (1882). Lazarus notes that Disraeli's famous egoism could be traced to his embrace of Sephardic ancestry: "There can be no doubt that a spark of fiery Castilian pride was transmitted, unstifled by intervening ages of oppression to [his] spirit. He knew himself to be the descendant, not of pariahs and pawnbrokers, but of princes, prophets, statesmen, poets and philosophers" (*Selections* 69). Lazarus's fascination with the visibility of the Jewish body is evident here: Disraeli's "peculiar manner and outlandish costume," she notes, were an idiosyncrasy that was "something deeper than the so-called Oriental love of show." But she is clearly attracted to the performative aspect of his identity: "it is probable that the wily diplomat adopted it deliberately as a conspicuous mark for the shafts of scorn." The earl's boundary-transgressing persona is clearly attractive to her, as is the fact that, though baptized a Christian, he boasted of his Jewish *racial* inheritance. This evocative response to Disraeli seems to encode Lazarus's own conflicted feelings about modernity and Jewishness.

Lazarus's discussion is indebted to her favorite social thinkers, Arnold and Emerson. Her strategy in viewing Disraeli as a consummately "representative" Jew immediately brings to mind Emerson's *Representative Men* (1850), which elaborates a theory of cultural representativeness that accounts for the unique national traits of literary figures as diverse as Shakespeare, Napoleon, and Goethe. And Arnold, in his work on Celtic literature (not to mention his famous distinction between Hellenism and Hebraism), had helped popularize the tendency to distinguish between ethnic groupings on the permanent basis of "racial" characteristics.[44] Like Arnold, Lazarus's representation of ancestry is complicated; she emphatically notes that the Sephardic Disraeli is not the descendant of ghetto "pariahs and pawnbrokers" but rather of "princes, statesmen, poets and philosophers."[45]

Lazarus discovered imaginative ways to portray the dilemma of the struggling newcomers with sympathy, albeit through rigidly assimilationist, universalist strategies. These condescending strategies are visible in Lazarus's famous "The New Colossus," which was commissioned in 1883 to aid a fund then being raised to furnish the pedestal for the huge statue that the French people were preparing as a centennial gift to America. Certain intimations of the great sonnet appeared earlier in a much different, more distinctly ethnic mode in the prose-poem "Currents":

From the far Caucasian steppes, from the squalid ghettos of Europe, from Odessa and Bucharest, from Kief, and Ekaterinoslav, Hark to the cry of the exiles of Babylon, the voice of Rachel mourning for her children, of Israel lamenting for Zion. And lo, like a turbid stream, the long-pent flood bursts the dykes of oppression and rushes hitherward. Unto her ample breast, the generous mother of nations welcomes them. (*Poems* II, 63)

Read alongside the sonnet, this palimpsest of America's most famous public lyric, reveals that Lazarus found a way to transform the diasporic experience of a particular wave of Russian Jews into the definitive representation of America's universal meaning.[46] Like Heine, she had dallied with the oppositional tension between "Hebraism" and "Hellenism" in earlier lyrics, but here, in what amounts to one of the most "public" American poems of the nineteenth century, Lazarus triumphantly links America to the former and Europe to the latter—to justify the Jewish immigrants' dream of "home-coming." The original name of the statue was "Liberty Enlightening the World," but Lazarus ingeniously transforms the French gift's rhetorical and symbolic function from that of a passive, austere symbol to a mission of active intervention on behalf of the oppressed in her image of the "Mother of Exiles":

> Not like the brazen giant of Greek fame,
> With conquering limbs astride from land to land;
> Here at our sea-washed, sunset gates shall stand
> A mighty woman with a torch, whose flame
> Is the imprisoned lightning, and her name
> Mother of Exiles. From her beacon-hand
> Glows world-wide welcome; her mild eyes command
> The air-bridged harbor that twin cities frame.
> "Keep, ancient lands, your storied pomp!" cries she
> With silent lips. "Give me your tired, your poor,
> Your huddled masses yearning to breathe free,
> The wretched refuse of your teeming shore.
> Send these, the homeless, tempest-tost to me,
> I lift my lamp beside the golden door!"
> (*Poems* I, 202)

By this time Lazarus was fully adept at using the literary techniques of acculturation to appropriate America's rhetoric of equality and liberty in order to defend the Jews. Indeed, these lines represent the culmination of that struggle. In what has become America's most famous public sonnet, Lazarus boldly opposes the immigrant, ethnic character of America to that of the classical and imperialistic "storied pomp" of Europe. In this regard, the poem craftily builds on Emerson's and Whitman's calls for the transfer of art and learning from the Old World to the New.[47] The unconscious irony should be apparent: this was after all a tradition to which, like Heine's, her earlier poetry had been exceedingly loyal. But now, though "The New Colossus" is an Italian sonnet, she contrasts classical Europe's public (masculine) monuments to culture to New Israel's powerful female, whose torch lights the way for the "tired," the "poor," and the "huddled masses" to find a refuge. More significantly, as Lichtenstein rightly argues, her idealistic anthem to America's welcome of its strangers exhibits a highly sophisticated sense not only of what exile felt like but of what it might be to poeticize a fully heterogeneous American landscape: "valorizing as it does the status of the alien who finds in America a home, a native ground composed of many alien grounds" ("Words and Worlds" 261). There is a compelling logic at work here. After all, the Puritan imagination had already identified itself with the struggles and visions of the Jews. Now Lazarus cannily reversed that appropriation rhetorically, if not practically, transforming America into a more accommodating host, preparing the grounds for the future poetic renderings of pluralism that we will later encounter in Charles Reznikoff's modernist opposition to nativism.

This is not to say that Lazarus leaves much room for the liminality of exile or "Diaspora" as such; she is too swayed by nineteenth-century nationalist rhetoric, not to mention the fixities of Darwinism, which are both an important part of the reason for her abiding interest in Jewish colonization of Palestine. Lazarus anticipates some of the most important assimilative strategies visible in later Jewish American writing, her great sonnet inaugurating a discourse that would culminate in the early-twentieth-century works of Mary Antin, Israel Zangwill, and Abraham Cahan. In their works, to varying degrees, the brutal history of the Jews in Europe is redeemed by the American melting pot. Similarly, this is a poet who, rather than poeticize Diaspora, embraces the modern nation. Later Jewish writers would view the Lady in the Harbor quite differently. Kafka (a writer who never saw America) and Henry Roth (who lived there his entire life, if unhappily as a recluse) both wrote novels where the protagonists perceive Liberty wielding a threatening sword rather than a welcoming lantern as if, like the angel with the flaming sword in the Garden of Genesis, she bars the way to the new Eden and inaugurates only another phase of exile.[48]

In the end, it may be that Lazarus is much more of a universalist than a particularist. Hence, whether this sonnet reveals to us a poet who actually reclaims her Jewishness seems uncertain. For instance, the line "the wretched refuse of your teeming shore" actually masks the questions of identification, her intended audience, and not least the veiled fear of the cultural corruption that the Jewish masses might bring with them. At the same time that her lyrics sympathize with the immigrant's plight, Lazarus positions herself at a great distance from the masses. But none of this should take away from the authentic compassion that is also encrypted in the poem, which David Bleich rightly heralds as an important "beginning of the modern Jewish spirit" in America, providing "a model for the solution to the problems of assimilation: the reenactment of the generous act by those who are [already] here to those seeking a just society" (180).

◆

Though her cultural, ethnic, and literary politics underwent a radical transformation, Lazarus was never confident of her position. The devastating insult the struggling poet received from Emerson severely diminished her claim to be counted among the creators of the American cultural canon. The heightened insider/outsider consciousness that guides "The New Colossus" can be further illuminated by considering her enduring attraction to Heinrich Heine, the Jewish poet of Germany who, like Lazarus, ultimately rejected the assimilation of his youth. Like Lazarus in her youth, he began his poetic career by conjuring lands of enchantment, princes and princesses. In "The Poet Heine" (1884), a late essay written for the *Century*, Lazarus explains her fascination with the poet who was born a Jew but baptized and educated as a Catholic: "A fatal and irreconcilable dualism formed the basis of Heine's nature. . . . He was a Jew, with the mind and eyes of a Greek" (*Selections* 93). In spite of Heine's conversion, apparently undertaken to breach the world of high culture from which his debilitating identity had excluded him in spite of the official decrees of Emancipation, Lazarus fully sympathized with his position. As a true poet Heine must be *both* Hellene and Hebrew. Lazarus describes his duality by uncritically adapting Matthew Arnold's dichotomizing between Greek traits such as intellectual clarity, "laughter and sunshine," and a "somber Hebrew" ethos.

Even if the act of conversion was morally reprehensible to her, Lazarus's sympathy was not shaken. And this returns us to her embrace of "race"—something admittedly hard for post-Holocaust readers to grasp.[49] It was blood, not faith, that tied the individual Jew to her people—and though it is challenging to understand it in twentieth-century terms, this actually afforded the poet the precious and expansive space of ambiguity. Although for Lazarus, Judaism denotes "race" (for which we might substitute *ethnicity*), it is clear that such identification requires little of the individual: in her confusion of heritage, blood, and identities, Lazarus manages to have it both ways. For what at first appears to be a bold act of identification is actually a veil for the strategic preservation of ambiguity.

After her death, those close to her spoke candidly of the poet in terms strikingly similar to Lazarus's own analysis of Heine. Joseph Gilder, her editor at the *Critic*, remarked that, "She died, as she lived, as much a Christian as a Jewess—perhaps it would be better to say neither one nor the other" (Young 43). Perhaps by the end of Lazarus's life, Heine also came to represent this for her—the potential repudiation of the Jew by his ostensible homeland.[50] It is important to remember that as late as 1878 she could write that, though "proud of my blood and lineage ... my religious convictions ... and the circumstances of my life have led me somewhat apart from our people.... Hebrew ideals do not appeal to me" (Friedman 221). But it is probably also true that if Lazarus's ambiguous relationship to her people conveys an unenviable sense of dislocation, that very distress provides a uniquely *divided* perspective, which enhanced her writing. In "The New Year," separations, divergences, and schisms remain important features of her relationship to Jewish nationalism:

> In two divided streams the exiles part:
> One rolling homeward to its ancient source,
> One rushing sunward, with fresh will, new heart—
> *(Poems* II, 2)

In this Janus-faced lyric, we witness the tension between Lazarus's own "nativeness" and her struggle to articulate the otherness of an inassimilable ethnicity. This lyric beats a hasty retreat from the literal as well as the collective aspects embedded in re-territorialization. Lazarus's "divided streams" rhetorically anticipate the ambiguous strains that would accompany well into the twentieth century the ascendancy of Brandeisian Zionism, which saw Palestine as a place for some but not all Jews.

Lazarus's dilemma survives in the ambiguous ways that American Jewry came to exhibit its attachment to the teleology of Return. Reflecting on his visit to the Skirball Cultural Center's permanent collection of Jewish American historical artifacts, Stephen Whitfield noted that the "first object to be encountered . . . is a Torah scroll opened to Genesis 12:1–3. Next to it is the translation: 'Go forth . . . and be a blessing to the world.' What is omitted refers to the prospect of a 'great nation' to be formed in the Holy Land. The ellipsis was necessary, the coorganizer of the core exhibit explained, to avoid undue stress on 'the middle lines, which promise a particular land and future to Abraham's offspring'" (226). In subsequent chapters we will return to consider the broader cultural implications of the Genesis imperative in the contemporary Jewish American milieu.

◆

Though no immigrant herself, Lazarus's is one of the first attempts to grapple—albeit reluctantly at times—with the possibilities of extending America's proud notion of "newness" to those who truly were new Americans. In this sense, she must be credited with founding a new textual dynasty of ethnic voices who still seek, even into the twenty-first century, to assert their cultural heritage against the dominant culture. Her body of work beckons us to the inevitable hybridity of one's present culture and tradition, which have been crucial in forming not only the Jewish but other hyphenated American writers' identities as well. On the other hand, in responding to her culture's obsession with the Jew by glorifying ancient martyrdom and martial culture, Lazarus reinscribed the dominant culture's marginalization of those who did not conform to national ideals—in this case the ghetto Jews. The latter are intrinsically opposed to her projections of the model Jew of Zion's future. Lazarus's miraculous Hebrew is a being who serves her present in ways that are highly suggestive of later generations of American Jews; they too would insist on vicarious identifications with redemptive activity in the Holy Land, in spite of (or because of) its manifest distance from their own reality.

Although, after centuries of gazing on ghetto Jews, the world could no longer recognize the authentic biblical spirit in them, could not countenance their claim to an immortal relationship to their homeland, that is precisely where Lazarus locates their potential for redemption—once the "accumulated cobwebs and rubbish of Kabbalah and Talmud" were swept away. But conflicts remained. Her epic prose poem, "By the Waters of Babylon," composed during one of her own "rootless" European treks (in 1883–84), reminds the world of the cosmopolitan contributions of Maimonides, Halevi, Moses Mendelsson, and Heine. Nevertheless, their female offspring is reduced to a defensive stance. The creature the world "has named an ugly worm"—"Nerveless his fingers, puny his frame / haunted by the bat-like phantoms of superstition in his brain"—is actually a "Chrysalis" about to burst forth, ready to embrace the "blessed daylight," the benefits of Enlightenment and homecoming:

But when the emancipating springtide breathes wholesome, quickening airs, when the Sun of Love shines out with cordial fires, lo, the Soul of Israel bursts her cobweb sheath and flies forth attired in the winged beauty of immortality. (*Poems* II, 65–66)

Lazarus's greatest ambition was to create a literary legacy that would inscribe the once-and-future Jew more fully within the modern world of nation-building. What is perhaps most remarkable about this modernization of the diasporic subject through the agency of nationalism is that the latter does not require an indecorous submission to the tradition and the law of the east-European Judaism she so disparaged. The great distance between her literary expression and the collectivity she invokes demonstrates the success with which the assimilationist process her forebears pursued effectively severed her connection to traditional forms of identification. Hence the open-ended ambiguity, the compelling model of congenial parting at her "two divided streams."

For Lazarus, her in-betweenness was never a reason for regret. In a late sonnet, written during a final trip to Europe as she was already dying of cancer, she paid a final tribute to Heine ("Venus of the Louvre"), asserting the Hebrew *and* Greek sources of her own inspiration:

> Here *Heine* wept! Here still he weeps anew,
> Nor ever shall his shadow lift or move,
> While mourns one ardent heart, one poet-brain,
> For vanished Hellas and Hebraic pain.
> (*Poems* I, 203)

At the end the poet would not surrender her cosmopolitan yearnings in order to explicitly identify herself wholly as part of a Jewish collective. Whatever Jewishness might have meant to her, it is not something that she expected to survive for long on American soil. For when she says that Palestine offers the only alternative that will allow the immigrants a way to preserve their "time-honored customs and most sacred beliefs," she is implying that in America this form of continuity would not—or should not—endure.

Conclusion

For Emma Lazarus, it was clear that unassimilated behavior led to racism. Her representations of Jews articulated an attitude that would eventually be ingrained in twentieth-century liberal American culture, taking it for granted that there must be something tangible about the nature of the minority that inspired the racism that awaited them. Moreover, identifying the modern Jew with an ancient landscape only exacerbated the problems she sought to overcome, since the race-based arguments of the nineteenth century frequently emphasized the essential atavism of the Jew. Like American nativists, Lazarus contributed to a nostalgic discourse that sentimentalized one-to-one relationships between person and place, specifically attachment to the land of origin.

Lazarus was greatly at odds with other Jews, particularly those in the Reform movement, who sought to distance Jews from their association with the primitive tribalism of biblical nationality. Instead of identifying Jews with the racialized and immutable geography of the Holy Land, Reform Jewish rabbis associated them with the founding of the United States, strategically appealing to Protestant visions of America as the new Jerusalem. The American republic, not Palestine, was the true fulfillment of the prophet's dream. Rabbi Emil G. Hirsch, a Chicago Reform rabbi who would later ridicule the Zionists' dream of Palestine to defuse the charge of dual loyalty, stressed universalism and Americanization, insisting that "the day of national religions is past" and declaring that "race and nationality cannot circumscribe the fellowship of the faithful."[51] And his contemporary, Rabbi Silverman, protested that "[t]he evolution which Judaism has undergone in the past two thousand years, seems to be an unknown quantity in the minds of many" (Kirshenblatt-Gimblett 63). The hastily organized response of the Jewish leadership to Lazarus's Hebrew nationalism expressed the difficult position that nineteenth-century American Jews still felt themselves to be in.[52]

Lazarus can best be understood in relation to the rest of her generation— an acculturated population of Jews who willingly extended philanthropic aid to east-European Jews but at the same time feared contributing toward the growth of too-visible populaces in their midst. Her poetry reveals the conflicts and contradictions of the creative effort to link self to collective and selectively reclaim a past confined within a contemporary ideological framework. Her individual confrontation with Jewish suffering was a to-and-fro movement, a process that took her deep into, and then in hasty retreat from, collective solidarity. In spite of her vicarious commitment to Jewish rebirth and philanthropy, she distanced herself socially and symbolically from most American Jews, let alone the unsophisticated and impoverished immigrants from the shtetls of eastern Europe. Yet in spite of the fact that this extraordinarily complex writer was unwilling to accept the totalizing grip of an identity anchored to the bonds of the past, she willingly determined a narrative for others that would bind *them* to collective identity, the remedy that Eliot had prescribed for Lazarus's people: "a great feeling that animates the collective body as with one soul" (*Theophrastus Such* 138). This is precisely the creative force of Lazarus's enigmatic legacy; those divided streams continue to run through contemporary Jewish American life: a preoccupation between reclamation and territorial autonomy on the one hand, and cosmopolitanism and open-ended dialogue with the Jewish past on the other.

The Jewish return to Palestine that Lazarus envisioned embodied her uncertainty over her own fragile connection to Western culture. How easily the canon-maker Emerson exposed the bedrock of her own marginality. It may well be that in his thoughtless snub, Emerson engendered the hyphenated Jewish-American writer. Like Lazarus, generations of Jewish American writers would be marked by an acutely ambivalent flirtation with both American literary canonical authority—and a more ancient tradition that was equally distant, if not more so. In the language of high culture, the international world of letters, Lazarus, like her beloved Heine, might at first presume to find refuge in the apparently neutral space of intellectual culture. But we have seen that she never overcame the problem of the extent to which Gentile culture would continue to define the Jew on its own terms. In this regard we have seen the powerful role that the representations of non-Jewish writers played in her efforts to explain Jewish identity. Lazarus's relentless dichotomizing between warrior Jew and shopkeeper relied on these sources—and contributed to their proliferation. Only through the cultural representations of Longfellow, Eliot, and Oliphant did she glean a way to become a successful mediator of the Jew's relation to the external world.

Epitomizing generations of Jewish secular intellectuals to follow, she had no Jewish religious faith to sustain her, no firm conviction about the validity of traditional observance in the present. She found it difficult to belong to a community beyond the pale of the cultural authenticity she locates in the glorious and empty time of antiquity. Gifted at lyrically validating the heroic Jewish past as once viable, Lazarus hesitated in imagining Judaism as a living religion. Perhaps she believed it would inevitably be sublimated in American Protestantism, the culture that most influenced her proto-Zionism. And if we look closely at what Lazarus understands of her ancestors' experience, we discover a powerful logic here: faced with expulsion from Spain, the Sephardim were forced either to convert to Catholicism or depart. Considering all the vicissitudes of Jewish history, it was not unreasonable of her to imagine the enduring relevance of this harsh proposition. Lyrics such as "1492" and "The Exodus" validate the Jewish presence in America without embracing the present as an irrevocable Zion. For this reason Lazarus deserves to be understood as the first Jewish American writer to intimate that perhaps America was not the Promised Land at all, but Diaspora, part of the unstable terrain of Jewish geography.

Lazarus's poetry produced an extravagant recasting of tradition to enhance the exploits of ancient heroes and embellish the legendary successes of the race. Of course, at times, the ideal vision that Lazarus's poetry conjures bears little resemblance to the Jewish American writing that was to come. Celebratory, epic, and even apocalyptic, her lyrics most resemble the kind of literature that would be valued by the early Yishuv, in which poets were expected to enact what Sidra Ezrahi calls "an aesthetics of the whole . . . a perfect fit between map and territory that excludes new narratives of longing, wandering or restlessness" ("Israel and Jewish Writing" 12). For ultimately Lazarus—ranging from the mentorships of great men of letters such as Emerson and James to masculine figures like Daniel Deronda and Bar Kochba—"excludes" the actual grounds of her own internal Jewish exile and estrangements. Besides her unique position as the first Jewish American writer to be canonized, Lazarus exemplifies the experience of the minority writer in democratic America, caught between complete assimilation into the public culture of letters and adherence to the self-compromising call of memory and ethnic identity.

What she shares with the modern Jewish writers considered in subsequent chapters is a two-sided component of communality and alienation. For at the same time that Lazarus's proto-Zionism might be construed as an effective political response to the interrelated crises of pogroms and emigration, this ideology "solves" an individual crisis in ways that would be repeated by other ethnic writers in later generations: a reunion with a nearly lost self that is somehow deemed essential, though uprooted from a sense of an organic relation to authentic origins and collective destiny. Though her opportunity to create an American Zionist consciousness was cut short, Lazarus was one of the earliest, and most self-conscious, contributors to Jewish image-making and image-consumption, an industry that would continue to proliferate alongside the manufacture of other American ethnicities throughout the early twentieth century. Her attempts to respond to contemporary pogroms in Europe produced a poetry and rhetoric of outrage that would not be equaled until the generation of Marie Syrkin and Charles Reznikoff, discussed in the next two chapters.[53] For whatever we think of the obfuscations of Jewishness in Lazarus's obsessive dedication to post-Enlightenment reforms and proto-Zionism, there is also a sense of the impossibility of constructing an artistic ego independent of the moral claims of the tribe.

Her nineteenth-century struggle toward a poetic fusion of prophecy and political rhetoric of course proved prescient. Today we are in a better position to appreciate the propagandistic power of heroic myths of manhood that fed Zionism. Indeed, by the late nineteenth century, the radical revolutionary climate in Russia produced a generation of Jewish youth who adapted a remarkably similar Jewish nationalist mythology to that articulated in her proto-Zionist rhetoric. They saw themselves as the heroic advance guard of the Jewish people and identified themselves as *haluzim*, a term derived from Moses's command to the tribes of Gad and Reuben to conquer Canaan: "We ourselves will cross over as haluzim, at the instance of the Lord, into the Land of Canaan; and we will keep our heriditary holding across the Jordan" (Numbers 32:32).[54] Gradually this heroic mythology spread with the movement of Eastern European immigrants to the United States and became an unparalleled source of cultural vitality and intellectual debate in Jewish American life.

Lazarus's life and poetry illuminate the personal anguish as well as the potential for an energizing response that the predicament of marginality would foster in Jewish American writing for decades to come. Like later Jewish American poets, she had an abiding if complicated relation to her Jewish past and an obvious desire to belong to her cosmopolitan present. Perhaps this is the key difference that remains: for Lazarus, the creative challenge is that whatever "Jewishness" might be, it must be safely contained within acceptable forms of "heritage," whereas later American writers, even as secular as the poets I will next describe, know "Jewishness" to be a far more disruptive presence, a way of rigorously engaging with alternative world views. Her utopian Zionism did not provide an alternative to the prevailing Western language of soil and rootedness, but rather submitted to its chief values. The rest of this study will discuss writers who challenge and interrogate the meaning of Jewish continuity in America by contrasting that presence with Zionism's bleak conclusions about the Jew's position in the host culture.

Chapter Two

"It Will Not Be the Saving Remnant"

Marie Syrkin and the Post-Holocaust Politics

of Jewish American Identity

> Zion became a utopian extension of the American dream, a Jewish refuge
> where freedom, liberty and social justice would reign supreme, an "out-
> post of democracy" that American Jews could legitimately, proudly and
> patriotically champion.... The Zion of the American Jewish imagination,
> in short, became something of a fantasy-land: a seductive heaven-on-earth
> where enemies were vanquished, guilt assuaged, hopes realized, and
> deeply-felt longings satisfied.
> —Jonathan D. Sarna, "The Israel of American Jews"

Introduction

In the three decades following Lazarus's death, the United States absorbed
approximately two million Jewish immigrants from eastern Europe. This up-
heaval caused assimilated and nonassimilated Jews to become intensely preoccupied with creating a meaningful cultural synthesis. As early as World
War I it was becoming evident that Jewish American identity and the Zionist
movement would necessarily intersect. In the critical years of crisis during
World War II and beyond, Zionism would represent the only viable answer
to an apparently inevitable fragmentation, constituting American Jewry's
greatest platform of unity, organization, and coherence. By the early decades
of the twentieth century, literary and public figures such as Horace Kallen
(1882–1974), Louis Brandeis (1856–1941), Hayim Greenberg (1889–1953),

and Maurice Samuel (1895–1972) had persuasively brought the message of Labor Zionism not only to the Jewish American community, but to sympathetic gentile intellectuals such as Randolph Bourne, John Dewey, Reinhold Niebuhr, Paul Tillich, and Mark Van Doren. Zionism made surprisingly rapid inroads into mainstream American life. With the rise of Hitler, prominent labor leaders voiced public support for the Jewish national home.[1] More important, as the social historian Mark Raider reveals, by the 1940s, a "quasi-Labor Zionist orientation had passed imperceptibly into the mainstream of American Jewish discourse" (124).

Even before the euphoria of the Six Day War, American Zionism provided Jews with a popular synthesis of Jewish secular messianism and American notions of pluralism, democracy, and cultural humanism. Jewish Americans admired the attractive self-images of youth, health, and virility that Labor Zionism afforded them. Jewish men and women alike were dazzled by the flattering details presented by the Christian observer, George W. Seymour, in a series of reports published in the influential New York *Evening Post* in 1923. Seymour witnessed *halutzot*, pioneer women who shared strenuous construction and agricultural work with the men. On the road to Tiberias he encountered women "lifting and carrying stones with their bare hands and devoting hours to crushing them." One English-speaking woman was "a Russian Jewess, a university graduate with an M.D. degree," whose "soft, blue eyes laughed with each stroke of her sledge hammer against the rock she was breaking. 'We are equals with the men in Palestine. We are all working for the same object: to build a nation, and we are in full accord as to the rights and privileges of each other.'" After providing readers with such vivid sensory details as "the steel head of the big hammer [which] came down with a crash on the face of the huge stone, which fell apart in many pieces," Seymour proclaimed the "new feminine militancy of a newborn nation which stands unflinchingly the test of the wilderness in the old land of Israel."[2]

The Zionist *haluz* (pioneer) in the Land of Israel, a product of Labor Zionism, was depicted in numerous posters, newsreels, and even films of the 1930s, providing attractive images that could serve a variety of ideological and cultural purposes. One of the most popular of these films, *Land of Promise*, was a German production written by Maurice Samuel and released in the United States in 1935, where it was viewed by approximately 1.5 million people. The film showed images of young men dancing and singing on the foredeck of a liner as they arrive in Palestine to work in Jewish farms and factories. As Raider observes, the "cast" of the film, which reportedly did not include any actors, was listed in the credits as "The Jewish People

Rebuilding Palestine." According to a *New York Times* review, the effect on audiences was "electric" (Raider 115). Cinematically, there had never been such a Jewish figure; the Zionist was at once "revolutionary, warrior, farmer, watchman, redeemer, builder, scientist, and even dashing young discoverer." Jewish Americans saw the pioneers as the flattering embodiment of their own Jewish vitality. By the end of the Second World War, the resources of American Jewry were harnessed for two immediate goals: to provide relief for the victims of Hitler; and to create a sovereign Jewish state. In the immediate postwar period, a nascent partnership was being cemented between Palestine and American Jewry.

But writers in the American Diaspora responded to the new Jewish narrative of nationhood in diverse ways, depending on the cultural milieu in which they found themselves. We have seen how homelessness, ethnic identity, and Americanization converged in the work of America's first major Jewish poet. There is little doubt about the political meaning of Lazarus's proto-Zionism: Palestine was to be a refuge for the rejected Jew of Europe and a source of pride for the assimilating American Jew. That homeland was to partake in the somewhat utopian vision shared by the integral nationalism of other countries. But the questions of collective destiny and obligation that inform Lazarus's verse surface in vastly different ways in the work of a poet who lived through both Zionism's actualization and the culmination of European persecution. In this chapter I offer a reading of Marie Syrkin's (1899–1989) translation of a utopian dream into a political drama of redemptive return. The political tug-of-war between the private poet and collective identity, between the American Diaspora and Zionism that we witnessed in Lazarus's poetry has even greater consequences in the work of this twentieth-century poet.

Like Lazarus, Syrkin is often neglected in recent histories of American Zionism, which tend to focus overwhelmingly on luminaries such as Kallen, Brandeis, and Felix Frankfurter. Moreover, her lifetime dedication to the Labor Zionist cause similarly places Zionism both in the context of public life and as a literary, subjective phenomenon. Unlike American Zionists such as Kallen and Brandeis, Syrkin had arrived at her Zionism almost organically as the daughter of Bassya Osnos Syrkin (1878–1915), a feminist revolutionary activist and Zionist, and Nachman Syrkin (1867–1924), the founding leader and theoretician of Labor Zionism, whose ideas inspired the kibbutz movement.[3] By the time he came to the United States, Nachman Syrkin had achieved an international reputation as a scholar-intellectual and Zionist theorist. His socialist ideas were later absorbed into Kallen's philosophy, though with a much milder dogmatic thrust.[4] Marie Syrkin was born in Berne,

Switzerland, and came to the United States as a nine-year-old after already having lived in Germany, France, and Russia during the years of her father's activities on behalf of socialist Zionism. Her friend and biographer, Carole S. Kessner, recalls Syrkin remarking that "Papa was always getting exiled— so we traveled a lot" ("Marie Syrkin" 53). In childhood, Syrkin encountered village children in Vilna who warned her to paint a cross on her house if the killing began. Later she recalled that when she repeated this advice to her father, he offered a different remedy: "The answer I was taught and grew up believing lay in a socialist society and a socialist Jewish state" (*The State of the Jews* 1). But after fleeing the Czarist authorities, Nachman Syrkin instead took his family to America, where he had been invited to edit *Das Volk*, the journal of the Socialist-Territorial movement, setting into motion the tug-of-war between American and Zionist identities that would preoccupy his daughter for the rest of her life.

Kessner tells a memorable anecdote of Syrkin's early adult life, an incident that occurred not long after Marie's mother had died of tuberculosis, in which her father, "who disapproved of her literary bent, blazed out at her because he thought she was frittering away her abilities." Syrkin told Kessner that it was at about the same time (Syrkin was nineteen) that her father remarked acerbically, "'There is a woman in our movement who is a remarkable speaker. I thought you'd be like her.' The unnamed woman was, not surprisingly, Golda Meir" ("Marie Syrkin" 54). Perhaps because of her father's lofty expectations, Syrkin committed herself to a public life that would ultimately deny her the luxury of seriously heeding her own subjectivity as a poet until her old age. Though she wrote her poetry over the years, the collected poetry discussed here did not appear in print until 1979, after years of tireless effort on behalf of Zionism, after serving as the faithful friend and authorized biographer of the great woman to whom her father had compared her unfavorably, and after decades of toiling to support the creative life of her husband the Objectivist poet Charles Reznikoff, whose own modest fame, no matter how slight, may have caused her some regret. *Gleanings: A Diary in Verse* is the long forgotten poetic record of Syrkin's activities, and its title is apt, for the work represents the great themes of her life: her great loves, losses, resentments, and political battles, and above all her devotion to realizing the dreams of Zionism.[5] The poet's early years in Czarist Russia, the postwar years interviewing the survivors in the DP camps of postwar Europe, and her frequent sojourns in Israel as a public figure in the Zionist movement, would culminate in a poetry of intense emotional and intellectual terrain. In ways that evoke Lazarus's verse, her works link the immediate threat to Jewish survival in the present with ancient Jewish dreams of transcendent and metahistorical proportions.

Like Lazarus, in spite of being excluded from most (predominantly male-authored) official histories of Zionism, Syrkin warrants consideration as one of the most influential Jewish American women writer-activists of this century. Besides contributing to the *Menorah Journal*, she wrote for *Commentary*, *Midstream*, and *The New Republic* during a career that lasted more than fifty years. Respected by American intellectuals for her withering critique of Hannah Arendt's response to Zionism and the Holocaust, she had already achieved a reputation for her intelligent coverage of the Moscow Trials of 1937. As the first female professor appointed to Brandeis University, Syrkin developed the first courses in the literature of the Holocaust ever taught on a college campus. Her 1980 anthology of often acerbic essays, *The State of the Jews*, testifies to her lifelong concern with the enigma of twentieth-century Jewish experience, offering candid reflections on such topics as the Holocaust, Israel and its relations with the Palestinians, and especially Jewish culture in America.[6] After her first trip to Palestine in 1933, she joined the staff of the *Jewish Frontier*, the new Labor-Zionist publication that had supplemented the veteran *Yidishe Kemfer*. Eventually she would write Zionist speeches for Chaim Weizmann and Golda Meir. Among her books is a famous oral biography of Meir, and they became such intimates that Syrkin was a guest in the former's home while researching her autobiographical account of her own father's life.[7] Together with such stalwarts as Hayim Greenberg, Horace Kallen, and Maurice Samuel, Syrkin would use her father's intellectual legacy and her own unique rhetorical gifts to shore up support for the Jewish state-in-the-making.[8] She remained a staunch defender of Israel even years after Labor Zionism's influence in this country had greatly diminished. Her life and writings, situated in the context of interwar and wartime society, provides hitherto unexplored perspectives on Jewish American ideology during periods of profound physical and existential crisis.

Syrkin's worldview had little in common with the Brandeisian Zionism that sought to accelerate the Jews' acculturation and acceptance in America; it conformed instead to the pessimistic strain of her father's European Zionism. Long before the Holocaust, Zionists argued that Jews could have no future in the Diaspora. For Zionists of Nachman Syrkin's generation who witnessed the atrocities of pogroms, Jewish national connection to the land and their failure at living as a minority in the Diaspora were inseparable tenets. For instance, in a Russian pamphlet of 1901, Nachman warned that all the "social and political needs of the constantly wandering Jewish masses could not be met by socialism alone" (M. Syrkin, *Nachman Syrkin* 239). Since *Galut* was inevitably linked to repressive political institutions and pogroms, the most logical hope for the Jews' continuity lay in a state of their own. In Syrkin's experience, it was the very fact that Jews had no homeland that made their existence in exile untenable. Hence, cultural nationalism must evolve into territorialism: "the Jewish proletariat [has] to fight for a Jewish homeland in Palestine, not as a holy land but as a territory" (240). Years before Syrkin would proclaim the State of Israel as the indispensable *resolution* of the Holocaust, her father described the Jewish proletarian masses (who were under the constant pressures of political and economic need and migration) as the "natural fulfillers of the Zionist idea [since] they are driven to Zionism by necessity" (242). Zionism is the natural complement and requisite of world socialism; if Zionism is thus the "natural" concern of the Jewish working class, as he argues, "assimilation becomes the concern of the Jewish bourgeoisie, and the ideology of Jewish defeatists, escapists, and traitors" (242). There was no room for ambiguity or compromise on the issue of Jewish sovereignty.[9] Nachman Syrkin's hard-core socialism was really a transformed messianism: "the messianic hope, which was always the greatest dream of exiled Jewry, will be transformed by political action. . . . Israel will once again become the chosen people of the peoples" (N. Syrkin, "The Jewish Problem and the Socialist-Jewish State," 349).

Rabbi Herbert Bronstein, who knew Marie Syrkin, is persuaded that, like her father, her understanding of the Jew in relation to society was European-Zionist in its origins and remained so throughout her life: "She believed in the Jews' inevitable alienation from culture in the Diaspora. . . . [S]he could never embrace American culture."[10] Syrkin's inherited variant of Zionism, unlike the discourse uttered by Kallen and Brandeis, is not persuaded by the Jews' emancipation from European ghettos and their transformation by the surrounding European culture of individualism. This rejection culminates in the articulation of a series of irrefutable principles:

that the Jewish people is viewed as alien everywhere in the diaspora; that the Jewish bourgeoisie invented the deception of assimilation to promote its power of exploitation, that a profound moral contradiction exists between the bourgeois lie of assimilation and the revolutionary truth of socialism; that the Jewish socialist is duty bound to aid the Jewish people and to accept Zionism as the instrument for the emancipation of the Jewish people and the spiritual redemption of the individual Jew.[11]

As with Emma Lazarus, the disillusionment that shaped Syrkin's perspective of Christian Europe eventually diminished her confidence in the Jews' position in America. Marked by a complete loss of trust in the host society, this ideology led to a fundamental lack of confidence in the very foundations of Jewish participation in Western culture.

◆

In October 1934, Syrkin, together with Hayim Fineman, chaired a committee of Labor Zionists to discuss plans for a new publication that would bring the message of Labor Zionism and the reality of Jewish settlement in Palestine directly to the Jewish American public on a greater scale than ever before. Hoping to attract a broad readership, the committee was determined to bring the creation of the kibbutz movement, the establishment of the Haganah self-defense organization, the Histadrut (the General Federation of Jewish Workers in the Land of Israel), and other achievements of the Zionist pioneers in Palestine into the center of Jewish American discourse. In December the *Jewish Frontier*'s premier issue appeared, announcing its founders' agenda:

We consider the creation of a Jewish labor society in Palestine as the chief task of our generation. This does not mean, however, that we will disregard the tormenting problems of Jews in the diaspora countries. We consider it our function to mirror the Jewish struggle for existence in the difficult transition period which whole countries and continents are now experiencing. Because we are "Palestinocentric," we cannot ignore the diaspora.[12]

The *Frontier*'s rhetorical assumptions could not have been stated in clearer terms; if Diaspora was worthy of attention it was only because it was a site of crisis and torment, not for its intrinsic worth. Besides presenting translations of the Hebrew nationalist poetry of Haim Nahman Bialik and Nathan Alterman and Hebrew articles by Palestinian leaders such as David Ben-Gurion and Berl Katznelson that were otherwise unavailable to English-readers, the journal attracted such writers as Hannah Arendt, Will Herberg, Mordechai Kaplan, Ludwig Lewisohn, and Maurice Samuel. The founders readily acknowledged the contemporary tension between Jewish socialists and those who had wholeheartedly embraced the American Dream. Moreover, they foresaw the conciliatory and unifying role that Zionism would eventually play in Jewish American culture: "We represent that synthesis in Jewish thought, which is nationalist without being chauvinist, and which stands for fundamental economic reconstruction without being communist. Only such a synthesis can answer the need of the disorientated modern Jew" (4). Here then was the tangible reward of Josephine Lazarus's promise to America.

It is important to note that, though Palestine was presented as the "chief channel for the flow of Jewish energy," there is no evidence of any official effort on Syrkin's part to negate *Galut* in this period. In their priestly ministering to the "disoriented modern Jew," Syrkin and the other founders of the *Jewish Frontier* did not depart significantly from the American Zionism of Brandeis and Kallen. The "rapture of pioneering" would also ennoble and stimulate Jewish life throughout the Diaspora. But when it seemed necessary, Syrkin and the other writers of the *Jewish Frontier* were capable of taking decisive stands on the politics of Palestine. Over the course of nearly a decade, the *Frontier* waged an impassioned, often bitterly ideological campaign in its pages against the hate-mongering right-wing Revisionist Zionist press, creating an implicit equation between Labor Zionism and American liberalism on one hand and Revisionism and American xenophobia and nativism on the other.[13] Syrkin's own 1940 essay, "The Essence of Revisionism: An Analysis of a Fascist Tendency in Jewry," was representative of this editorial trend toward the left.[14]

From the beginning, Syrkin's public life was marked by similar confrontations with Jewish and non-Jewish adversaries of Jewish culture and Zionism, which seems to have led gradually to the conclusion that only the latter could serve as a safe haven for the former. In the 1930s, the utopian imagination of American writers was often blemished by nativism and antisemitism. Syrkin's defensive responses to the latter underscore the success with which these forces drove home the Jews' irreconcilable otherness in these years. Her husband, Charles Reznikoff, recounted one of the earliest of these attacks—and its emotional aftermath—in a letter where he mentions her hard work to formulate "an answer to Jay Nock's slimy articles in *The Atlantic*" (*Selected Letters*, 301).

Nock, a member of an emerging breed of nativists and race ideologues who favored the "Nordic" races of northern Europe, had been invited by *The Atlantic* to inaugurate a series of articles on "The Jewish Problem in America," which were published in the June and July issues in 1941. Interestingly, Nock portrays the Jew much as early American Zionists had several decades earlier—as an exotic "Oriental." After her sister's death, Josephine Lazarus had argued that the great gift the Jew could offer America was not the "modernized, occidentalized, liberalized" Judaism of the congregations, but rather the authentic Oriental essence that is in fact the Jew's eternal nature. The Jew belongs "more to the East than to the West," but by Zionism's consolidation of the Eastern and Western worlds through "interdependence and interchange of gifts spiritual and material," the prophetic visions of Amos and

Jeremiah will be fulfilled. Paradoxically, it was as though only by thoroughly "Orientalizing" the Jew could the Lazarus sisters remove the taint of European decadence and the stigma of modernity. But now, in a way that suggests just how slippery these essentialist terms were in the age of nativism, Nock had seized on precisely the same trope to prove the irreconcilable difference that would always prevent the Jews' successful acculturation within any occidental civilization. In her response, published in the fall by *Common Ground*, Syrkin began by dispassionately summarizing the essence of Nock's argument:

> The Jewish problem is essentially an "Oriental problem." The Occidental world cannot accept an Oriental people on the same terms it does another Occidental people. This makes for perpetual suspicion and misunderstanding. Furthermore, anti-Semitism is always of "proletarian or sub-proletarian" origin. In times of stress, the resentment of the masses forces the rulers of a state to take cognizance of the anti-Semitism of the "mass-man." Finally, no matter how mistaken the prejudices of the mass-man may be, the "intelligent Occidental" must take the views and bigotries of the Occidental mass-man into account when passing legislation or planning the social order. ("How Not to Solve 'The Jewish Problem'" 74)

What should interest us here is Syrkin's unwillingness to acknowledge the rhetorical parallels between Nock's analysis and the doctrine of "shelilat-ha-golah" (negation of Jewish Exile) articulated by the first generation of Zionists, including her father. Yet at this moment, Syrkin's indignant response is directed against what was clearly an insidious attempt to "other" Jewish Americans, setting them in opposition to Western culture at a particularly precarious time: "Fascist elements in the United States are deliberately striving to make of the diversity of American national strains a disruptive factor, using anti-Semitism as an entering wedge. No greater disservice can be rendered American democracy than to yield to this blunt device under the pretense of honoring the wishes of the Nazi-stimulated 'mass-man' (78). Syrkin was disturbed by the devastating ease with which Nock manages, positioning himself as "a Conscientious Gentile," innocently to distance himself from the Hitler regime's "barbaric" persecution of the Jews and yet within the same pages to insinuate that inevitably—"within my lifetime"—much worse would happen to them in America. She quotes from Nock's less inhibited reflections on the Jews in the late thirties: "'Thinking over Hitler's anti-Semitism, [Nock writes,] one is forced to admit, I believe, that the Nazis could not have carried their programme through and made it work without clearing the Jews out of Germany.... [M]ost of the Germans played the game fairly and loyally. . . . [T]he Jews on the other hand, cut every corner they could—and there you are'" (77). The inevitable outcome, Nock merrily hinted, was the coming "cataclysm."

At the very least, this episode seems to have confirmed her father's views as prophetic and greatly diminished her sense of at-homeness in America. Unlike Reznikoff, whose masculine sense of American freedom and mobility (much like Alfred Kazin's) was somehow rekindled by every walk in Central Park, Syrkin's role as public defender of the Jews often left her so emotionally drained and alienated from her American milieu that she would flee—to Palestine, Europe, and elsewhere—treks that never seemed to provide her with a true sense of rest. The combative role Syrkin assumed in the Nocks episode seems to have taken a toll, for when it was all over, Reznikoff told a friend that Syrkin has fled to England for a "brief vacation" (*Selected Letters* 301).

Syrkin was appalled by the frequent betrayals of the liberal American press: in this instance, not only had *The Atlantic* presented Nock's views, but they had also left little space for pretending that their position was one of editorial detachment and objectivity. In fact, "with [a] special editorial note, [they] endowed them with significance worthy of the widest consideration" (78). Nock was only the first of the "liberal" intellectuals who would anger her in the ensuing decades. For where Emma Lazarus had only Madame Z. Ragozin to contend with, Syrkin came to find herself in the embattled position of defender of the Jews, not only against antisemitic misreadings of Jewish experience spawned by non-Jewish intellectuals such as Arnold Toynbee,[15] but in reply to cultural figures she saw as shameless Jewish self-haters, such as Hannah Arendt and Philip Roth. Over time these heated rhetorical battles—though emotionally taxing—led to creatively productive lyrical entanglements with the invigorating question of Jewish identity.

Stormtroopers in Madison Square Garden: Marie Syrkin and Wartime Angst

In spite of her international reputation as social thinker and Zionist, Syrkin's literary criticism and poetry were crucial to her identity. In the 1920s she was still one of the most prominent translators of Hebrew and Yiddish poetry.[16] Her own lyrics, collected in *Gleanings: A Diary In Verse* (1978), an undeservedly neglected work, explores the marked disparity between the fulfillment of the poet's private and public selves. It also provides a wonderful resource for comparing her Zionist lyrics to Reznikoff's diasporic verse and for thinking more deeply about the variety of imaginative constructions of Jewish identity in this century.[17] Ironically, Marie Syrkin herself, as was true of her father and so many Zionists of a particular generation, knew much more about "exile" than she did about inhabiting a homeland. This painful fact often surfaces in her lyrics. Living outside the Land and its language, she was intimately acquainted with five languages of the European Diaspora, including Yiddish. And it is worth remembering that in the pre-Holocaust years, Syrkin had enthusiastically investigated the culture and life of the European past through her critically praised translations of the poetry of Yehoash, which originally appeared in the *Menorah Journal*.[18]

Her lyrics, like Lazarus's, often contrast the promise of a living Jewish culture with evidence of the ruin of its oppressors. For instance, touring the archaeological decay of fallen Rome, once the ravager of Jewish civilization, the Jewish poet marvels instead at the miraculous rebirth of the site of the ancient Temple:

> Among fallen columns,
> Broken pedestals,
> The Arch of Titus, triumphal
> For Jerusalem fallen.
>
> Among the ruins on Mount Palatine,
> I remembered Mount Scopus;
> The University of Jerusalem
> Whole
> On the greening slope.
>
> (*Gleanings* 67)

"In Rome" confirms that she had accepted the classic Zionist view of Jewish history, a narrative trajectory from Catastrophe to Redemption that silently effaces the twenty centuries of Diaspora. Syrkin would never write such a paean to the renaissance of Jewish culture in America. This effacement of the Jewish present can be traced to Syrkin's guilt-inflected struggle to come to terms with the Holocaust.

The *Jewish Frontier* was among the very first of the Jewish American print media (in English) to receive reports of genocide.[19] Syrkin would later acknowledge being present at a small meeting of Jewish journalists held in August 1942, where she first heard that a Nazi extermination plan had begun. As Syrkin later admitted to Kessner, the response of the entire group was incredulity and skepticism, in spite of the fact that "only a week earlier the *Frontier* itself had received a document from the Jewish Socialist Bund which was an account of mass gassings of Jews in Chelmno." Many years later Syrkin felt compelled to confess to her friend that "we hit on what in retrospect appears a disgraceful compromise: we buried the fearful report in the back page of the September issue in small type, thus indicating that we could not vouch for its accuracy" ("On Behalf of the Jewish People" 214). In November, however, the magazine belatedly printed the first American report of annihilation: "In the occupied countries of Europe a policy is now being put into effect whose avowed object is the extermination of a whole people. It is a policy of systematic murder of innocent civilians which in its ferocity, its dimensions and its organization is unique in the history of mankind."[20] The editors concluded that a "holocaust" had "overtaken the Jews of Europe." To my knowledge, this was also the first time this word was used in relation to the persecution of the European Jews.

Not surprisingly, the naysayers who had opposed Zionist militancy were utterly discredited in the Jewish American community, which came to see the Zionist movement and the Yishuv in Palestine as the only source of salvation. And as Raider explains, "[b]y default . . . the burden of the Zionist cause now lay at the doorstep of American Jews [and] the fact that no country would admit European Jewish refugees increased the urgency of the American Zionists' activity" (208–9). Because of this harshly pragmatic reality, from this moment on Zionism became inextricably a part of mainstream Jewish American life. As for Syrkin, when she came so close to the reality of the Holocaust, it intensified her European pessimism to an even more radical degree, diminishing her faith in the viability of Jewish life anywhere outside the Jewish state. But it also inspired practical action: more than anything else, being a Zionist meant saving Jews, bringing them as refugees to any safe haven. Efforts in securing such a haven outside of Palestine were tragically ineffectual. Syrkin's wartime editorial addressed to Roosevelt expressed outrage in the face of the frivolous response to the refugee crisis: "If the United States can permit itself to declare to the world that its maximum contribution to the refugee problem is the admission of 1,000 people, what answer can be expected from smaller and poorer nations, who have coped with sporadic streams of refugees for years?"[21] From this anguished rhetoric grew the reasonable logic that would lead her to conclude that the best single hope for the future lay in Palestine.

Immediately after the war, Syrkin gathered material for a book on partisans and Jewish fighters that highlights the final days of the parachutist

Hannah Senesch.[22] In her poignant translation of Senesch's "Blessed is the Match," we see that genocide's aftermath casts a very long shadow over Syrkin's own poetry:[23]

> Blessed is the match that is consumed in
>   kindling flame
> Blessed is the flame that burns
>   in the secret fastness of the heart.
> Blessed is the heart with strength to stop
>   its beating for honor's sake
> Blessed is the match that is consumed
>   in kindling flame.
>   (*Blessed is the Match* 24)

If we are to take seriously Syrkin's desire that *Gleanings* be read as an autobiographical record of her inner turmoil, then the transcendent emotion of these lines—"Blessed is the heart with strength to stop / its beating for honor's sake"—seems to be a literary and emotional milestone in Syrkin's own verse, a sort of poetic and philosophic covenant.

It must be noted that Syrkin had already begun to distrust the liberal consensus that had dominated Jewish *belles-lettres* prior to the war. Any lingering temptation to reconcile with the cosmopolitans had been scuttled by her shock following the Moscow Trials and Stalin's mass execution of Yiddish writers: "for those who were Socialists as well as Zionists the Moscow Trials would be the first in a bitter series of shocks and disappointments (*The State of the Jews* 2)."[24] Kessner recalls Syrkin's dedicated work in this period:

Marie read through six hundred pages of the Russian stenographic typescript of the January 1937 trial. In May the *Frontier* published her long article that challenged the authenticity of the defendant's confessions and concluded that these trials were nothing less than Stalin's method of destroying dissent. "These deductions," Marie asserted, "seem inescapable after reading the record. They are not pleasant, but no service is done to socialism . . . by refusing to face what one conceives to be the truth." ("On Behalf of the Jewish People" 213)

Syrkin's published analysis was the first American exposé of the trials. In these years she was acutely aware of the expanding presence of antisemitism on the left and right in America and Europe. Together with her experiences in Europe and among the ghetto and concentration camp survivors in Israel, these threats persuaded her of the ubiquity of evil and the utter inadequacy of American liberalism. This article opened up a rift between Syrkin and the Jewish left that would never heal.[25]

Her prewar unease, exacerbated by Father Coughlin's radio broadcasts, and her uncertainty over just what affronts American democracy was prepared to ignore at home and abroad form the painful theme of "Current Events":

> Cautiously I ask, my voice quiet,
> "Will any one speak for the other side?"
> Tentatively I glance at the unraised hands, the indifferent eyes
> And I say,
> "Then we will go on, since no one will speak for the other side."
> Or I urge,
> "What about democracy? Was his talk democratic?"
> I fold myself in the stars and stripes, I clutch the constitution,
> I wait.
>
> But suppose I said, "There is no other side."
> Suppose I said, "This is the hour of choosing."
> Suppose I said, "This is the hour of anger."
> Suppose I screamed to the Nazi visitor in my room
> Affably smiling,
> Brought by the principal to observe American methods,
> "Get out of my class."
>
> Some day we will have to stand up at our desks
> Unmindful of the sure job, the summer money,
> The pension after the long years.
> We will have to say,
> "This is the truth, my class,
> This is the truth."
>
> *(Gleanings* 48–49)

This is an electrifying admission, a passionate articulation of a painful and guilt-ridden memory of a personal role in the complacency that once gripped American Jewry as a whole. It is difficult for younger generations of Jews and non-Jews alike to understand the depth of Syrkin's fears for Jewish well-being in this country. But of course these were the years in which Henry Ford circulated *The Protocols of the Elders of Zion.* As Syrkin tells it, the decay of her trust in America began in the late thirties and early forties, which were to introduce old terrors into the consciousness of American Jewry. . . . Home-grown rabble-rousers, emboldened by Nazi victories, had come out of the closet. Pro-Nazi Father Coughlin rallied his disciples in popular radio broadcasts that influenced a periphery extending far beyond the circles of such rabidly anti-Semitic groups as the Christian Front or the Silver Shirts. The German American Bund strutted openly in full stormtrooper regalia in Madison Square Garden at huge meetings . . . against American Jews scheming to inveigle the United States into the conflict. . . . In the high school in which I taught, pro-Nazi pupils propounded their creed during the current events period with little objection from their classmates. . . . Few teachers ventured to challenge this tolerance. (*The State of the Jews* 4–5)

Syrkin's alienation from a democracy that apparently allows for the dissemination of evil in the name of "pluralism," as well as from the company of liberal intellectuals who failed to grasp the enormity of the century's evil, would culminate in her furious critique of Hannah Arendt's anti-Zionism.[26]

◆

In the immediate aftermath of genocide, approximately eighty thousand Jews were crowded into DP camps in American-occupied Europe alone, and by 1947 their numbers would triple, with no apparent asylum but Palestine. In America, retention of the biased national-origins principle continued to prevent the accommodation of many Jewish refugees. The quarter-million stateless refugees in Europe provided living proof of Zionism's most pessimistic assumptions about the countries into which Jews had unwittingly entrusted their lives. That Syrkin was able to bear witness to the essential humanity of the survivors was itself significant in ways long since forgotten. But at the same time such recognition was not always forthcoming from postwar visitors to the DP camps. For instance, General George Patton, commander of the Third Army (in whose zone of occupation most of the Jews were held), noted his repulsion in a diary entry following a Yom Kippur visit to a DP camp outside Munich, where the Jews "were all collected in a large wooden building which they called a synagogue . . . which was packed with the greatest stinking bunch of humanity I have ever seen" (Sachar 1992, 554). Back in America, Harry Truman's verbal expressions of sympathy did not extend to modifying the nation's immigration quotas for some time. Having already witnessed the restrictionist xenophobia of America and the Allies that prevented sufficient wartime rescue during the Nazi persecutions, Syrkin went directly to the refugee camps to confront the unwillingness of the world—whether the result of continued indifference to the fate of the Jews or simply of bureaucratic callousness—to get these traumatized survivors out of the camps. In January 1947, she received permission to visit the DP camps in the American Zone "for the purpose of gathering first-hand information on the DP problem. An additional purpose was to screen suitable candidates for admission to American colleges, who would be allowed to enter the United States above and beyond the restrictions of the immigration quotas" (*The State of the Jews* 10).

The prose that she wrote during the same years that the poetic "diary" was conceived sheds important light on the traumatic impact of the Holocaust on her literary representations of Jewish identity. Above all else, Syrkin was struck by the immediate impulse of the survivors themselves to transform horror into art—"It had to be said or sung somehow" (318). She felt that representation of this catastrophe constituted the greatest responsibility of the Jewish artist and of the survivors themselves. During her 1947 visit to the DP camps, she was "startled by many of the songs composed in the concentration camps and sung by survivors" (318). Shaken by the "contrast between the grim content and the music," she is yet cognizant that the survivors themselves apparently feel no sense of "impropriety" or "dissonance" (318). Even here, ideology shaped her perceptions of what she witnessed. For instance, she reports her satisfaction that though the DP children were initially taught in their native Yiddish, instruction was later changed to Hebrew. Furthermore, "[t]he emotional tone of the DP camps was preponderantly Zionist" (34). The greatest portion of her own verse, pointedly organized under the rubric "Holocaust and Israel," necessarily conflates these two; for Zionists the sacred sacrifice of one is always put to the service of legitimating the other. For Syrkin, Jewish politics and art would be inextricably linked after the catastrophe, and her lyrical mourning would assume intensely collectivist forms.

After returning to America, Syrkin was deeply troubled by the forms that post-Shoah Jewish identity might take in America. For instance, in a chapter, "Have American Jews a Jewish Future?" she wonders what could possibly remain to pass on about Jewishness to a generation beyond the cusp of assimilation, beyond the pitiable legacy of suffering:

How does one explain a gas chamber and a slaughterhouse to the potential victim— to the one who might have been there? The horror of this confrontation is intolerable and I understand the successful young Harvard professor of my acquaintance who tries to keep such knowledge from his ten-year-old son. The reluctance had a deeper reason than sheer horror. The young professor is a Jewish intellectual who is already one stage beyond suburbia. The values he brought from there are no longer meaningful in his present world. His Jewish attachments are of the most tenuous;

consequently, he cannot weigh down his child with a burden of irrational, zoological suffering which only a profound religious or national piety can transmute into the endurable. (*The State of the Jews* 268)

Only two paths will requite an otherwise endless cycle of "zoological suffering": religious or national life. Lacking religious faith, secular Jews must accept the alternative palliative of nationalism; Diaspora identity has diminished to the negative value of irrational suffering. Even the material success of Jewish life in America is a mere subterfuge; for within the space of a single generation, "the Jewish origin of a gifted parent becomes only a piquant curiosity with no relevance for his descendants. Much Jewish talent and intelligence are quietly departing from the Jewish people at the present time," and this is occurring at a far greater rate "than the sociologists with their variable figures of intermarriage rates indicate" (268). Yet even without the prospect of intermarriage, Syrkin was acutely discouraged by the post-assimilationist phase of Jewish American culture, for each successive generation in America is more diluted than the previous: "What is their present active bond with the Jewish people, the Jewish faith, or both? Frequently none." Caught between two worlds, the Jewish intellectual "can no longer take refuge in the village atheism fashionable among Jewish immigrants, or first generation intellectuals—an atheism often propounded in an excellent Yiddish—nor has he the compensating secular nationalism of that group" (269).

Syrkin found the cynical withdrawal of this breed of Jewish intellectual to be incomprehensible. By the 1960s, she was especially alarmed that the campus activism that had claimed so many Jewish students—their liberal infatuation with "the interrelated human family"—excluded Israel:

There is too often one exception to the all-embracing sense of social responsibility. If our idealist joins the Peace Corps, he would feel cheated were he to find himself shipped to the Negev rather than the Congo. At a time when he is personally affected by the national liberation movements of various African or Asian peoples, he views Jewish nationalism as restrictive. (271)

Rather than call for a renewal of Jewish American life, Syrkin repudiates the viability of America as a haven for difference. Rejecting the optimistic pluralism that *The Menorah Journal* espoused earlier in the century, she argues that "Whereas all American slogans appear to encourage what we loosely call "cultural pluralism," American reality opposes it." The genuine essence of "difference" disappears in the American abyss of indifference: all that remains from distinct nationalities are the charades of slogans and parades: "The Irish may parade on St. Patrick's Day, the Ukrainians may dance folksily in colorful costumes, the French may remember Lafayette—all to the accompaniment of general applause and speeches reminding us that the American heritage is richer for its many strands" (272). Although it is undoubtedly true that maintenance of one's culture can be a generally daunting task in America (a "difficult and complex endeavor" that Syrkin hints may lie beyond the ability of any group), it is also true that, in making this claim, she ignores the resilience of the Jewish Diaspora—as if its traditions hadn't thrived, and evolved, throughout thousands of years in exile.

The past was shattered, only its shreds remained. What was left required a radical act of restoration. For many of the survivors, Zionism represented the only avenue of permanent refuge. Years later she would recall the "Jewish DP who told me with brutal simplicity, 'They killed us because we had no land of our own'" (10). Paying heed to the voices of Holocaust survivors drove home the lesson of national sovereignty as the only viable escape from the European charnel house. Hence, it is easy to understand why Syrkin came to idealize Zionism's communal organization and ordering of Jewish life. Agitated by the anti-Zionist camp, she resented the "view commonly held by assimilationists of the Council for Judaism stripe, on the one hand, and 'radicals' of the old school on the other. In this view every affirmation of Jewish national awareness is culpable and to be strictured either as multiple loyalty or treason to a larger national ideal" (196).

Where Kallen and Brandeis once found an adaptable strategy that organically linked Zionism with the viable Americanization of the Jew, Syrkin suggests only that a "crisis for Zionism is a crisis for Judaism" (275), not the reverse. In Syrkin's collected essays there is no evidence of trust in a Jewish American life of any lasting value: "The core will remain, but it will not be the saving remnant: neither in its ethnic culture nor in its religious intensity will it be significantly Jewish. It will be American, as it must be" (276). This classic statement of Syrkin's pessimism might be usefully juxtaposed with the culmination of her husband's epic *Holocaust*. The latter ends with a small victory, as a group of Jews evades the Nazi killing machine by escaping to Sweden. In Reznikoff's texts of Jewish history, a small community of Jews escapes every new Haman—even remaining Jews. But for Syrkin the crisis of Jewish life everywhere would only be resolved when Zionism is accepted as the exclusive wellspring of authenticity. Like many Zionists in her generation, Syrkin's rhetoric overcomes the spectre of separate Judaisms drifting apart because they have reconciled difference under the rubric of the state:

In this period of history, a complete Jewish life can only be led in the Jewish state. There the secular Jew and the religious Jew, the radical kibbutznik and the rigid fundamentalist, whatever their violent differences and disputes, are both engaged in the creation of a Jewish land and a Jewish life with all the scope the terms permit. In language, in culture, in purpose, there the one people emerges. (276)

Today it seems clear that "violent differences and disputes" in the Jewish State are not so easily resolved. Nevertheless, for Syrkin, whereas diasporic memory was eminently untrustworthy, excessively reliant on "artifice [or] attachment by catastrophe," in Israel "parents need not fear that Jewish symbols and festivals will pale into invisibility before the brilliance of the Christmas candles" (276).

It seems ironic that, at the same time that Nachman Syrkin reconstituted the Jewish past and advocated the benefits of cultural separatism, he failed to provide a linguistic foundation for his daughter's future sense of at-homeness among the Zionists in the Jewish state. Syrkin's estrangement from Hebrew as a living connection to the Zionist dream was particularly irksome to her. As Kessner points out, Syrkin always claimed that "this lack . . . was a major reason for her own failure to make aliya." Responding to a comment that she was "fortunate to be the daughter of Nachman Syrkin," Syrkin ruefully remarked: "yes, but one thing he failed to provide me. He did not teach me Hebrew at an age when one could have learned it. It's maddening. . . . That he didn't teach me Hebrew was a serious loss" ("An Exemplary Life" 53).[27] Indeed, the most visible form of the elder Syrkin's nationalist legacy to his daughter was a mournful form of messianism, a seed that grew until it left her increasingly unhappy with the circumstances of Jewish life in America—and with the Diaspora as a whole. In Syrkin's famous rebuttals to Arendt, Roth, and ultimately in her response to Charles Reznikoff, it becomes evident that her father's Manichaean formulation was adapted into her own thinking.[28]

Whereas for Reznikoff the crisis of the present may unpredictably turn out to be a source of creative ferment, itself a kind of continuity, Syrkin sees only the prospect of vacuity. Turning again to the poetry, we repeatedly encounter this paradigm. For example, in "Shirley" she despairs of the unfinished, sadly diluted Jewish products of American culture that she observes in her classroom with helpless bewilderment:

> Her name is Shirley and not Deborah.
> There's one in every class; I know the look.
> She'll never read what's called a worthwhile book.
> She'll stay at home on Yom Kippur but not fast.

> She tinkles when she walks—bells, bracelets, charms
>> but with the rest
> Of late, a Shield of David on her breast.
> I ask her why; she knows no word sublime;
> She hesitates, "I guess it is the time.
> Besides, the other girls wear crosses now."
> I bow.
> What makes these little girls
> With heavy lipstick and with silly curls,
> With voice too loud,
> So proud?
>
> (*Gleanings* 47)

A generation of crassly materialistic Jewish women and their daughters, symptomatic of American Jewry's rapid rise to postwar prosperity, stand behind "Shirley." Syrkin was probably making coy reference to the archetypal middle-class Jewish woman of the decade, for Shirley is the name of the heroine in Herman Wouk's 1955 satirical *Marjorie Morningstar*, a novel that depicts the transformation of a young, "emancipated" Jewish girl into a complacent suburban matron. According to Joyce Antler, these and other books of the postwar period

defined the Jewish American Princess . . . in the popular mind. Members of the new Jewish suburban middle class: pushy and materialistic, they dominate their families, living through their children and belittling their weak and ineffectual husbands. Though they might belong to Hadassah and other Jewish or community charities, neither these volunteer activities nor their families provide adequate scope for their innermost desires. The failure to realize their potential is destructive to all around them. (234, 266).[29]

In Wouk's novel, Shirley is all "tricked out to appear gay and girlish and carefree," but suffers from "a terrible threatening dullness jutting through" (*Marjorie Morningstar* 172). As Charlotte Baum observes, according to this comic representation of the Jewish female, this dimly conscious third-generation Jewish woman, born in America, is driven only by the material rewards of matrimony, preoccupied only with her own selfishly narrow interests: "The princess inherited the mother's *chutzpah*, her energy, her lack of deference; but while the Mother focuses her attention on her children, the daughter is portrayed as concentrating on her future husband—someone whom she, too, can dominate and manipulate, and who will provide her access to the material possessions she is said to covet" (Baum 251).

Invoking the stereotype of the coarse Jewish American Princess that rapidly infiltrated popular culture, Syrkin humorously bemoans the fate of an assimilated and thoughtless American Jewry sadly incapable of measuring up to its own prophetic traditions: "Her name is Shirley and not Deborah" says it all. In ironic contrast to the sole pursuit of excess and material success that vapid Shirley has been trained for, Syrkin alludes to Deborah, judge, warrior, and prophetess of the Book of Judges, famous for defeating the Canaanites who oppressed the Israelites with their nine hundred iron chariots and for predicting that the enemy general Sisera would be killed by a woman. The triumphant narrative of Deborah is told in Judges 4–5. Undoubtedly drawing from the lesson of her father's stern contrast between herself and Golda, she compares American Jewry's woeful progeny with the heroic Hannah Senesches, Bassya Osnos Syrkins, and Golda Meirs she has known throughout her life, all proud zealots. Instead of the biblical political emancipator, Syrkin's debased American remnant is embodied in the crassly "tinkling" Shirley.

Similarly, in her poems about the European catastrophe, nothing remains to compete with the past. Syrkin mourns her alienation from the sacred language, notably in Holocaust lyrics such as "My Uncle in Treblinka," which traces the pathos of the German Jewish experience from the rarefied days of its highest academic achievement to its destiny in the gas chambers and lime-pits of Europe. Syrkin judges harshly the barren choices she, and by extension her entire generation, has made. Facing the loss of a relative murdered in a death camp and the world he represented, this acutely self-conscious poet confronts the sheer inadequacy of her own subjectivity to perform the task of witnessing:

> The Germans led my uncle to Treblinka.
> He went with his prayers and equations,
> His psalms and logarithms.
> At the door of the slaughter-house
> Both were with him—
> The angels at his side.
>
> God of Israel,
> Light of reason,
> In the chamber of gas, in the pit of lime,
> Did my uncle, gentle and hard of hearing,
> Feel their pinions
> Over his head?

In this elegiac lyric, mourning for the European past is overtaken by a sense of pessimism and inadequacy toward the present. Implicating herself for lacking the sacred language to respond as she should to the legacy of the ancestral past, Syrkin again portrays the uncommitted present as woefully unequipped to live up to its vigorous heritage, as if she is no better than the Shirleys of her classroom:

> To the seat of justice,
> Where prayers are heard
> And problems solved,
> I, ignorant alike
> Of Hebrew and mathematics,
> Send these words for my uncle,
> Murdered at Treblinka.
>   (*Gleanings* 60–61)

The same pessimistic current surfaces in her prose reflections on Jewish intellectual life in America as a whole. For if the grim prospect of intermarriage and dislocation is not enough permanently to cripple Jewish life in America, then the morbid cynicism of its intellectuals and novelists will finish the job. The literary Jews' rootless existence in America is symptomatic of the erosion of the standards of Jewish communal life as a whole:

The report we receive from the ablest Jewish writers about American Jewish life—the Jewish community—is anything but reassuring. Each in his fashion, allowing for variations in talent and style, if he is a serious American Jewish writer of the second or third generation, describes a middle-class existence oppressive in its vulgarity, without ideas or ideals, and without genuine commitment to the religious or social values it professes. (*The State of the Jews* 270)

Castigating the unholy trinity of Malamud, Roth, and Bellow (though in later years she would compare the latter favorably to Roth), she notes that their male characters are "uprooted, erotically mobile." Above all they are weak, subject to "disintegrating on the analyst's couch" (270). Syrkin complains that "[t]he fictional characters who inhabit the [literary] scene are gross and trivial, as are their activities and ambitions" (270). What distresses her so much in other writers, particularly the contemporary Jewish novelist, is what she takes for excessive negativism: "One suspects he [the American Jewish novelist] is engaged in a valedictory. This is his farewell to a world from which he has emerged and is leaving. And the mood of his farewell is distaste rather than nostalgia" (271). Jewish writers are singled out because "they formulate their disenchantment in words. Among other sectors of the intellectual community, there is a less demonstrative, passive fading away" (273). Elsewhere, she concludes a brief survey of the Jewish American novel with the unhappy remark that "for many of the ablest of its sons, 'being Jewish' has become a dry well" ("Jewish Awareness in American Literature" 226). Always attentive to the treachery of literary representations, Syrkin was highly skeptical of the ability of Jewish Americans to comprehend the insidious work of such representations:

Jewish self-hatred has reached an overwhelming degree. It takes very devious forms. And curiously it is sometimes totally unaware of itself. For example, I have met intelligent Jews who think that *The Little Drummer Girl*, Le Carré's new novel, is a very fair account. I read it because it is a number one best-seller, so I thought it important to read; otherwise I never read detective stories, I can't stand them. Now if ever there was a blatant piece of propaganda, very cleverly done, and in which the writer editorializes, that's this book. But the book is not the problem. The problem is that apparently perceptive Jews fall for it. That's a very subtle form of Jewish self-hatred—the unwillingness to recognize what the enemy is doing to you. ("A *Moment* Interview" 239)

Syrkin never doubted the role she had to play in what she regarded as a high-stakes cultural war. In Emma Lazarus's poetry, the enervated shtetl Jew is replaced with martial prowess and agrarian images of vigor and strength. Nearly a century later, Lazarus's prophecy seemed to be fulfilled. Accordingly, Syrkin exults that Israel in her time had enjoyed incomparable success in replacing one set of popular images of the Jew with another, more positive group of symbols: "A striking instance of the effect of Israel's emergence on popular attitudes is that for the first time in generations a code word for Jew is no longer the medieval 'wandering Jew' or 'rootless cosmopolitan' but 'Zionist,' the individual fiercely rooted in his soil—the exact opposite of the former stigma" (*The State of the Jews* 287). Syrkin wants her readers to see this exchange as incontestable progress; the record of thousands of years of catastrophic encounters between the Jew and the Gentile world is wiped clean now that s/he is as "fiercely rooted" as they. The existence of Israel absolutely compels a particular Jewish identity, "even though the individual may demonstratively decline to honor the connection" (287). Furthermore, this shift in Jewish history is so monumental that "its very immensity makes comment superfluous" because life in the Diaspora has come to mean either "benign assimilation" or "active persecution," nothing more.

During the Hitler years, when she was teaching high school English, Syrkin confesses to having felt repugnance for the "cringing Jew" that she saw represented everywhere: ". . . it was painful to teach *Ivanhoe*. The one German refugee in my class would wince visibly each time the cringing Isaac would get another taunt or buffet. And the noble Rebecca was too clearly the unreal creature of romance to be of much help." Like Emma Lazarus in her response to the European pogroms, Syrkin pushes for a Zionism that replaces the old model of ghetto Jew with more heroic images: "the modern Rebeccas [of Israel] are on the front pages and the Isaacs have become sturdy Itzhaks," adding that, "they provide a more effective refutation than a learned disquisition on medieval barbarism and the status of the Jews in the days of stout King Richard" (*The State of the Jews* 290–91).[30] For Syrkin the best answer to one stereotype is simply another stereotype: "by and large images of vigor and independence have replaced those of cowardice and obsequiousness in the consciousness of the gentile world" (290). This is precisely the substitution that we witness in her poetry.

◆

In this regard it is telling that Syrkin's biography of her father recalls his disapproval of the artful evasions and compromises of the Jewish community in his childhood town of Mohilev. Many of the town's Jews were intent on "Russification" and hoped to send their most gifted boys to the *gymnasium* so that "they could become lawyers, doctors, and engineers" (*Nachman Syrkin* 19). The problem was attendance on Saturdays: the boys could walk to the *gymnasium* but not carry anything on the Sabbath, according to Jewish ritual. Yet under Jewish law it is possible to transform a public domain into private property. As Nachman Syrkin later told his daughter, the school authorities were unwilling to compromise on the matter of carrying the required books, even on the Jews' sacred day:

Obviously there was only one solution for the dilemma: the town had to be transformed into an *eruv*. Naturally, city officials had to be kept in the dark in regard to this scheme. They could not be expected to condone even the symbolic transformation of a Russian town into Jewish property. The undaunted Jews of Mohilev literally pulled wires at night stringing them secretly at strategic points. When the required section was completely "enclosed" by invisible wires, the triumphant Jews declared it a private domain, *ergo*, a "home!" (*Nachman Syrkin* 20)

By enclosing the area with rope or wires, an *eruv* ("mixture" in Hebrew) was established so that bread or water might be carried between the private space of the home and the public space of the synagogue. In simple terms this meant that within a circumscribed space objects might be carried. But in a richer, psychological sense that Syrkin overlooks, this ingenious suspension of normal prohibitions enabled the Diaspora Jew to "reconquer" space and time. By transposing a rich symbolism onto material reality, Jews could cope with Exile. As Dan Miron argues, the shtetl was essentially "the Jewish 'body politic.'" As Jewish territory, it was "carved out and separated from the continuum of space in which it was embedded but to which, ostensibly, it did not belong" (34). Hence, in this unique compromise with spatial exigency, the *eruv* (often a mere cord tied to tree branches) marked the edge of the non-Jewish wilderness, or Nature:

> An essentially non-Jewish feminine entity, beautiful, seductive, and subtly demonic. Conversely, the territory within the limits of the shtetl was not only Jewish in and of itself but also had a Judaizing effect upon almost everything with which it came into contact—including plants . . . and animals. (*The Image of the Shtetl* 35)

Yet beyond its anecdotal value as an amusing relic of the quaint past, Marie Syrkin says that his memory of this "ritualistic hocus-pocus" disgusted her father, "fill[ing] him with a distaste for 'slavish' adaptation through trickery, no matter how innocent. These were the servile shifts of the oppressed" (20). He was unimpressed by the philosophic dimensions of the *eruv*, the dim illusion that such a symbolic dispensation might actually allow one to move through a mixed, sometimes hostile world still proudly centered as a Jew.[31] For Nachman Syrkin, the Jewish masses are the "proletariat of the proletariat," the "slave of slaves"—miserable peddlers, tailors, shoemakers, and so on—whose "sole redemption lies in Zionism."[32] Here, in the classic rhetoric of the first generation of European Zionism, we can find the nullifying strain of pessimism that Marie Syrkin would pointedly invoke in her own appeals, from her indictment of Philip Roth to her scathing critiques of American culture as a whole. In her abhorrence for the "weak" Jews of American literature, there is no celebration of the resilience of tradition or the *Galut*'s ingenious adaptations to the norms of the host culture. The rich tradition of the ostensibly defeated schlemiel enduring as a moral victor in language is no longer viable in the totality of the Auschwitz universe:

> If you cannot be David,
> You will be Samson.
> One thing is sure,

You will not be Isaac.
You will not walk trustingly toward the altar.
You know
No ram will appear.

(Gleanings 72)

Here Isaac's submission stands in as a marker of the entire, fatal tradition of Jewish meekness—augmented by a fatalistic fear that "David" will falter on the battlefield. Like Lazarus, Syrkin yearns in her verse for the security of the ancient period of Jewish sovereignty. The radical reversals that may yet occur in the present evoke dread throughout *Gleanings*, particularly in this lyric written on the brink of Israel's 1948 War for Independence:

> Suppose, this time, Goliath should not fall;
> Suppose, this time, the sling should not avail
> On the Judean plain where once for all
> Mankind the pebble struck; suppose the tale
> Should have a different end: the shepherd yield,
> The triumph pass to iron arm and thigh,
> The wonder vanish from the blooming field,
> The mailed hulk stand, and the sweet singer lie.

(70)

But in other instances, Syrkin's post-Holocaust poetry, though positing a vision of a harsh universe dominated by the rule of force, is not altogether devoid of a sense of humor. As with other poets of trauma, her pragmatic ethos often has clever, albeit morbid effects, as in the wittily titled "Illiterate," where, "In the farmyard / White and brown chickens / Scratch peacefully in the gravel / Unwitting of the sign above them / 'Broilers'" (21). Although it is difficult to determine just how far we are intended to take this witticism, one of Syrkin's last poems, there is certainly an oblique allusion to the Holocaust. Is the farmyard of "white and brown" chickens doomed in spite of, or because of, their idyll of pluralism? Is coexistence always ill-fated? Here the poet touches her Jewish readers' awareness of the ease with which the harmony of multilingual and multicultural worlds could be destroyed. A similarly dissonant experience issues from the ironically titled "Coexistence":

> Grant the gray cat
> Find a warm sunning
> Far from the bird,

Young, without cunning,
That fell.

May the mute fish
Dart past the baited
Rod—and the angler
Homeward go sated
As well.

Foolish the wish,
Human in error,
While the soft worm,
Writhing in terror,
Hangs there unheard.
(*Gleanings* 25)

Substituting the vulnerable human for the "soft worm," Syrkin brutally wears down our hopes for the seductive but ultimately naïve attractions of the quotidian, the kind of small moments of unanticipated compassion that make urban civilization endurable in the wake of immeasurable loss. Reading this dark poem as a blunt allegory (that echoes Syrkin's chilling prophecy of an infinitude of "zoological suffering"), we find her striving to overcome the uncritical optimism that she felt characterized Jewish American liberalism. Invoking a postwar Jewish identity now "writhing" and "muted" by a secret dread of the universe, these lines resurrect the "lachrymose" view of *Galut*. The Diaspora Jew as innovator in her or his own right, intrinsic to the tradition of Western individuality, is undermined by Zionism's rhetoric of collective fate.

Though I am persuaded that *Gleanings* is overtaken by an ominous tone that embodies Syrkin's resistance to validating the open-ended flux of reality, it is crucial to note how successfully Syrkin's poetry anticipates the poet Jerome Rothenberg's disturbing call for a Jewish poetry "altered, transformed down to its roots" by the reality of Auschwitz and "mankind in extremis." For Rothenberg, a new lyric voice of "uglinesss" must counter the easy "temptation of the beautiful":

This, then, is also poetry's real voice—its most real voice perhaps, given the revelations of the Khurbn & of the century through which we have just been living. It is not an easy thing to say, since I too have been smitten by Beauty—& have felt that as an antidote to the murder & madness of the other dispensation. But that was to forget that the perpetrators themselves so often held to a cult of mindless beauty, while committing the ugliest . . . of crimes & degradations—as the final issue, so to speak, of a false & lying art. (Rothenberg 145)

There is a distinct sense that Syrkin already embraced the terms of Rothenberg's quest for a more sober poetics for an age of catastrophe, and "The Lie" might serve as her own philosophic manifesto. Here is her early realization of the enormity of loss and emptiness that Rothenberg (following Adorno) says must now haunt the poet:

> Do not believe the lie
> Life springs from death.
> The phoenix will not fly
> No ash has breath.
>   (*Gleanings* 39)

Even though Syrkin shares her Objectivist husband's keen fascination with the contingencies of modern urban life, here open-endedness gives way to foreshadowing disaster. Unlike Blake, *all* of Syrkin's songs are "Songs of Experience." Thus, the inevitable outcome in the cruelly titled "Safe":

> One old woman in Central Park
> Daringly feeds birds in the snow,
> Unafraid of muggers,
> Guarded by pigeons.
>   (22)

The inherent fatalism of these sardonic lines may be obvious, but there is something rather sadder that surfaces here—almost a tone of contempt for the hopeless complacency of the weak. An impending threat of urban violence looms over the scene. Even a child's innocent investigation of her environment is shrilly jettisoned by the traces of the adult's unendurable knowledge of the past:

> This small obstructive child
> Screams when I swat a fly
> And will not eat her lamb chop.
> She must be taught good behavior
> And how simple is killing.
>   (22)

Invariably, these scripts of doomed domestic and urban life are inflected by a far greater script of devastation. In a crucial analogous development, just as Syrkin's knowledge of the European devastation infiltrates and ultimately skews her critique of American urban and domestic complacency, her Holocaust poetry is similarly bound to Zionist conventions. For the Holocaust lyrics are featured in a section that also includes celebrations of Hebrew street names, dancing and conversation about Bialik in the streets of Tel Aviv, and the triumphant reburial of her father on the shore of Kinnereth in 1951: "Could you but see what flag flies from the mast / What comrades wait beside Kinnereth lake / What walls have risen at the trumpet blast / of vision!" (*Gleanings* 83). Committed to the inseparable epics of European genocide and statehood, Syrkin rarely pauses for the ordinary, never commits the mundane to lyricism, except to overshadow it with catastrophe. Uneasily joined to verses about Treblinka and Auschwitz are lyrics such as "David," the most anthologized of her poems, about Israel's War for Independence, and a poem about the 1973 Arab-Israeli war. Though today the juxtaposition of threats to Israel's security with the Nazi genocide may seem less reasonable, we have to grant that for Syrkin this relation bears an incontestable logic. For instance, she finds no reason not to conflate Russian MIGs and the death camps:

> Doomsday can break even in this bright air
> By these clear waters.
> The blue Mediterranean will stay blue;
> No ghosts will spring
> From smokeless chimneys in Treblinka's square,
> Or roll from Babi Yar.
>
> (78)

◆

An early scholar of international Holocaust poetry, Syrkin deserves our admiration for her urgent attention to those early texts written by victims and survivors of the ghettos and camps, who had written much of their work on fragments, "preserved by chance or smuggled out" (*The State of the Jews* 317). In addition to Reznikoff's ambitious project, *Holocaust*, she was familiar with Yevtushenko's Russian *Babi Yar*, as well as the Yiddish poetry of Jacob Glatstein and Yitzhak Katzenelson. Syrkin had already contributed to this genre herself by translating the poetry of Nobel Prize winner Nelly Sachs. We have seen that in Syrkin's own poetry of witness the subjective is deferentially muted. Hence it is revealing that Sachs is the Holocaust poet who most pleases her precisely because of Sachs's selflessness in transmuting "personal anguish" into a *collective* vision (*The State of the Jews* 317–30).

Describing her moral and aesthetic preference for Sachs's lyrics above all other renderings of German bestiality, Syrkin applauds the absence of any messy taint of ambiguity, no "murky confusion between victim and evildoer" (*The State of the Jews* 319). For Syrkin, dismayed by Hannah Arendt's unwelcome parallels between victim and persecutor in her analysis of the European Jewish establishment, the aesthetic representation of the totality of loss and evil must not be diminished: "Sachs knows fully the helpless terror of children; she does not romanticize their destruction by endowing it with metaphysical consolation" (323).[33]

Sachs's Blakean portrayal of a victimized ghetto child, a piper who perishes in an act of lyrical resistance seems especially congruent with her own vision:

> And when Eli saw
> With his eight-year-old eyes
> How they drove his parents along the cow path, the cow path
> He took his pipe and piped.
> He did not pipe as one pipes to cattle or in play.
> He threw his head back
> As the deer, as the roe,
> Before they drink at the spring.
> He turned his pipe to the sky,
> He piped to God, this Eli.
>
> (*The State of the Jews* 322)

Sachs's eight-year-old Eli audaciously angers a stormtrooper by playing his pipe "to God" and thus perishes in the obscurity of a ghetto street. Ideologically consistent with Zionist historiography, Syrkin embraces Sachs's vision in casting the shadow of the Holocaust *back* into history, through this contemporary martyrdom: "Eli is the innocence of Israel attacked throughout history because of a divine dedication" (323). In Sachs, Syrkin grimly discovers a kindred spirit, one whose vision (at once brutal and sentimental) of a universe filled with bestial suffering blurs the luxury of a normative distinction between human and animal:

The image of dust, the common denominator in the universe, recurs in a poem about the suffering of animals, whose "fate turns with small steps, like the second hand on the dial in the unredeemed hour of mankind." Sachs does not hesitate to write of the calf torn from its mother, the mute fish, the bloody flesh of a horse on a battlefield. She is not afraid of the triteness of straightforward compassion, nor . . . does she seek unusual symbols for its expression. However, in the midst of poetic commonplaces there occurs the magnificent line: "How much creeping and feathered dust clings to the soles of our shoes, which stand like open graves in the evening." The "graves of air" of the Jews of Europe do not obscure the leather graves in which we tread on life, that "creeping and feathered dust". . . . The shoes torn from his feet remind her that they were made of "calf-skin once stroked by the warm tongue of the mother-animal before it was torn off." (326)

For both poets, death, whether as imminent prospect or lingering sensory awareness, fills the universe. The Holocaust transformed Syrkin's poetic and critical voice to such an extent that nothing remains in the way of consola-tion, at least not until a politics of redemption fills the vacuum. A line from Sachs seems to account eloquently for her own morbid perception of quo-tidian reality: "Superfluous is the embrace of emptiness, a circling ring that has lost its finger" (327). Syrkin sees that Sachs's great gift is to pose "the question-mark which hangs over our century, the mystery of its moral col-lapse" (329). But that question is only rhetorical, having just one possible resolution.

Throughout her reading of Sachs, as well as in the narrative structure of *Gleanings*, Syrkin performs what Michael André Bernstein has cogently described as the kind of retroactive foreshadowing in which the collective knowledge of an outcome is used to judge the participants in earlier events.[34] Taken as a whole, her poetry moves us along what has proven to be a seduc-tive trajectory for many Jewish writers—from collective tragedy to collective redemption—in which the challenges of individualist human agency and hard choices give way to inevitable futures. In the later stanzas of *Gleanings*, the Holocaust's shadow is present in Syrkin's Zion in ways that dismantle human agency, the extreme individual freedom that had in fact molded the spirit of American Jewry. Leaving behind the interiority of the earlier lyrics, the private heartbreak of her own solitude, she takes up the heavy burden of articulating the outbreak of collective grief, as the enormity of loss settled in. As with much of Lazarus's late poetry, *Gleanings* reads as a work torn between the very premises of autobiography and the need to subsume indi-vidual experience within a historically deterministic narrative of collective experience.

Syrkin's commitment to the power of the spare, illuminating detail in-forms much of the section called "Holocaust and Israel," which forms the subject of her middle years. The caustic wit is all her own, but the razor-sharp imagery and observation that create such stunning moments of witness provide evidence of her early respect for Reznikoff's commitment to imagism and objectivism. Indeed, Syrkin, no less than Reznikoff, was writing Objectivist poetry, and her lyrics of witness from this period certainly stand the test of time, particularly the starkly nullifying "Niemand," a lyric of excruciating pain, inspired by the story that, in 1938, a Jewish woman driven out of the Sudeten area gave birth to her son in a ditch and named him *Niemand* or "Nobody":[35]

> You with the cross and you without the cross,
> Come quietly.
> We go to Maidanek; all roads lead there
> And every sea.
> The summons is for all; the pilgrims wait.
> It is not far.
> You will find stations: shelter in Zbonzyn,
> A bed in Babi Yar.
>
> *Niemand* will greet you; *Niemand* knows the way
> From ditch to doom.
> [Hear the Annunciation: cursed art thou,
> And cursed thy womb.]
> A little child shall lead you—it is he,
> No One, my son.
> No one, Nobody, Nothing—now he calls
> On everyone.
> The house of death is big; its walls will hold
> A multitude;
> And of this sacrament you must partake,
> Body and blood.
>
> You with the cross and you without the cross,
> On each the sin.
> Seek absolution in no other place.
> Come, enter in.
>
> (58)

The stark fact of the child born in a ditch is interwoven with what may be references to Blake's cruel Nobodaddy. Yet this is perhaps a more radical denunciation, a bitter subversion of Judaism's traditional refusal to name the Divine Presence, now at best truly a remote absence who has left his children homeless—and now nameless. The reader cannot escape an even more terrifying prospect—that of a bitter deity who has contrived a new covenant, of death, for His people. Such a convention often informs the poetics of Yehudah Amichai, Paul Celan, and Dan Pagis. The emotive effect of Syrkin's sometimes lamentative, usually angry, lyrics of this period is often as compelling as these more renowned poets, particularly when she invokes Christological motifs (though hardly in a spirit of ecumenicism) to drive home the West's betrayal of its Others:

> Give me back Jesus
> He is my brother.
> He will walk with me
> Behind the gray ghetto-wall
> Into the slaughter house.
> I will lead him into the lethal chamber;
> He will lie down upon the poisoned stone.
> The little children pricked with the death-bubble
> Will come unto him.
>
> Return to him the yellow badge.
> Give me back Jesus;
> He is not yours.
>
> (53)

◆

It is hardly unreasonable that, in the immediate aftermath of the Shoah, her work urgently calls for an immediate change of circumstances in the lives of victims. But the effect is still jarring when her sequence of Holocaust lamentations breaks off abruptly, as a martial ode introduces a new tone: "To Comrades in Palestine" marks the tonal and thematic shift from mourning to zealotry, as a triumphant Judean lion symbolizes the new Jew who will at long last resume responsibility for his fate and "Roar into Galilee / Past the Judean hills / Beyond the Shattered Sea!" (64). During Syrkin's lifetime, the Shoah became an intrinsic feature of contemporary Zionist discourse and Israeli culture. Hence, in what is at once the most awkward and revealing of this group of verse, "The Silent Army," the desert landscape itself observes the formula of an inescapable logic as it merges with the European atrocities. It is as if the empty Negev desert melts away like a fata morgana to reveal the six million it did not shelter, a reality that is somehow more tangible to the poet's experience:

Do not believe that we are few . . .
   Though few the figures on the hill;
A host ascends the mountain-side
   Whose solemn ranks are marching still.

Along the waste six million trudge
   Up to the Negev's burning rim,
The bodies seared at Maidanek
   Can bear the flame at Nitzanim

(76)

Here the high rhetorical style of Israeli leaders such as Ben Gurion seems to overtake her own voice as she links the European martyrdom to a visit to the Negev, where Ben Gurion's Zionism reaches its fulfillment.

An important clue to the pervasive influence of this limiting aesthetic may be traced to Syrkin's biographical studies of Golda Meir. These include her own authoritative biography *Golda Meir: Israel's Leader* (1969), as well as *A Land of Our Own: An Oral Autobiography of Golda Meir*, which Syrkin edited. Touted as "autobiography," the latter is actually a compilation of formal addresses, press interviews, and public statements. There is surprisingly little evidence of the kind of reflective narrative of the self—the site where we might expect to encounter the doubts or textual ruptures produced by the subjective voice—with which most people associate the genre. Yet Syrkin accepts this deception on face value: "at no point was there a real dichotomy between the demands of [Meir's] personal life and her imperious need to take part to the fullness of her ability in the social and political movements in which she believed." *A Land of Our Own* purports to capture "the totality of her experience as woman and stateswoman" (12). There is never a conflict between one's inner life and Zionist ideology: "Because of this unyielding commitment to her cause, her addresses, for all their variety of subject matter, have an inner harmony and progress dramatically to their climax—the establishment and defense of Israel" (12). There are no doubts or contradictions in this record—only a seamless, unfolding narrative whose outcome is predictably exemplary: "The youthful dream, which to all save a dedicated few seemed an illusory spark, blazes into the steady light of her old age" (12). In his astute analysis of Zionism's displacement of individualism, Yaron Ezrahi notices that, "[a]lthough Israel is committed to basic liberal-democratic principles of order, such as the dignity and freedom of persons, the value of self-narration has been limited not only by the poverty of personal space, personal time, or personal language but also by the omnipresence of the collective social voice" (*Rubber Bullets* 81). The precipitous change from Syrkin's individualist poetry of loss, intimacy, and irony to the kind of impersonal and declamatory poetics that Ezrahi alludes to should not surprise us. For Syrkin, Jewish poetry and politics were twin expressions of a single impulse. Since no individual voice can suffice to mark the catastrophe, one must instead surrender to the collective groupspeech of ideology. As Ezrahi asserts, in Zionist narrative, "death at the hands of the Nazis and liberation by means of a Jewish army were too monumental to be regarded as autobiographical events" (99). Parting judiciously from the traumatic narrative of the Holocaust and turning away to welcome the new epic, the unfolding drama of statehood, it is as if Syrkin's own voice is deemed insufficient to evoke martyrdom or heroic sacrifice. In this regard *Gleanings* provides instructive insight into the self-limiting cultural forms that would mediate Zionist experience for decades to come. For whether it expressed religious, nationalist, or socialist yearnings, or a potent combination of all three, the Zionist enterprise was intensely collectivist in nature. The Western tradition of liberal-democratic individualism was simply not a factor, except perhaps among the exceptional Brandeis-Kallen efforts to "Americanize" Zionism, and this movement was not influential in shaping Zionist ideology either in the Yishuv or the Jewish state itself. Set against this collectivism, Syrkin's poetry shifts from her private vocabulary of selfhood to the transformation of that self into an agent of ideology.

Unlike what we witnessed in Emma Lazarus's work, the poetic and critical components of Syrkin's oeuvre blend well together. Having fully committed herself to representations of the European Diaspora as singularly violent and the American Diaspora as uniformly vacuous, Syrkin's poetry and polemics both propose Zion as the only alternative for a viable Jewish existence. The sad irony, of course, is that, in the end, the irresistible power of the collective narrative of Zionism does not bring her home. With the failure of Labor Zionism and the ascendancy of the far right, she was effectively estranged from Israel in her last years. Although Zionism's irrefutable truths had been etched onto her identity by her father, she falters, bereft of the certitude of terms that had once provided her with an ultimate position in relation to Israel and the world. Rhetorically however, she was impressively unwavering and liked to repeat her lifelong friend Golda Meir's remark that: "When I meet my American friends, women who are my contemporaries, I am sorry for them. They worry about their grandchildren. My grandchildren are . . . in a kibbutz in the Negev, but I am absolutely certain about them" (276). In spite of physical danger, Meir and Syrkin were persuaded that "a complete life as a Jew can only be experienced in full sincerity in the Jewish state" (*The State of the Jews* 277).

Accordingly, Syrkin's poetry exhibits an understanding of Jewish trauma that has been accepted by many others: the return of the Jewish people to statehood must be understood against the shadow of the Shoah and even prior persecutions. Besides her father's lingering influence, there is some evidence to suggest that her fatalism was reinforced by her careful reading of one of the most pessimistic of Zionist theoreticians, Ber Borochov. For Syrkin, invoking the latter's foreboding statement that the Jews are unassimilable because they are inevitably forced into the interstices and margins of economic life makes perfect sense: "there is an inevitable dynamic process in every society which at some point drives Jews out, when they have achieved a certain measure of success. The point comes when they can be replaced by other elements in the majority or other section of the native population."[36] Unable to compete in economies dominated by non-Jews and arousing anti-semitism everywhere, the Jewish masses would be compelled to migrate to Palestine, the only territory in which they will achieve economic "normalcy." Building Palestine is the only possible response to the catastrophic record of dissolution and impotence. In the strategic thematic arrangement of *Gleanings*, the dark nights of Europe apparently dissolve forever in the cheerful sunshine of "Tel Aviv": "Hora, they dance the hora" / . . . / Stamping, along the pavements / They circle singing, to left, to right" (68). Written shortly after one of her visits to Palestine, no later poem exhibits such a wistful or wondrous dream of rest, comradeship, and homecoming:

> In Tel Aviv the camels slowly
> Trudge on the edge of the soft-sea-sand
> The whiff of the foam is salt and sudden
> And the houses are white on the sunny strand
> I am glad in my heart for the quiet camels
> The good white houses and the silver sea
> I am glad in my heart for the fine friends strolling
> Arm in arm in the dusk with me.

After her harrowing lyrics of atrocity, the readers may feel rewarded by a calm resolution as Syrkin contemplates the solidity of those white houses in Zion. This is also the only poem of *Gleanings* notable for its expression of camaraderie. But after wandering numerous streets named "Balfour," "Bialik," or "Herzl," she comes to solitary rest on the street that commemorates her father: "But when I stood on the unpaved 'Syrkin' / It felt pleasant to my feet" (68–69). In spite of the poet's professed sense of "pleasant" home-coming, there is an unspoken sense of incompletion and unease that lingers at the lyric's end. *Unpaved*, it is as though her father's ghostly presence in the Land represents an unfinished project—the unfinished landscape express-ing her own sense of incompletion, as if she herself, a sojourner in *Galut*, has failed to complete the promise of her father's vision.

A "home" that is beyond her own grasp forms the pivotal trope of her Zionist poetry, a logical but morbid link between two generations of dead Syrkins that leaves her bereft outside the Land, to cope alone with a memory of loss, like any other diasporic poet. Like the collective trauma of the Holo-caust, the pain of her private losses is put to rest in Zion:

> I have never gone back to Ithaca,
> Afraid of the small headstone, the weed-choked plot.
> Now there is a plaque with your name
> In a kindergarten in Jerusalem.
>
> In Jerusalem
> In a house for children
> With eyes dark as yours,
> Prattling in Hebrew
> And laughing,
> I took heart to face your name:
> Benyah.
>
> (94–95)

Is there a note of envy here for the Sabra children "prattling in Hebrew," the language of homecoming that forever excluded her? Only the comfort of her father's reinterment in Israel, the material artifacts of an unpaved Tel Aviv street, and a plaque in memory of her first child in a Jerusalem kinder-garten remain left to contemplate.[37] For ironically, Syrkin and other Ameri-can Zionists would inevitably find themselves excluded from the privileged vocabulary of the Zionist utopia: *aliyah, yerida, Eretz Yisrael, ha'aretz, ba'aretz,* and *hutz-la'aretz*.[38] As most American Zionists gave little thought to uprooting themselves, the rhetoric of Zionism was unable to accommo-date their identities.

By the time of her own death, on February 2, 1989, just a month short of ninety years, Marie Syrkin had earned a reputation as a gifted thinker and educator who consistently engaged and experienced the political world as a Jew. Facing the historical forces of political antisemitism, her response was to produce prose and poetry intended to counter fascism and defenseless-ness. The Holocaust—and the decaying remnant of a rootless Diaspora—confirmed her conviction that Jewish survival in the modern world required the politics of Zionism. Her mission-oriented poetry and polemics are angrily invigorated by a coherent and unified vision of a meaningful Jewish destiny, in spite of the ever-widening schism between that dream and her own lived experience. The manifest failures of Zionism—"social inequities, deprivation among Oriental Jews, endless struggle with the Arabs"—and the fading of utopian dreams notwithstanding, she found justification in the medieval sage Maimonides' famous speculation on the days of the Messiah:

> Let no one believe that when the Messiah will come anything in the world will be destroyed, or that there will be some change in Creation. This will not be so. The world will go on even as it had before . . . there will be no difference between the present day and the days of the Messiah except for the fact that the Jews will cease to be subject to alien domination. That is all. (*The State of the Jews* 292)

In her commentary on this passage, Syrkin observes that the single "condition for the ideal time . . . is independence—the ability of a people to act according to its lights. From this all else follows: the rescue of victims of persecution, the building of a cooperative society or whatever else the vision may inspire. But the precondition is the sovereign right to act. The capacity for the search for solutions marks the days of the Messiah, not their attainment" (292).

Until the end, she was a vigilant and embattled warrior against the naysayers, as her posthumously published "'Phony Israel': An Exercise in Nastiness" reveals. Written in reaction to a 1988 article by Hebrew University professor and leftist activist Avishai Margalit that denounced Israel's propagandistic uses of Jewish history and putative compassion for its enemies (he calls the latter "shooting and crying"), Syrkin lashed out at what she saw as moral charlatanism.[39] Citing Kundera's definition of the vicarious sentiment, rather than true involvement, that cultural kitsch always masks, Margalit condemned a broad range of revered institutions in Israeli life, from famous speeches by Golda Meir to its "Holocaust kitsch" and war memorials. In her eloquent and characteristically trenchant rebuttal, Syrkin insisted on adding another term to her adversary's lexicon: " 'Critical kitsch,' that is, phony criticism and political distortion in which an opponent, instead of attacking straightforwardly, disguises stale accusations to make them more 'marketable.' Since Margalit occasionally sounds grace notes of regret, it may also be [defined] as 'hooting and sighing,' a more honest variant of shooting and crying" (271). She had faced down a lifetime of such foes. At once intellectually acerbic, rationally and emotionally persuasive, what were to be Syrkin's last public words on "Israel-bashers" offer us a synthesis of some of her best qualities as a lifelong defender of the essential compatability of Judaism and the Jewish state:

'Holocaust kitsch.' Yes, that's the term Margalit uses. Many Jews have reservations about the sometimes unseemly exploitation of the Holocaust and may agree with Adorno that, for so immense a calamity, silence is fittest. But what has such aesthetic restraint to do with the genuineness of the emotion? When I was in D.P. camps in 1947, I collected songs and verses composed by survivors. *"Dos Shtetl Brent"* would have failed any literary criteria, but the singers and the listeners wept. . . . Whatever may be wrong, it is not the reality of Israel, its achievements, suffering, and beliefs, for which Jews gave their lives. The 'blood, sweat, and tears' have been all too genuine. (271)

Though she had written that "[t]he phoenix will not fly," Syrkin fervently sought to link the Holocaust's ashes to the rebirth of Israel as parts of a coherent continuum. And yet toward the end, the ideological lines of *Gleanings* are inflected by an unexpected late confession of disillusionment and fading idealism that bursts forth:

FACTS

Remember how the heart rode high
Upon the gallop of young hope?
And now the nag is winded, lame,
And where it leapt must weakly grope.

The course long lost—yet in my need
I still cling to the silly steed.
Dismount? And face the facts alas:
This trot was all along an ass?

(31)

Though she has gone too far to "dismount," the once self-evident "truths" of this "silly steed," ideology, are no longer persuasive. It is as though, if she paused to "face the facts," Syrkin would be unhorsed and find herself ideologically unsettled. Sincerely appalled by the intransigence of the Right in Israel, she tried to make belated amends to the Left by signing the first Peace

Now statement.[40] Hardly a conventional conservative, in one of her final interviews she remarks sadly: "Look at the small group of wonderful individuals who started the American democracy. Enlightened people, full of liberal ideas—and now we have Reagan. That's certainly a monumental decline" ("A *Moment* Interview" 239). At the same time she is painfully aware of an even more precipitous decline that has occurred in Israel: "from Ben-Gurion to Begin." "From this point on," says her sister Zivia Syrkin Wurtele, in reference to the election of Menachem Begin and the defeat of the Zionist Labor party, "she was far less hopeful about the future."[41] Syrkin even confesses her own ideological alienation resulting from the deterioration of Zionist vision into the cynical excesses of Occupation: "I can disagree with an ideological member of Gush Emunim who sees biblical patrimony that he must act on— but when I read of a real estate boom on the West Bank, fueled by speculators for no other reason than to make money, I am shocked" (238–39). In her essays published in 1980, she again made plain her revulsion at Begin's "betrayal" of the Zionist dream. But it would be inaccurate to claims that she wavers: "Zionism and the reality of a Jewish state are the chief forces making for Jewish spiritual and physical survival in this secular age" (239). "Facts" appears to insinuate that she never really enjoyed the sense of autonomy necessary to reject the political identity she was born into—without rupturing her sense of personal integrity and authenticity.

Syrkin remained a nuanced and thoughtful critic of Israeli policies even in her final months. In the early days of the Intifada, when asked by *Commentary* to respond to the question of what had changed in her attitude toward Israel, she expressed her dismay over "the espousal of the Likud program by half of Israel. The vision of a . . . secular, democratic society now competes with extremist chauvinism and pseudo-messianic bigotry." But for the most part she was unapologetically loyal to her earliest views: "I still believe that Herzl's naive vision of happy Arab-Jewish coexistence, as well as the theoretical socialist-Zionist program for Arab-Jewish cooperation in the reclamation of Palestine, affirmed a moral principle integral to a rational world order. That [such] views . . . sound like sentimental drooling indicts those who shattered generous hopes rather than those who held them" ("American Jews and Israel" 74–75).

Ironically, as far as the situation of American Jewry was concerned, it is often the case that although the very things Syrkin feared the most have indeed transpired, these have often *enhanced*, not diminished, Jewish culture. For instance, it is true that the public school system, which served earlier Jewish generations so well, has declined. But as Henry L. Feingold points out, the direct consequence (at least from the perspective of the last few years) is that "Jewish day schools are growing in number and impact." Further-more, American "Jewish rabbinic academies suffer no dearth of enrollment, and university presses and commercial publishers produce more books on Jewish subjects than ever before in Jewish history" (*Lest Memory Cease* 18). Five decades after the biological and cultural losses that so anguished Syrkin, "Jews seem to have regained the confidence to go forward":

> What we are witnessing . . . is not disintegration but transformation. That does not mean an abandonment of faith but rather the transmutation of its basic principles to accord with the modern sensibility. The messianic impulse appears again as the search for justice and world peace, exile is transformed into a priestly mission to the nations, chosenness becomes avocation. Most importantly, the religious sensibility that was once public, commanding, and communal becomes, in modernity, internal-ized, private, and searching. (18)

But it is precisely this crucial trope of modernity, the notion of "transmuta-tion," that Syrkin zealously rejected, remaining ever distrustful of the liberal individualism of American culture. In her lifetime, various discourses of op-position to Zionism enjoyed a lively resurgence on the American scene.[42] But in her allegiance to the absolute justice of Zionism she abstained from fully examining the justice of those arguments. At the same time, it must be under-stood that her poetry of witness represents a highly ethical Jewish response to the recent past. Her lyrics speak for a guilt-ridden identification that many Diaspora Jews feel when they think about the Shoah. But it seems likely that these guilt-inflected lyrics were more informed by her Jewish American identity rather than Zionist affiliations. Unlike Arendt, Syrkin refused to see any significance in the Zionist leadership's contempt for the victims of Hitler and their leaders who had lacked the vision to emigrate to Israel. Even years after the war, the attitude of the Zionist leadership's attitude toward the Nazi victims was markedly ambivalent. And yet, in Syrkin's prose and poetry, she managed to remain persistently loyal to both groups. Throughout her life she attempted an impossible task: to graft the political and military victories of Zionism onto unspeakable losses.

For Syrkin the ontic grounds for a viable Diaspora were sorely tested in the mid-twentieth century. The Holocaust was nothing less than the dread fulfillment of the Zionist's worst-case scenario and, in response, this mani-festly Zionist poet recast the Jewish struggle as one poignantly constituted by a search for wholeness and healing that culminates in the recovery of place. For this reason I will now turn to consider the poetry and prose of Charles

Reznikoff, Syrkin's husband for some four decades, to directly contrast the features of a liberal, anti-essentialist notion of Jewishness with a Zionist's perspective on Jewish history and identity. Since my chief hope is to encourage alternative perspectives on the traumatic century we have just emerged from, the two chapters that follow place greater emphasis on the two poets' disparate efforts to thematize Jewish experience. Then, by considering Reznikoff and Syrkin in close proximity, we can draw a tighter mesh around the slippery ways that Diaspora and Zionism haunt the post-Holocaust consciousness of the Jewish American writer.

Chapter Three

Convivencia, Hybridity, and the Jewish Urban Modernist

One need be neither a religious fundamentalist nor a mystic to believe that there is some exemplary meaning to the singularity of Judaic endurance, that there is some sense beyond contingent or demographic interest to the interlocking constancy of Jewish pain and of Jewish preservation. The notion that the appalling road of Jewish life and the ever-renewed miracle of survival should have as their end, as their justification, the setting up of a small nation-state in the middle east, crushed by military burdens, petty and even corrupt in its politics, shrill in its parochialism, is implausible.

—George Steiner, "Our Homeland, the Text"

Over and above its national significance, Jewish history, we repeat, possesses universal significance.... The effective educational worth of the biblical part of Jewish history is disputed by none. It is called sacred history, and he who acquires a knowledge of it is thought to advance the salvation of his soul. Only a very few, however, recognize the profound, moral content of the second half of Jewish history, the history of the Diaspora. Yet, by reason of its exceptional qualities and intensely tragic circumstances, it is beyond all others calculated to yield edification to a notable degree.

—Simon Dubnow, "An Essay in the Philosophy of History"

Where is the wisdom
with which I may be medicined?
I will walk by myself
and cure myself
in the sunshine and the wind.
—Charles Reznikoff, *Poems* II, 29

Introduction

"Diasporism" has long been a creative current in postmodern Jewish philosophy and poetics. Variously voiced by Paul Auster, Daniel Boyarin, John Hollander, Edmond Jabès, George Steiner, and many others, it posits that language is the only natural homeland of the Jew.[1] Together, such writers have transformed nomadism into a source and justification of the Jewish text. They participate in a post-Shoah literary culture for which (even for non-Jewish theorists) the ambivalent nature of the Jewish Diaspora has increased its fascination. In other words, they have created a discursive space in which the Jewish self-image has been projected onto other identities, as well as the vocation of literary writing as a whole. When absolute national identities begin to show signs of decay, this ambivalence suddenly seems to be a universal condition applicable to other Others. The category of Diaspora, which has long had critical resonance for Jews, whose survival engendered a constant dialectic between Homeland and Exile, has become increasingly important in postcolonial theory.[2] In the postmodern world, various groups of people increasingly identify their liminal status between home and homeland as one of diaspora. As Sidra Ezrahi notes, "the postromantic, democratic language of personal quest and the role of personal alienation within the general condition of collective exile [evolved] into a peculiarly American diasporic agenda" (*Booking Passage* 30). But this creative paradigm has not often been traced to a pronouncedly diasporic current that was present in the early twentieth-century works of Charles Reznikoff (1894–1976). Yet Reznikoff's contribution to this historically significant paradigm led later generations of poets into an exploration of the prospects for a Jewish consciousness that lays stress on the humanity of the individual rather than upon a rigid chauvinism with a strict allegiance to a tribal collective. It is in the context of early Zionism's reinvention of Jewish identity that I suspect a new generation of readers will want to discover the works of Reznikoff, one of the first identifiable Jewish American poets of the twentieth century. This chapter examines the fertile intellectual and cultural debates that inspired Reznikoff's unique response to both nationalism and Jewish fate. Establishing the fascinating historiographical and cultural milieu that shaped his poetics should prepare the reader for a comparative discussion of Reznikoff and Syrkin and the closer readings of poetry that follow in chapter 4.

Though they first met in 1927, Marie Syrkin had become familiar with Reznikoff's poetry during her studies at Cornell nearly ten years earlier.

Immediately following the outcome of her prolonged divorce from Aaron Bodansky, she and Reznikoff were married in 1930; they lived together sporadically until Reznikoff's death in 1976.[3] Though it endured into a harmonious old age, this was not an easy marriage. Almost immediately they had to assume responsibility for the economic woes of Charles's immigrant parents, producing tensions candidly described in Syrkin's essay memoir (*Man and Poet* 37–67). But there was a more oblique source of tension that warrants further investigation. After a decade of marriage their awareness of ideological and vocational differences caused an open rift. Recalling that "[t]he forties were an unhappy time for us personally," Syrkin remarks that her "absorption in the unfolding Jewish catastrophe" came at a time when "Charles' own deep involvement expressed itself in verse not public activities" (51). The thought remains undeveloped, but it does seem to hint at a divide, as if she was disappointed in his failure to publicly embrace her ideological commitment to ethnic nationalism.[4] Though strongly committed to the idealistic plurality of *The Menorah Journal* (1915–1962), to which he contributed verse, drama, and prose narratives for over three decades (eventually serving as contributing editor), Reznikoff's involvement with American Jewish communal organizations was reluctant at best. And this would mark the schism of their warring Jewish identities.

From Syrkin's own account we also know that during the years of his editorial work for the *Jewish Frontier*, the Labor Zionist monthly, Reznikoff had little appetite for the propaganda and polemics that she readily admits were "its stock-in-trade" (54).[5] For Syrkin and the Labor Zionists at the *Jewish Frontier*, Zionism had returned the Jews to a grand epic narrative called "History," but for Reznikoff they had never been absent from it. Acknowledging only that he "despised the facile generalizations . . . and the superficial editorials that would have to be dashed off in response to a current crisis . . . [for these] were rarely of the literary caliber he was likely to admire" (53–54), Syrkin alludes to Reznikoff's exacting standards in matters of style, depth, and aesthetic taste. There is no pause to consider that Reznikoff might have found the *Jewish Frontier*'s ideological content itself distasteful. Beyond a terse acknowlegement that Reznikoff was no "[Jewish] nationalist with political affiliations," she does not bother to develop this thought, as if she has no appetite to pursue the deeper implications of his unrest. But for Syrkin, it is as though Reznikoff's stance constituted little more than a *lack*, not a position worthy of closer examination on its own terms. And in this regard it is worth noting that of the dozen lyrics she quotes in her memoir essay in the *Man and Poet* volume, none of these reflects Reznikoff's abiding preoccupa-

tion with the ways that exile and homelessness spoke to his modernist identity as an artist.

In Reznikoff's sidelong look at perhaps the most famous nonessentialist
of the age of modern Jewish artists, we are rewarded with a more revealing
glimpse than Syrkin offers of his own preoccupation with the endurance of
Jewish consciousness in spite of polyphonic attractions:

> We have a print of Marc Chagall's picture of a green-faced Jew:
> like a corpse, a doctor visiting us once said.
> But the green-faced Jew is smoking peacefully,
> holding tightly in his opened hand between thumb and forefinger
> a cigarette stub or bit of a cigar—
> to smoke the very last of it—
> and looking at you calmly.
> An open book, brown with age, such as my grandfather used to read,
> is in front of him,
> and behind him a silken hanging over the scrolls of the Torah.
> The hanging is green, too;
> embroidered on it, the shield of David
> and a single word in Hebrew, "hai,"
> meaning "life."
> When we moved, the moving-men dropped the picture
> and the glass that protected the print cracked;
> the crack ran over the word "hai"
> but the cracked glass held in the frame.
>
> (*Poems* II, 121)

The reader is left to imagine the fate of the painting as it remained on the
poet's wall in ensuing years. Was Reznikoff so taken with the crack juxtaposed with the symbol of life that he found the thought of replacing the glass
unbearable? Unlike the conspicuously gravity-defying figures of Chagall's
famous figures, the painting meets with the disfiguring condition that is
the inevitable fate of vulnerable objects and beings in the real world. But
Reznikoff embraces the fall, as if finding greater aesthetic pleasure in the eerie
accident and the cheerfully defiant "hai" than in the intact work.

For Reznikoff, Chagall was a representative figure of Jewish creativity and
endurance, having witnessed three Russian revolutions, two world wars, the
Holocaust, and the birth of the Jewish State. At the same time Chagall provided Reznikoff with an exultant paradigm of how the diasporic artist might
be at home in multiple worlds without sacrificing a Jewish selfhood, since,
along with modern secular Yiddish literature, he also embraced the Russian

language, the achievements of the Russian and French avant-gardes, as well as the aesthetic traditions of earlier Christian painting. In the two chapters that follow, we will examine the literary permutations of the poet's diasporic poetics—a response to what he saw as the unnecessarily reductive sense of identity and rootedness produced in Zionist discourse. In proposing an alternative meaning for Jewish continuity, Reznikoff's poetry speaks to the acute schisms that continue to divide Israel and the Diaspora.

◆

In the aftermath of a dinner party in early 1930, Reznikoff wrote a letter to Syrkin, describing a conversation with Maurice Samuel, her first husband. Samuel had dismissed the Zionist "mob and their idols," to which Reznikoff remarked that "these are very small idols [Stephen Wise and Hillel Silver], local gods: Herzl was a fraud" (*Selected Letters* 76). It is impossible to say with absolute certainty what Reznikoff meant by this atypically political out-burst, but it is likely that Herzl's famous condemnation of the Jewish Euro-pean past provoked him. Herzl had largely accepted the antisemitic portrait of Jews as unprincipled, parasitic, and vulgar, even when he argued that Christian oppression had "deformed" the Jewish character.[6] The shaper of political Zionism had been deeply hostile to the form of cultural Zionism articulated by Ahad Ha-Am (who had won a significant degree of accept-ance among the *Menorah Journal* intellectuals Reznikoff respected). Instead, Herzl claimed that the only "present day" work of a Zionist was the propaga-tion of settlement; anything designed to improve conditions in the Diaspora was useless (Heymann 228).

Similarly, for Emma Lazarus, the defining feature of Jewish identity was *absence*, the loss of an organizing reality. Writing for an America that had created an identity within its own biblical narrative, with its own reference points for events described in the Bible, Lazarus's rhetorical agenda was to show that Jews were territorially rooted, that they came from a definite land-scape that might yet be reclaimed. In her desire to divorce the Jews from their host societies and return them to a homogeneous space, her lyrics idealize ancient periods of Jewish sovereignty. For the Labor Zionists of Marie Syr-kin's generation, struggling to satisfy both a yearning for normality and the imperative of uniqueness, a mythopoetic imagination generated national realities. But for Reznikoff, writing in a radically shifting landscape of both European immigration and black migration, the Jews' loss of their territory meant that they had long anticipated the existential condition and displace-ments of other peoples. Hence, the experience Lazarus translated as a lack,

Reznikoff imagined as a new form of "authenticity." In contrast to Lazarus's and Syrkin's struggles to solidify the Jew's native grounds, vacillating between America and Palestine, erasure and memory, Reznikoff's poetry responds to Jewish traditions that strain against coercive narratives of nationalism. He drew from these traditions in ways that helped illuminate other marginal identities.

It is clear that for Reznikoff a positive encounter is created whenever a culture has an inner, vital power that manifests itself as openness to elements from without. Such an ethos is particularly evident in a parable included in the volume *Inscriptions: 1944–1956* where, though the speaker's lonely estrangement is presented sympathetically enough, as an inescapable yearning for recovery and wholeness (part of what makes us all human), such nostalgia is gently overcome by a call for fully dwelling in one's present moment:

> As I was wandering with my unhappy thoughts,
> I looked and saw
> that I had come into a sunny place
> familiar and yet strange.
> "Where am I?" I asked a stranger. "Paradise."
> "Can this be Paradise?" I asked surprised,
> for there were motor-cars and factories.
> "It is," he answered. "This is the sun that shone on Adam once;
> the very wind that blew upon him, too."
>
> (*Poems* II, 75)

Here the Jewish diasporist exploring the New World meets the modernist embrace of "profane" space. Stephen Kern evocatively describes the latter as the post-Nietzschean geography where modernist artists "learned to love their fate in the face of the void. If there are no holy temples, any place can become sacred; if there are no consecrated materials, then ordinary sticks and stones must do" (179). Idiosyncratically evoking both Hebraic exile and Wordsworthian Romanticism—"As I was wandering with my unhappy thoughts"—Reznikoff suggests that history flows out from sacred Eden into secular Exile, into the modern cityscape strewn with "motor-cars and factories." In its folkish analogy of Creation and the urban present, the lyric enacts a sanctification of diasporic space. Reznikoff's poetry transfers the sacredness sometimes reserved for the pastoral spaces of Arcadia to the American, urban present, a space where his insistent rebukes to insularity, bigotry, and indifference form a corollary for his poetic examinations of Jewish history.[7] Indeed they are inseparable.

Modern sources, from Hegel to Jung to certain trends in contemporary environmental philosophy, erroneously contend that Judaism's story of the Garden in Genesis is responsible for our unhappy relationship with the natural world, but Reznikoff draws on the Hebrew Bible to imaginatively promote the attunement of the individual to his or her environment, suggesting that Paradise is wherever one lives fully in the present: "This is the sun that shone on Adam." The present may or may not contain both Eden and Exile —that is for the individual to determine—but there is no return, no way to find your way back. The fiery sword that God places at the gates of Eden means that we can never regain the locus of origin. For a poet content to dwell in the gap between an inner and outer reality and between ideal and real worlds, nostalgia for the past must not monopolize one's identity.[8]

I mention this lyric's nod to rural romanticism because it is one of those instances that mediates separate realities. But whether he is resisting the monopolizing tendencies of pastoral sentimentalism or a politicized ethnic identity, a similar sensibility illuminates his response. As in the case of the urban setting, this means that he is not caught up in measuring the city of the present moment against some mythical ideal. Reznikoff's vision of Diaspora is resolutely post-Edenic in a way that no nostalgic quest for nationhood could ever achieve. Much like the model increasingly invoked by postcolonialists and multiculturalists alike—it cannot and does not wish to be assimilated or fused with society at large, but neither can it return to its idealized origin. As such, his vocabulary of alienation is actually a profound claim to being-at-home. Reznikoff's historical poems invite the reader to interrogate the relationship between the Jewish ethical tradition and the paradoxes and limitations of nationalist or even group identity.

Then too, it is no accident that a palpable reflection of Emersonian Romanticism haunts these lines. For there is a sense of yet another Jewish poet (born a mere decade after Lazarus's death) struggling to inscribe a space for himself within Emerson's vision of American poetics. For what else lies behind the constructive energy of Reznikoff's immigrant call to self-reliance in the fragmented present than these lines from *Nature*:

Every spirit builds itself a house; and beyond its house, a world; and beyond its world, a heaven. Know then, that the world exists for you. For you the phenomenon is perfect. What we are, that only can we see. All that Adam had, all that Caesar could, you have and can do. Adam called his house, heaven and earth; Caesar called his house, Rome; you perhaps call yours a cobbler's trade; a hundred acres of ploughed land; or a scholar's garret. Yet line for line and point for point, your dominion is as great as theirs, though without fine names. Build, therefore, your own world. (*The Collected Works* I, 45)

Taking the monumental step from the inner sanctum of the Jewish home into the unexplored urban spaces of New York City, Reznikoff resolves the challenge of the "familiar and yet strange," resolutely embracing the American experience of mobility and self-creation (if not Emerson's project of nationalism), a peculiar sensation of extraterritoriality that was somehow enough to sustain inexhaustible lyrics of the lonely narrating self. There is more than an act of self-legitimizing here; transferring the Transcendentalist ethos to the urban scene, he both fulfills and enlarges Emerson's charge. What he observed in the American city reflected his Jewish modernism and vice versa: a sense of homelessness (literal and metaphysical).

In Reznikoff's poetic rendering of Jewish history, Diaspora proves to be a daunting series of temporary dwellings or ephemeral refuges, but each successive displacement adds a new spiritual or intellectual paradigm to the world at large. In at least one notable instance that will be described, an exilic ethos is imported even into the Jews' sacred land. These features are commonly noted, but why, we must ask, did Reznikoff feel compelled to eulogize Jewish wandering for a secular world of alienated ethnic enclaves? The child of east-European immigrants who had fled the 1881 pogroms, Reznikoff was born in Brooklyn and spent his youth in Brownsville on the Lower East Side, eventually studied both journalism and the law, and served briefly in the U.S. Army. In his early years he witnessed the arrival of his paternal grandparents from Russia and the emigrant struggle of numerous relatives. Many of his close relatives suffered antisemitism in the United States, and their experiences, together with the childhood beatings Reznikoff himself endured, emerged as important themes in his later work. With Louis Zukofsky and George Oppen, he founded the Objectivist Press in the early thirties. His poetic influences came from a diverse range of modernist movements, including Imagism, Objectivism, and German Expressionism. Beginning in 1918 and during the next sixty years, Reznikoff published three novels, numerous translations, historical and edited works—and nineteen individual collections of poetry. In most of this prodigious body of poetry, Reznikoff traces the scattering of just about everything: "Another generation of leaves is lying / on the pavements; / each had a name, I suppose, / known to itself and its neighbors / in every gust of wind" (*Poems* II, 79). In his Jewish poetry the poet follows the inexorable logic of just such scattering, emphasizing a subjectivity linked to: exile from the Old Country; from the dreams of his parents' generation; from Jewish ritual; and increasingly, from Zion:

> We must build in Babylon
> Another Zion
> Of precepts, laws, ordinances and commandments
> To outlast stone or metal
>
> *(Poems* I, 141)

A belonging to nothing and therefore everything feeds the humanity that persists in his poetry. The Jewish diasporic experience is deeply embedded in the way he imagines the economic, political, and cultural struggles of other human beings. The liminality of Jewish identity suggests to him a new way of thinking about the American urban experience, the paradoxical condition of organic continuity coexisting with ultimate estrangement. Enacting a myth of self-making as epic as Emerson's, it also constitutes a refusal of assimilation in the broadest possible sense. At the end of Reznikoff's life, an interviewer expressed bewilderment: How could it be that the husband of Marie Syrkin —"editor of Herzl Press and a prominent Zionist," who wears "the obligatory badge of Judaism"—meaning her numerous trips to Israel—"had never set foot in Israel?" To which Reznikoff responds simply that ". . . certainly I feel Jewish regardless." And then he names a few of the diasporic sites of triumph and catastrophe that he has commemorated throughout his poetry: "I would be Jewish whether it's here or whether I'd been born in Alexandria, Russia, Germany—anywhere" (Rovner 15–16).[9] For those who suspect that when American Jewish identity situates itself exclusively in relation to Israel or the Holocaust (frequently both), it diminishes the radical prospects of fulfilling the promise of all the multifarious Jewish worlds before World War II—and the Torah itself—Reznikoff's poetry serves as an alternative model of ethnic identity. Just what did it mean to be a member of a group considered by some to be among America's unmeltibles and to observe the birth of the Jewish state from afar? A thoughtful chronicler of the major currents in Jewish history, including the events of his time, Reznikoff refrains from mentioning the doctrine of Zionism directly in his Jewish poetry and fiction (and only rarely in his letters), an absence that provides an important window into his thought. In the complicated syntax of Jewish American life, Reznikoff's "silence" masks an alternative vision of Jewish life.

Reznikoff's resistance to full recovery of "Jewishness" is informed by the same logic that refuses the temptation merely to parrot the idiom of the hegemonic culture. If he chose to write in English, rather than the Yiddish of his childhood, it is not because he had any illusion of entering the modernist canon of intrepid self-creators but so that he might more emphatically pursue a difficult tradition that was far more important to him: the creative liminality of Jewishness in relation to the host culture. In its ambivalent and competing identifications, Reznikoff's poetry comments on the enlarged and ultimately permeable borders of all the worlds he inhabits, while aspiring to avoid the exclusionary practices of any particular majority culture. Preservation of this enigmatic space has important consequences for his aesthetic responses to Jewish politics.

"He is brave to whom every land is home": Reznikoff, *The Menorah Journal*, and *Convivencia*

Among the readers of *The Menorah Journal*, Reznikoff found a more welcoming environment for his verse than he would ever again achieve in his neglected career. To fully appreciate his poetics of exile, it is important not only to come to terms with the cultural resistance to Zionism articulated by Jewish intellectuals in the pages of *The Menorah Journal*, but to recognize that they themselves struggled to lay claim to a form of national belonging. But first, I intend to introduce a theoretical trope that has never before been applied to the study of Jewish American modernism. Best translated as coexistence, *convivencia* was first used by Spanish historians to describe the intermingling of Jewish, Muslim, and Christian cultures in the "Golden Age" of Spain, the intellectual interchanges and cultural influence of Spain's pluralistic medieval society. This paradigm is as nuanced as befits any theoretical framework that presumes to describe the intricate work that diasporic Jewish poets do. Rather than denote a state of "harmony" or an actual Golden Age, it suggests a cosmopolitan setting in which "separate communities engaged in business with each other and influenced each other with their ideas and cultural forms until 1492" (Mann, Glick, and Dodds vii–xviii). Despite the politics of competition, mistrust, and mutual suspicion, unusually rich cultural exchanges flourished, and medieval Hebrew poets revolutionized the prospects for Jewish poetry by adapting imagery and themes from Moslem poets. By arming himself with evidence of Judaism's adaptive genius in earlier centuries, Reznikoff questions whether a static and insular Zionism might not cripple Judaism's historical potential for interchange and growth. Moreover, this ethos challenges that most tenacious of Zionist myths—that the Jewish people ever behaved or thought as one. For Reznikoff and many other *Menorah* writers, the Jews have always been "fragmented"; but as this innovative Sephardic account of cultural fusion suggests, this condition contains the enabling potential of *intermingling*.

I embrace this recent historiographic paradigm of *convivencia* because its fundamental logic was already embedded in the methodologies of some of the earliest and most celebrated *Menorah* writers, who often expressed their modernist identities in compelling terms borrowed and refashioned from the Jewish Hellenic corpus. Among these, Reznikoff's historical poems, verse plays, and even the historical novel *The Lionhearted* show us ways of existing between the polarities of absolute absorption by and absolute expulsion from non-Jewish populations. Whatever they may have wished, the Jews Reznikoff writes about rarely succeeded in such insulation, and the poet's lived experience bore the fruit of dynamic exchanges. For instance, when asked in his final interview, which took place only ten days before his death, how a poet "so deeply Jewish" could be inspired by the blatantly antisemitic Ezra Pound, Reznikoff did not evade the question but stressed his lifelong interest in an ethos of influx, experimentation, exchange, and adaptation: "I don't see why I can't benefit from the work Pound did, whatever his prejudices. I was very interested in the music of everyday speech and in free verse, and along came Pound, experimenting with these very things. I found all that very useful and illuminating; and frankly, I'm still very grateful for those ideas. Whatever motivated his anti-Semitism—and remember, this was no Hitler— it isn't related to what he taught me as a poet" (Rovner 16).

This stubborn desire to learn from Pound and communicate with the non-Jewish world finally brought Reznikoff some degree of material reward. Years after *Family Chronicle* had been rejected by Jewish publishers, the new British publishing firm Norton Bailey (which had no Jewish editors) was impressed enough to make it their inaugural venture. The work was then enthusiastically reviewed by the London critics. And it was the Irishman, Seamus Cooney, who edited Reznikoff's collected works, and C. P. Snow who wrote a moving introduction to his New Directions paperback. Reznikoff's response to this unexpected attention juxtaposes his understatedly wry modernism with his modest desire to situate himself in some way within Jewish textual tradition: "You never can tell who will be moved by what you write. That's as true today as it was in the time of Amos the Prophet. The king wanted to have him thrown in jail for what he was saying—but he kept on." Reznikoff's reply (as it turned out it was his final public statement) at once bears a specifically Jewish knowledge and underscores his cosmopoli-

tan credo, ruefully noting his unfortunate neglect by the Jewish establishment after the halcyon years of the *Menorah*: "Whatever the difficulties, your
business is to write what you think you should. You owe that much to yourself, and to other humans too" (Rovner 18).

Reznikoff's resistance to the Zionist insistence on ending Exile may be at
least partially accounted for by considering his unequivocal representions of
Judaism as an extraterritorial culture, a textual landscape enriched by a living
stream of ideas (even from antisemites), enlivened by its propinquity to other
discourses, one in which Jews were not so ethnically bound that they could
not interact on a par with members of other groups. A telling exemplar of the
kind of polemic that seems to have contributed to the presence of such an
ethos in Reznikoff's lyrics occurs in Cecil Roth's *Menorah* essay "Paradoxes
of Jewish History," where the historian stresses the ways in which Judaism's
growth in the ancient past often seems to have occurred at its best *only* when
surrounded by dominant, "alien" cultures. For Roth, the condition of the
Jew in Hellenistic Alexandria is "indistinguishable in essentials" from the
Jew in modern New York.[10] Reznikoff and Roth never succumb to invoking
the authority of the past as a means to recover "authenticity"; rather, they
seek out the potential for difference within the rubric of community. This
is surely what is intended by Reznikoff's frequent panegyrics to the open-
endedness of contingency in such early poems as "Samuel": "Chance planted
me beside a stream of water; content, I serve the land, whoever lives here and
whoever passes" (*Poems* I, 73).

Today we know how well this "Chance"—the Jew's intellectual gamble
on America—has paid off. As of this writing, Jews in America are reaping the
unexpected rewards of *convivencia*: unprecedented numbers of widely read
Christian journals publish articles that urge Christians to study rabbinics as a
wellspring of religious insight. Post-Holocaust Protestant and Catholic theologians and professors of religious studies read and teach Buber, Levinas,
Heschel, and Scholem. But for the poet such blessings do not mean that the
stream where the poet "think[s] in psalms" is "homeland," or that America is
his Zion, but rather, as he patiently explains in the title chosen for a prose
work and poetry collection, "Babylon." Consider what a representative *Menorah* writer like Roth makes of the "ancient" literature of Jewish Hellenism:

The literature which was produced—without exception, in Greek—was incredibly
modern in tone. There were anticipations of Graetz, of Mendelssohn, of Zangwill . . .
and all imagined that, by writing in Greek, and not in Hebrew, they were assured of
immortality. There were historians, anti-nationalist and assimilationist. There were

philosophers who endeavored to prove that Judaism was rational, and antiquarians who discovered that it anticipated all that was best in Hellenic lore. There were dramatists who elaborated biblical themes for their plots. . . . There were anti-Semites who attacked Judaism, and apologists who defended it. It would never surprise me to find that there was an Alexandrian Jewish Publication Society to foster Jewish literature, or a *Menorah Journal* to present it in periodical form: Maintaining, perhaps, a Summer School which invited Caecilius Rossus from across the sea to deliver its inaugural address. (19)

Certainly Jewish political restoration could hardly claim to guarantee the continuity of such cultural vigor: for Reznikoff the latter invariably develops, in spite of circumstances of potential vulnerability, alongside other groups open to exchange.

◆

A few years before Reznikoff became acquainted with them, the members of the nascent *Menorah* group of students and intellectuals had earned a certain notoriety for their distinctly anti-Zionist tendencies. In 1919, an influential essay published in *The New Republic* attacked the basic arguments of American Zionism. Morris Raphael Cohen, a philosopher and a colleague of Horace Kallen's at City College, argued that Zionism was "false and profoundly inimical to liberal or humanistic civilization":

A national Jewish Palestine must necessarily mean a state founded on a peculiar race, a tribal religion and a mystic belief in a peculiar soil, whereas liberal America stands for separation of church and state, the free mixing of races, and the fact that men can change their habitation and language and still advance the process of civilization. There is not a single opportunity offered by Palestine that is not open, to a larger extent here. Even if the history of ancient Palestine were glorious . . . the glory of Palestine is as nothing to the possible glory of America. (182–83)

Reportedly, Cohen's thesis had a great impact on Cohen's students at the City College of New York, including Irving Howe and Sidney Hook.[11] The key terms of Cohen's pluralistic argument—"that men can change their habitation and language and still advance the process of civilization"—meant a great deal to a generation of modernist intellectuals struggling to make sense of their relation to the past. During the difficult years of Jewish settlement, the *Menorah* itself often expressed ambivalence (or "evenhandedness") and eventually antipathy in its role as witness to historical events in Palestine. The members of this group were not opposed to a Jewish refuge in Palestine per se, but they chose to interrogate a nationalist ideology that seemed to discourage free and critical discourse and even the very concept of Diaspora culture.[12]

To better appreciate the ways in which Reznikoff's poetry is representative of a generation that was unsettled by the Zionist rhetoric of consensus and homogeneity, it seems worth setting forth an explicit account of how he came to perceive the political situation in Palestine. Understanding the intellectual influences of Reznikoff's resistance to the negation of diasporist identity requires some attention to the intellectual culture of *The Menorah Journal*, a venue in which both Syrkin and Reznikoff published. Throughout its years of publication, writers in the pages of *The Menorah Journal*—without romanticizing the actual circumstances of Jewish life in the Diaspora— tended to claim that much of inestimable value had been achieved during the exilic period. Visiting some of the controversial aspects of the contemporary correspondence of Henry Hurwitz, the journal's editor and founder (and an enthusiastic reader of Reznikoff's verse), should help us gauge the strange eagerness of many of the Jewish intellectuals in the Menorah sphere to bear witness to Zionism's failures.[13] Gaining some perspective on Hurwitz's own ambivalent and at times hostile attitude toward American Zionism should strengthen our appreciation for the contemporary significance of Reznikoff's poems for the audience that read the poems this editor chose to publish in the twenties and beyond.

Hurwitz and the Menorah group shared at least one attitude with Zionism: neither showed much interest in assuming defensive postures toward antisemitism. As Elinor Jean Grumet points out in the *Menorah Bulletin* (1917–1923): "Henry Hurwitz forcefully expressed Menorah hostility to admitting the psychological power of anti-Semitism, even in the teeth of a threatened quota. Jews must stop whining about prejudice, he said, and betraying such softness of moral fiber as to 'fall back upon their race or faith as the cause of their "undeserved" sufferings or deprivations'" (32). It is essential to recognize the striking correlations between the competing narratives of the *Menorah* writers and Zionist ideologues. Without the major transformation of Jewish confidence secular Zionism inspired, few American Jews would have engaged in such radical rethinking about their Jewishness. While the Society may largely have rejected Zionism, it also published "materials warning against capitulating one's Jewish spiritual and intellectual life to the majority culture" and, most significantly, "against espousing a false universalism" (Grumet 32). And even though the *Menorah* generally struggled to avoid the polarized positions embedded in Zionist rhetoric, there was clearly a period when the notion of *cultural* Zionism was attractive. In its earliest days, and throughout the 1920s, *Menorah Journal* writers often expressed sympathy for Ahad Ha-Am's cultural Zionism at a time when American Jewish immigrants were indifferent or hostile to Zionism.[14]

Expressing a pacifism that was antithetical to the conflict destroying Europe, the cultural Zionism of Ahad Ha-Am had immense appeal even for non-Jewish *Menorah* writers such as Randolph Bourne, who approved of an ideology that apparently conformed to his own pacifist and internationalist paradigm:

> as I understand it, the Jewish State which Zionists are building is a non-military, a non-chauvinistic State. Palestine is to be built as a Jewish centre on purely religious and cultural foundations. It is not to be the home of all the Jewish people. Zionism does not propose to prevent Jews from living in full citizenship in other countries. ("The Jew and Trans-national America" 284)

The sympathy of non-Jewish intellectuals such as Bourne and John Dewey inevitably increased Jewish intellectual interest in a movement that at first glance had seemed to compromise their status as loyal citizens. According to Grumet, "[Bourne] used to feel Zionism undesirable, because it put the Jew in a position of conflicting loyalties; but he understood it now as a spiritual and cultural allegiance that would keep America diversified without threatening its unity" (51). But now, reversing the Enlightenment's claim that Judaism presented an obstacle to full participation in the Jew's land of exile, Bourne claims that "the Jew in America is proving every day the possibilities of this dual life"; if Zionism accelerated that process, all the better. And Dewey, who published a short article in *The Menorah Journal* in 1915, was similarly enthusiastic, welcoming Zionism "as a cultural movement . . . rather than one of political nationalism" (Grumet 51–52).

What Grumet's otherwise authoritative account leaves out, however, is the powerful postwar influence of Bourne's essential pacifism on many of the *Menorah* intellectuals. As Leslie J. Vaughan points out, Bourne's "famous charge [that] 'war is the health of the state,' was meant as a warning to his fellow intellectuals to refuse cooperation with the state, whose new form of warfare depended above all on the cooperation of the intelligentsia . . . on managed information designed to mobilize a domestic consensus" (445). When it became apparent to them that Zionism had manifestly disintegrated into an ideology of statism and territorialism, the *Menorah* writers emerged as its most skeptical American critics.

In the beginning, the *Menorah*'s interest in Zionism and Palestine was remarkably nuanced, in spite of the passions roused by the violence in Palestine. Though it covered the Arab uprising of 1929 through eyewitness accounts and provided thoughtful analysis through such writers as Maurice Samuel and Cecil Roth, the effect was quite different than the discourse in contemporary mainstream Zionist publications. During these months of ferocious violence, Salo Baron's deeply reflective series "Nationalism and Intolerance" appeared. Overtly concerned with the ghetto, nationalism, and intolerance in Europe, these articles nevertheless had unmistakable bearing on the Palestinian conflict between Jews and Arabs in the Yishuv. Reznikoff's poetry would often appear alongside these and similar articles in the pages of a journal that its irascible editor Henry Hurwitz increasingly intended as a goad to the Jewish establishment, particularly the Zionist movement. In a widely circulated letter written in 1918, Hurwitz sets forth what he tentatively calls "the official Menorah attitude" toward a number of movements, including Zionism:

Our movement would not be the Menorah anymore, in my opinion, if it swerved from the purely academic, non-political, non-ecclesiastical, non-partisan character which has given us being and distinction. . . . I think far-sighted Zionists, for example, see that. Nothing, it seems to me, could be worse for an ardent, intensely propagandist and specialized organization like that of Zionism to-day than to feel that within its own mansion lie all chambers of wisdom, all casements of vision. We must have an untrammeled, academic spirit brooding and breeding "above the battle" if Jewish life as a whole is to grow in nobility and sound self-determination."[15]

Essentially a statement of far-reaching editorial policy, it seems more than likely that Reznikoff would have seen it. Hurwitz's letter came at a time of increasing competition and antagonism between the Intercollegiate Menorah Association and the Intercollegiate Zionist Association: there was a great deal of tension between those who wanted to include Zionism as a subject for thoughtful analysis and debate and those who saw only the urgency for its immediate implementation.

For their part, the Zionists were contemptuous of the *Menorah*'s intellectual neutrality. It is true that Hurwitz saw his journal as an essential nexus for shaping a distinctly diasporic identity: "essentially we must develop our Jewish character here through our own exertions and thought and education. We cannot be spoonfed from Jerusalem or Daganiah."[16] When Zionists charged that the journal was little more than an assimilationist organ, an infuriated

Hurwitz claimed that it had sacrificed more for "authentic Jewish ideals" than "a lot of Zionist critics and ballyhooers":

> There is a good deal of confusion about "assimilation." In one respect, the Zionists are the greatest assimilators of all. In spite of scolding other Jews for not supporting a positive Jewish life, the Zionists have not been contributing so much to a more abundant Jewish cultural life in America. On the contrary, a deplorable fanaticism has developed which has been denigrating constructive Jewish efforts unaffiliated with the sect. I think that a little self-criticism and self-reform among Zionists themselves would perhaps do Jewish life in this country as much good as a lot of confused scolding of other Jews.[17]

What Hurwitz means when he calls the Zionists "assimilators" was expressed more artfully by Hannah Arendt in the pages of the *Menorah* four years later: "[t]he hollow word struggles between Zionism and assimilationism has completely distorted the simple fact that the Zionists . . . were the only ones who sincerely wanted assimilation, namely, 'normalization' of the people ('to be a people like all other peoples'), whereas the assimilationist wanted the Jewish people to retain their unique position" ("Zionism Reconsidered" 230). Both Hurwitz and Arendt were concerned that it was Zionism that posed the greatest normative threat to Jewish difference, by transforming the Jew into a Hebrew, or an Israeli, an uncritical citizen of the nation-state.

From 1932 the *Menorah* abandoned its earlier efforts toward reconciliation. An informal relationship was even formed with the radically anti-Zionist American Council for Judaism, a group that Marie Syrkin abhorred and that, like Reznikoff, experienced the vigorous responses of Zionist institutions.[18] After Hurwitz rejected the idea of a Jewish state in Palestine as a "hopeless aberration" (Alter 1965, 55), the mounting tension would accumulate until the explosive appearance of Arendt's "Zionism Reconsidered" (Autumn 1945). Reznikoff admired Arendt's eminently diasporic critique of political Zionism.[19]

As Robert Alter argued in a 1965 *Commentary* article: "their [the *Menorah* intellectuals'] freedom from party, sect, or institution strengthen[ed] their ability to offer both a variety of perspectives on a given problem and the perspective of variety on the subjects which they regarded as Jewish" (54). Such unorthodox and critical discourse undoubtedly strengthened Reznikoff's resolve to remain a political outsider, a poet profoundly skeptical of ready-made solutions and the new stereotypes of Jewish identity that discouraged debate, especially when that discourse appeared to repudiate the validity of Jewish American life or the Diaspora in its entirety. For Reznikoff this came to mean a Jewish identity that was pluralistic and creative, a resilient response to historical contingency rather than a rigid ideology. *The Menorah Journal* confirmed for him that a poet could be at once literary, Jewish, and autonomous.

◆

It is time to consider how Reznikoff's lyrics illuminate this expansive notion of Jewish modernity. Dan Miron's astute reading of I. B. Singer's wielding "a deep distrust in human willpower and an absolute aversion to both the Nietzschean 'will to power' and the liberal faith 'in progress'" deeply resonates with my interpretation of Reznikoff's poetics (*The Image of the Shtetl* 340). Always an openness to contingency and a spiritual skepticism to grand master schemes is encrypted in his Zen-like lyrics: "If you ask me about the plans that I made last night / of steel and granite— / I think the sun must have melted them / or this gentle wind blown them away" (*Poems* I, 120). In March of 1933 the *Menorah* published his more forceful response to political developments as "A Dialogue: Padua 1727," whose last lines declare that, "as our God was never of wood or bone / Our land is not of stones or earth" (*Poems* I, 127). These lines echo a 1929 letter Reznikoff wrote to Elliot Cohen (managing editor of *The Menorah Journal*) in which he describes the *Menorah* itself as a sort of homeland: "The land that we Jews hold in common . . . free of any mandatory power . . . is ideas expressed in words: this is the only land of Israel. We have been in possession three thousand years and are a people only because of it. I think of the *Menorah Journal* as a colony."[20] This anticipation of George Steiner's nonterritorial Judaism reads today as a gentle subversion of Zionist rhetoric of the 1920s and a profound expression of his advocacy of Judaism as a living stream of ideas that did not require a territory.

Far from indifferent to the Jewish condition abroad, Reznikoff closely followed what was happening in Palestine, just as he kept attuned to the growing crisis in Germany. There is good evidence that he had been thinking long and hard about the situation of the Jews in the Yishuv, even before his marriage to Syrkin. In large part, this may be due to the sheer abundance of nuanced and provocative reportage from the Yishuv that appeared in the *Menorah*. In 1932, when the Jewish presence in Palestine was limited to a population of 180,000, Reznikoff singled out for editorial praise Zacharia Shuster's "Progress and Problems in Palestine."[21] By this point, the utopian idealization and identification with the Arabs of Palestine had faded. The romantic emulation of the proud Arab by the horsemen of Hashomer gave way to deep suspicion and violence. Since Reznikoff rarely referred to *any* reportage about this subject, it seems worth taking a brief look at what Shuster had discovered. By no means the first or the last word on the subject, this report nonetheless provides a valuable foundation for any serious consideration of the basis for Reznikoff's ambiguity toward Zionism. Reznikoff must have been struck by what the author said about the precarious condition of the Yishuv. Shuster enumerated a number of serious problems: the general intensification of conflicts between Arab and Jewish labor, frequent deadly attacks on Jews, and the militant nationalism of the Zionist Revisionist group: "[t]he whole country was agog, riots were imminent" (162). Interviewing a young Arab in Jaffa, Shuster heard of the inevitability of a seemingly endless conflict: "the Christian Arabs are deadly enemies of their Moslem brethren, yet both are united against the 'Jewish invaders.'" Then too, the Yishuv itself is split between extreme factions, notably Brith Shalom (the Jewish Communists) and the Zionist Revisionists. But for Reznikoff the report taken directly from a Hebrew newspaper of May 3, 1932, must have been even more disturbing: "The lawyer M. Cohen, who is a member of the Central Committee of the Revisionist Party, stated before the Court in Jerusalem: 'If the Hitlerites would have eliminated from their program the enmity to the Jews, then we would have lined up with the Hitlerites. If not for the Hitlerites, Germany would have been lost. Yes, Hitler saved Germany'" (164).

Though the impassioned ideological conflicts of the Jews were often the subject of his historical treatments of a vigorous people, this linkage of Jewish territorialism with fascism must have seemed abhorrent to a poet as alarmed by the growing threat that Hitler posed as Reznikoff was. And though he would hardly have failed to be impressed by Shuster's account of the heroic struggle of Jewish workers to build ports, factories, and agricultural colonies, the inherent animosity between Jews and Arabs, the depressing *inevitability* of territorial struggle and violence as indicated by Shuster's young informant, must have had an impact on him, as would Shuster's foreboding tone: "the foundations driven deep in the soil, with the greatest love and sacrifice and confidence, but at the same time eyes are alert and scanning around in all directions over a vast, brooding sea" (166).

At one point Shuster discovers that though the Palestinian Communists were outlawed by the British Mandate, their leaflets are everywhere, distributed among Bedouins as well as the Jewish workers of Tel Aviv. It isn't necessary to ignore Reznikoff's evident distaste for communism to suspect that he might have found the ethical grounds of the complaints articulated in the Jewish Communist platform (from which Shuster quotes to a surprisingly generous degree, as if he too is half-convinced) persuasive. An Arabic pamphlet, published and distributed by the Central Committee of the Palestine Communist Party, encouraged attacks on Jewish settlements:

What are they that are the cause of your ruin? The foreign Government who occupied your country. The Zionists who rob you of your land, your work and sources of livelihood. The Zionists have already taken possession of the best of your soil. . . . The lands which they have acquired were formerly Arab villages. They do not content themselves with casting you off your land, but they are also excluding you from work on your plundered lands. . . . Fight against the admission of Zionist immigrants who intend to expel you from your lands and to take away your work. Make an end to disagreements among you and elect revolutionary committees to defend your land against the Zionist invasion. (165–66)

In spite of the manifestly propagandistic quality of this incitement, Reznikoff might very well have been struck by the essential charge of injustice as well as been chilled by the prospect of impending violence. What if the Zionists had indeed caused the violent geographic dispersal and economic disenfranchisement of the native population? Not only were some Jews inciting Arabs to violence against other Jews, but there seemed to be a core injustice that was at least partly responsible for the irresolvable tensions.[22] The disparity between the utopian formulations of the American Zionists and the reality in Palestine would have been all too apparent by now. To say the least, Zionism could not very well have seemed to be a safe haven, even less a Jewish "homeland." In his brief reference to Shuster's article, Reznikoff refers somewhat obliquely to the "nostalgia" it evokes in him, perhaps an allusion to the halcyon days when *Menorah* writers like Dewey, Veblen, and Bourne could proclaim the Zionist cause as a spiritual world citizenship and a shedding of ethnocentrism. But now, the utopian road to Zionism's fulfillment would have begun to seem an unacceptable surrender to nationalist violence. As if in partial response to Shuster's bleak report, Reznikoff would intensify his poetic explorations of the Jews' heterogeneous experience in the past.

In the same period, Reznikoff's own "prophetic" view of how utterly ideology could scuttle the intellectual life was made apparent when he attributed the demise of his beloved *Menorah* to two rigid ideologies: Communism— "When you become a Communist, you must check your brains"—and Zionism. Of the latter he will say only that, "when Zionists found more and more in Palestine and in the State of Israel to attract and hold them . . . as a rule [they] found the *Journal* of declining interest." He seems to be hinting that the Jewish American community had been thoughtless in its rush to adopt Israel as an anchorage for ethnicity, a substitution for discourse and debate.

As the years passed, the Zionists dismissed the *Menorah*'s discourse as "belonging to a Diaspora that at its worst was spawning Nazis and, at its best, would end in complete assimilation. . . . *The Menorah Journal* remained only a light in the Diaspora and many Jews were looking away."[23]

◆

In his three-page poem that appeared in *Inscriptions* (1944–1956) Reznikoff addressed a subject that would remain, for decades to come, an unmentionable topic, let alone a proper subject for twentieth-century lyric poetry:

> One man
> escapes from the ghetto of Warsaw
> where thousands have been killed or led away in tens of thousands,
> hundreds of thousands, hundreds of thousands,
> to die in concentration camps,
> to be put to death in trucks, in railway cars, in gullies of the woods
> in gas chambers,
> and he who escapes—
> of all that multitude—
> in his heart the word *Jew* burning
> as it burned once in Jeremiah
> when he saw the remnant of Judah
> led captive to Babylon
> or fugitives,
> from that man
> shall spring again a people
> as the sands of the sea for number,
> as the stars of the sky.
> *Blessed are You, God of the Universe,*
> *delighting in life.*
>
> (*Poems* II, 60)

Originally titled "A Compassionate People," this lyric appeared as American Jewry was receiving the darkest reports about the fate of European Jews, and it led off the thirtieth anniversary issue of *The Menorah Journal*. It is worth pausing to compare its haunting juxtaposition of extermination and continuity, a nightmare of the secular world and divinity, with Reznikoff's conclusion to *Holocaust* (1975):

> Fishing boats, excursion boats, and any kind of boat
> Were mustered at the ports;

And the Jews were escorted to the coast by the Danes—
Many of them students—
And ferried to safety in Sweden:
About six thousand Danish Jews were rescued
And only a few hundred captured by the Germans.

(111)

What both poems have in common, the lyrical poem of the 1940s and the spare, sober lines from the poet's last year, is a shared investment in what is sometimes called the "Doctrine of the Saving Remnant," which constitutes a greatly muted but undeniable presence in *Holocaust*. Hence, though his radically unsentimental, violent, and unvarnished record of atrocity dares not speak of hope, its mitigating clause embraces the totality of the Holocaust, which meant its rescuers and survivors, as much as its sadists and corpses. In other words, the prophetic imperative of the Jews' ultimate survival and creativity in their dispersal remains every bit as binding on his poetry as is the actuality of persecution.

Here I should pause to explain that the notion of the saving remnant, more often the purview of theologians, constitutes a dynamic presence throughout Reznikoff's poetics. In Hebrew, this phrase (*sheris ha'pleyte*) probably derives from Genesis 45:7: "And God sent me before you to give you a remnant on the earth, and to save you alive for a great deliverance."[24] Though this understanding of Judaism's destiny harmonizes with an ethos secularized by the editorial worldview of the *Menorah* editors, it should be emphasized that this vague faith, this upstart confidence in Judaism's viability in exile, was indebted to countless generations of Jews who survived successive waves of persecution and saw in their endurance the proof that God ultimately guaranteed their continuity, if not their safety. But in the modern period, this ethos was refined to a remarkable degree by the historiography of the distinguished historian Simon Dubnow.[25] Reznikoff would have been among the recipients of an essay written by Dubnow that was highly praised by other Menorah intellectuals. Understanding the intellectual currents encrypted in Reznikoff's Jewish verse means coming to terms with Dubnow's unconventional historiographical speculation that in the future all nations should depend no longer on a particular territory but would be distinguished by their cultural and historical heritage. As Irving Howe observes, Dubnow saw world Jewry "as a spiritual community held together by historical, cultural, and religious ties, despite the absence of a common homeland or territory, and he urged the Jews to struggle for cultural and religious autonomy in whichever country they happened to find themselves. . . . [I]n opposition to the Zionists, he desired the preservation of Jewish identity in the Diaspora" (19). With the possible exception of Franz Rosenzweig in the third part of his *Star of Redemption*, Dubnow articulated what is arguably the most elegant counter-argument ever to confront the Zionists' negation of Diaspora. Whereas Zionist cultural custodians had to repress the cultures they chose to discard, he proposes to create autonomous national and cultural Jewish institutions in every country where Jews find themselves. Just as they succeeded in establishing local centers of autonomy throughout the Diaspora, Jews would again assume their prophetic role as teachers to the nations. Much like the Bundists of Eastern Europe, Dubnow sees that Jewish spiritual self-realization is perfectly achievable without recourse to conventional nationalism or territorial ambitions: "Jewish history possesses the student with the conviction that Jewry at all times, even in the period of political independence, was pre-eminently a spiritual nation, and a spiritual nation it continues to be in our own days, too."[26] Dubnow argues that the most significant potential contribution of Judaism as a spiritual phenomenon resides in its lived experience in the Diaspora, the *second act* of Jewish history, alluded to in the quotation that began this chapter. Dubnow's Jews warrant the attention of the philosophers of history not only for the time in which they enjoyed independence, but for "the period of [their] weakness and oppression" (*Nationalism and History* 255).

Reznikoff too, in his explanatory notes for his 1944 story "Pharisee," describes the ancient kingdom as if its true significance for him resides in its service as a launching point for the great adventure of Jewish exile: "It is a time of war and civil war and the growth in power of the Pharisees. These, by their teaching and discipline, are to enable Judaism to survive the disasters and suffering of the twenty centuries that follow."[27] Accordingly, an early version of "A Short History of Israel" was published in *The Menorah Journal* with the following epigraph from Hugo of St. Victor (as quoted in H. O. Taylor's *The Medieval Mind*): "He is brave to whom every land is home."[28] This is a vision that poetically fulfills Abraham Joshua Heschel's evocative rendering of the spirit of Judaism: "What is retained in the soul is the moment of insight rather than the place where the act came to pass" (*The Sabbath* 6). Or to put it another way: like the innovative historiographies of Dubnow and Baron (and the work of postmodern theorists such as the Boyarins), Reznikoff presupposes the permanence of Diaspora as both an historical and a metaphysical condition that humanizes culture.

It is striking how often explicit references to this theological tradition were expressed by other supposedly secular *Menorah* intellectuals. For instance, the historian Cecil Roth confessed that: "Personally, I have a deep-rooted belief (and here I am at one, I believe, with the vast majority of Jews, even in this unregenerate age) in the eternity and indestructibility of Israel" ("Paradoxes of Jewish History" 18). This otherwise exacting historian's unscientific confession of faith, undoubtedly appealed to Reznikoff's own historical engagement with tropes of endurance. For Roth, the destiny of the Jews must not lie exclusively in Zionism ("for Zion has not been able to save itself from overthrow on repeated occasions, nor has it been able to preserve the communities of the countries in closest touch with it from complete decay" [18]). On the other hand, Roth argues that there is no historic instance "that any body of Jews imbued with their ancestral culture has withered away." By this he seems to both echo the doctrine of the saving remnant and imply a textually obsessed society: "[t]he ancient tradition of the genuine Jewish scholarship has alone succeeded invariably in perpetuating itself and perpetuating those who immersed themselves in it" (18). The secret for Roth, as for Reznikoff, whose interest in different periods of Jewish scholarship is insatiable, is Jewish learning, "the one tried preservative, rather than nationalism or even religion" (18).

Reznikoff's poetry responds to the imbalance in representation that Dubnow describes, the imperative to accord "the same treatment" to the exilic period.[29] For both men, Judaism's textual heritage must do more than memorialize the past, it must be put in dialogue with the present; for the poet this means "continuity" despite the paradoxical modernist literary form of its renewal. If there is a significant difference between Dubnow and Reznikoff, it lies in the latter's more emphatic resistance to the myth of a *forced* Diaspora and a culture of martyrdom. Instead of mourning the destruction of the Temple or thinking of the Jews as a Palestinian people, Reznikoff draws our attention to their already dispersed cultural identity in *ancient* times, undermining the myth of a lost homogeneity beloved by Zionists. This is why the narrative voices in a relatively late work such as "Jews in Babylonia" (a "collage" that Reznikoff says he wove from translations of Talmud [1969]) explicitly refrain from expressing the myth of a forced Diaspora.

Whether one is "at home" or in "exile," the richly sensual world described by the "Babylonian" poet is filled with contingencies that must bear the memory of hope: "If the ship you are traveling on is wrecked / a plank may come floating your way / and on it you may ride wave after wave / until you walk again on dry land" (*Poems* II, 194). Reznikoff recognizes that some of the most central practices of Judaism, its ancient rituals of life and death, were formed in proximity to a landscape and people alien to it, transposed into a key resonant with Jewish history and monotheism. Accordingly, the diasporic setting that most interests Reznikoff (apart from New York City) is Babylonia, because this is the archetypal site wherein Jews learned to assert themselves vis-à-vis Others. As much historian as poet, Reznikoff knew that the displaced Judeans in Babylonia not only entered the mainstream of Babylonian culture but were even in a position to extend significant economic aid to those Judeans who returned to their homeland in 536 B.C.E. (much as Jewish Americans extended aid to Israel in the twentieth century). Accordingly, "Jews in Babylonia" do not "weep" for Zion but rather retain the everyday world of continuity and pragmatic activity, exiles getting-on-with-it where the sun continues to shine and the rain falls: "Plough, sow and reap / bind the sheaves, thresh and winnow / shear the sheep / wash the wool / comb it and weave it" (*Poems* II, 191). Even where a few vestiges of catastrophe linger in memory, the consciousness that consolidates the poetic collage is present-centered. And in *The Lionhearted* (1944), Reznikoff's novel of Jewish martyrdom during the Crusades, a character facing imminent destruction remarks wryly that, "The fire with which they attack is also a sign to those who will send us help" (106–7). In the aftermath of the Holocaust and the world's refusal to provide shelter for the Jews, these lines will necessarily provoke the reader's skepticism. Nevertheless they provide a direct conduit into the poet's triumphant vision of contingency, continuity, and restoration in the wake of seeming annihilation.

"King David was partly Moabite": Transgressions of Hybridity

I have been arguing for a discernible consistency that links what Michael Davidson calls Reznikoff's "more expansive view of narrative—one truly heteroglossic and hybrid in its impulse" (169)—to his representations of the Jewish past as a vigorous site of translations and exchanges. For it is Reznikoff's *particularism*, the "narrowness" of his self-acknowledged origins and heritage, that enables him to sanction so many other varieties of Americans. Davidson's description closely parallels the kind of dynamic that Thorstein Veblen claimed in his 1919 argument about the relation between Jewish culture and the host community. Veblen had hoped that the Jews would never succeed in reifying a nationalistic movement of their own since this would be an irrecoverable loss to world culture. Though Zionism was more distinguished by its "sobriety and good-will" than other nationalist projects, it too threatened to succumb to a "dominant bias of isolation and inbreeding." It is "by loss of allegiance, or at the best by force of a divided allegiance to the people of his origin, that he finds himself in the vanguard of modern inquiry" (33, 38). Veblen suggests that the "pre-eminence" of modern Jewish intellectuals was due to their proximity to other cultures and their willingness to detach themselves from traditional nationalisms. Similarly, Leslie J. Vaughan observes that this kind of cosmopolitan Jew, idealized by both Veblen and Bourne, "enjoyed a dual citizenship with divided loyalties and multiple perspectives" and "represented not so much alienation as a healthy self of fluid identity, 'at home' in several worlds" (454). And in considering Reznikoff's cosmopolitan formulation of Jewish cultural history we can see that, though no more a utopian than Syrkin, he celebrates the positive striving for meaningful survival that does not preclude exchanges with the host culture.

This reality of multifaceted motives and actions in the Jewish Diaspora was not always acknowledged by historians, Jews and non-Jews alike, who understood the flow of history as an exclusive narrative of institutions and their trappings, decrees, and the will of the powerful, instead of seeing it as a multifaceted portrayal of the richness and complexity of human lives and societies. In contrast, a new generation of Jewish scholars offer a perspective that, though less immediately advantageous ideologically, reveals a reality with many more dimensions. As Max Weinreich argues, "the close and continuous ties of the Jews with their neighbors, which used to be severed only for a while during actual outbreaks of persecutions, manifested themselves in customs and folk beliefs; in legends and songs; in literary production" (2204). And in Martha Krow-Lucal's nuanced portrayal of multivalent responses to the Inquisition within the Marrano culture, she recognizes that

the ballads . . . sung by Jews for centuries . . . contain innumerable references to Christian institutions, festivals, rites and saints. . . . [T]his Christian substrate in songs sung by Jews means that there was constant contact between Jews and Christians for centuries, for otherwise [they] could not have learned these songs and this tradition, and created new ballads within the same artistic tradition after the Expulsion. Even if we wish to discount all Inquisitorial documents, we cannot discount this living cultural evidence of what Américo Castro has called *convivencia*—a living together that makes possible cultural exchange and intermingling. Even if all the *conversos* were true Christians and ardent assimilationists (a sweeping generalization that is belied by the records of individual lives left in *responsa* and Jewish communities across the world), Jews knew them and they knew Jews. And together, as Spaniards, they created and preserved an art form that is living proof of their *convivencia*. (57–58)

The cultural innovations and values of Jews, Christians, and Muslims were idiosyncratic to each population and yet were selectively available for appropriation by members of other communities that, in varying degrees, exhibited a cultural openness.

In a similar, but perhaps somewhat idealized vein, we have Daniel Boyarin's ethnopolitical claims that Jewish diasporism is "a positive cultural product" that puts to rest the myth of the ghetto, or ethnic absolutism. For Boyarin, the interactive and adaptive Jew of modernity comes "into contact with the dominating society . . . free to act out a mediation of one sort or another between the 'native' and Metropolitan cultures." Though they do not invoke the term, Daniel and Jonathan Boyarin, nonetheless manage to delineate the essence of *convivencia* in their celebration of "those situations in Jewish history when the Jews were relatively free from persecution and yet constituted by strong identity—*those situations moreover, within which promethian Jewish creativity was not antithetical, indeed was synergistic with a general cultural activity.*" Hence, Muslim Spain was both culturally rich and paradoxical: "The same figure, a Nagid, an Ibn Gabirol, or a Maimonides, can be simultaneously the vehicle for the preservation of traditions and of the mixing of cultures" (721). Without reducing the long history of the Mediterranean world to a romanticized cultural pluralism, this analysis recognizes in it a vividly cosmopolitan culture.[30] Wherever its origins might lie, this account of Judaism's growth as a border culture, *convivencia*, can bring us closer to understanding a receptive quality that is often observed in Reznikoff's oeuvre. In light of the cumulative impression of Jewishness we may glean from Vaughan, Weinrich, Krow-Lucal, and Boyarin, I am proposing that against the ethnic absolutism that operates as an imperative in Syrkin's poetic and political vision, Reznikoff poeticizes an interactive and adaptive idea of Jewish identity.

In his romantic search for a Jewish "essence," Marie Syrkin's father, Nachman Syrkin (1878–1918), had claimed that the Greeks conceived of the world as a "garden of art and play," whereas the Hebrews saw it as a "holy place where the universal idea must triumph." In America, Horace Kallen seemed to concur, arguing that "the Jews isolated man in the universe . . . while the Greeks made the spirit of man at home in the world." But unlike Syrkin's polarized realms, Kallen was arguing for a Hebraic/Hellenic nexus that was "intimate and interpenetrative."[31] Reznikoff's strategy of combining seemingly opposed forces can best be understood in the context of his exegetic readings of the Hellenic and Hebraic traditions in *Jerusalem the Golden*, a collection published by the Objectivist Press in 1934. He weighs in on this schism in "Hellenist," where Jewish "jealousy" of the Hellenist's sensual at-homeness is actually sublimated within his aesthetics, in the form of erotic cohabitation:

> Shameless moon, naked upon the cloudless sky,
> showing your rosy and silver bosom
> to all the city,
>
> King Davids, we meditate business, and you
> must now be bathing on a housetop in the pool of evening,
> Bathsheba.
>
> (*Poems* I, 107)

To discover the poet's keen interest in the existential paradoxes and disturbances produced by hybrid identities, we need look no further than the creative tension generated by his confession in these lines that he is "guilty" of an intensely self-conscious attraction to Nature's/Hellenism's surprisingly seductive intrusions into his field of vision. This is a compelling representation of the individual's private struggle to align himself with a demanding tradition; the Jew is supposed to seek proximity to God, but this very nearness causes a sense of alienation from the earth. And the very God in whom the Jew would seek consolation is—unlike the intimately "shameless moon," the poet's "sole companion many a night" (108)—utterly remote, because of a prevailing metaphysics of abstraction.[32] But what is most compelling in these lines is not the ostensible tension between Judaism and Nature (or even Reznikoff and the "Greek"), but rather the poet's eagerness to illuminate his own hybrid essence and the confused yearnings that invariably ensue whenever one is ambiguously poised on the margins of two cultures.

Instead of the homecoming and homogeneous culture Zionism promised, Reznikoff probed the possibilities of illicit confluences between seemingly disparate worlds. Unlike the Zionist hunt for "authenticity" in the past, most of the *Menorah Journal* writers, with whom Reznikoff was increasingly affiliated, were drawn to Hellenistic Alexandria as the preeminent site of liberating textual and individual translation and transformations. Similarly, Reznikoff struggles to conceive of a poetics that would combine an ethics of Jewish witness with the modernist's interest in new forms of perception. As a passionately engaged walker in the city, he alternates the immediacy of direct observation of the urban scene with Jewish memory and rich allusions to Judaic textuality (biblical and talmudic discourse).

In a section titled "Hellenist" Reznikoff describes the strangeness of coming in conflict with his own fissured "identity." The first four poems set forth the problem of his division. Apparent fragments, these lyrics eventually emerge as an intricately woven, thematically continuous narrative:

> The moon shines in the summer night;
> now I begin to understand the Hebrews
> who could forget the Lord, throw kisses at the moon,
> until the archers came against Israel
> and bronze chariots from the north
> rolled into the cities of Judah and the streets of Jerusalem.
> What then must happen, you Jeremiahs,
> to me who look at moon and stars and trees?
>
> (*Poems* I, 107)

At least two questions are posed here. After two thousand years of displacements and exile, what new catastrophe can possibly be unleashed against the poet's imagination? But more importantly, precisely what constitutes the transgression of the subject who gazes longingly at "moon and stars and trees"? The latter question might best be addressed by considering Hegel's Abraham—the Hebraic archetype whose wandering at the behest of an abstract deity causes him to become indifferent to Nature in an organic sense until he "objectifies" or pragmatically masters physical matter. In a superficial sense this may be the poet, whose careful observation of the surfaces of reality exhibits a mode of perception in which the transcendent Word struggles to overcome and eventually substitute for the reality of the Thing. In contrast, Hegel's enlightened Hellenist rightly seeks in Nature an animate spirit. For Hegel it is precisely because they are "the people of the Book" that the Jews produce a mode of thought that is like cancer, forever consuming the living object of their incessantly analytical inquiry, a dichotomizing argument that prefigures Matthew Arnold's Hebraic/Hellenic polarity.[33]

With the notable exception of a few poets (such as Allen Ginsberg and Harvey Shapiro), Reznikoff has never before been considered a trendsetter in the larger Jewish world. But if we take note of how the newly dynamic world of Jewish Studies has come to explain its intense fascination with the confluence of Hebraic and Hellenist literary culture, and its interest in the resulting acculturations and adaptations, we awake to his enduring relevance—and prescience. Consider David Aberbach's recent observation that ancient "Hebrew literature was infiltrated by Greek vocabulary and concepts. . . . The entire system of rabbinic discussion of Jewish law which predominates in the Talmud and Midrash was influenced by the symposia of the Greek philosophers. . . . [T]he immense work in the 2nd and 3rd centuries C.E. on the codification of Roman law left its mark on the Mishna" (22). Moreover, according to Erich S. Gruen, even the Palestinian Jews "engaged actively with the traditions of Hellas, adapting genres and transforming legends to articulate their own legacy in modes congenial to a Hellenistic setting" (xv). Similarly, in his extensive study of the long history of encounters between Judaism and Hellenism, Israeli historian Yaacov Shavit stresses that, had the self-modernizing Jews who accepted Hegel's and Arnold's formulations at face value delved a bit deeper, they would have discovered that the vitality of ancient Judaism owed much to outside cultural influences (470).

Contrary to Zionist historiography, these three scholars are representative of a new wave of thinkers who insisted that even the Jews of Hellenistic Palestine had to find a means of defining and expressing their singularity within a cosmopolitan milieu. Provocatively, Shavit argues that "Greek" and "Hellenistic" concepts have been internalized even in the secular Jewish culture of modern Israel itself:

A secular Jew is not merely a *Hellènistès*, one who behaves like the Gentiles by participating in the foreign culture: the foreign culture is an inalienable part of his own new culture and provides him with the concepts and definitions with which to test his old Judaism, define his new identity, and form his cultural life. . . . Athens is an integral part of Jerusalem. Without it, Jerusalem, namely the modern secular Jew and modern secular Jewish life in Israel, would not be what they are today. (471, 480)

But this is not "news." Reznikoff's poetry is already immersed in what this "recent" paradigm describes: the Diaspora Jew does much more than merely choose between succumbing to or resisting the surrounding culture. Reznikoff's own dismissal of Jewish "essence" may be partially indebted to his contemporary Horace Kallen, who says much the same about the ancient origins of "Hebraism" in *The Book of Job as a Greek Tragedy* (1918), a work that Reznikoff admired. In describing the proximity of the "Yahwistic party" to other tribes, Kallen argues that the

nomadic tradition which it drew from was a memory turned into an ideal, a historic social organization of which its divinity was the name and the symbol. The agricultural life which it denounced was a condition, oppugnant to its heart against the nomadic past. The confrontation of the two meant mutual *interaccommodation*; an *interpenetration* and *confluence* whence sprang the new constitution of the state and the new definition of the nature of God." (48–49; emphasis mine)

Note the way in which Reznikoff furthers Kallen's logic, ultimately arguing for the Hebrew Bible itself as a multifaceted and diverse fabric of many
cultures:

The thing to bear in mind in reading the Old Testament is that it is really an anthology covering at least a thousand years and, most likely, including the unwritten traditions, much more than that. And, unlike other anthologies where each contribution
is arranged according to the date of composition, early and late material and material
from various districts and countries are more or less interwoven and much early
material has been revised again and again. (*Selected Letters* 302)

For Reznikoff, a narrative is never complete; whether it is his family history or
the family history of the Jews, the story is only put to rest with the greatest
reluctance. There is something in this resistance toward the text as a static
entity that ultimately informs Reznikoff's indifference to Zionism's coercive
readings of the Jewish past and to its definitive resolution of Jewish destiny.
Above all, his poetry and prose argues for a history of cultural choices rather
than an organic unfolding of a single cultural impulse—which was essentially
his reason for rejecting Zionism as well.[34]

◆

The discursive tension between homogeneous ethnocentrism and a universalizing vision of Jewish continuity that shapes the thought of Aberbach,
Gruen, and Shavit, frequently surfaces in Reznikoff's thought as well. For
instance, on one occasion, Reznikoff's old friend, Albert Lewin, a Jew who
spent years as a player in the big Hollywood studios, called him to task for
overlooking the Old Testament's ostensible reverence for warrior heroes and
xenophobic violence. But in spite of Exodus's manifestly dramatic and epic
qualities, Reznikoff was unwilling to represent it as a story of heroic resistance in the Western manner, with its own unequivocally "native" son. For
Reznikoff, Jewish tradition discourages idolatrous impulses in all forms, even
veneration of its prophets. In his epistolary response to Lewin, he remarks
pointedly that "Moses is not mentioned, except once I think, and if so in a
very minor way, in the *Haggadah* which the Jews read at the Passover celebration of the Exodus. . . . The reason given is to discourage hero worship."
His evident pleasure in musing over these particulars suggests that he was
finding a way to link his condition as a modernist Jewish artist with the actual
ambiguous, even hybrid, origins of Jewish ethnicity rather than with the
chauvinist or nativist reading his friend posits. Which is why Reznikoff liked

to keep his Jewish heroes within human, and sometimes even diminished, dimensions:

> The Pharaoh of the Exodus is eight feet tall;
> of black granite; a god and a sun.
> You must have seemed very small, Moses,
> standing before him pleading for Israel;
> hide, Jacob,
> between two rocks in the water, bow down
> among the bushes of the desert!
>
> *(Poems* II, 21)

Reznikoff quietly denied that the biblical emphasis on genealogy constitutes a racist ideology, for "Moses might have been an Egyptian." The poet pointedly compares the insignificance of the ancient prophet's racial origins to "the great leaders of the proletariat, Marx, Engels, Lenin, and Trotsky, none of whom was a member of that class. It should not be hard for Jews to believe that race, per se, means nothing. King David was partly Moabite" (*Selected Letters* 303–4). Reznikoff is alluding to the king's great grandmother, Ruth, whose conversion to Judaism points to the strangely hybrid origins of Judaism's ancient monarchy (Ruth 4:17–22). Delighting in the myriad ways that ancient stories could be read to instruct the multiple self of American pluralism, a new being that would be the inevitable product of the hybridized and multiethnic American culture that surrounded Reznikoff.

The poet's reticence to cooperate with the Zionist program can be understood by considering yet another ironic reference to the narrative of King David. Besides providing a pleasurable moment of whimsy, this lyric quite seriously challenges the mythic significance of all messianic/nationalist narratives, Jewish and Christian alike:

> I do not believe that David killed Goliath.
> It must have been—
> you will find the name in the list of David's captains.
> But, whoever it was, he was no fool
> when he took off the helmet
> and put down the sword and the spear and the shield
> and said, "these weapons you have given me are good.
> but they are not mine."
> I will fight in my own way
> with a couple of pebbles and a sling.
>
> *(Poems* II, 29)

Always a careful reader of Scripture, Reznikoff seems to have in mind the disparity between the famous account of Goliath's demise in I Samuel and a more cryptic reference in II Samuel, where it appears that an obscure warrior named Elhanan does the deed. Besides playfully reducing the epic scale of biblical figures to more manageable proportions, Reznikoff implicitly confronts the uses of myth in the present. Many religious and secular Zionists have justified the right of Jews to Eretz Israel by tracing their presence to the tenth-century biblical precedent of the Davidic kingdom. Thus in 1948, the State of Israel's Proclamation of Independence spoke directly of the "re-establishment of the Jewish State" (not its establishment), which implied the repossession of a nation-state ceded to the Israelites by divine covenant, the state that reached its apogee under David and Solomon. David also sits atop the genealogy of Jesus (according to the Gospel of Matthew), and so he has always been vital to Christian theology as well. In his wry midrash, the poet undermines the divine glory associated with an exalted pedigree crucial to both traditions.

Deflecting the reader's interest from the usual highlights conjured up by this scene—martial victory, the gore, a fallen giant, a jubilant mob, and the ascendancy to power—Reznikoff points instead to images of resiliency and adaptation, the peculiar triumphs of *smallness*. Our reading might also lead us to think a little more about the identity of this profoundly humble poet— nearly unknown even today—who has done his best with a couple of pebbles and a sling. Ultimately, this vision is entirely congruent with the ancient rabbis' metahistorical approach to life. For the talmudic sages, "ultimate meaning [is] contained within small and humble affairs" (Neusner, *The Way of Torah* 36).

The point is so subtle it *almost* seems as if nothing profound is being said in this lyric, except perhaps for the wryly humorous and softening intrusion of the Yiddish inflection—"whoever it was, he was no fool"—which anachronistically tones down the opulence of the biblical version with its assumption of regal dominance and disrupts the hegemony of the sacred and canonical text with a stylistic heterogeneity that embodies the linguistic boundary crossings of the diasporic poet. Of course, to many, the story of how a young shepherd triumphs over a Bronze-Age giant with the aid of a slingshot might already seem a sufficient celebration of smallness. But Reznikoff seems to want to burrow even further into the biblical narrative, causing us to wonder whether this crucial dimension of the story has not been immoderately overshadowed by his powerless people's increasing desire to locate monarchic grandeur and heroism in its distant past. This is quite the opposite of what we observed in Lazarus's lyrical recovery of Maccabean virility or Syrkin's advocacy of heroic Return. As we have seen, there is a striking difference in the latter's foreboding treatment of the same biblical narrative in the previous chapter.

The active reader always feels invited to speculate on how Reznikoff adds to and subtracts from the biblical narrative itself; here the lyric seems to hint that it might almost have been better if the slayer of Goliath had remained a forgotten nobody rather than become a Jewish king, whose traditional eminence might further contribute to the mythologization of violence. As Daniel Boyarin has pointed out, the form of resistance most visibly sanctioned in the Talmud is *evasion*:

> The arts of colonized peoples of dissimulation and dodging are thematized . . . as actually running away, the very opposite of such "masculine" pursuits as "standing one's ground." The central Babylonian talmudic myth of the foundation of rabbinic Judaism involves such an act . . . the "grotesque" escape in a coffin of Rabbi Yohanan ben Zakkai from besieged Jerusalem, which the Rabbis portray as the very antithesis of the military resistance of the Zealots who wanted to fight to the very last man and preserve their honor." (*Unheroic Conduct*, 93–94)

Authorizing a Dickinsonian gap of mystery and indeterminacy ("It must have been—") over a cherished Jewish narrative of a recovered heroic past, this poet advocates a past that is not compelled to serve ideological formations in the present but instead remains available for open investigation. Always a supreme skeptic and minimalist, Reznikoff is indifferent to the myth of an ancient dynasty that has a royal king at the head of its ancestry; instead he shifts the story's focus to valorize individualist idiosyncrasy and unconventional strategies born of contingency. He defies those who would plow through the complex literary strata of Jewish tradition for the sake of a single-minded goal, such as "proving" the Bible in order to propagandistically buttress Jewish claims on the land. Instead, we make do with a schlemiel, the singular vocation of the run-of-the-mill, a long-forgotten quick thinker of indeterminate origin who just happened to be present on the scene.

◆

Though a determined "secularist," Reznikoff's poetry leads the reader to an ironic understanding: that Exile (and paradoxically even the expulsion of heretical individuals) is also the theological idea that makes most sense of Jewish history *and* modern identity, the very paradigm that is rejected by the classical Zionist perception, since the latter replaces it with a motif of

"Redemption" within contemporary history. That he rises to this cultural challenge stands as a credit to him but also to a small number of Jewish and non-Jewish intellectuals in his generation who sincerely believed that the Jews are not only a people who live most creatively, productively, and humanly precisely at the intersection of universalism and particularism, but who might possibly persuade others to question the anomalous features of territorialism, nationalist ideologies, and the modern state itself. In contrast to his famous contemporary Ludwig Lewisohn, who saw Eretz-Israel as a revivifying spiritual influence on a worn-out Diaspora, a vortex for Jewish life, Reznikoff ironically *amalgamates* the cultural strata of ancient Israel and the *Galut*. Even when he poeticizes themes or motifs from the Bible, he frequently ironizes these through layers of cultural perspectives and attitudes acquired over centuries of diasporic living. And so the chief referent always remains his present position, not a distant landscape or a yearning for recovery.

The resulting vision is at once singularly Jewish and cosmopolitan. This is a poet whose literary output repudiates all forms of happy resolution and stasis, rather than directly challenging the politics of Zionism. Reznikoff's opposition to absolutist identities, particularly insofar as they deny the likelihood that *change* and shared vulnerability are the only constants in human experience, is evident in his poetic recasting of an allegorical dream. Instead of homecoming or rest, Reznikoff dreams of his ancestor, always situated on the brink of departure—and open doors:

> In my dream,
> long dead, he stood in front of me
> before an open door;
> head high and confident,
> looking as he used to
> when about to leave on a business trip.
> And, indeed, he had his hat and coat on
> and held a valise.
> At the moment I was as fond of him
> as I used to be when a boy; and I called out, "Uncle, uncle!"
> But he paid no heed to me
> and was going away.
>
> Through the open door I could look into other rooms with open doors
> that led into other rooms—
> all with open doors.
>
> *(Poems* II, 100)

As the Jewish poet who refused to trade Central Park for Palestine, Reznikoff confirms the poetic and theological imperative of deferral. Instead of arrivals, the poem enacts the repeated gesture of departure, as if through a funhouse mirror. Through its spare imagery of the silent and heedless relative, its enigmatic suggestion of abrupt exits, determination, and freedom, this lyric seems to define Reznikoff's peculiar sense of "Diaspora": what the open door might lead to, neither the dreaming boy nor the adult poet is privileged to determine. Dwelling in *Galut* is a mysterious vocation: in the present moment the poet is only a limited creator, not privileged to know the unseen, which will be revealed only over a greater expanse of time than he will be privileged to witness (as his apparent riff on Psalm 90 reveals):

> The tree in the twilit street—
> the pods hang from its bare symmetrical branches
> motionless—
> but if, like God, a century were to us
> the twinkling of an eye,
> we should see the frenzy of growth.
> (*Poems* I, 110)[35]

Well acquainted with Job's protest and the celestial reply that is not an answer, Reznikoff is humbly content with the gift of a modest, human-sized reflective capacity, which means knowing that his own gaze (or even Marx's or Herzl's) is not "like God's," that he cannot construe the final pattern of growth, must only have a kind of faith in its process. For Reznikoff, ours is not an intelligible universe but rather one that is brutally arbitrary. At best we are left with only a dim understanding that humanity is trapped in an enigmatic process of change. But what may appear to be terrifying endings (those encoded in classical Zionism) are invariably swept away by new beginnings:

> If there is a scheme,
> perhaps this too is in the scheme,
> as when a subway car turns on a switch,
> the wheels screeching against the rails,
> and the lights go out—
> but are on again in a moment.
> (*Poems* I, 120)

And that is the cycle of Jewish history, at least as imagined in the exquisitely intertwined modes of exile that form the landscape of Reznikoff's sense of an unfolding narrative. This is a poet who knows how to juxtapose the schemas of history with the randomness of the urban present. As Milton Hindus says of this relatively early poem, it evokes an existential moment:

> when we feel as if we were suddenly plunged back into the primeval state of chaos and disorder that preceded the creation. What tides us over at such times is the "antiseptic" of faith which we may not even know we possessed, the conviction that all will be well again, that the lights which have gone out for us will come on again "in a moment," though it seem an eternity. ("Charles Reznikoff" 266–67)

Embodying a deep skepticism as to whether we can thwart fate through rational remedies, these lines are nevertheless something much more than a nihilistic argument. Rather than an outright dismissal of individual moral agency, this lyric invites us to read it as an interrogation of human wisdom, a "gentle" chastening (especially if we think of Job) of the intellect's natural enthusiasm for synthetic and deficient remedies inherent in all the collective ideologies that pretend to account for the future. Perhaps uncertainty is the most ethical mode for the modern Jewish poet.

Reznikoff's historically literate perspective contrasts one epoch with another, until the reader begins to understand Jewish history as a way toward broadening one's awareness of the phenomenal unfolding of Jewish—and frequently, in a broader sense, human—continuity across time and place. In his close reading of "A Compassionate People," one of the most revealing and truly exemplary diasporic narratives of the poet's middle years, Stephen Fredman (22–26) considers this 1944 poem's historical situation, coextensive not only with the thirtieth anniversary of *The Menorah Journal* but determined by the poet's gaze toward catastrophic events in Europe—and already looking beyond. Throughout its seven stanzas, the poem insists that "the healing quality of the scriptures has arisen." In the next chapter, I will return to the pivotal question of the poet's faith in the "healing" dimensions of tradition. For now it is enough for us to consider, as Fredman suggests, the complexity of Reznikoff's lyrical achievement in: commemorating Judaism's endurance; drawing attention to the Nazi persecutors; and laying stress on "cultural survival as an ultimate value." That all this occurs in the same poem is a remarkable achievement, particularly considering the date of its composition. But perhaps the poem's most stunning act of cultural imagination resides in its stubborn refusal to turn in desperation to the redemptive remedies of Zionism, even in such a terrible crisis: "Reznikoff makes the point that the sacred writings of Judaism are the products not of an attachment to a sacred land but of a condition of exile and suffering." Stripped of territorial ambition or the exercise of force, the Jewish imagination wields an awesome range of symbolic and theological strategies.

Here, then, in Reznikoff's simultaneous nod to both this spirit of the past —the enduring vitality of Judaism's textuality—and his incomparable struggle to look ahead to a Judaism that might survive even the Holocaust, we find what is perhaps the most explicitly prophetic moment in his entire oeuvre:

> As when a great tree, bright with blossoms and heavy with fruit,
> is cut down and its seeds are carried far
> by the winds of the sky and the waves of the streams and seas
> and it grows again on distant slopes and shores
> in many places at once,
> still blossoming and bearing fruit a hundred and a thousandfold,
> so, at the destruction of the Temple
> and the murder of its priests, ten thousand synagogues
> took root and flourished
> in Palestine and in Babylonia and along the Mediterranean;
> so the tides carried from Spain and Portugal
> a Spinoza to Holland
> and a Disraeli to England.
> *God, delighting in life,*
> *You have remembered us for life.*
>
> (*Poems* II, 60)

Though its tone is somber, this lyric's confidence in recovery is undeniable. Depending on the reader's perspective, the allusive effect of the invocation of the Jews in the Diaspora as "seeds," "the sands of the sea," or "the stars of the sky"—in spite of their "death by gas, in trucks, in railway cars, in chambers hidden in the woods"—may be audaciously sanguine or simply heartbreaking. As Yaron Ezrahi declares, in the absence of military power, "the word of God, the Holy Scriptures, and the words of the rabbis became the ultimate means of world-making, of acting and interpreting, of shaping and protecting life, of resurrecting the ruined Temple, the conquered Holy Land, and the Lost Kingdom" (178).

There is, at the same time, another layer of meaning that presses for our attention. For in the poem's fifth stanza we learn of the remarkably fecund properties that reside within the fertile soil of *dispersion*. Privileging Torah over terrain, the speaker asks first: "Where is that mountain of which we read in the Bible—/Sinai—on which the Torah was given to Israel"; then, "Where was the Bible written?" (59); only to ultimately dismiss the significance of geography altogether. Rather, Jewish history is one of constant tension as a new center of authority rises to wrest control of the shaping of tradition from its predecessor: hence Babylonia from Judea; Spain from Babylonia; Portugal, Holland, and the rest in their turn. Furthermore, this modernist's reference to Spinoza tells us that, though tradition is engraved on one's subjectivity, the individual also creates new patterns in response to changing times (as, on a larger scale, it is the role of the Jewish people to do in history). Reznikoff remained fascinated by Jewish "modernists" such as the Prophets, Maimonides, Spinoza, and Marx precisely because, for these figures, the "Golden Age" always lies in the future, not the past.[36] In an important sense, Reznikoff's recovery of these figures constitutes a search for his own Jewish essence.

In Lazarus's effort to mediate between American and Jewish myths, we saw that early Zionist rhetoric adapted its nationalism from notions of a racial essence that was somehow inextricable from *place*. Zionism emerged at a time in which most people regarded as axiomatic the connection of race to place and the biological determination of thought. Implicit in their debates was the problem of where the spirit of Israel was really shaped—in Palestine or in the wilderness? In Reznikoff's recovery of the past, history prevails over geography. In fact, this poem's territorial landscapes melt into inconsequence (as opposed to the tangible landscapes of Lazarus's poetry), leaving in their wake only the textual dwellings of "the prophecies and the psalms," "the Torah and the prophecies / the Talmud and the sacred studies, the hymns and songs" (*Poems* II, 61). There is no attempt to wrest from these the promise of a nationalist redemption. What another poem, "Exodus 3:13," elegantly underscores is that, for very good reasons, the Jewish tradition had long ago situated its origins in the empty desert:

> Day after day in the wilderness,
> Year after year,
> Until you see a bush burning.
> Yes, but you have to climb a mountain
> to speak with God.
>
> (*Poems* II, 206)

There is a double move here, for though these lines (like the aforementioned "I do not believe that David killed Goliath") may speak first and foremost to Reznikoff's lifelong vocation and private struggle in the "wilderness," they also link that solitude to his Jewish identity, his sense that Jewishness has evolved not in collective safety and insularity but as the fruit of wandering and transcending one's place. Such a notion is supported by numerous rabbinical interpretations, wherein the desert is a no-man's land in which the Torah could be given without any hindrance whatsoever, free of any influences from a settled environment. Others have claimed that the desert was selected as the ideal site for the people's growth because it was not a paradisaical garden, and that sanctity and wisdom do not come forth from pleasure. But of course for the Zionists this was now unthinkable. A modern national ideology has to prove its at-homeness by demonstrating an intrinsic relation to the territory it seeks to possess.

As those interwoven strains of race and geography that we first noted in Lazarus's thinking continued to evolve, race served not only as an historical but also as a *psychological* principle that sustained one's claim to belongingness and continuity, an ostensible shelter against assimilation. Zionist theorists like Nachman Syrkin had argued that the Jews were a specific "race," a group possessing unique "psychic and physical properties," insular endowments that passed from one generation to the next (quoted in Sharit 397). Interestingly, as a socialist, Nachman Syrkin could exult that "the spirit of the desert is a monotheistic spirit . . . [a]nd the nomadic God is social. In the nomadic life there is no private land and the animals and goods belong to the tribe as a whole" (*Prophecy and Politics* 305). But for most Zionists, an historical explanation for Zionism required that the narrative of the Jews' formative years shift from Sinai to Palestine. In Lazarus's time this locale had already received much support in the mystical travel literature about Palestine, written mostly by Christian visitors. Throughout the nineteenth century, the distinctive properties of the landscape even provided an explanation for the universal monotheism that was thought to be its natural outgrowth.

The rabbinic notion of the wilderness as the source for Israel's monotheistic faith was weakened most of all by Heinrich Graetz, who stressed the Jews' "genetic" origins as much as their spiritual and moral inheritance. Arguing that prophetic ethics developed within Israel during its days in its own land and not during its years of wandering, Graetz portrayed a Palestine as a sublime landscape:

Whilst the eye surveyed, from a prominent standpoint, the objects encircled by an extensive horizon, the soul was impressed with the sublime ideas of infinitude. . . . Single-hearted and single-minded men, in the midst of such surroundings, became imbued with a perception of the grandeur and infinity of the Godhead, whose guiding power the people of Israel acknowledged in the early stages of its history. Sensitive hearts and reflecting minds may well be said to perceive "the finger of God" in this region. (Graetz, 49)

Many members of the Russian Jewish Zionist intelligentsia accepted the logic of Graetz's milieu theory and applied it frequently to authorize the modern return to Zion. The genius of Judaism was the product of the material conditions of its homeland, and thus only a return to Eretz Yisrael could restore the Jewish people to its autochthonous culture. Reznikoff was troubled by the seductive logic of the Zionist polemicists, whose radical shift away from a conception of Jews as a dynamic group capable of adapting to—or even being in the vanguard of—social change, toward a static linkage of race to place, he saw as a challenge to his own vocation as an individualist urban dweller. In the chapter that follows, we see that Zionism's conclusion that the Jews must return to their only authentic home in the new/old landscape of Palestine inspired the poet's most confrontational poetics.

Chapter Four

"Palestine Was a Halting Place, One of Many"

Diasporism in Charles Reznikoff's Nine Plays

and Beyond

In deepening my analysis of Charles Reznikoff's poetics of exile, I turn now to a critically neglected and long out of print source, the poet's *Nine Plays* (1927), which amount to the most vibrant expression of an explicit diasporism in the history of early Jewish American literature. In the previous chapter I hinted at the poet's ardent resistance to Zionism's claim that the Jew's experience in their land was the sole precipitator of Jewish ethics. Before returning to consider the cultural vision of Marie Syrkin, it behooves us to confront the most demonstrative evidence of Reznikoff's opposition to both the messianic politics of return and possession and the usurpation of Jewish subjectivity by ideology. Reznikoff's poetic/political dramas, the poet's earliest and most neglected works, are the foundational texts of his efforts to work out the linkage he perceived between ethics and the experience of dispossession.

It is in relation to this work that Reznikoff encountered an unexpected source of editorial resistance. His first awareness of Zionism as a censorious discourse occurs in a 1922 letter to a friend. Reznikoff was momentarily vexed by the fading prospects for publishing his playlet, "The Black Death," a short work inspired by German Expressionism that examines medieval antisemitism during the time of the bubonic plague, in a Jewish venue. An editor had "read it, and accepted it, but then hesitated because some of it seems anti-zionistic and the special issue is to be very zionistic."[1]

This is precisely the moment that American Zionism began to flex its institutional muscle. Sensing the distance between his own conception of

Jewish history and that of classical Zionist discourse, this already marginalized poet now faced the possibility that his work was unsuitable for ideologically predisposed Jewish readers. This encounter is an outstanding example
of the power-knowledge nexus within Zionist discourse and of the political
repercussions of Jewish creativity.

It is not difficult to identify the ways in which "The Black Death" would
have displeased the nascent Zionist American audience. For example, in the
first scene, set somewhere in western Europe at the beginning of the four-
teenth century, two old Jews, the master of the house and his guest, converse
pessimistically about the present, with the tough-mindedness of an ongoing
investigation. The uneasy host asks his guest: "Do you know that Christians,
in debt to us / Say that we spread the plague?"[2] Inexplicably, their conversation abruptly shifts from the scene of disease, and from the immediate prospect of persecution that faces them in the present, to a meandering exchange
on the enigma of Judaism's extraterritoriality:

> **The Guest.** Had Israel a land? Was Canaan ours,
> Which we took a while and never held
> Against Assyrian or Roman?
> When Solomon was king was the land Israel's?
>
> (76)

Intoxicated by his sense of Jewish destiny, the guest's speech exhibits an
increasingly cavalier attitude toward historical exigency. Even while recognizing the distinct possibility of imminent destruction, this diasporic voice
becomes more timeless—and resolute:

> Palestine was a halting place,
> One of many. Our kin, the Arabs,
> Wander over their desert. Our desert
> Is the Earth. Our strength
> Is that we have no land.
> Nineveh and Babylon, our familiar cities,
> Become dust; but we Jews have left
> for Alexandria and Rome.
> When the land is impoverished, as lands become,
> The tree dies. Israel is not planted,
> Israel is in the wind.
>
> (76)

If "halting" in the first line denotes uncertainty or hesitancy, it also suggests
a stumbling, perhaps even a momentary lapse from a chosen path. At this

juncture we might take stock of Reznikoff's ironic reversal of Zionist rhetoric, for the latter conventionally constructs Diaspora itself as a lapse, an aberrant exit from history. Ultimately this is a lyric that challenges a naïve faith in the permanence of any home, setting a brake on the thralldom of the individual to the nation. But it seems something of a paradox that Reznikoff would choose a well-known instance of one of the Jews' most futile struggles against a hostile environment in order to present his case for Diaspora. If he means to persuade us of something, why not argue it in the context of the numerous instances of benign coexistence? And is the case not weakened further by the fact that the guest's rather idealistic exposition of his belief in Judaism's viability is spoken into the reader's awareness that the cruel massacre is imminent?

Perhaps this apparent slippage may be understood as Reznikoff's determination to fully acknowledge the events of Judaism's dark history—which were so often the privileged territory of the Zionist polemicists—in order to produce an argument that could not possibly be accused of utopianism. In fact, the guest's speech exemplifies Jewish literature's traditional symbiotic relation to catastrophe. For Reznikoff, the collective memory that recounts this grim history is understood as an emphatic affirmation of continuity. A keen knowledge of the poetic tradition of Jewish lamentation privileges the poet to argue: "Take no threats to heart / This may be the end of you and me / But for all the grains of sand blown / From the desert, the desert is" (76).

For Reznikoff, "Israel is in the wind" signifies diasporic "geography"—the *luftmensch* movement of Jewish civilization through time and space. It is around the time of "The Black Death's" composition that he expresses his preference for the pristine tropes of wilderness and struggle—"rocks," "sand," and "glaring sun," in short, what he thinks of as "the Hebrew" (and this is the desert imagery of Sinai not Canaan)—over "towns," "fields" "rivers," "lakes," and "woods," which he considers the comparatively tame, rooted pleasures of "the English" (*Selected Letters*, 38). In the modern canon of Jewish poetry, we have no poet more faithful to the ethical dimension of exile than the French Jewish philosopher Emmanuel Levinas, who describes Judaism's "difficult freedom": "The Jewish man . . . is at home in a society before being so in a house. He is in a sense exiled on this earth, as the psalmist says, and he finds a meaning to the earth on the basis of a human society. . . . Man begins in the desert where he dwells in tents, and adores God in a transportable temple" (23).

A constructive diasporism does not lead the poet to a utopian denial of the inevitability of evil in the universe. Hence, it is entirely consistent that, an indeterminate number of years after the Jews have been massacred for their "guilt" in the plague, two characters speak of the likelihood of future atrocities:[3]

> The Guest. Evil to Man—like the plague—and
> evil men do,
> Like sores upon a healthy body,
> Scab and fall off.
> The Host. If the body is healthy—sores?
> The Guest. Those at least are gone, your city once
> more crowded.
> The Host. The disease is in the blood to break out
> again.
>
> (84)

We have seen that, for the Zionists, such catastrophes, invoked frequently enough, justified their negation of *Galut*. For Syrkin they were singularly "corrosive." But Reznikoff claims, again and again, that though barbarism indeed poses a severe threat, far from discrediting the Jewish presence in Europe, more often than not, it actually strengthened Jewish civilization by acting as a stimulus for its culture. His lyrics obstinately avoid any suggestion that the trauma to which Jews have been subjected justifies or necessitates an embrace of nationalist identity, since the latter had only led to greater suffering. It is revealing that *Nine Plays* appeared in the wake of the 1929 Arab riots in Palestine.

In this regard, Reznikoff's alteration of his original title for a 1934 volume of historical poems seems to announce a decisive moment of rupture. Originally, the typescript that includes the full-length versions of "Babylon," "The Academy at Jamnia," "The Synagogue Defeated," "Spain," "Poland," and "Russia," bore the title "If I Forget You Jerusalem: In Memoriam, 1933."[4] But in the final revision—faithfully reproduced in all subsequent appearances in print—only the *second* phrase is preserved, and in two additional places the phrase "If I Forget You, Jerusalem" has been vigorously crossed out by Reznikoff's hand. In this boldly diasporic effacement we know that Reznikoff made a startling, some would say regrettable, choice. In spite of the growing crisis in Europe and Palestine (not to mention the severe admonition of the psalm: "let my right hand wither"; Ps. 137:5), he elects to affirm the radical autonomy and creativity of Jewish dispersal, not its manifest hopelessness and deferral of arrival. That decision underscores Reznikoff's self-conscious determination that the individual poet must break off from the whole, from the communal. The fracture produces a radically individuated voice and sensibility, one uncertain of regaining either a rootedness in the collective or the uncomplicated piety of the poem's pre-text. And yet, as Maeera Shreiber explains, for a certain breed of Jewish poet, what "begins as a liability becomes an asset; loss is recovered as gain . . . the question, 'How can we sing God's song in a foreign land?' is also itself the answer—as the song of exile becomes the master narrative in which all poems begin" ("The End of Exile" 273). For Reznikoff, certainly, "radical displacement" is transformed into the starting point for altruism and compassion. It meant taking a stand against those who, with the best of intentions, would force the end of history.

Many years after writing "The Black Death," Reznikoff would make several remarks to interviewers that greatly clarify his idiosyncratic attitude toward antisemitism and the entire tragic history of persecution: "Occasionally you have situations like the Holocaust or during the Crusades, where there were lots of killings, or [when] they were blamed for the Black Death in Europe. . . . [M]y own feeling about it is, that the effect of anti-Semitism is double; in one case you have assimilation, and in the other, you have a strengthening of whatever the person thinks is Judaism."[5] The phrase "whatever the person thinks is Judaism" exhibits a radical openness to the unpredictable ways in which American Jews might respond to modernity and yet still draw from a genuine wellspring of Jewish textual traditions and belief. Weeks before his death, Reznikoff offered an interviewer a singularly unpretentious, yet profound, analogy that may underscore *all* his Jewish lyrics about vulnerability. Though it would probably never have been voiced in quite this way by most intellectual Jews of his generation, it might, one suspects, nonetheless have resonated with them: "you know, anti-Semitism can sometimes bring out the best in you. In my case I know it strengthened my identity and my resolve. Americans are often spurred to do more precisely because of prejudice—blacks are a good example" (Rovner 16).[6] In his clear-eyed consideration of struggle as a welcome catalyst, Reznikoff advocates an exilic Judaism that does not cleave to a messianic-redemptive resolution of its history.

As always, Reznikoff's material struggles as a Jewish poet greatly enriched his respect for the struggles of other ethnic communities.[7] Unlike many Jewish American intellectuals, such as Syrkin, Irving Kristol, and Gertrude Himmelfarb, Reznikoff did not, in the aftermath of the Shoah, turn toward the right as an act of recovery. Instead, catastrophe sustained his earlier view, perhaps mediated by the socialism that had been the predominant Jewish discourse of his age, that organized society is always a war of the powerful against the disenfranchised. Though it would probably never have been voiced by most intellectual Jewish Americans of his generation, it might, one suspects, nonetheless have resonated with many of them: "Maybe it's something like a cold bath. It's unpleasant while you're in it but when you get out, you feel braced . . . a warm bath can be *too* relaxing" (Rovner 16). As a screenwriter in Hollywood's world of artifice, Reznikoff had experienced the stultifying effects of just such a warm bath. His preference for a "bracing" struggle is evident in his dismissal of his wasted months among the rich and priviliged in what he called "Lotus-land,": "very little, if anything is done here" (*Selected Letters* 174).

Nine Plays is most intriguing when it cleaves to an ethos of mutual struggle and accommodation that remains intact even when the poet examines the ancient Jewish relation to the Land. Reznikoff's "Genesis" is inflected by the fact that, in the twentieth century, the "peoples of the Book" are poised to devour each other in order to possess the Land. It would be difficult to imagine a verse less palatable to a territorial ideology than Genesis 26:15–31, a strange account of a series of submissive accommodations and withdrawals that Isaac—born to a sojourner perpetually on the road—relates in order to resolve disputes with local tribes over the rights to various wells and grazing lands. In the Hebrew Bible this idiosyncratic narrative of a weary tribe of desert sojourners stalls the inexorable momentum of conquest and possession that otherwise distinguishes the text. Reznikoff's imaginative discovery of the biblical text's diasporic intentions is typically understated:

> **The Eldest of the Herdsmen.** If Ishmael
> were the master, they would not dare this.
> **The Eldest of the Shepherds.** How gentle
> Isaac was beside Ishmael,
> When he was here to bury Abraham:
> Isaac has lived in booths and tents,
> His clothing woven from the hair of goats and camels;
> Ishmael was in the skins of the wild deer he has killed.
> Isaac's face is like honey, Ishmael's
> Like the black rocks among which he hunts;
> Ishmael's hair and beard are two bushes,
> His glances arrows and his hands fists;
> Isaac's eyes are like a father's on his grown son,
> His palms open as if to help or bless—
> Here he comes.
>
> (110–11)

Reznikoff is alert to the fact that Isaac is very different from the heroes of other ancient myths and traditions. Neither hunter or warrior, he is a herdsman who meditates in the fields. Perhaps even more than his hospitable father, he is a Jewish universalist. Isaac's refusal to act aggressively is interpreted as a radical resistance toward the seductive power inherent in exercising control over the land. After the desert chieftain Abimelech demands that he remove his flocks and herds from the very land God has promised to his father, Abraham, Isaac instantly surrenders. The biblical text does not explain why, though of course the nearly sacrificed son must have grown up with an unusual understanding of the uses of power. In Reznikoff's version, Isaac seems to be naively reimagined as an anachronistic surrogate for the poet's modernist Jewish soul. But perhaps he has it right; after all, Genesis is an utterly self-divided text of migration and rootedness, where successive waves of exile and resettlement continually scramble human destinies. For the modernist poet this unsettled narrative represents a critical juncture in which the ancient Hebrew writers (possibly composing the text in exile) judiciously appraised their relationship to God, the Land, and Others with equal claims to their land. At any rate, the poet's characteristic sense of "apartness" is also present in "Isaac's" Bourne-like idealism, which is clearly incomprehensible to his herdsmen and shepherds:

> Isaac. My wealth is the wealth of the land in which
> I am,
> In a time of hunger yours as well as mine;
> My men in a time of need are also yours.
> My father, Abraham, took no man's, but if one said of
> his,
> This is mine, he answered, It is yours;
> Nevertheless, he grew richer.
> And this my father did, not out of fear—
> . . .
> Abraham gave because of friendliness.
> I am my father's son in this:
> That I wish all men well;
> Surely the stars send them sorrows enough.
> But if you say that there is no room for us,
> My father, Abraham, and his father, Terah, wandered
> far;
> The Earth is wide,
> And as they prospered, their son may hope to prosper.
>   (112)

After digging a well, an action that declares sovereignty, Isaac's herdsman enters to complain that the men of Gerar have claimed its water as their own.

The patriarch responds simply, "Let them have it." A second herdsman soon enters, to declare that he has gone on a "day's journey" from the first contested site only to have his rights to the well also challenged by the valley inhabitants. Isaac, who for unknown reasons seems perpetually to defer the occupation of the land of Canaan, announces that this well too should be abandoned. The play quietly concludes with the arrival of another herdsman who observes: "We dug a well / beyond the valley and are not troubled" (113). Reznikoff's skillful rendering translates an ambiguous moment in the ancient narrative as a triumphantly universal plea: The Land must be shared by peoples with competing claims, rather than possessed. Undoubtedly, the ethical vision articulated in Reznikoff's lyrical drama was intended to be applied to contemporary Jews and Arabs, as if to suggest that these groups need to recover Isaac's gentle skills to achieve accommodation. Today we might profitably read Reznikoff's treatment of the ancient intertext against the grain of what Michael Lerner has called "Settler Judaism"—whose adherents so distort Judaism that they not only believe that God gave them the West Bank as an eternal inheritance, but that whatever is done to hold on to it is somehow "righteousness," a messianic-redemptive act (*Jewish Renewal* 248). Whatever the biblical source's original intent, Reznikoff's midrash warns about the cost of ideology in the present.

Though there is no textual instance in which Reznikoff ever referred directly to the conflict between Arabs and Jews, it is revealing that "Genesis," so disruptive of the discourse of territorialist hegemony and statism, was chosen by Reznikoff to be his final statement in *Nine Plays*. There is a marvelous moment in a 1974 interview that sustains the spirit of my reading here. Reznikoff expresses his delight over an episode in the Hebrew Bible he has just encountered, "in which David, who has been hiding or fighting Saul," is greeted by friends to whom "he happens to say . . . how wonderful the water was in the village in which he was born, they go and bring him some, and he wouldn't drink it. He said human life was risked for it" (Charles Reznikoff: *Man and Poet* 123).

◆

Reznikoff's critique of the Zionist recovery of sacred territorial origins grew in sympathy with the way he viewed the fatal consequences of the European invention of America as terra incognito, with its own narratives of innocence, self-invention, and rebirth:

> They landed and could
> see nothing but

meadows and tall
trees—

The reverie of a lush landscape in an apparently empty paradise is suddenly broken by the revelation of a mysterious, hitherto unseen presence:

In the twilight,
through the thickets
and tall grass,
creeping upon all
fours—the
savages, their
bows in their
mouths.
(*Poems* I, 122–23)

Here the poet reveals that the earth's ostensibly empty paradises are invariably informed by the presence of an Other. Even this subtle deconstruction of American history, titled "The English in Virginia" (1930), written in the same period as the verse dramas, seems informed by the seething territorial tensions in the year following the Arab riots. "Landing" and not "seeing" seems to unify the stories of all territorial interlopers. Since the time of Emma Lazarus, Palestine was frequently represented as essentially "empty" because it was not inhabited by Europeans. This conception was manifested in the early Zionist slogan: "A land without a people for a people without a land." In Nachman Syrkin's early theoretical and programmatic works, in which the ontological status of the land is apparently influenced by contemporary colonial discourse, there are no references to the Arab population. Though deeply concerned about the plight of the Jews in the Yishuv, it is also likely that the poet of these lines had grown uneasy about Zionist certitudes about the "empty" land they wanted to inhabit.

Where Zionists stress the fact of ancient Jewish life in Palestine, Reznikoff enunciates the *how*—artfully evoking the original text's special attention to the moral nature of that presence in the land, as in Isaac's patient willingness to wander to the next valley: Land-loss does not mean the end of history or identity. Whenever Reznikoff turns to the past of the sacred text (or, as in *Testimony* [1934], when he turns to America's violent, secular past), he does so with a particular moral imperative gained by situating himself in the present of that past. History is thus personalized. It is a mode of writing that enables him to relate to others on the ground of their common humanity. This poet's temporal inclusivity works against the grain of Zionist ideology, which, according to Israeli sociologist Yaron Ezrahi, is a discourse that largely "base[s] the Book of Life on the last chapters" (93). In contrast,

> liberal democrats anchor the meaning of the narrative in the middle chapters, in the present. They continually rewrite the past and the future from the perspective of the present. They are the only group that has an open conception of meaning directed simultaneously toward the past and the future. This, of course, is the strategy that subordinates the narrative of life to the autonomous present and a maximalistic conception of human freedom.... The sheer plurality of perspectives and stories undermines the mobilizing power and authority of any single master narrative. (94)

Reznikoff's poetry is unashamedly informed by just such liberal strategies of free agency and of choice amid multiple perspectives. This holds true for his historical works about his own country. Having carefully examined America—in the present moment of its urban frenzy as well as its rural past—the Jewish experience with homelessness provides him with an imperative to address the needs of others. Reznikoff became the rare kind of modernist poet who, by virtue of his outsider status, somehow knew that he was emblematic of America, that America was full of aliens like himself, and that through "the sheer plurality of perspectives" these represented, they undermined univocal notions of the nation. For instance, in the following lyric, his own sense of homelessness is muted, but nonetheless underscores a civic and intimate space of mutuality.

Judaism may seem to be of casual significance here, but in some fundamental way it transforms the meaning of all the forms of wandering he encounters in the American city. The commanding thing about Reznikoff's lyrics is the sense of a metaphysically demarcated space of Diaspora that always envelops his poetic speakers. Wherever he goes he meets literal and existential émigrés like himself:

> The new janitor is a Puerto Rican;
> still a young man with four small children
> He has been hired because he is cheap—
> not because he is the handy man
> A good janitor is supposed to be.
> I doubt if he ever saw any plumbing
> before he came to this country,
> to say nothing of a boiler and radiators.
> Anyway, he was soon overwhelmed by requests from the

tenants to do this and fix that.
He does his best and spends hours at simple jobs,
and seldom does them well—or can do them at all.
He was in my flat once
to do something or other and, when he was through,
asked me if he might sit down.
"Of course," I said and offered him a drink,
but he would not take it.
"It is so quiet here," he explained.
And then he began to talk about a man who lived in the house
and taught Spanish.
"He talks to me in Spanish," the janitor said,
"but I do not understand.
You see I am not an educated man."
His eye caught the print of a water-color by Winslow Homer
which I have hanging: a palm tree in the Bahamas.
"That is my country," he said,
and kept looking at the print
as one might look at a photograph of one's mother
long dead.

(Poems II, 114–15)

There is an acute sense in this poem that America is filled not only with other Diasporas but with inhabitants haunted by similarly fissured identities. I think that there is another reason why the janitor's condition is so compelling—and familiar—to him. Like the poet, the janitor is linguistically bereft. In his autobiographical lyrics, Reznikoff repeatedly and almost ritualistically mourns his dislocation, identifying it as a yearning for Hebrew. Haunted by a longing for linguistic wholeness, as though he has lost the divine language and the certainty of belonging to a people, he writes: "How difficult for me is Hebrew: even the Hebrew for *mother*, for *bread*, for *sun* is foreign. How far have I been exiled, Zion" (*Poems* I, 72). So far that he is utterly estranged from the primary forms of nurturance, at least in their "native" forms. Reznikoff was highly stimulated by T. S. Eliot's insistence that between a textual heritage and an inheritor there is no continuity, but a generational fracture in transmission, an anamnesis, and an effort of reappropriation. Eliot's imperative that "[t]radition cannot be inherited, and if you want it you must obtain it by great labour" meant a great deal to him. And perhaps most importantly the poet, estranged from Zion, is struck by how the Puerto Rican janitor finds himself gazing at the prospect of a distant homeland, one whose tangible dimensions are melting away in a mythic landscape. Like each of us, the janitor is seemingly fated to suffer the loss of a cherished world. That is the essential condition of Reznikoff's Diaspora.

Reznikoff's radical interest in the narratives of Others also emerges forcefully in his reworkings of traditional Jewish sources. For example, his acknowledged source for "Kaddish" (which appears as the introduction to the poem) is the *Kaddish de Rabbanan* as translated by R. Travers Herford in 1925, which appears as an epitaph in his translation of the Talmudic text *Pirke Aboth* (*Sayings of the Fathers*):

Upon Israel and upon the Rabbis, and upon their disciples and upon all the disciples of their disciples, and upon all who engage in the study of the Torah in this place and in every place, unto them and unto you be abundant peace, grace, lovingkindness, mercy, long life, ample sustenance and salvation, from their Father who is in Heaven. And say ye Amen. (*Kaddish de Rabbanan*)

Reznikoff's version is more complex. Since America is filled with homeless outsiders, then the outsider poet must create a new/ancient modal embodiment of moral authority. Instead of echoing the traditional invocation of Jerusalem and Return, he pleads for a sovereign existence sanctified only by a living relationship with the Text. For Reznikoff, the collective homelessness of a people seems to be a situation wherein a utopian potentiality endures. Something can be learned from this condition and applied to a movement resembling "progress," though this is not construed as a linear narrative free of catastrophic setbacks. Hence, the poet imagines himself as a being contented to be a guest and a stranger, committed to coexistence with other guests and strangers. And so in "Kaddish" he wishes for *all*

> who live
> as the sparrows of the streets
> under the cornices of the houses of others,
> and as rabbits
> in the fields of strangers
> on the grace of the seasons
> and what the gleaners leave in the corners;
> you children of the wind—
> birds
> that feed on the tree of knowledge
> in this place and in every place
> to them and to you
> a living
>
> (*Poems* I, 186)

In the original there is no explicit allusion to Others, but Reznikoff's secular alternative, while insistently evoking the darkness that besets Jewish life in Europe during the 1930s, repeatedly beckons in every stanza to a reader with an uncertain identity: "to them and to you / peace." The xenophobic and racist shadow of fascism is all the more reason to resist an exclusively ethnocentric voice. On the one hand, it does no good to deny the need to belong to a community; in fact, it is futile to deny this claim of identity. There is nothing reprehensible about the desire to form a strong identification with a cultural tradition and with a people. But for Reznikoff this does not mean that in our dealings with strangers we may neglect the principles of equality. As "Kaddish" and other poems of the 1930s are acutely aware, rejecting these principles facilitates deportations and exterminations. There are times when, to remain human, one must speak and act *outside* the interests of one's group. So rather than preserve the original text's emphasis on the singular burden of Israel's "chosenness," he prefers a liturgical form that yearns for an abundance that might be enough to go around to all the earth's deserving, an urgent address that might speak to the crisis of any moment (including the contemporaneous Depression in America). The dispersal of humanity into separate nations no longer serves the poet as a satisfactory paradigm. In Reznikoff's recasting of the *Kaddish de Rabbanan*, prayer is a direct address to a reader whose own identity remains an open question, rather than an assumption—something provisional and not reified.

By failing to make any explicit claims about who the Other is, Reznikoff transforms the piety of the traditional prayer of talmudic study into a response not only to the fascism of the thirties, but to any form of ideological imperative that engenders territorialism and the persecution of Others. Reznikoff's profoundly American poem transforms the mourner's prayer into a reinvigorated statement about continuity. As David Bleich observes, for a startling number of later Jewish American poets and composers, like Leonard Bernstein, Allen Ginsberg, David Ignatow, and Melanie Kaye/Kantrowitz, the new/old Kaddish "can be read as a collective name for the death of Jewish life in Europe and its rebirth in America; its not mentioning of death or passing makes it especially eligible for this role" (192). But perhaps, as Reznikoff intimated, it is the kind of prayer one might hope to find in the liturgies of the multicultural era now upon us.

Just as Reznikoff's Jewish epics typically culminate, not with the triumph of territorial redemption, but with the scattering that always engenders diversity and experience, his urban American poems celebrate the city's shifting terrain of difference. Even the poet's slyly humorous studies of birds and animals illustrate the unpredictably heterogeneous character of the metropolis. We find an instance of this in "Neighbors," where two species inhabiting a claustrophobic space, with irrevocably separate and hostile agendas, are forced to come to terms with the existence of the Other:

> the horse that draws a cab through the park
> now digs his mouth into the pail
> in front of him
> and is annoyed at the pigeons
> pecking away at the oats he scatters
> as they are at his active hoof.
>
> (*Poems* II, 93)

Similarly, this seemingly inconsequential gaze at the beasts in the city zoo wryly critiques the status quo on the other side of the cage:

> the camel and zebra are quarreling:
> trying to bite each other
> through the bars between them.
> Of course, they come from different continents.
>
> (*Poems* II, 95)

Though whimsical, these blunt Aesopian lyrics are thoughtfully inflected by the problem of nationalist identities and territorial struggles of the human world. It is not difficult to see why Reznikoff might extrapolate from the tense encounters of the camel and zebra and other exotic species to wryly comment on the claustrophobic urban spaces that surround them. Throughout Reznikoff's oeuvre, the street is the place where the sheer fact of pluralism (as well as its promise), is most explicit and this is the theme of many of his recollections of his childhood. As Marcus Klein observes of the early-twentieth-century metropolitan clusters, "[t]he street was a metaphor for territory . . . something to be possessed and defended, and sometimes extended. Since the urban ghetto was in fact a warren of ghettos, one's own street—meaning one or two city blocks—was likely to have an ethnic definition created by the ethnic differences of the neighboring streets" (*Foreigners* 30–31).

Leslie J. Vaughan's meditation on Randolph Bourne's early-twentieth-century attraction to the urban spaces of modernity further illuminates Reznikoff's sensibility: "In the city, one reaches another state of consciousness, expressing oneself in ways not directly reducible to the past, in particularistic blends of current and past cultures and traditions. Modern urban trans-nationalism contained elements of diversity and a little disorder" (457–58). Like his contemporary, Reznikoff's early poetry reveals the presence of many diasporic communities in America. We immediately notice that these allegorical encounters between animal species issue no special plea for *transcending* racial and ethnic differences in the name of universalism. Rather they intimate a kind of immigrant cosmopolitanism that is not color-blind (or color-bound as current identity politics requires) but simply color-curious, acknowledging that difference might be a source of civilized attraction.

Such attraction to the exotic American streets was certainly common to the experience of Russian Jewish immigrants and their children. Consider the experience of Maurice Hindus (uncle of critic Milton Hindus), who, upon arriving in America in 1905, was "overpowered with curiosity":

The streets lured me irresistibly. They were my first American school. It was in the streets that I saw for the first time Negroes, Chinese, Italians, Hungarians, Irish, others of the multitude of nationalities that made up New York. I had read of these people and now I saw them in the flesh. I yearned to speak to them, to learn all I could about them: how they lived, what foods they ate, what books they read, what they talked about when they were by themselves, what they thought of the peoples among whom they lived, and how they differed from the muzhiks, the Jews, the intellectuals I had known in the Old World. But language was a barrier I couldn't hurdle —not yet. I contented myself with watching and wondering about them—the Chinese in the laundries, the Negroes as day laborers, the Irish as truck drivers, policeman, and saloonkeepers, the Italians as shoe-shiners, ice and coal carriers, peanut vendors, and organ-grinders. (41–42)

Like Reznikoff, the immigrant's Whitmanesque catalogue of New York diversity does not presume that one can really "know" the Other—there is that linguistic hurdle at the very least—but he is clearly delighted to be enriched by the pluralistic proximity he shares with these ethnic and cultural identities. In spite of admitting to a feeling that he is "bewilderingly alien" to his new surroundings, Hindus desires neither to return to the insular shtetl his parents have left behind, nor to seek refuge in the relatively homogeneous Jewish East Side. His passion for multiplicity is reflected in his reading of the twentieth-century American city as an unprecedentedly promiscuous intermingling and dispersal of the worlds' peoples. In Reznikoff's own linguistic estrangement, he embraces the fate of America's Babel of strangers, each of whom loses the intimate world of community and common sociolinguistic origins. Reznikoff's reader is invited to form an identification with a wide-ranging humanity composed of differences: immigrants, the poor, minorities—the powerless rather than the strong.

At the same time, Reznikoff imports the notion of Jewish space into New York City so that everything within its continuum embodies a particularly Jewish resonance. In ways that bear comparison with Sholom Aleichem, Reznikoff conceives of his urban survivors as a kind of schlemiel people. Though powerless, they are psychologically and sometimes even culturally the victors in defeat. In this regard, Maurice Samuel's reflective analysis of Aleichem's ironic technique of reversal offers an illuminating way of understanding the role of weakness and disenfranchisement in Reznikoff's poetry:

It is more than a therapeutic resistance to the destructive frustrations and humiliations of the Exile. It was the application of a fantastic technique that the Jews had developed over the ages. . . . They had found the trick of converting disaster into a verbal triumph, applying a sort of Talmudic ingenuity of interpretation to events they could not handle in their reality. They turned the tables on their adversaries dialectically, and though their physical disadvantages were not diminished thereby, nor the external situation changed one whit, they emerged with a feeling of victory. (54)

Keenly aware of the textual permutations of this ethos, Reznikoff—though he richly layers his relationship to tradition with irony and discontinuity— enlarges on this paradigm again and again. In the following lines from a variation on a verse of Zacharia that anti-might ethos is plainly apparent:

> Go swiftly in your chariot, my fellow Jew,
> you who are blessed with horses;
> and I will follow as best I can afoot,
> bringing with me perhaps a word or two.
> Speak your learned and witty discourses
> and I will utter my word or two—
> not by might or power
> but by your spirit, Lord.
>
> (*Poems* II, 68–69)

This lyric's seemingly mild repudiation of power will perhaps be best appreciated by those who read it against the grain of Zionism's mission of rejuvenating the bodily representation of the Jew, as in the post-Enlightenment orientation we experienced in Lazarus's verse-dramas and polemics. Disdaining the "weakness" and "femininity" of Diaspora Jews, the virile rhetoric of classical Zionism is distinguished, in part, by a deluge of body-building, hyper-masculine imagery. But, transcending that anxiety, Reznikoff's poetics expand on the problem of what it meant historically for such Jews to interact with the larger world and not merely abide within a ghetto.

It is worth pausing to consider Reznikoff's language because it provides an important clue to his struggle against totalizing ideologies and identities. Though Reznikoff was drawn to Hebrew to gain entry into the living stream of Jewish thought that creatively engages with each new historical crisis, his textual orientation is not quite the same as Marie Syrkin's in her frustration at not being able to speak the *living* language of national rebirth. In spite of Reznikoff's oft-stated love for the learning of Hebrew, he much prefers to write lyrics that declaim the difficulties it causes him than to actually gain fluency in it. Reznikoff began life with a relatively assimilated cultural upbringing (though his Russian-immigrant parents spoke Yiddish), became deeply conversant with the most experimentalist literary trends of his time, and yet created a poetry that often journeys into the premodern world. Straddling the two worlds, he expresses the tension between them in lyrics marked by a considerable degree of ambivalence as well as humanity. Ultimately, they emphasize that the individual is both fixed in the present moment and inseparable from the past. Thus, the poet's verse-plays surveying the possibilities of Jewish history, and his dramatic studies of figures from Abraham to Uriel Acosta, all strive to engage the specificity of each crisis.

Not having a Jewish language, Reznikoff is far more interested in experimenting with the multivocal possibilities of English, the majority language, in which Hebrew and Yiddish might surface as destabilizing currents. I say "Hebrew" and "Yiddish" here because there is in Reznikoff's work both a current of suffering, outrage, and sublimity, informed by the poet's reading of prophetic literature, and a gentle buffoonery, self-deprecating and antisublime, through which the Yiddish of his forebears speaks. More successfully than any other Jewish American poet of his generation (though George Oppen and Louis Zukofsky sometimes strive for similar effects), Reznikoff integrates the ironic, vernacular Yiddish with the classic, prophetic Hebrew.

What does this choice (or is it a not-choosing) to blend Hebrew and Yiddish into English tell us? For one thing, it is a choice not to work in Hebrew, which, since its revival by Chaim Nachman Bialik and Shaul Tchnerichovski in the 1890s, was increasingly associated with reterritorialization of the language and its ascendancy to a majority culture. Interestingly, as his poetry matured, Reznikoff often found himself working in the company of Zionist ideologues at the *Jewish Frontier* (the Labor Zionism monthly). There he served alongside Ben Halpern, Hayim Greenberg, and Marie Syrkin, who issued such declarations as the following: "Eastern Europe and what it represents is no longer a viable symbol for us. We study Hebrew today not because Akiba did, but because the modern Israeli Jew does" (Israel 9).

In his creative work, Reznikoff insists that Rabbi Akiba is every bit as relevant to the modern Jew as is Ben-Gurion, not because he is nostalgic for a lost religious vocabulary, but because as a modernist he respects Judaism's self-renewals in the wake of subsequent catastrophes. Keenly aware that Hebrew survived as a *minority* linguistic culture over three thousand years, Reznikoff is drawn to its layered strata of creativity and crisis, to the mysterious way that it empowers the powerless.[8] It is telling that his favorite Hebrew writers are those of the prophetic period (Jeremiah and Ezekial), *exiled* as a result of imperial conquests, as well as the authors of the Mishna—rabbis who were exiles or the sons of exiles from post–Bar Kokhba Judaea. Similarly, he is attracted to the Hebrew rabbi-poets of the "golden age" of medieval Spain, all self-conscious exiles in one way or another.

There is a sense in which Reznikoff chose to be simultaneously an exile *and* an immigrant. The child of people forced by circumstance to leave their home, he could operate effectively in the new culture. Except that he did not become a full-fledged member of the latter because he was a material failure, and even worse, a poet, and even worse, not a refined modernist but a *Jewish* poet. In other words, Reznikoff did not rush into an uncritical embrace of the dominant culture. On the other hand, there does not seem to be any lost or abandoned culture he wanted to recover. He is simply willing to not be at home, either on the dais of Jewish community or in the marketplace:

> Not because of victories
> I sing,
> having none,
> but for the common sunshine,
> the breeze,
> the largess of spring
>
> Not for victory
> but for the day's work done
> as well as I was able;
> not for a seat upon the dais
> but at the common table.
> (*Poems* II, 75)

In spite of envisioning the diasporic tradition of the text as the locus of personal and national homecoming, Reznikoff severely qualifies his Jewish knowledge—"we had little Jewish learning and knew no Hebrew nor the prayers which our fathers had repeated since they were children"—linking his Jewishness to a distinctly modernist self-awareness of loss, distance, ignorance, and alienation.[9] Hebrew is frequently alluded to in his poetry, though chiefly as a trope of irrecoverable absence. But Reznikoff was hardly unique in his ignorance and eventual sense of a loss of spiritual language. For David Shearl, the young hero of Henry Roth's *Call It Sleep*, Hebrew is an untranslated and mystical beckoning, a "strange and secret tongue. . . . If you knew it, then you could talk to God. . . . That blue book—Gee! It is God" (227). Reznikoff's representation of *The Menorah Journal* (1915–1962), the site of some of his earliest publications, as "a land where we were welcomed" is an implicit corrective to his own estrangement as well as a gentle subversion of Zionism's denigration of a Judaism in which the Text is recognized for its radically transcendent mobility, from one space to another, from one generation to the next.

For Reznikoff, like his forebears, the word remained the medium of this struggle, even if his idealized text was a site of translation and perhaps hybridity. The *Menorah*, memorably evoked by Robert Alter as "one of the most exciting episodes in the history of the American Jewish intellectual community," did not embody a "pure" identity.[10] Fredman describes it as a place "where Jewish writers could invent a [new] form of American intellectualism" (personal communication). More than a mere journal, the *Menorah* was an intellectual and cultural movement created by Jewish humanists who sought to put the question of their Jewishness into a language fully commensurate with American intellectual life. Reznikoff saw the journal as the very embodiment of how the Jewish intellect, though homeless and restless, could find fulfillment in the American idiom.

Reznikoff's rejection of Hebrew as the direct medium for his Jewish modernism (though he spent years trying to master it) is hardly a mystery. But why did he choose not to experiment with Yiddish verse? After all, the Russian Yiddish of Reznikoff's childhood was a radically "cosmopolitan" idiom, even more so than the German Yiddish that earlier Jewish Americans brought with them. Encountering Reznikoff for the first time, Yiddishists I have spoken to, familiar with the vigorously *international* modernism of Yiddish poetry movements in America and abroad, invariably raise an interesting question: Why did Reznikoff write in far greater isolation than was strictly necessary? I do not have a definitive answer, but I would argue that

Reznikoff's attraction to deterritorialization as an essential aspect of modernity is so radical that he is unwilling to contribute toward *any* pretense of full recovery of a native dimension. The Yiddish and Hebrew elements that are present within his poetry serve to interrogate the homogeneity and wholeness of English. Instead of enjoying the certainty of a Yiddish audience, Reznikoff was fully aware that his verse was a uniquely solitary form of writing. He intentionally constructed a perversely minor position within a hegemonic literary environment, and this resulted in some of the earliest—and by far the most innovative—Jewish American poetry in English in this century. Just as his poetry claims *partial* affiliation with modernist poetry, his metatextual narratives draw on interpretive forms available to him within both Hebrew and Yiddish literary traditions, including parable, midrash, and textual commentary (though these are often presented ironically). Thus his American poetry provides a space in which neither Hebrew nor Yiddish is privileged but rather both are present—and sometimes ironically so. This too is diasporism.

◆

Significantly, the philosophical stance that informs Reznikoff's lyrical illustrations of the relevance of the Jews' centuries-old Exile for living fully and ethically in spite of the instabilities wrought by linguistic and territorial losses was a stance increasingly challenged by the *Frontier*'s other editors, particularly Ben Halpern:

Exile meant for the Jews a forcible sacralization of their religion. For an action-oriented, transcendalist faith this was no less than a calamity. Exile thwarted the ethical impulse of Judaism. . . . A religion of ethical activism projected through an organized society can *only* flourish when the society is free to determine policies relating to the whole range of social action. In Exile the Jews are not free to act." (12-13)

It would be difficult to formulate a more precise antithesis to the historical acumen I am claiming for Reznikoff's Jewish works. Like Halpern in the statement above, Reznikoff regards ethical action—not religious ritual—as the definitive realm of Judaism. He boldly undermines, however, the basic premises of Halpern's conclusion, not only by demonstrating the vitality of the ethical impulse throughout the history of Exilic Judaism, its rich heritage of choices and decisions, but through ultimately claiming this "calamity" as the basis for a compassionate civilization in the present. Reznikoff's numerous midrashim on Jewish history and scripture, though usually evoking one crisis or another, nearly always avoid a sense of doom or fatalism. Even when darkness descended upon the Jewish people, in the poet's own time, Reznikoff found a mooring in language's imaginative capacity for responding to crisis. In the following lyric we see how his advocacy of a "powerless" people residing only in time and in the allure of the text differs considerably from a monolingual centeredness in space and the will to sovereignty:

> Those who lived in villages and alleys
> in huts and cellars,
> selling a calf shrewdly
> and buying a sack of wheat cheap
> to sell cupfuls
> for a copper—
> who were pillaged and murdered
> in the cities of Germany,
> in Spain and Russia,
>
> from York to Isphan—
> their sons
> stand up to plead—
> in every language—
> for the poor
> and wronged,
> teach by formula and picture,
> speech and music—
> heal and save!
>
>   (*Poems* II, 20)

Clearly preferring the wisdom of experience, the retrospective mood that poetry's depth of vision provides, the poet refrains from merely evoking the frenzy of the immediate moment. This preference is especially apparent in two versions (written decades apart) of a lyrical narrative of his family's experience with antisemitic street thugs. Published as part of *Uriel Accosta: A Play and a Fourth Group of Verse* (1921, self-published), the earlier version presents the events in terse detail, overlaid by the uncomprehending fear of the horrified narrator, and leaving the reader with no comfort, only the visceral aftermath of brutality: "Uncle came, bare-headed, blood oozing out of his hair" (*Poems* I, 46). But the 1969 version, without sentimentalizing what must have been a traumatic moment, suggests a hidden resource not explored by the first, as if the poet senses there is something unvoiced in that familial scene that had not been sufficiently integrated into his initial telling:

> My grandmother was muttering that this country
> was no better than Russia, after all;
> and my parents and I felt ashamed,
> as if somehow we were to blame,
> and we tried to explain that what had happened was unusual,
> that only the neighborhood we lived in was like that,
> and what a wonderful country this was—
> that all our love for it and our praise
> was not unmerited.
>
> (*Poems* II, 155)

This time it is the ironic argument between the generations that completes the poem, conquering the vicissitudes of persecution through language. Now, having told his story, his wound washed and bandaged, the uncle leans quietly against the hot-water boiler. He is replaced in the foreground by the other members of the family, who, instead of being shocked into silence (as in the apparent resolution of the older poem), are prepared to *argue*, to struggle for the "meaning" that will somehow account for (or efface) raw experience, just as the reader is left to choose which of the narrative's disparate Americas most resembles his or her own experience.

In this poem Reznikoff surely does not set forth the naive notion of language as "redemptive." After all, these were the years he spent poring over the Nuremberg and Eichmann trial transcripts for *Holocaust* (1975). But language can perhaps render something besides the unrelieved horror of Syrkin's verse; there is also the sheer tenacity of one's own response. Anne Stevenson illuminates this paradoxical juxtaposition of horror and faith in Reznikoff's relationship to language: "The only justification I can see for Reznikoff's documents of 'real' revelation is that he believes that the will of God is manifest in a world of horrors, and that to turn away from the horrors in the name of literature is to turn away from God himself" (185). The tensions between the shtetl's cruel certainties and the immigrant's disruptive relation to the new culture produces a poetics that refuses to settle on a singularly optimistic or pessimistic vision. Pogroms, atrocities, persecutions (and finally genocide) are always filtered through the poet's *present* position in history, not to diminish reality but to affirm the need to experience the past through the dispassionate messenger of time. At the same time, readerly attention to the vicissitudes of the Jewish past requires that we read the last four lines with the full weight of their intended irony.

In contrast to that lyric's balance, here an almost gleefully perverse attitude defies the contingencies of a challenging universe. It is not the least of

Reznikoff's gifts for confronting darkness that he is often very funny. In a lighter moment, for instance,

> People think walking in autumn the
> pleasantest season
> but I don't.
> I was hit on the head by a falling leaf.[11]

It is worth paying special heed to the ironically titled poem "Pessimist," not only because it was apparently Reznikoff's last, composed shortly before his death, but because it amazingly distills the essential qualities of his anti-epic and measured response to vicissitude. Here, Reznikoff transfers the Jewish code of exile to a mute universe wherein falling leaves, like all organic beings (and even the Chagall painting that inaugurated this discussion in chapter 3) share an impersonal fate. Written by an eighty-one-year-old man who had in his last years suffered a brutal mugging, the poem points to a deep reservoir of quiet resistance. Besides the initial amusement it provides (again we witness Reznikoff's perverse enjoyment in scaling epic ideas down to small truths), this lyric wryly reassures us of the poet's psychic resilience in the face of a lifetime spent becoming closely acquainted with an appalling textual tapestry of death, suffering, and cruelty, not to mention his own struggles. He knows that in its essence *Galut* indeed contains the "tragic." But it also constitutes a source of energizing influence for the world—and the poet— perhaps because only under trial, in the most severe circumstances, does the individual have the opportunity to discover the unexpected within:

> Now that black ground and bushes—
> saplings, trees,
> each twig and limb—are suddenly white with snow,
> and earth becomes brighter than the sky,
> that intricate shrub of nerves, veins, arteries—
> myself—uncurls
> its knotted leaves
> to the shining air.
>
> (*Poems* I, 117)

It is the same kind of cavalier discovery made by an impassioned character in "The Black Death," who, even as his community teeters on the edge of crisis, proclaims his willingness to dwell under the precarious circumstances of adversity rather than yearn for a return to Zion. Or like Reznikoff's favorite persecuted heretic, Uriel Acosta, on the verge of excommunication: "Now I am fixed within them like a weed / That torn up, trampled, grows again / The hardier for its torments" (*Nine Plays* 11).

Distant Origins and the Immediacy of Witness

"Our forefathers, strangely enough—and this I believe is the real root of mankind's problem—originally came not from Kana'an, not from an earthly Jerusalem, but from the far Euphrates with its source in Eden, from an impossibly remote and primordial home. We cannot forget it, or ever find it again. I believe this fact has afflicted us to the present day."
—Aryeh Lev Stollman, *The Far Euphrates*

As we noticed earlier, Reznikoff's "Jewishness" embodies a call to resist arrival and resolution. Now we will witness another form of this tug-of-war between home and exile. Self-consciously Jewish American poets often represent the present in ways that constitute a break with the past. Like other poets, they often argue with ideological constructions of "community." Fully awake to the ambiguity that contaminates the identity of the modernist ethnic intellectual, Reznikoff undergoes a privatization of Jewish consciousness, an apartness that inevitably strains the stable enclosures of collectivist narratives.

Discovering an original way to interpret the past almost certainly demands an acute sense of separation from the sanctuary of community and collective memory. Reznikoff contributes to this heretical paradigm when compelled to confess—even in the very heart of a collection devoted to the memory of his mother, grandparents, and their east-European origins—that "only the narrow present is alive":

> I like this secret walking
> in the fog;
> unseen, unheard,
> among the bushes
> thick with drops;
> the solid path invisible
> a rod away—
> and only the narrow present is alive.
> (*Poems* II, 39)

In the end, he proposes that one can only live in the world with *uncertainty*, another word of pivotal importance to Reznikoff's notion of exile. This is a lyric that fully embodies what Gerson D. Cohen describes as "the play of tension between the demands of tradition and what are felt to be the requirements of the present, between the desire for continuity, represented by tradition, and the desire for adaptability and relevance, characterized by change" (162). And poetry is the reward for learning how to respect that instability. Rather than prescribe a "redemptive" resolution for this crisis of communal erosion that would mimic the efficacy of either political ideology or tradition in its narrowest sense, Reznikoff's lyrics express the tension between "pure seeing" and the call of tradition. The very endurance of this struggle signifies the gap between his poetry and Zionist homecoming.

The poet is lured by that which "has constantly evolved," not what has been codified or resolved into permanence.[12] Even in his use of the Bible, Reznikoff delights in the fluidity of a midrashic ethos, hoping that his "selections and use of verse may have the same effect as when in a congregation a new cantor sometimes gives a slightly new version and renews the glitter of the precious metal dulled by use."[13] Precisely where we witness the poet's personal apprehension of existence as an *exile*, an unseeing of "the solid path" that one intimates—or imagines—may be there but cannot easily integrate into immediate perception, we find the wellspring of the poet's individualist sense of Jewish selfhood. "Secret walking": the formation of an inner world that is only ostensibly solipsistic, an act that transforms the Jewish experience of exile into an expression of one's modernist sensibilities. Invigorating as a way of understanding the ethical relation between the isolated self and the surrounding community, these lines also boldly negotiate between a discontinuous present and the epic of history, without the consolation of return that Zionism proposes: "the solid path invisible / a rod away— / and only the narrow present is alive."

Other modernists would soon adapt similar strategies in drawing together the halves of their seemingly disparate Jewish and American selves. I am thinking particularly of Alfred Kazin, who in 1942 inaugurated an innovative critical vocabulary to delineate this form of willful apartness, the peculiar argument that alienation from the past provided the surest way to mediate both Jewish and American identities. In a rhetorical move reminiscent of Emma Lazarus's distillation of the Jewish American immigrant's schism from the Old World, Kazin represents the essence of American writing as one of deep and abiding alienation. "The greatest single fact about our modern American writing," he asserts, is our writers' absorption in every last detail of their American world together with their deep and subtle alienation from it. There is a terrible estrangement in this writing, a nameless yearning for a world no one ever really possessed. . . . What interested me here was our alienation *on* native grounds—the interwoven story of our need to take up life on our own grounds and the irony of our possession. (ix)

Reading Kazin's meditation on the writer's alienation from collective tradition hastens our awareness of Reznikoff's ambiguous relation to collective narratives of either American or Jewish fate. Knowing that there might be a "solid path" of historical continuation is not at all the same as possessing any assurance that one has inherited an organic relation to the past. Yet for Reznikoff, there may be a way to find consolation even in this gap. Robert Alter probably has it right when he argues that, in the end, "the sense of exclusion from the continuity of Jewish history of which Reznikoff wrote so plangently was not absolute: if you can talk about being in exile with such feeling, that may mean that at least some small part of you belongs, after all, to a realm of rootedness against which the condition of exile is defined" ("Poet of Exile" 55). Granting the perspicuity of Alter's perception of the poet's "realm of rootedness," perhaps the ultimate question that Reznikoff's lyrics converge on is: "What does it mean that someone as open to the world as I am is essentially a Jew?" In other words, where is the precise meeting point between continuity and present experience, Jewishness and the inner self? This search is entirely congruent with Reznikoff's avoidance of ideology as well as his interest in the larger question of what it meant historically for Judaism to be a sect interacting with the larger world and not merely a ghetto. Even when historical circumstances contained Judaism within the ghetto, its walls, Reznikoff suggests, were permeable like a membrane; through the resulting osmosis there was much mixing. Hybridity is the inevitable outcome of dispersion.

◆

The extent to which Reznikoff saw himself poised always at the boundary, as natural antagonist to self-righteous political collectives that discourage individualist critical thinking, is evident in an uncharacteristically impassioned 1938 letter to Syrkin. He tells her that he so despises all "majorities, whether they call themselves Nazis or Bolsheviks, Christians or Mohammedans" that he is "ready to burst with rage when I think of their stupidities and injustice." Reznikoff proceeds to indict the collective evil of these jungles of the world— "the potent handful"—contrasting Italian and German Fascism's destruction of civilization in Europe with the Jewish, highly "individualistic" tradition embodied in men such as "Blum, Trotsky and Brandeis" (*Selected Letters* 219–20). Reznikoff's election to be an Emersonian witness apart from the mainstream of American literature, even from the inner circle of Jewish American intellectual life, is reflected in the lonely figures he wrote about— the Spinozas, the Uriel Acostas, the Chattertons, and others exiled from their origins. The theme of "apartness" resonates throughout Reznikoff's most personal lyrics: "I listen to the chatter of my fellows— / alien as a bird / who cares, who cares? / I see their smiles / but am the silent dog that hurries on / nose to the ground / busy about his own affairs" (*Poems* II, 79). Many modernist artists might see themselves as dedicated to overcoming a variety of "elites." But often they only established new elites and, having arrived, rarely sought to interrogate the brutality directed toward outsiders or to question the solidity of the boundary line between insider and outsider. In contrast, Reznikoff's poetry proposes that the isolated individual, whether alienated from popular ideology or a member of a persecuted minority, remains a moral touchstone.

It has long been a common presumption that the highly ethical, intersubjective mode of Reznikoff's poetry compensates for an apparent reticence toward the political world. The observation that his verse is distinguished by compassion for the plight of strangers, particularly ordinary people—the *kleine menshele*—has rightly been the catalyst for much critical commentary. Recently a few readers have begun to suggest that there is a more radical practice embedded in Reznikoff's poetics. I am thinking particularly of Michael Davidson, who persuasively argues that Reznikoff's magnum opus of American history, *Testimony*, constitutes a highly charged political act. In my investigation of the specific values Reznikoff associates with Diaspora, I welcome Davidson's suggestion that Reznikoff's American poems are acutely awake to the possibilities of narrative for "a critical reappraisal of nationhood" (138). Moreover I see a consistent correlation between what Davidson heralds as Reznikoff's rejection "of a unified national [American] story" and my sense that Reznikoff was alarmed by Zionism's homogeneous rendering of the multifarious history of the Diaspora.

Though Davidson may be somewhat reductive in his casual identification of Reznikoff as a political leftist, he nevertheless provides a valuable insight into the wider ideological significance of the poet's interest in the multiple voices of legal testimony. He sees Reznikoff as "part of a new documentary culture, that was trying to 'brush history against the grain' by reading American history not as a narrative of Adamic discovery and perfectibility but as a material record of diverse constituencies" (140). To illustrate this point, a good case could be made for linking Reznikoff's counternarrative of American history and the radical social criticism of the iconoclastic Randolph Bourne (himself a WASP) who, in the pages of the *Menorah* and elsewhere, challenged the solidarity of the "100% Americanism" of Anglo-Saxon culture in the 'teens by proposing a theory of "trans-nationalism" in which the diversity of ethnic identity and even cultural hybridity were elevated as values in themselves: "It bespeaks poverty of imagination not to be thrilled at the incalculable potentialities of so novel a union of men." Here Bourne asserts that hyphenated Americans (German-Americans, Jewish-Americans, Polish-Americans, Irish-Americans, and so forth) would create an antiassimilationist culture: "America shall be what the immigrant will have a hand in making it, and not what a ruling descendant of those British stocks, which were the first permanent immigrants, decides that America shall be." [14]

Expressing confidence that the position of the Jew would be strengthened by such a fragmented culture, his poetry argues with the binary terms of Hannah Arendt's political assertion that the Jew in Western culture would inevitably remain either a pariah or a parvenu excluded from an ethically effectual cultural role. Reznikoff's example suggests that an openly emphatic avowal of Jewish identity might inscribe a different ambition altogether: that is, to write a poetry for an American society not yet fully acquainted with itself, but one that would increasingly come to terms with the myriad forms of displacements that it contained. His own exilic awareness reportedly came early to him: in an intensely personal retrospective poem he recalls his acute sense of solitude as he prepared to leave the sanctuary of home for the University of Missouri: "perhaps, because in spite of all the learning I had acquired in / high school / I knew not a single word of the Torah / and was going out into the world / with none of the accumulated wisdom of my people to guide me" (*Poems* II, 167).

Post-Holocaust Identity: Reading Marie Syrkin and Charles Reznikoff in the Twenty-First Century

They gathered some twenty *Hasidic* Jews from their homes,
in the robes these wear,
wearing their prayer shawls, too,
and holding prayer books in their hands.
They were led up a hill.

Here they were told to chant their prayers
and raise their hands for help to God
and, as they did so,
the officers poured kerosene under them
and set it on fire.
　　　　　—Charles Reznikoff, *Holocaust*

There is an oft-quoted phrase that comes to us from the mishnaic tractate of *Pirkei Avot* (The Ethics of the Fathers), a Hebrew saying attributed to the first-century-C.E. rabbinic sage Hillel: "If I am not for myself, who is for me? And when I am for myself, what am I? And if not now, when?" The disparate components of this tripartite aphorism have received different degrees of priority in different settings. In Israel, it is the first line that is most frequently cited, because Zionism always stressed the Jews' need to stand up for themselves against a hostile world. But for liberal Jewish Americans, especially for those who lived through and understand their identity in some relation to the civil-rights era, it is the second line which has been invested with the greatest cultural value, reflecting a desire to translate Jewish values into terms of a struggle for universal social justice. It is the latter that has been most enthusiastically transmitted in the non-Jewish world. I invoke Hillel's ancient challenge because the two diametrically opposed premises seem to reflect a hitherto unspoken tension between the Zionist and the non-Zionist Jew and therefore illuminate the difficult conclusions reached by Syrkin and Reznikoff as Jewish American poets. But here is the crux of the matter: since these questions ("If I am not for myself, who is for me? And if I am for myself, what am I?") do not occur in isolation, an uneasy coexistence must perpetually be sought, or something essential is sacrificed. Syrkin and Reznikoff's lyrics live this conundrum as a defining tension.

Reznikoff and Syrkin were both children of Yiddish-speaking immigrants and grew up in a generation that had no rich Old World memories of its own. At best this generation had vestigial memories of deformed Jewish customs and traits, fragments of Hebrew phrases, and a debased Yiddish vocabulary. It is important to remember that only a very few writers or poets of this generation urged remembrance of the European Diaspora as a principal base for an advance into an American Jewish future, and therefore, in different ways, both Syrkin and Reznikoff wrote against the grain. What I intend here is to contrast Syrkin and Reznikoff's disparate understandings of what a commitment to Jewish identity actually entailed.

In examining this tension between their careers, it occurs to me that

Syrkin, in spite of a lifetime identifying with the Jewish state, remained "homeless" in a vital sense, caught between America and her love of Zion and ending her days estranged from both. Perhaps because Reznikoff not only embraced homelessness as his personal heritage but recognized that it was shared by a great many Others—that it was the great unexplored epic of America's past and future—he was able to draw strength from it and, in the end, perhaps even feel more at home in America as an Emersonian poet. Though his plunge into the atrocities of the Holocaust sorely tested his confidence, the poetry affirms a people that can endure any displacement, no matter how grotesque, without losing its course. But it would be unjust to conclude that, because of its strain of prescriptive pessimism, Syrkin's verse is less authentically situated in relation to Jewish tradition. Quite the opposite is true. I'm thinking of sources such as Amos, often credited as the most ancient of Judaism's prophetic books (c. 750 B.C.E.), wherein the Northern Kingdom heads toward its doom: "The city that went out by a thousand shall have a remnant of a hundred, of that which went by a hundred, ten shall remain." As Steiner points out, it is here that "[t]he long terror of the Diaspora is precisely promised: the songs of worship 'shall be howlings' "(10).

Israel's wanderings, warns Amos, are all in vain. Syrkin's post-Holocaust lyrics bear somber witness to that truth. But as a lawyer, Reznikoff seems equally attentive to the peculiarly mitigating clause in the divine sentence, the doctrine of the saving remnant, an ethos that is highly consonant with *The Menorah Journal*, the intellectual milieu with which Reznikoff felt most at ease. In the absence of religious certainty or any sustainable political ideology, Reznikoff creates a kind of covenant with the reader. Together he and we acknowledge that we are poisoned by bottomless grief and atrocity. But with the utmost imagination and moral vision we defy it, not allowing it to annihilate the Good. In a secular sense, this tenet informs his entire poetics—from "the girder, still itself" so beloved by George Oppen and others, perhaps illuminating the defiant poet himself:

> Whatever unfriendly stars and comets do,
> whatever stormy heavens are unfurled,
> my spirit be like fire in this, too,
> that all the straws and rubbish of the world
> only feed its flame.
>
> (*Poems* II, 211)

In contrast, as one of the very few Jewish American writers in the forties to come to terms with the scope of the devastation, Syrkin is incapable of indulging what must have appeared a servile fantasy, woefully detached from the reality of annihilation. In 1945, at the close of the war, she saw her mission in Palestine as gathering testimony from Palestinian Jewish parachutists, ghetto fighters, and partisan survivors. The least she could do was strive to erase the myth of Jewish passivity. For Syrkin, like many others, the meaning of terror could no longer be accommodated by what must have come to seem an obscenely Romantic incarnation of the Wandering Jew myth.[15] Like Amos's prophecy, Syrkin's *Galut* has almost exclusively tragic dimensions. Thinking of their poetry in argument, we might find the ultimate expression of her dialectical rejoinder to Reznikoff's "Pessimist" in the chillingly apt "Optimism": "How hopeful are fingernails! / They keep growing / On a corpse" (*Gleanings* 27). This is the judgment she passes on the false signs of life in Jewish American culture, the luftmensch dreaming that defers the inevitable.

One might fairly call Reznikoff's almost theological faith in the remnant— in contrast to Syrkin's projection of inevitable disintegration—"Diaspora triumphalism" (a phrase I borrow from Todd Endelman), insofar as it is just as ardent an ideology as classical Zionism. After the Holocaust it becomes even more vital for Reznikoff to keep faith with the tradition in its philosophic and cultural entirety. The prophetic imperative of the Jews' ultimate survival and creativity in their dispersal remains every bit as binding on his poetry as is the actuality of persecution. More importantly, Reznikoff seems fully prepared to reenvision American Jewry as sharing the contingency of history with other cultural groups in a cosmopolitan milieu, whereas Syrkin, like Norman Podhoretz and others among the postwar intellectual Jewish Americans, seems unwilling to give up a sense of Jews as the paradigmatically tragic minority (a chauvinism that provokes unnecessary tensions with the African American community to this day).

A passionate reader and sometime translator of the Talmud and even more esoteric texts such as the apocalyptic Ezra, Reznikoff devoted himself to constructing a Jewish reality that is something like a permeable text, containing interpretable norms, rather than claiming an insular "homeland." This is precisely why Hellenism as a hegemonic cultural force had faded into the past, while Judaism, after adopting some innovative Hellenistic elements, thrived. Rather than undermine his Jewish identity, "Hellenism" expands and reinforces it. Without denying that modernity has fragmented the wholeness of what had been religious fabric of life, Reznikoff asserts that Jewishness remains, in spite of Syrkin's not unreasonable demographic premise that the secular "Hellenism" of America eventually *overwhelms* collective Jewish life via its alien culture of self-realization and hard individuation.

Reznikoff's celebration of the achievements of Diaspora need not compel us to conclude that the poet is explicitly anti-Zionist, but simply to acknowledge that he resents the Zionist tendency to impose a monolithic interpretation of Jewish identity. The here and now of one's surroundings, whether neighborhood or nation, will suffice. For Reznikoff, fulfillment must depend on interior life, as well as an openness to one's exterior circumstances. He may not find himself at home anywhere, or is at least aware that the active intellect invariably makes foreign what is most familiar. The poet knows there is a spiritual homelessness that cannot be conquered by any form of political intervention. Yet in the meantime there is the solace of one's present moment and the immediate surroundings, which invite closer investigation: the "familiar and yet strange." Desire is never satiated, and so there is no thought of a return Home.

I have argued that Reznikoff's silence on the matter of Zionism cannot be construed as a mere problem of distance. For he did endeavor to write as an authoritative witness—from a far greater cognitive reach—to that other great epic of twentieth-century Jewish history. The trauma of the Shoah informs the internal dynamics of his Jewish poetry—whether as a mute corrective to his own comfortable American identity or as witness to the oral testimony of others. There is an inescapable correlation between, on the one hand, the lyrical challenge he makes to the cohesiveness of American nativism by amplifying the seemingly inconsequential narratives of immigrant ethnic experience in American cities and, on the other, his unease with the way Zionists defined Jewish identity.[16] For Reznikoff, a political ideology that neglects the diverse forms of Jewish life and historical experience ultimately fails to grasp the full dimensions of what it really meant to be a Jew in history. His "Jewish" poetry argues for reviewing our perception of the meaning of that past, in search of possibilities not anchored in the theodicy of exile and redemption constantly invoked by Zionists. In opposition to that narrative he explores the problem of alienation as a voluntary moral stance. Boldly, he replaces the notion that wandering is a curse with the idea of mobility as a uniquely American opportunity.[17]

Undoubtedly there will be thoughtful readers for whom Reznikoff's tenacious reticence on the hard issues of ideology and politics may complicate what I have set forth here. It is true that this is a poet who had deep reserves and was often willing to let an idea illuminate softly from within rather than be explicitly *said*. Nevertheless, there is a crucial distinction between the worldly values embedded in Reznikoff's and Syrkin's thinking. Both writers recognize the importance of the surface of reality. Their difference lies in the degree to which they accept the potential *open-endedness* of that reality. Though I have argued that, in her post-Holocaust phase, Syrkin is not content to allow Jewish history or identity to remain unfixed and unresolved, this warrants further qualification: in their postwar literary endeavors both Syrkin and Reznikoff boldly determined to unsettle their readers' complacency, to fill their present with the disquieting traces of the ravaged past. In the remarkable collections of witnesses' voices that constitute both *Holocaust* (Reznikoff's mosaic of testimony gleaned from the Nuremberg and Eichmann trials) and Syrkin's chronicle of resistance, *Blessed Is the Match*, the poets struggle to shock the world into recognizing what it had allowed to happen.

There are other important similarities between the two, of course. Both allegorize the dynamics of human interaction by examining the adjustments of domestic animals to their urban situation and their proximity to one another. But in contrast to the unrelentingly tragic universe of Syrkin, the beings (persons, animals, and objects) of Reznikoff's poetry are not explained or interpreted, nor is the universe in which they are situated. In Syrkin's poetry, we are forced to accept as calculated fact that the feral instincts of the predator will *always* rise to the surface and that the weak are doomed. Not so in Reznikoff's poetry, where there are always the surprising accommodations and adjustments whenever the subject encounters the vagaries of existence. Significantly, even in his retellings of the received epics of Jewish history, Reznikoff provides us with a way of seeing details, of relating to the world through contemplative attention without prior assumptions. To interpret as the Zionist does is to impose meaning rather than to perceive it, as the diasporist might. But even in Reznikoff's earliest poems there are no "interpretations"; only facts. It is part of Reznikoff's genius to create a poetic universe of real and simply presented human beings, objects, and language in which each thing is acknowledged to have its own integrity. Avoiding the absolute pessimism of Syrkin's didactic poetry, this poetry expresses a faith that a fully exercised moral imagination might come to terms with the world's darkness without the shackles of ideology.

The existential responses to Jewish destiny that divide Syrkin and Reznikoff illuminate their disparate ways of framing Jewish cultural traditions. Ultimately, their contrasting oeuvres might be understood as the modern echo of an ancient distinction that lies between what might be called the prophetic and priestly worldviews of modern poetry. The prophetic poet places the highest possible value on individual choice as the reliable route toward justice and salvation. The priestly antithesis (T. S. Eliot personifies this trend) mistrusts this ethical capacity of the unharnessed individual, demanding deference to a voiced and ordered hierarchy of set norms established for the collective. Denigrating individual choice, this voice beckons toward a coerced order. The priestly/prophetic distinction begins in the wandering in the wilderness, under the vastly different forms of leadership embodied by Moses and Aaron, and intensifies when the Jews establish themselves in the land of Israel. Michael Walzer elegantly reveals the underlying assumptions of these dissimilar visions:

Whereas the priests act for the people, the prophets call upon the people to act; and whereas the priests represent the ritual requirements of the covenant, the prophets, denying the centrality of ritual, represent the ethical requirements. The priesthood is the vanguard grown old, the vanguard entrenched, conservative. . . . The prophets sustain the pedagogical role of Moses, though their teaching often takes the form of a savage indictment. . . . The prophets teach the law to the nation. (52–55)

Placing Reznikoff in this "prophetic" category does not immediately validate him as a more genuine witness to Jewish experience than Syrkin—both are necessary—but rather emphasizes that his idiosyncratic individualism frees him of the ideological limitations of self-satisfaction and the relief that one has arrived at the certainty of a frozen status. This view of Reznikoff is sustained in a comment he once made about the American rabbinate: "perhaps the future of Judaism is not in the rabbis, if by 'rabbi' we mean what it seems the title has come to mean—the spiritual leader of a congregation of business men. Perhaps we may look to the rabbis to be at most guardians, *but not creators*—unless they are freed from their petty, but multitudinous tasks."[18] Hence, it is not surprising that Reznikoff returns, again and again, to prophetic narratives.[19] Virtually all of his lyrics dealing with such figures are attentive to the biblical text's emphasis on the peculiarities of the prophetic personality—traits linked to subjectivity, and thus strikingly "modern": hesitations, anger and despair, loneliness and alienation.

As an acutely self-conscious secularist, Reznikoff suggests through focusing on such personal attributes that the prophet is not presented as God's representative on earth, but as an altogether human emissary.[20] These intimations of prophetic humility are distinctly antithetical to the uncritical certainty of the priestly tradition. But more important, the argument between priest and prophet originates in the animosity that separates nationalism and universality. Steiner calls this the "mortal clash between politics and verity, between an immanent homeland and the space of the transcendent" (21). The prophetic poet's (i.e., Reznikoff's) chutzpa lies in a resolute commitment to resist normalizing the Jewish people. There must be a *significance*, even if beyond the reach of his or her own cognizance, in the phenomenal way that Jewish pain and Jewish preservation have remained fused. This is the source of Reznikoff's motif of the saving remnant, a recognition of the singularity of Judaic experience, which Steiner so aptly describes: "when the text is the homeland, even when it is rooted only in the exact remembrance and seeking of a handful of wanderers, nomads of the word, it cannot be extinguished" (24). The medieval persecutions that set the stage for *The Lionhearted* and "The Black Death," the various narrative versions of his family's immigrant struggle, and the capsule histories of his poetry are filled with centuries of risks and losses, but for Reznikoff the sacrifice on which Steiner speculates—the choice to settle for a material homeland—is the one that causes him the deepest sense of loss: "Locked materially in a material homeland, the text may, in fact, lose its life-force, and its truth values may be betrayed."

For the prophetic poet the truth is always untethered and extraterritorial, whereas the priestly poet is entrapped by dogma. Though no utopian, Reznikoff's investigations of Judaism led him to conclude that its genius is its ability to foster sociality and society without a state. Keenly aware that there is a tradition of self-determination and autonomy to be gleaned from the biblical and rabbinic texts, Reznikoff's lyrical reworkings of these sources crystallize their rejection of the state to assert an apolitical cosmopolitanism that is highly commensurate with individual moral autonomy. This is a poetry that takes heed of Abraham Joshua Heschel's warning that "it would be suicidal to reduce Judaism to collectivism or nationalism. Jewish existence is a personal situation."[21] Though his spiritual radicalism does not readily acknowledge it, Heschel's preoccupation with "the self" is indebted at least as much to such liberal and democratic heralds of the Enlightenment as Locke, Rousseau, and John Stuart Mill as it is to traditional Judaism. But the debt is paid in full because of course the West's own inclination toward spiritual self-narration owes its genesis in turn to the prophetic subjectivity of the Hebrew Bible. These unpredictable ripples of influence are what I mean by the surprising permutations of *convivencia* that can nurture a poet as surprising as Reznikoff.

Syrkin's priestly lyrics can be seen to respond to cultural rupture and genocide by aptly leaning heavily on a collective identity. Unlike Reznikoff's claim that ambivalence and fragmentation are the pabulum of Jewish creativity, her poetry, under the dark shadow of the Holocaust, demonstrably declines the "privilege" of remaining homeless and all its attendant catastrophes. But the tension that ultimately divides their poetry cannot be summed up merely in their disparate responses to the Shoah. To be sure, Syrkin transformed the Holocaust into an icon and herself into a mourner of incomparable loss. But she also participated in a traditional Jewish literary orientation that was markedly different from that of Reznikoff. Like the priests of the ancient Temple, she writes in a historical-messianic tradition, one that grasps the intrinsic meaning of events and stresses their immediate significance. Authorizing a monolithic interpretation of the meaning of the Holocaust, such a poet sees the creation of Israel as an imperative, a confirmation that in this world it is not possible to survive without the sanction of a protective territorial space.

In contrast, Reznikoff refused to see himself primarily as a mourner. Ultimately, this entails rejecting the relevance of *guilt* to his identity, for that would disfigure the authentic vigor and relevance of the past and present. This is a poet who struggled mightily to avoid utopianism, to delineate what Eliot Weinberger calls "a world of injustice without ultimate justice, of disembodied outbursts of violent passion, *of suffering without the illusion of a political or spiritual redemption*" (78, emphasis mine). Nowhere is this more apparent than in "The Black Death," where the poet commits himself to the power of the surviving remnant (rather than the historical-messianic emphasis of the Zionist), to a construction of transcendence and a way of honoring a tradition that is not engulfed by the waves of history. But he will not rationalize the Holocaust and refrains from systematizing the unspeakable, where Syrkin represents the State of Israel as the only legitimate answer to Jewish vulnerability in the wake of Auschwitz. Sanctifying the Jews as History's paradigmatic victim, Syrkin translated the old theology of chosenness into sociological rhetoric.

This trope of an ennobled *extinction* helps us understand a crucial difference between Syrkin's and Reznikoff's approaches to the "remnant." Both poets were made heartsick by the fact that one out of every three Jews in Europe had perished precisely as the liberal institutions of governments and churches stood idly by, exposing liberalism as an empty sentiment that could never again be taken seriously as an adequate counter to evil. Both are eager for us to share in their loss of innocence. Whereas Reznikoff saw fit to continue, in his guise as a poet of the Holocaust, to describe unexpected encounters with endurance and resilience, even in the midst of catastrophe, in his famous, gently ironic style, in Syrkin's work the enormity of the Shoah prevented any faith in *Galut.*[22] Her poetry and polemics embody a different way of finding meaning in the past, revealing the Holocaust's substantial work in contributing to the inward and rightward shift, to some degree even a collective narcissism, that increasingly characterizes the political profile of American Jewry. Here I am thinking about that sadly revealing joke about the *Forward*'s apocalyptic banner headline, which will inevitably read "World Comes to an End—Jews Suffer the Most."

Whereas Reznikoff saw America as a patchwork of vulnerable outsiders, Syrkin saw a largely homogeneous culture in which difference was invariably expunged and what remained was not enough to sustain cultural knowledge. But Reznikoff does not fret about "identity" as such, and so *Diaspora* becomes a rubric encompassing enough to accommodate the endless forms of longing, memory, and (dis)identification shared by a broad spectrum of American minorities, migrants, and immigrants.

Perhaps Reznikoff's diasporism was as much a hybrid condition—formed in relation to the Hellenic/Odyssean tradition where it is the searching that counts—as it was a traditionally Jewish concept. He knew that, from the moment Jews successfully transcended various forms of tribalism and ghettoization in attaining the diversity of a full civilization in America, they would never again be privy to the kind of unified vision avowed by either Zionism or Orthodoxy. They would not be the same. And this is one of the vital ways that his poetry speaks for an entire generation; his lyrics are deeply permeated by a knowledge of the weakening of the corporateness of Jewish life, the lessening possibility of truly belonging to "one's people." That was apparently one of the necessary sacrifices that would have to be made by those who accepted a hospitality unparalleled in the history of the Diaspora. For the children of the immigrants, the historic memory that had bound them gradually dimmed. And it is this challenge that serves as a stimulus for Reznikoff's poetry.

◆

From the time of Lazarus until the beginning of Reznikoff's career (between 1880 and 1920), roughly twenty-eight million people arrived, and by the early 1920s more than half of New York's population was first- or second-generation immigrant. By 1920, only one million of the city's six million residents were native-born white Protestants. Hence, Diaspora is a condition that Reznikoff universalized because he understood it to be intrinsic to the modern experience of disenfranchised and dislocated immigrants, African

Americans, and even the general population of modern American city dwellers. Reading his lyrics while attentive to this universalist move, we may recall Lazarus's accommodating strategies. But here is the difference: where Lazarus sought to demonstrate the Jewish immigrant's suitability for being granted an American identity (and Syrkin insinuated the essentially illusory nature of that hope), Reznikoff drew from Judaism's history and textuality to reflect on the condition of just about everyone else. This is not to say that Reznikoff ever loses sight of the specificity of actual Jewish history, because his "American" works embody a significant struggle against American conformity as much as his "Jewish" lyrics contend with Zionism's effacement of Jewish memory.

Inevitably, there will be thoughtful readers, perhaps occupying a different space on the spectrum of Jewish politics, who will contest my account of Reznikoff's ethical diasporism as an act of agency or principled position. What I have described may seem something quite different, less autonomous and more a noncritical result of historical circumstance. After all, this poet who extols wandering and "open doors" strived to stay precisely where he was. Although it is true that Reznikoff was attentive to Jewish identity at a time when few other poets writing in English were doing so—what was really at risk for a poet who largely did not venture beyond New York's cosmopolitan scene, with its decidedly Jewish component? If I am to avoid romanticizing this poet I must be grudgingly reconciled to the fact that such readers may feel justified in concluding that his ambiguous poetry succeeds only in transforming Jewishness into a vicarious, ultimately insincere trope of alienation (or perhaps generic tropes of Americanness), whereas Syrkin's tangible Zionism means a well-defined community, conventionally lived experience, and commitment. A more troubling issue is the matter of the poet's post-Holocaust community. For, unlike the pious generations that fled from Palestine, Spain, and similar catastrophes recounted in his lyrics, the afflicted secular community of Reznikoff's age has not yet produced a new perception of Jewishness or of the role of Jews in the world. Certainly the still young State of Israel, reeling from its wars, violent border clashes, Intifadas, and dominated by its fundamentalist rabbis, has not yet provided even a remote hint of a renewed theological eschatology. Certainly the symbolic "remnant" that Reznikoff knows best, the American Jew, has not yet risen to the challenge. This absence is not accounted for in his poetry—and so he halts precisely at the juncture where Roth's assimilationist nightmares begin.

Perhaps as a liminal artist Reznikoff *was* exploiting an image of the Jew as fragmented to serve his own circumstances. But such an argument does not mean that we can ignore the full dimensions of this achievement, the challenge of having to think about Jewishness as it is presented to the reader: a series of continual renegotiations in new and ever-changing circumstances of dangerous and sometimes rewarding coexistence. This Jewishness was constantly made and remade, vitalized by its contact with other groups. Reznikoff chooses to inhabit that difficult, liminal instability between assimilation and otherness, a migratory identity that will not rest in Zion. Above all there is a sense of a contemplative poet whose roving inner world is timeless and homeless. According to Abraham Joshua Heschel, though Jews "appreciate things displayed in space," tradition teaches them that what is "genuinely precious" is experienced "not in space but in time" (*The Earth is the Lord's* 13). Reznikoff's works are deeply sympathetic to this paradigm, bearing witness to the movement of a Jewish subjectivity across time, the plural and multiple aspects of Jewishness in history. His poetry is a counterargument to the notion that Jews would regain their vitality only by becoming as comfortable as other peoples, by reintegrating with soil and myth.

Reznikoff rejected the path of contemporary writers who in their early life intentionally sought merely to "transcend" Jewish particularity by escaping from the past. It is always illuminating to compare him to a certain generation of Jewish and non-Jewish writers and critics (the oft-cited example of Lionel Trilling comes immediately to mind) for whom the mark of the successful Jewish writer was to create an utterance wherein Jewishness actually receives exceedingly short shift so that more "universal" concerns might surface. In contrast to these, Reznikoff somehow managed to be faithful to his own notion of Jewishness, which entailed a commitment to a particular vision of Jewish history and culture that never overshadows but rather illuminates his interest in finding ways to highlight the experiences of a variety of other marginal groups in America. His childhood experience with antisemitism and an early sense of isolation eventually led him to create a poetics of deep-seated sympathy for other lonely and disenfranchised city dwellers. Instead of adapting one of the redemptive ideologies that attracted Jews in his generation, he is attentive to a broad spectrum of newly displaced urban inhabitants—immigrants, homeless, African Americans.[23] His intense interest in Jewish identity pivots on the unexpected results that follow the Jews' historical adjacency to disparate groups. For Reznikoff, the ominous term "assimilation" is hardly a synonym for disappearance. After all, as Ira Katznelson observes, this unwieldy notion really "connotes a strategy for transacting with the wider society" (181), rather than erasure. For Reznikoff this needs to be emended to include other groups on the outside margins.

Although at the uneasy beginning of this new century it is impossible to dismiss Syrkin's grasp of reality, I have leaned quite heavily toward Reznikoff's vision because I think that his poetry not only recognizes the ephemeral nature of conventional communities and the sins of tribalism, but sees beyond the naysayers who base their predictions on the surfaces of trends and demographics. All of which is to suggest that many of the boldest post-Zionist and postmodern debates over Zionism's limitations are already well foregrounded in this poet's voice. Ultimately, the centuries of exilic history that Reznikoff responded to contained more revolutionary potential than Zionism, which only succeeded in redefining the Jewish people for their participation in an age of nationalism that may already be waning, in spite of its violent legacy. His early-twentieth-century apprehension of the American Diaspora as a site in which the descendants of Lazarus's immigrants would become self-exiled forms the point of departure for the narratives of Philip Roth.

Chapter Five

"No Coherence": Philip Roth's Lamentations for Diaspora

Our rejection . . . of the Christian fantasy leads us to proclaim to the world that we are Jews still—alone, however, what have we to proclaim to one another?   —Philip Roth, "Jewishness and the Young Intellectuals"

"Who you supposed to be?"

   "No one," replied Zuckerman, and that was the end of that. You are no longer any man's son, you are no longer some good woman's husband, you are no longer your brother's brother, and you don't come from any-where anymore, either.   —Philip Roth, *Zuckerman Unbound*

On the last page of Philip Roth's (b. 1933) memoir *Patrimony* (1991), he tells of a terrifying dream that came in the weeks following the burial of his father, an assimilated secular Jew who had never exhibited any particular inclination toward faith. Responding to the mortician's request that he choose a suit for the burial, he inexplicably acted on a pious impulse to bury his father in an old prayer shawl. In the dream, Herman Roth appeared bitterly to condemn his son's choice:

one night some six weeks later, at around 4:00 A.M., he came in a hooded white shroud to reproach me. He said, "I should have been dressed in a suit. You did the wrong thing." I awakened screaming. All that peered out from the shroud was the displeasure in his dead face. And his words were a rebuke: I had dressed him for eternity in the wrong clothes. (237)

Though Roth has often disputed claims that his fictional representations of familial strife are in any way autobiographical, passages such as this recollection of a Kafkaesque nightmare suggest that the novelist has long harbored anxieties about his relation to the secular legacy of his parents' generation, in a private and a public sense. More recently, in *Sabbath's Theater* (1995), he has the title character emerge from the funeral of his closest friend to muse ruefully that "it's putting corpses into clothes that really betrays what great thinkers we are" (413). The acutely psychological problem of dressing his dead father "for eternity in the wrong clothes" hints toward a textual correspondence with his vacillating representations of "Jewishness" throughout his controversial career. One needs to approach Roth's novels with an awareness of their double status as "faithful" representations of the condition of the American Diaspora and as portraits of an altogether interior drama that, at times, has very little to do with the public reality of Jewish American culture.

From the outset, Roth's career has resembled the history of Jewish American culture—a complex history of border crossings between the "Jewish" and the "American" that has scrambled the exclusive nature of both. It is no longer news to most that the story of American Jews can be told in terms of the erosion of a more stable identity and that the quixotic search for the "essence" of Jewish identity at the vortex of the modernist maelstrom has long been the focal point of Jewish American writers. In Reznikoff's poetry this indeterminate subject is often translated as a buoyant identity that constantly transforms itself, producing a concrete Jewish subject who is continually repositioned in relation to narratives of the past. There are readers who have long thought that it is possible to read Philip Roth through a similar prism. But the truth is, he has always questioned the viability of a tangible Jewish self in the American milieu. For instance, as early as a 1963 conference in Israel, he remarked that Jewish identity was something fabricated, rather than inherited from the past. It is as though, from an early moment in his career, the tangible reality known as the Jewish self seemed to be fading. There was "no body of law, no body of learning, and no language, and finally, no Lord. . . . [W]hat one received [was] in strands and little bits and pieces . . . one had to invent a Jew" ("The Jewish Intellectual" 58). Few Jewish American writers have more readily acknowledged the uneasy mixture of disappointment and bewilderment that accompanied this awareness so early in their career, as Roth's precocious remarks in a long-forgotten 1961 *Commentary* symposium of writers now confirm:

Small matters aside—food preferences, a certain syntax, certain jokes—it is difficult for me to distinguish a Jewish style of life in our country that is significantly separate and distinct from the American style of life. . . . There does not seem to me a complex of values or aspirations or beliefs that continue to connect one Jew to another in our country. ("Jewishness and the Younger Intellectuals" 351)

Decades later, the diasporic "Jew" has altogether unraveled and the "bits and pieces" remain in his narratives, like poignant confessions of communal failure. For nobody knows better than Roth, whose characters range restlessly between Newark, Prague, and Jerusalem, that he forged his novels in the tumultuous intersection of a five-thousand-year-old contiguous community and the uniquely American experience of assimilation, forgetting, and the triumph of individuality. The tribal separatism that was once distinguished by unending dedication to faith under repeated cycles of martyrdom and persecution has diminished to a blurring of identity, for "it is not the sort of kinship . . . that produces solidarity and trust between us—for the strength with which Jesus continues to be rejected is not equaled by the passion with which the God who gave the Law to Moses is embraced. . . . [T]he result is that we are bound together, I to my fellow Jews, my fellow Jews to me, in a relationship that is peculiarly enervating and unviable." When the young Roth produced adjectives such as "enervating" and "unviable," he was, in effect, not only describing a failure of communal identity in diaspora, but announcing the very terms that would preoccupy him until the beginning of the twenty-first century.[1]

Roth's oeuvre represents the most somber reevaluation of the "freedom" that Reznikoff's poetry uncritically sets forth as the foundation of his Jewish modernity. For, unlike Reznikoff, Roth concluded that America's secular Jew, including its writers, lacked the poetic imagination to "*will* oneself into a community today on the strength of the miseries and triumphs of a community that existed in Babylonia in the seventh century B.C.E. or in Madrid in 1492, or even in Warsaw in the spring of 1943" ("Jewishness and the Younger Intellectuals" 351). Not long after writing this early observation about group dissolution, Roth was forced to confront perhaps the most painful obstacle ever to come between a Jewish American writer and the Jewish reading public. It was the problem of *piety*, the defensive impulse of certain prominent Jewish critics to construe ethnic literature as a form of cultural propaganda. For the majority of his readers, it no longer matters that the novelist, referred to as the Baruch Spinoza of American Jewry by more than one critic, was once excommunicated by the self-appointed guardians of the Jewish heritage and *Yiddishkeit* (Jewish culture and its traditional values). Yet it continues to matter to Roth, for he has always conflated his personal experience of adversity with the greater epic of Jewish struggle against complacency.

◆

In one way or another, the poetry of each of the writers hitherto addressed in this study responded to Judaism's "ideology of affliction," in other words, a tradition that Jews must live in a singularly hostile world ("as a lamb among seventy wolves") until the arrival of the Messiah or, according to the Zionists, until the Jewish people repudiated *Galut* and returned to their natural homeland. As Bernard Susser and Charles S. Liebman persuasively argue, more than any "other element of Jewish existence, this sense of collective trauma, the feelings of anxiety and foreboding born of long and painful experience, have been faithfully passed on from generation to generation" (26). The Jewish experience of martyrdom, exile, global wanderings, and immigrant struggle has translated into a continuity of words, texts, and books. But for Roth, what has served as the ineffable center of Jewish identity is cast into disrepute by America and Israel's tough Jews, whose relation to the increasingly remote experience of victimhood is little more than a knee-jerk response that masks the erosion of Jewish knowledge and authentic Yiddishkeit. In Charles Reznikoff's poetry, Gentile hostility was seen as a consistently reliable catalyst, for Judaism's liturgical imagination as well as its secular poetry. And Susser and Liebman contend that, in our generation, "[t]he brute fact of persecution has become more than a simple historical datum; it has, over time, become an obsessive, tenacious, and pervasive mental fixture. It is not too much to say that ever since the destruction of the Second Temple and the Exile, Jewish consciousness has been built around it" (25). Taking a cue from Susser and Liebman's study of what has remained "a virtually unbroached subject" for Jewish sociologists, it is imperative to consider Roth's imaginative response to an American Diaspora "in which Gentile hostility has ceased" (25). Any understanding of either Roth or the Jewish American literary present is dependent on coming to terms with Susser and Liebman's cogent argument that "although the idea of chosenness is often awkward and embarrassing to contemporary liberal American Jews, the uniqueness of Jewish suffering remains an unassailable given. . . . With Jewish substance shallow and diluted, few other alternatives remain" (62).

Following an early period of infamy, Roth has long been appreciated, even revered, as a writer whose parodies and caricatures of Jewish assimilation actually celebrated Judaism's more robust forms of survival. Moreover, there is an inspired new generation of Jewish readers who rightly celebrate their sense of discovery that "what most absorbs Roth's artistic consciousness is not his own identity but the plethora of alternate, often tragic Jewish identities and fates throughout the Diaspora and in Israel" (Furman 2000, 38–39).

But what has not been sufficiently examined is the extent to which this secular writer's oeuvre has been shaped by a realization that an end to the theological category of affliction leaves in its wake much uncertainty about the prospects for a genuinely Jewish future in Diaspora. Roth's narratives are driven by a singular motif that one notices as early as *Goodbye Columbus* (1959) and as recently as *The Human Stain* (2000)—the downfall of communal identification and the precarious selfhood left in its wake.

Some of the brief cues and almost imperceptible hints of this paradigm that prevail throughout Roth's fiction are well worth examining. One of the strangest deaths in Jewish American literature occurs as the conclusion to *The Anatomy Lesson* (1983), the third Zuckerman novel. The scene is set in 1970 in Miami Beach, where the Jewish American novelist's mother is on her deathbed. Selma Zuckerman is a woman whose writings otherwise consist only of recipes on index cards, knitting instructions, and thank-you notes. Yet when she dies, she leaves him with a scrap of paper ominously inscribed with the word "Holocaust." After the attending doctor gives the note to Zuckerman, he finds that he is unable to throw it away and is compelled to carry the fragment in his wallet throughout the rest of the novel, presumably until the end of his days.[2] As the Zuckerman epic, and much else in Roth's oeuvre, has continued to evolve, the little piece of hidden paper has taken on a mysterious life of its own. Selma's deeply encoded legacy to Zuckerman encapsulates the immutable, even congenital quality of Gentile hostility that once formed the Jew's sense of destiny.

The ephemeral relic that Zuckerman carries in his wallet bears the primordial and binding memory of persecution. The "literary heritage" of the Holocaust also crops up as an insurmountable obstacle in *The Ghost Writer* (1979), the first Zuckerman narrative, in which Nathan, in the New England home of E. I. Lonoff, his literary idol, meets Amy Bellette, a mysterious young writer of foreign background. Hearing her described as "some impassioned little sister of Kafka's" (170), Nathan's overheated imagination transforms the indeterminate young woman into Anne Frank, the paradigmatic victim of the Holocaust. Her presence in the Lonoff household inhibits Zuckerman's own identity as a writer ("If only I could invent as presumptuously as real life!" he exclaims [121]). Most of the novel follows Zuckerman's anxious attempts to overcome the enigma of Anne/Amy, by telling her "real" story. Of course he fails, and the mystery of Amy/Anne haunts the novel. It is as if Zuckerman/Roth is tormented by the intimation that the Jewish American novelist can never measure up to the "real" Jewish story. In its place he has struggled to mythologize the struggle of the "self" against the persecuting "collective," an alternative epic that has its origins in Roth's own construction of a literary identity.

The Writer and Literary Piety

As is well known among aficionados of literary scandals, for the sins of *Portnoy's Complaint* (1969) as well as the short stories eventually collected in *Goodbye Columbus*, Philip Roth attracted a number of dismayed detractors. Chief among these was Marie Syrkin, who, along with establishment figures such as Irving Howe, Ruth Wisse, Hillel Halkin, and even Gershom Scholem, exemplifies the influence of piety in Jewish criticism. Syrkin was the first to charge the young novelist with "self-hatred." In "The Fun of Self-Abuse" (1969), she challenged the wisdom of the *New York Times* praise of Roth as the unmatched authority on the Jewish condition in America's "gilded ghetto."[3] After faintly praising the novel's authentic "intonation of dialogue," Syrkin harshly criticized Roth's "vicious caricature" of Jewish domesticity: "Sophie, the mother, is a synthetic production, an amalgam of clichés, with touches from the Orthodox shtetl alternating with bits from middle-class suburbia. . . . By virtue of Roth's transforming malice, [Sophie] becomes a grotesque festooned with dirty toilet paper, the whole held together by a thick glue of elementary as well as alimentary Freud" (*The State of the Jews* 332). In his portrayals of "Sophie with the breadknife, the father defecating, the son masturbating," the irresponsible writer had not only waged war against the "trinity of the Jewish family" but was guilty of nothing less than a "contemptuous dismemberment of personality" (332, 333). Syrkin concludes that Roth's intent was wholly malicious (336). But, like many of Roth's later adversaries, Syrkin disconcertingly found herself in the no-win situation of repeating the charges of one of Roth's own characters. For at the end of *Portnoy*, a comely kibbutz member, a six-foot Sabra named Naomi (Roth's first Israeli character), appears like an avenging angel to enumerate his shortcomings: he is a self-hating Jew, a decadent project of the neurotic *Galut*. It is as if Roth wrote in ironic anticipation of Halkin's unyielding imperative that "a Diaspora Jew in Israel can be only one thing: a person on trial" (16).

Enraptured by the prospect of self-renewal in the Zion of Uris's *Exodus*, Portnoy (though anxious that he may have brought over "some kind of venereal infection" from *Galut*), pulls out all the stops in his effort to seduce the Jewish Other (just as Zuckerman would later attempt to seduce "Anne Frank"), one of Roth's earliest representations of the desperate act of self-transformation. But like so many of Roth's diasporic males, Portnoy proves impotent in Zion:

> By dawn I had been made to understand that I was the epitome of what was most shameful in "the culture of the Diaspora." Those centuries and centuries of home-lessness had produced just such disagreeable men as myself—frightened, defensive, self-deprecating, unmanned and corrupted by life in the gentile world. It was Dias-pora Jews just like myself who had gone by the millions to the gas chambers without ever raising a hand against their persecutors. (265)

Unmanned, fatally exposed as the "ironical" and "self-deprecating" creature of "ghetto humor" that he is, Portnoy's self-hatred and impotence (a fate to be shared by subsequent protagonists over the years) are the price to be paid for centuries of *Galut*.[4] Repelled as much by his "Ghetto humor" as by his las-civious wooing, the "wholesome ideological hunk of a girl" kicks him in the chest, leaving the hapless Portnoy to roll on the floor: "Ow, my heart! And in Israel! Where other Jews find refuge, sanctuary and peace, Portnoy now per-ishes! Where other Jews flourish, I now expire!" (*Portnoy's Complaint*, 258, 271). The fact that Naomi's rhetoric ("The Diaspora! The very word made her furious" [265]) "steals" from Syrkin's own instinctive recoil somehow enflamed the critic further. Roth wasn't playing the game fair: "Naomi's blunt description of Portnoy as a self-hating Jew takes the edge from anticipated ac-cusations and enables the author to appear above the battle. To quote Roth against Roth would be a *reductio ad absurdum*" (*The State of the Jews* 335).[5]

Many defensive Jewish readers stopped reading Roth after *Portnoy*, un-able to view the novel as anything but a social document, insider testimony that would "prove" the authenticity of the most extreme antisemitic claims. Syrkin spoke out as part of a post-Holocaust Jewish establishment that shud-dered in its nakedness. For besides the unproven loyalties of the author him-self, there was the matter of the near-masochistic attention lavished on his efforts in New York Jewish literary circles and beyond. As Roth's critical and popular success appeared in the excruciatingly public space of American let-ters, an indignant Syrkin felt compelled to minimize the damage by taking the issue back into the comparatively domestic enclave of Jewish debate, sur-rounding the controversial novelist with the familial inquisition of the Jewish establishment. In *Midstream*, Syrkin critiqued what she saw as Roth's uncrit-ical internalization of the worst forms of antisemitism:

> under the cartoon of the Jewish joke leers the anti-Jewish stereotype. Portnoy pol-luting his environment is one such. When he graduates to the fascination of female

"apertures and openings," his penis never loses its Jewish consciousness. Like Julius Streicher's Satanic Jewboy lusting after Aryan maidens, Portnoy seeks blonde *shik-ses*: . . . There is little to choose between [Goebbels] and Roth's interpretation of what animates Portnoy.

Well acquainted with the victims of Nazi propaganda, Syrkin saw only the smoky and ash-filled horizon beyond the "joke." The America she lived in might yet prove to be vulnerable to the kind of antisemitism that would surely follow in the wake of the self-confessed threat posed by Portnoy to Gentile culture. Scoring Roth's caricature of Jewish life as "vicious," Syrkin complained that though Roth claimed to explore "a disorder in which strongly felt ethical and altruistic impulses are perpetually warring with extreme sexual longings," the evidence indicated a far less worthy achievement: "Acts of exhibitionism, voyeurism, fetishism, auto-eroticism and oral coitus are plentiful but where are the other symptoms? Where is a single scene in which the patient suffering from this conflict appears as an ethical or moral being?" (*The State of the Jews*, 334).

Such intense disapproval may derive in part from Roth's onanistic reversal of Syrkin's privileged perspective. In other words, where Syrkin was devoted to the history of the *collective*, the presumptuous Roth apparently spoke from the narcissistic perspective of individual experience. Ironically, the ardent Zionist failed to appreciate the joking confirmation of Jewish distinctiveness Portnoy actually provides, in chronicling his difficulty assimilating into Gentile America. Syrkin remained unforgiving. Several years later, when it was already far less fashionable to engage in Roth-bashing, she issued a more scathing indictment in response to Irving Howe's own discussion of Roth in *Commentary* ("Philip Roth Reconsidered" [December 1972], 69–77).

Though Howe, no friend of Roth's, had actually been critical ("*Portnoy's Complaint* . . . contains plenty of contempt for Jewish life . . . an unfocused hostility"), Syrkin again felt the need to abandon the posture of literary criticism and to speak more bluntly about the effects of Roth's offense on Jewish communal sensibilities. Though still acknowledging that the novelist's "unrelieved picture of Jewish grossness" might be dimly situated within the tradition of the "extended Jewish joke," Syrkin, invoking the "Goebbels-Streicher script" more explicitly than before, charged that there was actually something worse in *Portnoy*, "a distillate of something describable only as plain unadulterated anti-Semitism."[6] Eventually Roth would answer Syrkin. But before beginning to address the terms of this defense, let me present all the relevant passages from Syrkin's culminating judgment of Roth.

All too familiar with the deadly effects of such stereotypes, Syrkin insisted that "while the pathology of anti-Semitism may be mysterious in its origins, its symptoms are all too obvious" (9). By portraying Portnoy not merely as "violator of the Gentile sexual background ... [but] as the enemy of the Gentile world," Roth showed his true colors:

For Portnoy, Assistant Commissioner of Human Opportunity, the phony Jewish liberal *par excellence*, offers as his prime achievement his exposure of an "Ur-Wasp" in the television quiz scandals: "Yes, I was one happy yiddel down there in Washington, a little Stern gang of my own, busily exploding Charlie's honor and integrity, while simultaneously becoming lover to that aristocratic Yankee beauty whose forebears arrived on these shores in the 17th century. Phenomenon known as Hating Your Goy and Eating One Too." This is not even funny. It's plain vicious. (8)[7]

Even though, as a vigorously loyal Labor-Zionist, Syrkin had sternly criticized the fascist-leaning Stern thugs during the years of Israel's struggle for Independence, she did not now appreciate Roth's flippant reference to Jewish power run amuck within America.

Syrkin was joined in her profound unease by a host of Jewish cultural luminaries, many of them from the same generation of Zionists. For instance, in two articles that originally appeared in Israeli academic periodicals (in Hebrew) and were promptly translated for Jewish American readers, Gershom Scholem weighed in with a similar condemnation. Too many readers had been fooled by "Roth's revolting book": "Let the Pollyannas not tell us that what we have here is satire. ... The fact is that the hero of a best-seller, avidly acquired by the public, proclaims (and lives his proclamation) that his behavior is shaped by a single lust which becomes the slogan of his life: to get '*shikse* cunt.'"[8] Alarmed that the novel had been rushed into German translation, Scholem warned that Roth had written "the book for which all anti-Semites have been praying," prophesying that Diaspora Jews would pay a heavy price:

I daresay that with the next turn of history, not long to be delayed, this book will make all of us defendants at court. ... This book will be quoted to us—and how it will be quoted! They will say to us: Here you have the testimony from one of your own artists. ... I wonder what price *K'lal yisrael* [the Jewish people]—and there is such an entity in the eyes of the Gentiles—is going to pay for this book. Woe to us on that day of reckoning! (57)[9]

For the latter, Roth was woefully unrepentant in his perverse portrayal of Portnoy as having precisely the desires the Nazis accused Jews of possessing.

It would take the passage of many years for a later generation of Jewish critics to uncover a deeper subtext, in which Alex actually seems to exhibit a sense of indebtedness to the struggles and dreams of his parents' generation: "Part of Alex's conflict with his father is his guilt about the old man's uncompleted emancipation. Alex feels responsible for that education and bringing its benefits home: 'in my liberation would be his—from ignorance, from exploitation, from anonymity'" (Cooper 121). As Alan Cooper's reading suggests, there seems to be something that Scholem, Syrkin, and numerous other Jewish critics, particularly from the Zionist establishment, overlooked.

Not only was Roth's "Jewboy" struggling with a doppelganger—a "nice Jewish boy"—but in assigning a pariah status to Portnoy, he was wistfully bestowing on him an enduring condition of apartness, commensurate with the notion of a people that "dwells apart." Hence, Roth *was*—as his critics charged—indeed obsessed with the Jew as transgressor and defiler of the West, particularly the American Dream. He would return again and again, in fine form, as David Kepesh, Mickey Sabbath, Merry Levov, and Iron Rinn— though the final section of this chapter will demonstrate that these pariah figures signify Roth's loyalty, not hostility, to Jewish difference.[10]

That Roth was hurt by the allusion to the Nazis is evident in "Imagining Jews" (an essay he reprinted in *Reading Myself and Others*), where, quoting from the *Commentary* letter, he protests Syrkin's willful misreading. But in answering Syrkin, Roth was in effect taking on the powerful *Commentary* establishment; for in three separate attacks that appeared during 1973, Irving Howe, Norman Podhoretz, and Peter Shaw had all launched pietistic attacks against *Goodbye Columbus*, as well as *Portnoy's Complaint* and its author:

Had she not been constrained by limitations of space, Syrkin might eventually have had me in the dock with the entire roster of Nuremberg defendants. . . . [I]t does not occur to her that sexual entanglements between Jewish men and Gentile women might themselves be marked, in any number of instances, by the history of anti-Semitism that so obviously determines her own rhetoric and point of view. (*Reading Myself and Others* 244–45)

Citing a variety of Jewish and non-Jewish movers and shakers, ranging from Nachman Syrkin, Meir Kahane, and Moshe Dayan to Jean-Paul Sartre and even Hitler, Roth insists that "imagining what Jews are and ought to be has been anything but a marginal activity" of the Jewish American novelist. For Roth, such a creative burden depends on "imagining Jews being imagined" and "given all those projections, fantasies, illusions, programs, dreams, and solutions that the existence of the Jews has given rise to, it is no wonder that [Jewish American novels are] . . . largely nightmares of bondage [and] baffled, claustrophobic struggle" (245). This leads to the crux of Roth's own literary intentions, namely the writer's struggle to thwart all the closures, limitations, and solutions that the world (not establishing establishment Jews) would impose on the Jewish self. As Roth says, "the task for the Jewish novelist has not been to go forth to forge in the smithy of his soul the *un*created conscience of his race, but to find inspiration in a conscience that has been created and undone a hundred times over in this century alone" (246). There is a striking disparity between Syrkin's and Scholem's Zionist assessment of Roth as a writer who said dangerous things about Jews but was incapable of generating a literature that issued from the ethical civilization and religious structure of Judaism, and Roth's contemporaneous sense of his own intrinsic relatedness to the prophetic tradition. For ironically, Roth claims that in this early period he "imagined fiction to be something like a religious calling, and literature a kind of sacrament. . . . The last thing I expected, having chosen this vocation—*the* vocation—was to be charged with heartlessness, vengeance, malice, and treachery" (Searles 65).

Roth was deeply offended at the time—"I had gravitated to the genre that constituted the most thoroughgoing investigation of conscience that I knew of, only to be told that I was a conscienceless young man holding attitudes uncomfortably close to those promulgated by the Nazis." Nevertheless over the years his writerly nerves have fed on, as much as they have been chastised by, the assaults of critics such as Podhoretz, Howe, Scholem, and Syrkin. As a Jewish artist, Roth has enjoyed something Reznikoff rarely had, namely a consistently engaged Jewish readership who closely interrogated his fictions, even the novelist's most solipsistic exercises, as if they held the very key to the Jewish destiny. But like the poet's quiet war with Zionism, Roth has indicated that he relished the schism between the writer and the collective. Indeed, on a number of occasions, Roth has acknowledged that it is hard to imagine from where the Zuckerman novels and much else would have sprung, if not from his antagonistic relations with those he dismayed.[11] In fact, the very structure of Roth's ambivalent and oscillating oeuvre, the text/countertext juxtapositions that mark its development, embodies agonistic repetitions of the foundational confrontation between the artist and his critics. Though Roth began his career emphasizing the American individualism of Epstein, Portnoy, and Zuckerman, virtually all of his latest novels represent a shift, one that testifies to the woeful state of the integrity of the collective. This early antagonistic relation with the Jewish mainstream has influenced the successive mutations and refinements of "diaspora" in Roth's works, including the recent humiliations to which Roth subjects this term.

As with Reznikoff and Syrkin, it is impossible to dissociate the Jewish artist's personal experience with adversity from the way "diasporism" gets encoded in his narratives. As Roth first acknowledged in the mid-eighties, "the furor coming right at the start probably has given my writing a direction and emphasis that it might not have had otherwise."[12] For some time, Roth's highly charged struggle with the Jewish establishment translated into an interest in Jewish struggle in a sense reminiscent of what we saw in Reznikoff's final reflections. A 1973 comment gets us close to answering why this perverse relationship with those enemies who had taken him seriously mattered so much to Roth:

[O]ne shouldn't conclude that a friendly, or enthusiastic, readership functions as a kind of . . . "ego trip," for the writer. The greatest value of an appreciative audience may even be the irritant that it provides, specifically by its collective (therefore simplistic) sense of the writer, the place it chooses for him to occupy on the cultural pecking order, and the uses it wants to make of selective, disconnected elements of his work and of his own (imagined) persona. (Searles 66)

The personal sense of persecution Roth suffered as a pariah figure became increasingly encrypted within the defiant destinies of his Jewish protagonists. Neil Klugman, Alexander Portnoy, David Kepesh, Nathan Zuckerman, and Mickey Sabbath share an existential exile, as well as fundamental uncertainties about the vitality of Jewish American life. Oddly enough, it now appears that no writer has more fully taken up Syrkin's assumption that the fertility and vitality of American Jewish culture was fated to vanish than has Philip Roth. His career constitutes a relentless examination of the claim that America is not merely an alternative Zion, as Lazarus would have it, but the *true* Zion, the site where Jews can most authentically fulfill their myriad possibilities. From *Portnoy* onward, Roth's expanding oeuvre sets the Israel-Diaspora dialectic at the center of an ever-widening examination of the complacency that is at the heart of Jewish American culture. There is a distinct correlation between a youthful enactment of conflict and the mature Roth's morbid nostalgia for the days in which his art mattered enough to create a scandal (or perhaps it would be more apt to say nostalgia for the community constituted by such a scandal).

One cannot overestimate the ways in which Roth's personal position has become enmeshed with public positions on Judaism as a civilization that has best thrived under adversity. Ever since the *Portnoy* fallout, Roth has exhibited an almost woefully nostalgic relation to his first emergence as a disturbing presence in the eyes of the Jewish establishment, as if his own pariah status was the privately cherished secret of his creative energy as a novelist: "I think now—I didn't then—that this conflict with my Jewish critics was as valuable a struggle as I could have had at the outset of my career. For one thing, it yanked me, screaming, out of the classroom. . . . Some people out there took what one wrote to *heart*—and wasn't that as it should be?" (Searles 65).[13] Describing an almost violently hostile audience that greeted him at Yeshiva University in 1962 in *The Facts: A Novelist's Autobiography* (1988), he concluded that his unfortunate encounter with the "fanatically insecure" as well as all the "angry Jewish resistance that I aroused virtually from the start—was the luckiest break I could have had. I was branded" (130). In his last two Israel-situated novels, the link between persecution of the individual and the high stakes of Jewish endurance are addressed quite seriously. In *The Counterlife* it is Zuckerman musing, but perhaps Roth insisting, that, "contrary to the charges by my detractors of literary adventurism, my writing had hardly been born of recklessness or naiveté about the Jewish history of pain; I had written my fiction in the knowledge of it and even in consequence of it . . ." (307). It is as though the novelist had begun to reconsider the dark vision of reality Syrkin had voiced twenty years earlier. This is a telling moment in Roth's oeuvre: "*I had written my fiction in the knowledge of it; and even in consequence of it.*" As this statement suggests, Roth places a high value on the responsiveness of his morally outraged audience. But the question looms large: What happens to the novelist when he no longer evokes that kind of dramatic response?

◆

Ironically, the writer who began his career carving out bitter portraits of Mrs. Patimkin, Aunt Gladys, Sophie Portnoy, Sheldon Grossbart, Milton Appel, and numerous others is lately concentrating most of his energy in creating oddly touching and elegiac tributes to that same generation. In a slyly confessional moment, Roth even has Zuckerman critique his changed sentiments in the "autobiographical" *The Facts*: "The truth you told about all this long ago you now want to tell in a different way. At fifty-five, with your mother dead and your father heading for ninety, you are evidently in a mood to idealize the confining society that long ago ceased impinging on your spirit and to sentimentalize people who by now inhabit either New Jersey cemeteries or Florida retirement communities . . ." (173). This may be why, in retrospect, the raging sex fever of Portnoy now seems almost an allegory of cultural vitality compared to the midlife impotence of the Zuckerman brothers in *Counterlife*.

In recent years, Roth has cast an increasingly elegiac gaze back toward the past, illuminating the struggle of his parents' generation as a heroism altogether lost to the present. Nathan Zuckerman has long played an intrinsic role in Roth's staging of the vanishing Jewish collective. This condition can be traced to *Zuckerman Unbound* (1981), a novel that concludes with Nathan struggling to navigate his way through contemporary Newark, a neighborhood scarred by riot and neglect. A black man steps out onto the street to stare at him.

"Who you supposed to be?"
"No one," replied Zuckerman, and that was the end of that. You are no longer any man's son, you are no longer some good woman's husband, you are no longer your brother's brother, and you don't come from anywhere anymore, either. (224–25)

This disquieting confession is a stark reminder that Roth's representation of Jewishness has long depended on mothers, fathers (including Sophie Portnoy and all the others he has vilified), and a sense of Jewish place, not in Halkin's sense of a native land, but wherever one properly feels at Home. This nearly biblical litany of grief and absence in the ruins of Newark provides an early intimation of the despair that has been steadily mounting ever since. For a long time, Roth has been wrongly considered to be the most autobiographic of Jewish writers, the maverick who celebrates the "I" as opposed to the communal "we." But in passages such as the one above this is not so.

Roth's later fictions return to revalidate what his earliest work seemed to dismiss as the coercive, incapacitating forces in the Diaspora—family, religion, and culture—but at the expense of unrelievedly gloomy representations of their present vigor. Two decades after Scholem's and Syrkin's condemnations, Roth is turning out aesthetically dazzling but relentlessly foreboding novels about the utopian impulse that first goaded Jewish Communists and other varieties of assimilationists in the thirties and was reawakened in the sixties. Seemingly confirming Syrkin's misgivings about the fate of the Jew in America, Roth's latest texts are parables she might applaud: quixotic statements about the inadvisability of lifestyle alternatives, of "passing," in spite of the manifest ease with which Jews not only do pass, but are rapidly making a massive silent exit from what once constituted Jewish difference.

Eager to conflate Portnoy with Roth, other critics even suggested that the author might heal his fragmented Jewish self by immigrating to Israel (Cooper 115). In spite of this fallacy, it seems to be from his attention to this prospect that Roth's artistry began to formulate itself in response to the problem of what constituted an inner Jewish self. Which site—Israel or America —would prove most viable for the long haul? Roth's antagonistic relation with Jewish America began precisely when Jewish difference had nearly vanished. Postindustrial and postwar prosperity neatly dispersed the Jews to suburbia and places like Los Angeles where the Jew nearly vanished into whiteness. Even the 1948 establishment of the Jewish state enhanced the Jews' whiteness. The Jew's rising status was strategically mirrored by Hollywood, notably Otto Preminger's crucial choice to cast the blue-blooded Paul Newman as Ari ben Canaan in his movie *Exodus*. As Matthew Frye Jacobson argues, "America's client state in the Middle East became, of ideological necessity and by the imperatives of American nationalism, a *white* client state" (188). Roth's own coming-of-age as a writer occurred under the influence of Jewish establishment figures such as Irving Howe, Norman Podhoretz, Lionel Trilling, and Alfred Kazin, who all insisted that they were speaking not as Jews but as "white," liberal/conservative Americans. Most of Roth's narratives examine the weakening of social ties accelerated by World War II, how, in America, "Jewishness" has become disaggregated from Judaism as it drifts away from the substantive domains of language, kinship patterns, and space. In a recent interview, Roth wistfully recalled that in the days "when I was growing up in Newark in the '30s and '40s, we were all—Irish, Italians, Slavs, blacks, Jews—settled and secure in different neighborhoods. There was barely any social overlap" (Interview 8). What Herbert Gans observes of the third generation of immigrants—"Symbolic ethnicity . . . does not require functioning groups or networks; feelings of identity can be developed by allegiances to symbolic groups that never meet. . . . Symbolic ethnicity does not need a practiced culture, even if the symbols are borrowed from it"—illuminates the shallow communal ties of the novelist's characters (9).

At the time of Syrkin's repudiation, Roth's arguably misogynistic portrayal of eros was intrinsically connected to a larger representation of the struggle between a putatively smothering Jewishness and this "liberating" assimilation into the American mainstream.[14] *Portnoy's Complaint*—with its hero's derogatory visions of castrating Jewish wives and mothers—appeared at a time when Jewish men's inner discomfort with their materialistic achievements stimulated the projection of spiritual emptiness and crass ambition onto the Jewish woman. As Paula Hyman notes, Roth's work captures a moment of transition, from the loving and tough Jewish mother to the loud harpy who consumes her husband and son's masculinity so that the "Judaism" Portnoy flees is a subculture struggling frenetically to remake itself in the image of a white and decidedly masculine middle class (*Gender and Assimilation* 159). What Syrkin missed is that, even when Roth's early characters seemingly abandon "Judaism," it is not Old World Judaism per se but rather an assimilationist culture of materialism and conformity. Similarly, in *Goodbye Columbus* the upwardly aspiring Neil Klugman's pursuit of Brenda Patimkin, daughter of a wealthy Jewish businessman, reveals a deep-seated ambivalence toward the empty consumerism of the American dream. The end of his own struggle is the temptation of temptations, a Moloch that would consume all vestiges of an inner Jewish self. In contemplating his relationship with a woman who will soon reject him in order to cleave to the nest of material affluence and leisure, Neil, an inept luftmensch unable to determine whether he belongs in the world of books or business, stumbles across the painful evidence of his loss of values:

What is it I love Lord? . . . If we meet You at all, God, it's that we're carnal and acquisitive, and thereby partake of You. I am carnal and I know You approve, I just know it. But how carnal can I get? I am acquisitive. Where do I turn now in my acquisitiveness? Which prize is you? . . . Which prize do you think, shmuck? Gold dinnerware, sporting-goods trees, nectarines, garbage disposals, bumpless noses, Patimkin sinks, Bonwit Teller. (*Goodbye Columbus* 100)

If Portnoy and Neil are indeed smothered by the feminine domestic space, it is largely because, in the postwar period when Jewish American men left the old neighborhoods in pursuit of worldly success, the synagogue they left became more woman-centered and domesticated. It is telling that the fathers in virtually all of Roth's works, from *Portnoy* to *American Pastoral*, are manufacturers, an occupation involving unrelenting work and economic struggle in a hostile world. Their sons invariably disdain this unrelenting toil—and its prizes. They struggle toward epiphanies of self-discovery.

Yet, unlike his fictional characters, Roth has actually spent a career resisting the crown of self-liberation his heroes wear so uneasily, circling around it but unable to break away. His recent novels are elegiac movements of this lonely and ceaseless circling, expressing the sadness of a Jewish writer who knows that there is no decision, only endless turning and doubt. Behind his parodic inventiveness, I suspect that the search for an authentic diasporic self that would never quite disappear remains the essential quest. In view of

Syrkin's negative comparison, one must recall that from the outset, unlike Bellow, Roth was quite comfortable with the label "Jewish writer" and even relished the distinction, making it clear that he never intended to follow the example of, say, a Lionel Trilling:[15]

One had to be careful about the temptation to become a gentleman. So many bright Jewish boys of my generation—and background—gravitated to literature because it was a prestigious form of assimilation that didn't *look* like assimilation. Not that I have any argument with what's called assimilation. I'm all for Jews reading Milton. But it was possible for even a Newark Jew to become a kind of caricature Noel Coward. . . . I wanted to be who I was from where I was. (Searles 283)

And yet there is something disingenuous here, not because Roth has by any means avoided representing Jewish characters, but because he has consistently done so through a variety of masks and impersonations. For many of Roth's critics, his countertexts exhibit the author's determined efforts to preserve the activity and open-endedness of a genuinely Jewish consciousness. But a close reading of the author's recent foray into genuine autobiography suggests that this arguably postmodern device enacts a dangerous negation.

In spite of the career Roth has built on dazzling displays of intellectual one-upmanship and countertexts, this smoke-and-mirror show has actually disguised an essential timidity that haunts all of the Zuckerman narratives and his subsequent oeuvre. The truth is that Roth backs off from ever defining "Jewishness." In spite of the fact that an exhaustive list of Jews can be catalogued in his novels and that the Jewish milieu, from the Holocaust to Israel, is woven into the fabric, there is a way in which his narratives undercut or negate *all* the forms of Jewish identity that appear in his work. For some time, Roth's texts have annihilated their Jewish protagonists, in one way or another. It is as if the further into the mainstream the Jewish American population drifts, the greater the perverse thrust of this novelist toward apartness, incommensurable alienation, and dissatisfaction with what has been achieved.

◆

It is no coincidence that the literary figures who have most interested Roth— Milan Kundera, Ivan Klíma, Primo Levi, Salman Rushdie—with some of whom he has formed close friendships, are, in his words, "writers in trouble." Ironically, Roth, like Syrkin, would explore the various cultural and literary after-affects of the Holocaust in Europe (six years abroad by Alan Cooper's estimate), resulting in the renowned Penguin series "Writers from the Other Europe," which made translations of hitherto unknown writers such as Bruno Schulz, Milan Kundera, and Tadeusz Borowski available to the West, as well as inspiring Roth's own essays and novels such as "Looking at Kafka" (1973), *The Ghost Writer* (1979), and *The Prague Orgy* (1985).

Nakedly envious of writers whose novels could still cause such repercussions in the world, he told *Time* in 1983 that "in America, everything goes and nothing matters [whereas] in Eastern Europe nothing goes and everything matters" ("Goodbye, Nathan Zuckerman," 89). Following the numerous trips that Roth took to Prague in the early 1970s, in which he played an active role in getting the Soviet-bloc dissident authors (many of them dislocated or exiled writers of Jewish descent) published in the United States and throughout the West, the novelist felt the need to rouse himself with more politically charged narratives of struggle than the American stories of assimilation he had been telling since *Goodbye Columbus*. In interviews of this period, Roth had begun to complain of the popular media's "usurpation and trivialization of literature's scrutinizing function": "The momentum of the American mass media is towards the trivialization of everything [which] is of no less importance for Americans than their repression is for the Eastern Europeans. . . . The trivialization of everything results from exactly what they do *not* have in Eastern Europe—the freedom to say anything and to sell anything however one chooses." Protesting "a looming American menace . . . the creeping trivialization of everything," Roth hints that Jewish writers like himself may suffer from "persecution envy . . . an envy of oppression and the compression of freedom" as if only in a condition of obstruction and repression could the writer's literary seriousness manifest itself (Searles 248–49).[16]

This has crucial implications for the unique psychology of his protagonists. For instance, around this time, Zuckerman, his most recurring character, complained that he is "Chained to retrospection. Chained to my dwarf drama till I die . . . Fiction now about losing my hair? I can't face it" (*The Anatomy Lesson*, 145). Though expressing exasperation with critics who sought to link his identity with Zuckerman's, Roth has his fictional author obsess that he is not "serious" enough, and in spite of a number of physical ailments, he fears that he has not suffered sufficiently and desires to enroll in medical school (*The Anatomy Lesson*), culminating in a journey to Soviet-occupied Prague in quest of a missing manuscript written by a martyred Yiddish writer, in the novella *The Prague Orgy* (1985).[17] Roth's own exploratory sojourns in Prague ended when the authorities revoked his visa in the mid-seventies.

The very fact that, at this point in his career, the old animosities had all but faded suggests one possible reason for the way Roth found himself drawn to the ever-beleaguered Jewish state, in ever-increasing degrees of engagement, in *The Counterlife* (1987) and *Operation Shylock* (1993). As first hinted in *Portnoy's Complaint*, in Israel he found a setting whose external geography nearly met the storms of his own internal consciousness, a place where, unlike the complacent haven of America, the Jews were still Jews. Israelis debated and contested the Jewish destiny with *passion*, as his own famous friendship and literary dialogue with Holocaust survivor and Israeli writer Aharon Appelfeld bears witness. Insisting that he was not the least interested in "the pride that may be inspired in American Jews by Israeli military victories or military might," the dominant expression of Jewish American communal solidarity, Roth felt that Jews would gain the most by "just the opposite":

[T]heir awareness of Israel as an openly discordant, divisive society with conflicting political goals and a self-questioning conscience, a Jewish society that makes no effort to conceal its imperfections from itself and that couldn't conceal them from the world even if it wanted to. The tremendous publicity to which Israeli Jews are exposed—and to which they're not unaddicted—has many causes, not all of them always benign, but certainly one effect of unashamed, aggressive Israeli self-divulging has been to lead American Jews to associate a whole spectrum of behavior with which they themselves may have preferred not to be publicly identified, with people perceived as nothing if *not* Jews. (Searles 246)

What a desirable milieu all this "unashamed" "exposure" must have been for Roth as he began to focus his own provocative lens on the fragmenting and fractious Jewish state. The politicized Israeli's "self-questioning conscience" and almost masochistic preoccupation with his naked imperfections allowed Roth to return with a vengeance to the subject he was born to witness, the fading struggle of Jewish modernity.

Beginning with *The Counterlife* and *Operation Shylock*, Roth began to weigh the apparent success of the Zionist movement in creating a coherent Jewish subject in Israel, against the erosions of Jewish life in the Diaspora. For instance, in *Operation Shylock*, the drug Halcion augments the character "Roth's" paranoid sense of individual mental and emotional disintegration to such a degree that dissolution begins to carry over into his representation of Jewishness as a whole. As the costs of personal debility and culture shock mount up, Israeli characters such as the Mossad operative Smilesburger tend to metamorphose into the embodiment of anchored and steadfast masculinity: "The this-worldliness. The truthfulness. The intelligence. The malice.

The comedy. The endurance" (394). But this apparently new development in Roth's representation of Jewish masculinity is simply grafted onto a much older and overriding concern, namely the question of the freedom of the isolated Jewish self versus the entanglements of tribalism and collective will.

"Forget Remembering": *The Counterlife* (1986), *Operation Shylock* (1993), and the Dissolution of Identity

> Circumcision makes it clear as can be that you are here and not there, that you are out and not in—also that you're mine and not theirs. . . . Circumcision confirms that there is an us. —Philip Roth, *The Counterlife*

If Roth's oeuvre is one that portrays the failure of American Jewry to consolidate an identity that preserves a tangible Jewishness, this invites some speculation on the novelist's allegorical encoding of "Diaspora" and "Zion" in his Israel-situated narratives. It may be interesting to accomplish this by situating *Counterlife* and *Operation Shylock* in relation to a moment in the late 1970s when the American-born Hebrew translator and critic Hillel Halkin made his elegant and memorable case in favor of aliya and against a viable Jewish life outside Israel. Praised in the pages of *Commentary* by Robert Alter as "an intellectual event" and by Marie Syrkin in *The New Republic* for its powerfully stark argument against "ease in a Fading Diaspora," Halkin's thesis, still striking today, dismisses many of the most cherished planks long associated with Jewish modernity. For example, rejecting the liberal Jewish "obsession with social justice and a passion for ideas," Halkin argued that these aberrations were not only ineffectual but incongruent with the heart of Judaism: "Ethical idealism and the philosophical traditions indeed, as if these were the distinguishing marks of historic Jewish existence rather than the very symptoms of its disintegration in modern times!"[18] These, Halkin argued, were essentially irrelevant to the authentic traditions of Judaism. Halkin's epistolary polemic is written in response to letters from an imaginary "friend" who will not immigrate to Israel because he fallaciously believes that these are intrinsic to the Diaspora.

I cite Halkin's often forceful argument for casting one's personal and historical lot with Israel because it provides an exemplary introduction to the communal concerns that surface in Roth's work in the same decade. For Halkin, his friend's error was to mistake for the "authentic" center of Jewish history and culture what was merely the cast-off rags and patches of nineteenth-century German Enlightenment. In one of the text's most poignant passages, Halkin casts his gaze on his newfound homeland, to seek out and praise the modest signs of what he hopes will become a truly "authentic" Jewish environment:

As a new housing development going up along a familiar road, carved terracelike into the hillside, looking almost in the distance—but no, as I approached it, its details gave it away—like an ancient Palestinian village, like someplace that had always been right where it was. . . . Perhaps in our children's children's time we really will come to be in this land like all the Gentiles, *k'khol ha-goyim*. . . . If we had as much true culture in this country as the Albanians or Finns, the Guatemalans or the Greeks, I would gladly say *dayenu*. . . . As if it were a little thing to be, like them, a people with a sure sense of itself, living as Zionism envisioned us doing, a healthy national existence on its land! (196–98)

Though at the end of this passage Halkin's wistful tone suggests that his quest for normalization is far from bearing fruit, he never once qualifies either his criteria for "authenticity" or his repudiation of *Galut*. Like classical Zionism, Halkin's gaze eclipses contemporary Palestinians, settling instead on "a new housing development . . . like an ancient Palestinian-village, *like someplace that had always been right where it was.*" Halkin's rhetorical strategy presents a seductive vision of new/old "authenticity." This is a profoundly triumphal vision of organic and continuous dwelling, undisturbed by either Diaspora or the prospect of the Land's Other indigenous inhabitants.

In the years since Halkin's appeal, no Jewish American writer devoted more creative energy to exploring the competing roles of Israel and Diaspora in the forging of Jewish American identity than Roth. As if to reacquaint himself all over with the invigorating stigma of guilt and shame thrust upon him by Syrkin, Howe, and other Jewish establishment figures years earlier, Roth has Zuckerman recall, in *The Counterlife*, a visit to Israel in that fraught year of 1960, where a friend in the Israeli army takes him to meet David Ben Gurion. A photographer is poised to capture what would be an indelible moment:

a picture of Israel's Founding Father shaking hands with Nathan Zuckerman. I am laughing in the photograph because just as it was to be snapped, Ben-Gurion whispered, "Remember, this isn't yours—it's for your parents, to give them a reason to be proud of you." He wasn't wrong—my father couldn't have been happier if it had been a picture of me in my Scout uniform helping Moses down from Mount Sinai. This picture wasn't merely beautiful, it was also ammunition, to be used primarily, however, in his struggle to prove to *himself* that what leading rabbis were telling their congregations from the pulpit about my Jewish self-hatred couldn't possibly be true. (*Counterlife* 55)

In turning to the problem of Israel at this phase in his career, having seemingly exhausted the narrative variations that could be spun from domestic Jewish angst, Roth, a writer in perpetual quest for a bigger staging ground for the Jewish soul, found a way to invigorate his chief literary talent, namely the formation of a dialectical perspective.

Numerous critics have seized on this, delighting in the extent to which Roth's narratives apparently subscribe to a poststructuralist view of subjectivity, by which the theater of the self possesses plural significance.[19] In this reading, Roth is viewed as keeping faith with the multiplicity of Jewish identities America offers: "The burden isn't either/or . . . it's and/and/and/and/ and as well. Life *is* and: the accidental and the immutable, the elusive and the graspable, the bizarre and the predictable, the actual and the potential, all the multiplying realities, entangled, overlapping, colliding, conjoined—plus the multiplying illusions!" (*Counterlife*, 306). Here Roth apparently underscores the existential relation between his fictional alter-ego's faithless and restless libido and the empty impulse of the Jewish writer to restlessly pursue multiple realities. In the novel's brutal descriptions of the ravished utopian dreams, homesickness, and mismatched alliances of its misfit cast, we can find the foundation for the darker counterhistories of Jewish life that would follow. This is the essence of Roth's dialectic.

In the century that witnessed the terrible consequences of Jewish complacency, Roth's incessant self-contradictions constitute an ethical response to that reality. But this kind of reading, to which many of Roth's fans are susceptible, depends on avoiding another possibility, that *The Counterlife* is not so much about the infinitude of the narrator, but rather that, in representing modern Jews as a coil of multiple self-reflexivities, there may be nothing substantial at the center to provide meaning to the pluralism.

On the surface, *The Counterlife* seems to engage sympathetically with the paradigm of adaptatation and transformation represented in Reznikoff's poetics of Diaspora. Virtually all the characters in *Counterlife* are engaged in a comedy of seemingly endless transformation and self-renewal, most of which circle around the question of Home. As one character says, although his Galician forebears came to America rather than to Palestine, *their* boldness constituted a form of "Zionism" as viable as those who returned to Palestine (*Counterlife* 53). Whereas later novels such as *American Pastoral* would move closer to Kafka's representation of transformation (to a bland conformity) as a monstrous process, *The Counterlife*'s competing narrative positions and acts of renewal read as playful comedic confusions that are profoundly sympathetic to the dreams and fantasies of its characters. Yet even here, the familial ties of the Jewish past are tragically severed. Most tellingly, we learn that it isn't long after the death of their parents that Nathan and Henry Zuckerman, good liberal diasporists, "weren't even like brothers." Anticipating more recent novels where the decay of Zuckerman's body accompanies the sad Jewish destinies he remorselessly delineates, the plight of Henry establishes a macabre correspondence: "Despite his dark good looks . . . he seemed to have passed overnight from his thirties to his eighties" (*Counterlife* 7). The bodily health of Roth's individual protagonists is always linked to the waning vitality of the collective.

Structurally, the five sections of *The Counterlife* constitute an intricately symmetric web of alternating texts and countertexts. Early on, the reader is exposed to the sordid erotic escapades of Nathan's younger brother, a dentist who dallies after-hours with his young assistant. Suddenly, facing the waning of his sexual prowess, Henry contemplates undergoing life-threatening surgery merely to restore his extramarital sexual potency. After describing the extent to which his sexual frustration has diminished his quality of life, Henry, emblematic of Roth's sense of post-affliction Judaism, is stunned by his cardiologist's cutting reply: "You haven't had a very difficult life then, have you?" (12). This uninvited judgment on his unfamiliarity with genuine struggle or suffering seems to reach the crux of the matter for Henry's creator.

For Henry, "it was impossible living alone any longer with his staggering loss," but for Roth, what "loss" actually entails is a diminished appetite for *struggle*, which is perhaps why, in the following section, "Judea," a resurrected Henry is shipped off to Judea as a reborn Zealot. In other words, for Roth, the Zionist fantasies of his fully integrated American character signify the frustrated appetite for *real* Jewish anguish and heroism precisely because neither of these forms any part of his reality.

"Basel" and "Judea" present two sharply divisive accounts of Henry Zuckerman's midlife escapism that pivot around the outcome of his impotence and subsequent heart bypass operation. We are teased with an alternative to Henry's humiliating demise: what if Henry hadn't died on the operating table, but instead had survived to abandon his family and immigrate to Israel? In his attention to the Israel-Diaspora nexus, Roth notices that, a century after its rise, political Zionism created a Jewish state whose borders have failed to preserve the coherence of Jewish life elsewhere. Instead of the homeland dissolving the Diaspora by successfully returning Jews to their land, the Diaspora has merely exhausted its waning energies. For Henry's self-proclaimed "liberation"—joining the religious-Zionist movement in Israel—seems mostly an escape from the unwavering rationalism of his immigrant forebears, and ultimately from his own subjectivity. Roth's awareness of this quandary is exhibited in the enviable certitudes with which his Israeli characters address Zuckerman or "Philip Roth"—the former interlocutors never doubt their identity. It is *land* and *language* that enable Israel's fundamentalist settlers, as well as its writers and intellectuals, to be confident that whatever a Jew does in Israel is necessarily a part of Jewish culture.

The markedly binary rhetorical struggle over Diaspora-Zionist identities is first articulated over a dinner in which Nathan's Israeli host, Mr. Elchanan, who immigrated to Palestine from Odessa in 1920, remarks to Nathan that "We are living in a Jewish theater and you are living in a Jewish museum" (52). This acerbic dismissal elicits one of Nathan's, and Roth's, most rapturous affirmations of diasporic genealogy:

I was the American-born grandson of simple Galician tradesmen who, at the end of the last century, had on their own reached the same prophetic conclusion as Theodor Herzl—that there was no future for them in Christian Europe. . . . But instead of struggling to save the Jewish people from destruction by founding a homeland in the remote corner of the Ottoman Empire that had once been biblical Palestine, they simply set out to save their own Jewish skins. Insomuch as Zionism meant taking upon oneself, rather than leaving to others, responsibility for one's survival as a Jew, this was their brand of Zionism. (53)

But in "Judea," Henry Zuckerman, ultra-assimilated dentist, happy victor of numerous sexual conquests of shiksas, and apparent surrogate for American Jewry, is badly shaken. Severe emotional distress following bypass surgery leads to uncontrollable weeping and then an uncanny encounter with an "inner-self." When his startled wife, Carol, demands to know what is disturbing him, he replies morosely that "It's staring me right in the face":

"What is?" Carol said. "Tell me, darling, and we'll talk about it. What is staring you right in the face?" "The words," he angrily told her, "the words 'it's staring you right in the face'!" (58)

The happy destiny that is staring Henry "right in the face" is the revolutionary prospect of recognizing a Jewish face that belongs to him, for, after being persuaded to join a few friends on a trip to Eilat and then Greece, Henry remains behind in Israel. While on a tour of Jerusalem, he breaks away from his friends and somehow ends up peering into the window of a yeshiva in the religious quarter of Mea She'arim, where he has an epiphany. Like numerous Jewish Americans before him, Henry "rediscovers" his missing "self" on the streets of Jerusalem. Filled with a sense of inner emptiness, Henry is primed for a radical discovery:

> And when I heard them, there was a surge inside me, a realization—at the root of my life, the very *root* of it, I *was them*. I always *had* been them. Children chanting away in Hebrew, I couldn't understand a word of it, couldn't recognize a single sound, and yet I was listening as though something I didn't even know I'd been searching for was suddenly reaching out for me. (60)

But precisely at the moment that Henry's Halkin-like vision of self-mastery seems most seductive, Roth demonstrates that an end to struggle and ambivalence effectively constitutes an erasure of personality. This is enacted by Henry's self-effacing attraction to the charismatic and fascistic West Bank settlement leader Mordechai Lippman. Henry's Halkin-like innocence at this point is emblematic of most Jewish Americans, who in this decade paid little, if any, attention to the fatal power relations and territorial discourses that Zionism actually generated.

As Paul Brienes provocatively suggests in *Tough Jews*, a pre-Intifada study of the transformation of Jewish American moral identity from weakling to warrior, for many years the Jewish conscience was rarely disturbed by the violent face of Israeli force: "[f]ar from being troubled over it, significant numbers of American Jews are in fact elated with what is often seen as a uniquely Jewish fusion of violent toughness and victimization that yields a new position, one that is at the same time protected and morally elevated." Writing in the decade of Sylvester Stallone's ascendancy in Hollywood, Breines termed this phenomenon the "Rambowitz syndrome" and analyzed the way that "roughly fifty" novels are "linked by their idealized representation of Jewish warrior, tough guys, gangsters, Mossad agents, and Jews of all ages and sexes who fight back."[20] Like the generation of pulp heroes Breines describes, Henry seems unfazed by the prospect of abandoning the timeless diasporic ability to distinguish sharply between the realities of power and the vision of messianic deliverance in an instant. Embracing the uncompromising ultra-Orthodox community, Henry is apparently unconcerned with the deep moral disfiguring that comes with the chauvinist xenophobia and violent racism of the settlers.

Interestingly, shortly after *Counterlife*, Roth recalled how he and his childhood friends at Weequahic High School often fled from antisemitic bullies. Instead of seeking revenge, according to Roth, this experience actually intensified their reverence for the nonviolent Jewish past: "The collective memory of Polish and Russian pogroms had fostered in most of our families the idea that our worth as human beings, even perhaps our distinction as a people, was embodied in the *incapacity* to perpetrate the sort of bloodletting visited upon our ancestors" (*The Facts* 28). But in the novel Roth does much more than champion a critique of Israeli violence. In what amounts to one of his most disarming forays into the unexamined assumptions of Jewish American culture, he offers a stirring examination of just why Israeli force proved so profoundly seductive a self-image.[21]

Much like Brienes, Nathan takes an interrogatory position against the complacent notion that "*real* Jews either vanished in Nazi crematoria or are soldiers in the Middle East. . . . It is as if the more fully Jews are integrated into American society, the more they experience their mediocrity as Jews—and the more they need fantasies of Israel avenging Auschwitz" (*Tough Jews* 52). As if anticipating the need for a Brienes-like critique, Nathan's old friend Shuki confirms that:

American Jews get a big thrill from the guns. They see Jews walking around with guns and they think they're in paradise. Reasonable people with a civilized repugnance for violence and blood, they come on tour from America, and they see the guns and they see the beards, and they take leave of their senses. The beards to remind them of saintly Yiddish weakness and the guns to reassure them of heroic Hebrew force. Jews ignorant of history, Hebrew, Bible, ignorant of Islam and the Middle East, they see the guns and they see the beards, and out of them flows every sentimental emotion that wish fulfillment can produce. (*Counterlife* 75)

As always, Nathan's enigmatic relation to the Jewish collective greatly complicates the possibility for uncovering his ultimate affinity toward any form of Jewish belonging. This is especially evident in Zuckerman's troubling response to prayer at the Western Wall: "Collectively they emitted a faint murmur that sounded like bees at work—the bees genetically commandeered to pray for the hive" (88). When approached by a member of this "hive" (a young Chasid), Roth repeats his offensive rendition of the Jewish uncanny: "The elongated fingers with which he was tapping my shoulder suggested something erotically creepy at one extreme and excruciatingly delicate at the other, the hand of the helpless maiden *and* of the lurid ghoul" (88). What frightens Zuckerman isn't the physical alterity of his coreligionist so much as what is required of *him*: "He was inviting me wordlessly, to take a book and join the minyan.... 'Come. We need you, mister.'"[22] A few pages later, Zuckerman is again summoned by the collective, this time in the form of the tough young members of Henry's Hebrew class in the West Bank settlement of Agor, after outraging a young ideologue by expressing doubt about the settler's extremism:

> Excuse *me*! What is *fanatical*? To put egoism before Zionism is what is fanatical! To put personal gain and personal pleasure before the survival of the Jewish people! *Who* is fanatical? The Diaspora Jew!... Believes that in their country he is safe and secure—an equal! What is fanatical is the Jew who never learns! The Jew oblivious to the Jewish state and the Jewish land and the survival of the Jewish people! *That* is the fanatic—fanatically ignorant, fanatically self-deluded, fanatically full of shame! (102)

Poor Zuckerman. This is the charge that has been laid against him since Judge Wapshot first called him to task at the beginning of his literary career, and as always his adversary gets many of Roth's best lines. Next Ronit, Henry's teacher (and also the wife of the Meir Kahane–like Zealot), charges Nathan with participating in "a second Holocaust" in the bedroom: "First there was the hard extermination, now there is the soft extermination ... spiritual suicide" (103). In the Zionist heart of darkness, Zuckerman finds the antithesis of the Jewish abnormality for which he professes so much affection, Ronit (reminiscent of Naomi in *Portnoy*), on whose shining countenance Zuckerman cannot imagine any of the characteristics Roth normally associates with Diaspora:

> Singing in the Sabbath, Ronit looked as contented with her lot as any woman could be, her eyes shining with love for a life free of Jewish cringing, deference, diplomacy, apprehension, alienation, self-pity, self-satire, self-mistrust, depression, clowning, bitterness, nervousness, inwardness, hypercriticalness, hypertouchiness, social anxiety, social assimilation—a way of life absolved, in short, of all the Jewish "abnormalities," those peculiarities of self-division whose traces remained imprinted in just about every engaging Jew I knew. (120)

The reader knows that, for Roth, it is precisely these blemishes that cause Jews to be *interesting*, as catalysts for the kind of jarring exchanges that enliven culture. No Jewish American writer has devoted more thought to the problematic of "Jewish self-hatred" and forgetfulness, and here in Zuckerman's letter to Henry is a bold statement about the kind of moral autonomy for Diaspora that Syrkin had claimed for the Zionists. "Self-love, confidence, and success" is perhaps "a world-historical event on a par with the history

you are making in Israel. . . . [F]lourishing mundanely in the civility and security of South Orange, more or less forgetful from one day to the next of your
Jewish origins but remaining identifiably (and voluntarily) a Jew, you were
making Jewish history no less astonishing than theirs" (146). As Zuckerman
proudly notes, he, like Israeli children of the same generation, did not have to
grow up cowering under the shadow of "an unnerving Catholic peasantry
that could be whipped into a Jew-hating fervor by the village priest." Moreover, unlike the progeny of the Zionist dream, "my grandparents' claim to
legitimate political entitlement had not been staked in the midst of an alien,
indigenous population that had no commitment to Jewish biblical rights and
no sympathy for what a Jewish God said in a Jewish book about what constitutes Jewish territory in perpetuity" (54). Nathan, embracing his role as
"Diaspora straight man" (101) to the nationalist excesses that swirl around
him, complains that the whole world applauded the Jews' effort to "un-Jew
themselves"—"no more Jewy Jews, great!"—noting that his brother's connection to Zionism in reality has

> little to do with feeling more profoundly Jewish or finding yourself endangered,
> enraged, or psychologically straitjacketed by anti-Semitism in New Jersey. . . . Zion-
> ism, as I understand it, originated not only in the deep Jewish dream of escaping the
> danger of insularity and the cruelties of social injustice and persecution but out of a
> highly conscious desire to be divested of virtually everything that had come to seem,
> to the Zionists as much as to the Christian Europeans, distinctively Jewish behav-
> ior—to reverse the very form of Jewish existence. . . . It was a species of fabulous
> utopianism, a manifesto for human transformation as extreme—and, at the outset, as
> implausible—as any ever conceived. (147)

This is one of numerous moments in which Roth not only began to look back
at Syrkin and other old Zionist antagonists to reconsider the terms of some
of those debates but, with a great deal of self-knowledge, was imposing on
Zuckerman the burden of his awareness of that false nostalgia, a writerly projection, as if without antagonism Nathan would perish. Later Shuki, who has
fervently remonstrated with Zuckerman not to include a Lippman-like figure
in his next novel, acknowledges that he has applied the kind of censorious
pressure to which the novelist has long been subject: "I'm not unaware that
you've been up against this sort of argument before from Jews in America.
American Jews are tremendously defensive—in a way being defensive *is*
American Judaism. It's always seemed to me, from my Israeli perspective,
that there's a kind of defensiveness there that's a civil religion" (161). As I've
stressed earlier, Roth's texts seem to circle around these old attacks because

they constitute the novelist's private understanding of Diaspora as a site of struggle. But at the same time, he has been outraged that this "defensiveness" has become an all-consuming industry that has all but expunged Judaism's self-critical and exploratory values from its discourse.

As Shuki acknowledges, this sad state of affairs owes much to Jewish guilt over its reticence to act in the past: "First the six million, now the three billion—no, it *doesn't* end. Cautionary exhortation, political calculation, subliminal fear of a catastrophic outcome—all this Jewish *fraughtness* . . . is something that your Gentile American contemporaries have never had to bother about" (162). Here Zuckerman is a surrogate figure, not merely for Roth but essentially for *all* contemporary Jewish writers—who are in some sense held in thrall by the twentieth-century epics of modern Jewish experience, Israel and the Holocaust, in spite of their relative isolation from these paradigm-shattering events. These urgent distractions have exacted a heavy toll on their ability to generate a space for the potentially counterhegemonic identity of the "Jewish American."

◆

Roth's plots have always been driven by what might be called a deconstructive impulse, one that exposed the shallowness of the compromised Jewish present, from the materialistic suburbs of *Goodbye Columbus* to the utter amnesia of *American Pastoral*. But in *The Counterlife*, he began to work in earnest to unsettle *every* safe perspective from which what had once seemed the real target might be viewed. *The Counterlife* is a text acutely aware that the Jewish politics of liberation come in the form of re-claiming, re-building, and repairing, rather than from the postmodern freedom of fracturing and multiplicity. As the two brothers debate, it becomes clear that this dichotomy is being set up.

The life Henry abandons in America represents mobility, secularism, and debased sexuality, whereas Israel embodies the roots of soil, the sacred past—and ironically enough (considering that Henry has shrugged off his, like the old clothes of Cahan and Yezierska's immigrants) even the family. In "Aloft" Nathan attempts to draft a dignified response to Henry's self-transformation, only to end up the naked, airborne victim of yet another visionary's plot. In the final two sections—"Gloucestershire" and "Christendom"—Zuckerman explores a final "what-if" scenario and concludes with an uncharacteristically redemptive reconciliation with his own Jewishness. But since Nathan replaces Henry as the frustrated midlife martyr to impotence, this detracts from the reader's willingness to accept the notion of a "real" Nathan at all, ultimately undermining the insistent assertions of a "conversion" at the novel's end. If Nathan dies in surgery in the previous section, the reader can have no confidence that the events of "Christendom" "really" take place. Has Nathan imagined his marriage to Maria, her pregnancy, and a life among a cluster of antisemitic friends and relatives? Or was the story of his fatal surgery just a literary conceit? The detail that remains most tangible for the bewildered reader is the condition of the brothers' impotence, Roth's metaphor for the waning energies of Jewish American life.

In constructing the elaborate hoaxes of death and rebirth that constitute *The Counterlife*, Roth obviously intended more than a postmodern gimmick. He seems to have had in mind the possibility of creating an allegory that captured the essence of Jewish history itself. For example, on one occasion, Roth sympathetically articulated the plight of *Counterlife*'s readers in terms that strikingly apply to the fragmentary, discontinuous reality of Jewish endurance in the Diaspora: "In this book the contract gets torn up at the end of each chapter. . . . It isn't that it lacks a beginning, middle, and ending; there are too *many* beginnings, middles, and endings. It is a book where you never get to the bottom of things" (*Reading Philip Roth* 11). This is a novel where the characters themselves are desperate to "get to the bottom of things." Accordingly, Henry (whose sojourn in the Occupied Territories is a variant of Eli Peck's transformation in Roth's early story "Eli, the Fanatic"), has a Jewish epiphany in which he abandons one identity for another, as if peeling back layers of an onion; the reversal of an Ellis Island immigrant changing clothes. In the moments between Nathan and Henry, tensions between the powers of collectivism and the culture of individualism come to the fore. Curiously reminiscent of Marie Syrkin's willingness to bury her private self, Henry lays down the ground rules for their impending discourse:

He'd talk about Agor, if I wanted to know what this place stood for, he'd talk about the settlement movement, its roots and ideology and what the settlers were determined to achieve . . . but as for the American-style psychiatric soul-searching in which my own heroes could wallow for pages on end, that was a form of exhibitionistic indulgence and childish self-dramatization that blessedly belonged to the "narcissistic past." (104–5)

In Nathan's observation that "[t]he old life of non-historical personal problems seemed to him now embarrassingly, disgustingly, unspeakably puny," one can't help but hear echoes of Roth's own complaint about America's trivializing present. Promising his younger brother "no psychiatry," Nathan nevertheless can't resist arguing about his old values of self-revelation and interior life. But Henry, who in leaving America has forsaken democratic individualism, surrenders self-authorship for the sake of the Jewish collective order. More than his brother's betrayal and abandonment of wife and children, it is this insensate collectivity that has taken over Henry's consciousness that unnerves Nathan: "Not me—we. That's where Henry's me had gone" (106):

"And no shit, please, about my name."
"Relax. Anybody can call you anything they want, as far as I'm concerned."
"You still don't get it. The hell with me, forget me. Me is somebody I have forgotten. Me no longer exists out here. There isn't time for me, there isn't need of me— here Judea counts, not me." (105)

As this defiant speech suggests, it is not the mesmerizing but ultimately brutish Lippman who is the chief target of Roth's caustic investigation, but rather ordinary Henry who, enjoying his newfound swagger, embodies a more substantial population of Jews. Through Henry we witness the paradox of the Jewish American made more "Jewish," transformed into a physically empowered citizen of the Western world. This passage embodies the novel's juxtaposition of the unprecedented freedom and mobility of twentieth-century Jewish life with the dangers of rootlessness. For instance, the intractable Henry, finding his "genuine" self in the stony landscape of Judea, decries his previous life among "Hellenized Jews . . . bereft of any sort of context in which actually to be Jewish": "Hellenized-hedonized-egomanized. My whole *existence* was the sickness. I got off easy with just my heart. Diseased with self-distortion, self-contortion, diseased with self-disguise" (111). Henry Zuckerman's experience confirms Halkin's notion that "Diaspora" is a distortion of the authentic spirit of Judaism.

Much of "Judea" is taken up by Zuckerman's dumbstruck attempts to cope with his brother's "conversion," as in this rueful critique of the sheer absurdity of such posturing: "what inspirational nomenclature! Moses against the Egyptians, Judah Maccabee against the Greeks, Bar Kochba against the Romans, and now, in our era, Hanoch of Judea against Henry of Jersey" (119). This is the crux of the novel, the challenge of writing out of an awareness of the artifice of a redemptive identity. For Henry, now incandescently consumed by the biblical landscape, the immediate past seems utterly vacuous and devoid of value—everything from "shtupping the dental assistant" (with whom he had planned to run away) to his kid's private schools. For his part

Nathan is staggered by the willingness of assimilated Jewish Americans to uncritically embrace the platitudes of nineteenth-century Zionist ideology that have "nothing whatsoever" to do with their lives. In Nathan's understanding of his brother's flight we hear an odd echo of another early, and in some ways foundational, Roth story, "Epstein" (*Goodbye Columbus*), a parable about an aging Jewish businessman. The latter's yearning to escape a lifetime of duty leads to a single extramarital adventure with the spectacularly humiliating denouement of sexual exposure and disfigurement.

This is repeated in Henry's subjugation to the desires of parents, spouse, children, and patients, which leads to his radical flight in search of an authentic self—and sexual redemption. In Roth's novels, the erotic is often hopelessly enmeshed in the protagonist's flight to—or from—"authenticity." Here it is important to remember Zuckerman's complaint in Roth's own "autobiography": "You've written metamorphoses of yourself so many times, you no longer have any idea what *you* are or ever were. By now what you are is a walking text" (*The Facts* 162).[23] It is as if a "Jewish self" were beyond recovery, bound to an abstract, unlivable textuality.

Perhaps because of this revelation, Roth could not permit himself merely to satirize satirizing settler fanaticism.[24] Impersonating Mordechai Lippman, Roth's language soars to Portnoy-like excess, subjecting the reader to the persuasiveness of what only moments before might have seemed entirely unacceptable premises. But here there may be a more personal reason for his acute act of ventriloquism. Ironically, both Roth and Zuckerman have attacked the assimilationist tendency toward the banal center just as the fanatic Lippman now does. Unlike mainstream Zionists, Lippman would preserve a marginalized, essentially "ghetto" existence in modern Israel. Readers who shudder at the presence of Ariel Sharon at the helm of Israel's government may dislike Lippman as well, but Roth doesn't make it easy to dismiss his arguments. Grandson of a Jew killed at Auschwitz and survivor of a brutal battle in the 1967 war, Lippman is a highly literate reader whose shelves are filled with German translations of Dante, Shakespeare, and Cervantes. And yet, Lippman is livid about diasporic cosmopolitanism, the "Hellenized" Jew's "civilization of doubt": "[T]he Hellenized Jew . . . is always blaming himself for what happens in Baghdad. But in Baghdad, believe me, they do not blame themselves for what is happening in Jerusalem. Theirs is not a civilization of doubt—theirs is a civilization of *certainty*" (117). From Lippman's perspective, the doctrine of affliction is the only sensible paradigm to apply to the Jewish condition and Elchanan's vision is dangerously vacant. Surrounded by a growing Islamic world, he persuasively argues that the Hellenized Jews

of Tel Aviv only have room for "the goy's approval"—not "Jewish survival"
—in their hearts. For Lippman, as for Susser and Liebman, persecution
remains the bedrock of Jewish existence. If some Jewish readers are startled
to find themselves even mildly sympathetic to Lippman's views it is because,
once Roth unleashes a character as outrageous as Lippman on us, we may
feel besieged, but we also experience the profoundly disorienting experience
of opening to the persuasiveness of the ideology of affliction he so forcefully
articulates—this is how the counterlife always works in Roth's novels. The
preliminary debate here pivots on the tension between acting in the world
versus inaction, being *in* the world or being *of* it:

All you see is escaping Momma, escaping Poppa—why don't you see what I've
escaped *into*? *Everybody* escapes—our grandparents came to America, were they
escaping their mothers and fathers? They were escaping history! Here they're *making* history! There's a world outside the Oedipal swamp, Nathan . . . not what decadent Jews like you think but what committed Jews like the people here do! Jews who
aren't in it for laughs, Jews that have something more to go on than their hilarious
inner landscape! Here they have an *outer* landscape, a nation, a world! . . . What matters isn't Momma and Poppa and the kitchen table, it isn't *any* of that crap you write
about—*it's who owns Judea*! (140)

In this dazzling round between Henry and Nathan, Roth subtly ups the ante
—a move that reflects soberly on his entire career of verbal one-upmanships.
It is as though the writer is masochistically offering up *his* career for judgment, as a passive and ultimately self-negating substitute for a life of action
and decisive identity.

The struggle for the authentic location of Jewishness in modernity continues on his flight "home," where an enraptured Jewish American tourist
presses Zuckerman for his "feelings" after visiting Jewish citrus farms and
air-force bases ("here are the Jews, who aren't supposed to be able to farm.
. . . You can't imagine my feelings when I saw those farms" (142). But an
unfazed Zuckerman stubbornly clings to the triumphs of his forebears' peculiar "Zionism":

I thought, while listening to him, that if his Galician grandfather were able to drop
in on a tour from the realm of the dead upon Chicago, Los Angeles, or New York,
he might well express just such sentiments, and with no less amazement: "We
aren't supposed to be Americans—and there are those millions and millions of
American Jews! You can't imagine my feelings when I saw how American they
looked!" (142)

This parodic reversal suggests at the very least that Roth is challenging Zionism's redrawing of the boundaries of the Jewish world by placing the achievements of Jewish immigrants and Zionist settlers on a parity: "How do you explain this American-Jewish inferiority complex when faced with the bold claims of militant Zionism that they have the patent on Jewish self-transformation, if not on boldness itself?" In this liminal chapter, aptly titled "Aloft," Zuckerman struggles to draft a letter intended to bring Henry to his senses. But the experience of being airborne, transported between two very different Jewish destinies, reinforces his preoccupation with Jewish grandfathers and their sterile descendents. What links the struggle of Zuckerman's grandparents to that of the Jewish state is not merely "that it worked" but that it derives from the same Jewish impulse toward self-emancipation, the existential struggle that distinguishes nearly all of Roth's narratives. But as it is the manifestly flawed Henry and Nathan who bear the legacy of his Galician grandfathers' New World struggle, this places their achievements into question. What one begins to notice about Roth is that his American defense of Jewish grandfathers and ethnic neighborhoods is all past-situated, *never* given a corollary in the American present.

Henry's wife, Carol, is one of numerous voices who sustain Nathan's antagonism toward Zionism's monolithic claim for the authentic site of Jewish selfhood. As devil's advocate for Henry's unconventional behavior, Nathan explains to his sister-in-law why religion is not the source of her husband's actions: "It's not the Orthodoxy that's inspired him, it's the place—Judea. It seems to give him a more serious sense of himself having the roots of his religion all around him." But to Carol, the notion of a Jew styling himself on Alex Haley is ridiculous: "What roots? He left those roots two thousand years ago. As far as I know he's been in New Jersey for two thousand years. It's all nonsense" (151). But in explaining Henry to Carol, Nathan can only articulate a sense of Nathan's struggle to confront the abyss of his own selfhood: "Authentic's his word—in Israel he can be an authentic Jew and everything about him makes sense. In America being a Jew made him feel artificial" (154).

Some Jewish American critics (including those like Emily Budick and Hillel Halkin who have immigrated to Israel) were rightly disturbed by what they saw as Roth's focus on an uncharacteristically extreme segment of Israel's Jews. But the xenophobic fanaticism of Henry's adopted community is almost beside the point. Nathan is less disturbed by the political dimensions of the ideology that Henry has accepted than by the fact that the latter sees himself in Israel as a unique creation, dissociated from any real ancestry, acting on a desire for autonomous self-birth. It is as if for Roth, such uncanny displays of the "true self's" rebellion surface aberrantly—but inevitably— almost as a genetic madness. Musing over Henry's shenanigans, Carol tells Nathan that *she* knows its source: "Oh, I know where. Living in that little ghetto when you were kids, from your crazy father—he's gone right back to the roots of that madness. It's that craziness gone in another direction" (151).

Counterlife is a warming-up exercise for the full-fledged arguments that would spring from Moshe Pipik in *Operation Shylock*. A precursor of Pipik, "Jimmy Ben-Joseph from the Diaspora Yeshivah," has carved out a manifesto that will "turn world opinion completely around on the subject of Israel" (165). American-born Jimmy has a number of concerns, chief among them "the immediate closing and dismantling of Yad Vashem." He attempts to hijack the plane on which Nathan Zuckerman flies out of Israel, in order to attract attention for his demands that Israel no longer situate the Holocaust at the ideological heart of its identity; he drafts a decree titled FORGET REMEM-BERING! Like Pipik, a would-be Moses who would lead the Israelites straight back to Europe, Ben-Joseph argues that:

I demand of the Israeli government the immediate closing and dismantling of Yad Vashem. . . . I demand this in the name of the Jewish future. THE JEWISH FUTURE IS NOW. We must put persecution behind us forever. Never must we utter the name "Nazi" again, but instead strike it from our memory forever. No longer are we a peo-ple with an agonizing wound and a hideous scar. We have wandered nearly forty years in the wilderness of our great grief. Now is the time to stop paying tribute to that monster's memory with our Halls of Remembrance! (165)

Of course Yad Vashem is one of Israel's most important national symbols, the one site that every foreign dignitary must include on the itinerary of state vis-its. More important, its strategic embodiment of Jewish trauma has set in motion a particular Jewish future that precludes other visions. Accordingly, Ben Joseph's startling slogans include "Forget Remembering!; Jews Need No Nazis To Be The Remarkable Jewish People!; Zionism Without Ausch-witz!"; and "The Past Is Past! We Live!" That we cannot safely determine Roth's position on the polarities his narrative reflects remains an intrinsic aspect of the novel's subtle power. The very structure of *The Counterlife* is a speculative tease, oscillating between the trendy postmodern conceit that self-division and fragmentation are intellectual or moral virtues and the grim alternative prospect that the flight from identity is merely shameful. As we have seen, with Henry's final words to Nathan, this is a novel of shrilly polar-ized positions. These embody schisms in the Jewish soul, the lines of division between hostile camps in modern Jewish culture. By shifting from Nathan

Zuckerman to Henry Zuckerman and back to Nathan's ghost, Roth disrupts the prospect of alternative existences, far more than he affirms them. Yet it is equally undeniable that at such moments his "alter-brain" craves the fading vigors of *Galut*.

Evidence of this desire surfaces in an odd passage that the reader might reasonably seize on as Roth's, not Zuckerman's confession. It comes toward the end of the book, in "Christendom," in the aftermath of a fight in which it has become evident that ethnic and religious worldviews will effectively prevent Zuckerman and Maria, his "English Rose," from reaching the marriage canopy: "I felt as though gentlest England had suddenly reared up and bit me on the neck—there was a kind of irrational scream in me saying, "She's not on my side—she's on their side!" Crossing back to Christian Europe nearly a hundred years after my grandparents' eastward escape . . . I still had to wonder . . . if I wasn't *wanting* the anti-Semitism to be there, and in a big way" (307). Indeed, it may be Roth himself who "want[s] the anti-Semitism to be there," not because the struggle of the European experience has "been negligible" in his life, but because he distrusts the endurance of a recognizably Jewish culture in its seeming absence. Roth is less interested in Jewish dispersal per se than in the enduring discomfort of the Jew, and it is with some justification that Barack-Fishman argues that, throughout his narratives, "one of the primary defining factors of Jewishness are the boundaries provided by antisemitism" ("Success in Circuit Lies" 149). That Zuckerman's relationship with Maria is apparently foredoomed is made explicit in all sorts of ways. Indeed, the overwrought exposure of the sister's and mother's antisemitism is hardly necessary for the familiar reader at this point. All s/he really needs to know about the certainty of impending catastrophe lies in Maria's own sense of romantic rootedness.

Visiting Maria's childhood village, the couple take long walks through Wordsworthian beechwoods and streams, gazing at "old hideaways" and Gothic ruins. Like Reznikoff, Roth makes a show here of disparaging the tame pleasures of the Wordsworthian sublime, which have too faint a correspondence with any reality wherein Roth is willing to locate the "Jewish." This romantic landscape of childhood dreaming is clearly embedded in Maria's current pastoral sensibilities: "This is where I'd have visionary feelings of the world being one. Exactly what Wordsworth describes—the real nature mysticism, moments of extreme contentment. You know, looking at the sun setting and suddenly thinking that the universe all makes sense . . . there is no better place for these little visions than a ruined mill by a trickling stream" (274). Much of the challenge the reader faces in "Gloucestershire" comes from experiencing just how elegantly Roth lays out the seductions of home for his character. For instance, Nathan imagines Maria (who is again linked to romantic fantasy) dreaming a dream in which she swims in the open sea toward a jetty from where young boys are shouting "Judea," encouraging her to swim beyond the horizon. Suddenly she glimpses a far more welcome prospect—"a little tiny boatyard"—to which she swims. Soon she recognizes her English husband, in "a green tweed suit," who has been patiently "waiting to take me home," to rescue her from displacement and the alien Jew who beckons (no wonder Zuckerman later ruefully calls the dream "the promised land versus the green tweed suit" [195–96]). Inheriting the old Kazin paradigm of the Jew as "walker-in-the-city," to which Reznikoff and a generation of literary Jewish Americans adhered, Roth has long been an active interrogator of the Jewish urban experience. Perhaps this accounts for why, in *American Pastoral*, in which "Old Rimrock," a lush exurb of New Jersey, lures a Jewish soul away from his origins, there are cruelly grotesque consequences for the man, his family, and even the liberal Gentile society that surrounds them.[25]

As Zuckerman understands it, the dream is, for Maria, a tempting vision of a stable sense of self, one that is inextricable from the domesticity of place. In fact, Maria incarnates Nathan's own unacknowledged desire for stasis, a desire that inevitably unravels the closer he comes to marrying his English Rose. For Roth, this placid dream is clearly as ruinous to Jewish identity as Zionist utopianism. What Maria embodies for Nathan in England resembles what Henry sought in Judea, namely the serene confidence that *place* affords him, a balm from the burden of writing about Jews. Ironically, the closer Nathan comes to actually escaping into marital bliss in England, the more he fears losing his "innate capacity to impersonate" (320). For Roth, a life devoid of marginalization and struggle is no life at all. Complete liberation paralyzes, rather than frees, Jewish energy. Refusing to settle for a Jewish literature without the scars of affliction, he invents Job-like trials of humiliation, madness, and decay for his characters to endure.

Throughout the "Gloucestershire" and "Christendom" sections of the novel, Roth juxtaposes the banal pleasures of English gentility with the hard edges of Jewish paranoia and unease. A telling instance of this occurs in an exchange between Nathan and Maria, who debate the writer's obtuse obsession with misery, conflict, and the "disfiguring" Otherness characterized by the rite of circumcision. According to Zuckerman's analysis, this most indecorous of religious rituals commemorates nothing less than humanity's struggle to apprehend the meaning of its own intrusive nature, the inevitability of a distinctly *un*harmonious existence:

[C]ircumcision gives the lie to the womb-dream of life in the beautiful state of innocent prehistory, the appealing idyll of living "naturally," unencumbered by man-made ritual. To be born is to lose all that. The heavy hand of human values falls upon you right at the start, marking your genitals as its own. Inasmuch as one invents one's meanings, along with impersonating one's selves, this is the meaning I propose for that rite. (323)

Ironically, the novel's depiction of the seduction of a variety of fictive escapes dissipates into permanent otherness. This knowledge propels Roth's alter-ego to argue for the existential necessity of circumcising his unborn child. For a stunningly unprecedented moment, Zuckerman celebrates a hereditary Jewishness, rendered in a son's birth (though poignantly one who never arrives) and the visual sign of circumcision:

The pastoral stops here and it stops with circumcision. That delicate surgery should be performed upon the penis of a brand-new boy seems to you the very cornerstone of human irrationality, and maybe it is. . . . Circumcision makes it clear as can be that you are here and not there, that you are out and not in—also that you're mine and not theirs. There is no way around it: you enter history through my history and me. Circumcision is everything that the pastoral is not and, to my mind, reinforces what the world is about, which isn't strifeless unity. (323)

In the heart of Christendom, Zuckerman apparently apprehends the cold fact of Jewish continuity's debt to the systematic insulation born of the ideology of affliction, described by Susser and Liebman: "this hatred did not imperil their national existence; on the contrary, it sustained it. First, because anti-semitism kept Jews apart *by blocking any exit from their pariah community, and second, because persecution and humiliation stung a proud and ancient people into resistance and defiance*" (20, emphasis mine). Similarly, for Zuckerman, there is no "miracle" of Jewish survival. It all comes down to the concrete reality of Jewish separatism, the messy entanglements of both suffering and group purity. And yet, as Jewish difference is now only "skin-deep," the reader is left to wonder what sustaining culture remains after the mohel's knife. As Roth surely knows, the intentionally tribal marker of circumcision long ago dissipated in an America where the foreskins of most males are removed at birth.

As if to overcome this absence, Roth subjects Zuckerman and other protagonists to grotesque humiliations, attempting to resuscitate the anachronistic condition of the pariah. And yet here Zuckerman's dramatic epiphany is undermined by the fact that, though fully aware of the anachronism of the pariah status, the "essence" of Judaism continues to elude him. Zuckerman appears to be talking here about peoplehood and "authenticity," not the Jewish religion per se. But in the book that calls itself a journey into the "Jewish heart of darkness," neither the wounds inflicted by the mohel's knife nor the novelist's pen reveal a tangible Jewish self. In a milieu in which the majority are circumcised, the sexual mark that once stressed the marginalization of the Jewish world is inverted as the boundary that contains the same. Perhaps because, as Roth himself admits in a 1988 interview, "the book progressively undermines its own fictional assumptions" (Milbauer and Watson 11), the endless, circular discourse about Jewish identity is essentially self-negating, an aggression directed as much toward the reader as toward his hapless characters. By sabotaging the reader's faith in any version of the contradictory texts, Roth performatively undermines the possibility of "authenticity." There is a point at which the dizzying language game of the "author," who constantly fades back into one countertextual oscillation after another, comes to resemble the problem of the vanishing Jew. There is no "Roth" there, nor is any "Jew" there either.

In "Gloucestershire" Maria is outraged by the novelist's projections and occupations of multiple identities (in response to the "Christendom" text), all in the service of wreaking emotional violence and controversy. Angrily condemning the novelist's manipulations, Maria expresses her dread of Zuckerman's rejection of his own "true" identity. In Zuckerman's rejoinder, he seems almost to concur: "It's *all* impersonation—in the absence of a self, one impersonates selves, and after a while impersonates best the self that gets one through" (320). Perhaps it was not the merits of the other side's argument that he missed, so much as the creative friction produced in his own struggle. It is entirely consistent with Roth's interest in the ways that persecution preserves diasporic identity that he should be "attracted" to Britain as a place where Jews are still made to feel more like boarders than like truly welcome members of society. Nevertheless, the whole "Christendom" episode rings false. The virulent antisemitism projected onto contemporary English characters is especially unconvincing (perhaps intentionally so). The artificiality of Zuckerman taking on English antisemitism only underscores the fact that, in America, persecution as a literary and cultural paradigm has outlived persecution as a reality; Roth is unwilling or unable to come to terms with what might lie beyond.

Initially, the question for many readers of *The Counterlife* may surround the question of the fate of the individual subject. First Henry, then Nathan "dies" after failed surgery. But in a novel where all endings are put into question, the mortality of any single individual or ideology is no longer at issue, but rather the fate of the text. Even the heat of carnal desire implodes, reduced to "textuality," as when an impotent Nathan explains in "Gloucestershire" that "there's to be no exquisite pleasure here that cannot be derived from words. My carnality is now *really* a fiction and, revenge of revenge, language and only language must provide the means for the release of everything" (184). After leaving Israel, it seems evident that the mysteriously disembodied Nathan no longer speaks from any locus at all, but rather from what Shostak has called "the eternity provided by textuality," as Nathan's fittingly enigmatic parting remark to Maria, who would lie to escape from his book, suggests: "It may be as you say that this is no life, but use your enchanting, enrapturing brains: this life is as close to life as you, and I, and our child can ever hope to come" ("Obsessive Reinvention of the Real" 201, *Counterlife* 324). If Roth pretends to adapt a Steinarian outlook here, it is also one that he is guiltily aware affords him an unending freedom to be *noncommittal*. There will always be readers who will read that oblique parting shot as self-reflective irony, but it is also one that heralds Roth's bleakest statements on diasporic identity in the novels that followed. Whether intended or not is a matter for debate, but the "lesson" of *The Counterlife* may well be that the endlessly multiplying and fracturing freedom of postmodernism is not a viable paradigm for a people with a strong communal sense of the "self" and a special understanding of history.

◆

Years before the debates over diasporism voiced in *Operation Shylock*, Roth's most resonant affirmation of the Jewish homeland as a mobile industry of narration was voiced in *The Prague Orgy* (1985), a neglected novella where Zuckerman, searching for a lost manuscript by a martyred Yiddish writer, records his startled discovery of the meaning of Jewish exile as:

the mining and refining of *tons* of these stories—the national industry of the Jewish homeland . . . the construction of narrative out of the exertions of survival [where] a joke is always lurking somewhere, a derisory portrait, a scathing crack, a joke which builds with subtle self-savaging to the uproarious punch line, "And this is what suffering does!" Wild with lament and rippling with amusement, their voices tremulous with rancor and vibrating with pain, a choral society proclaiming vehemently, "Do you believe it? Can you imagine it?" (63–64)

For a stunning moment of coherence, there is no division between the Jewish self and the collective: "That such things can happen—there's the moral of the stories—that such things happen to me, to you, to us." Anticipating and perhaps transcending Moshe Pipik, the redeemer of Diaspora in *Operation Shylock*, Zuckerman's euphoria implicitly supersedes *Hatikvah* (Israel's national anthem) with the "national anthem" of the true, nonterritorial "Jewish homeland": "By all rights, when you hear someone [in Prague] begin telling a story—when you see the Jewish faces mastering anxiety and feigning innocence and registering astonishment at their own fortitude—you ought to stand and put your hand to your heart" (64).

In a vital sense, Roth's next Israel-situated novel seemed to renew this affirmation of a creative Diaspora of ever-renewed imaginings. In the *New York Times Book Review* interview that followed *Operation Shylock: A Confession*'s publication, a strangely troubled (or exuberantly playful?) Roth insisted on the veracity of the absurd plotlines of the novel, involving an anti-Zionist doppelganger, resulting in "an astonishing affinity between myself and the audience that has long considered me exactly what I considered him: deformed, deranged, craven, possessed, an alien wreck in a state of foaming madness" ("A Bit of Jewish Mischief" 20). Perhaps the most unsettling moment in the novel arrives when the character named Philip Roth telephones his impostor's room in Jerusalem's King David Hotel. Upon inquiring if this Other is Philip Roth, he is told, "It is, and who is this, please?" (40). That profound question has always been the most unanswerable of queries for this author, and the dissolution of identity that spirals out of control in this novel begins here.

In *Operation Shylock*, the reader joins "Roth" to experience a dizzying collage of the hits and misses of contemporary Zionism—the bungled trial of the Nazi John Demjanjuk, the touchingly banal details of the final entries (fictional) in terrorist victim Leon Klinghoffer's diary, and the high-camp shenanigans of the Israeli Mossad's spy service. Roth's enduring fascination with the tension between a "coercive" Zionism and a "liberating" Diaspora reaches its triumphal culmination in this novel, a work John Updike not entirely enthusiastically called "an orgy of argumentation."[26] Here the character named "Philip Roth" learns that his identity has been usurped by an impostor who preaches an exotic doctrine the stranger calls "Diasporism"—a program that would return all Jews of European descent back to Europe. In many ways, the individual violation that the character called Roth suffers is not unlike that perpetrated by Zionist ideologues who, in claiming that Judaism in *Galut* was no longer tenable after the founding of the state, essentially usurped the meaning of Jewishness. This counter-Zionism would not only challenge Zionism's vision of the Jew but seek to provide an alternative destiny.

After listening to "Roth's" anguished account of his plight, his friend, the fictional version of Israeli novelist Aharon Appelfeld, advises him to consider the matter merely as an "aesthetic outrage" that can be reversed as easily as any other textual misfortune: "The great wonders performed on the golem by Rabbi Liva of Prague you are now going to perform on him. Why? Because you have a better conception of him than he does . . . you are going to rewrite him" (107). This, of course, proves to be the remedy; "Appelfeld's" invocation of the magical clay sculptor of the ghetto parallels Roth's plastic ability to anticipate every counternarrative, the crafty elusiveness that had so enraged Syrkin. "Appelfeld's" citation of the rabbinic legend is enough to jar "Roth" into remembering his gift for avoiding precisely the kind of ideological prison that his impostor would impose on him. After some one-hundred-odd pages of torment, "Roth" begins to gain some psychological mastery of the situation by the act of naming his aggressor. Like Rabbi Liva of Prague, who wielded the great supernatural power inherent in the Diaspora, "Roth" effectively reverses the situation by ironically naming the impostor "Pipik," a Yiddishism that immediately diminishes the latter's gothic weight: "Yes, name him now! Because aptly naming him is knowing him for what he is and isn't, exorcising and possessing him all at once" (115).

Later, he increases this advantage by impersonating his own impersonator, even allowing his old Palestinian friend George Ziad, to mistake him for precisely the kind of messianic ideologue that Roth has taken pains to avoid becoming. By exercising the prerogative of "naming," "Roth" disables the stranger's menacing capabilities, for "Moishe Pipik" translates literally to the joke name Moses Bellybutton, which, as "Roth" disarmingly observes,

probably connoted something slightly different to every Jewish family on our block —the little guy who wants to be a big shot, the kid who pisses in his pants, the someone who is a bit ridiculous, a bit funny, a bit childish, the comical shadow alongside whom we had all grown up, that little folkloric fall guy whose surname somehow designated the thing that for most children was neither here nor there, neither a part nor an orifice, somehow a concavity and a convexity both, something neither upper nor lower, neither lewd nor entirely respectable either. (116)

This extravagantly comic passage not only reduces his nemesis to a derisive butt of Kafkaesque liminality but allows "Roth" to stake his preference in the tension between the comic Yiddish and the Hebraic sublime. Though for some readers, "Roth's" jocular assault may be unexpected—after all *Counterlife* appeared to be leaning toward precisely the conclusions Pipik reaches— we can still find a strong correlation to the "real" Roth's inability to get on board with any ideology, whether Lippman's fascist "Zionism" in *Counter-life*, or the upper-case "Diasporism" of a Moishe Pipik. Both men are convinced that their vision of Jewish destiny is the only viable one. Pipik prophesies a new, Arab-sponsored Holocaust if the Jews remain in Israel, whereas Lippman foresees both catastrophic levels of intermarriage and assimilation and a "Great American Pogrom out of which American white purity will be restored" (128).

To some readers, *Operation Shylock* seemed a brave expression of a new Jewish zeitgeist. Not since the short-lived Breira (Hebrew for "alternative") peace movement of the sixties, which was eventually hounded out of existence, had such an apparently sincere critique of Israel emerged from the Jewish polity. The novel appeared to confront readers with the painful prospect that the "Jewish people" and the "Jewish spirit" were exposed to grave perils in Israel. But at the heart of the novel lies an essential conservatism. For as much as the Palestinian Ziad (who loves Diaspora Jews but hates Israelis) and Moishe Pipik's diasporism may speak to a reader's heart, Roth forces the rhetoric of both characters to such absurd extremes that the moral validity of their arguments collapses. In both *Counterlife* and *Operation Shylock*, it is not the Israeli (embattled though he may be) but rather the diasporic Jewish personality that remains a troubled enigma. For Pipik meets the figurative and literal fate of other Jews in the diaspora—impotence. Having lost his physical manhood he can only have intercourse with one Wanda Sue Posseski—a once virulent antisemite of Polish descent—by wielding a mechanical penile implant.

In the end, Moishe Pipik is not the prophet of a vital Diaspora at all, but rather the embodiment of a diseased community, grotesquely tumescent only through artificial means. Though I admire Sylvia Barack-Fishman's reading of *Operation Shylock* "as a quest narrative in which the protagonist is engaged in a baffling search for an authentic Jewish identity" ("Success in Circuit Lies" 137), I see little room for her optimistic conclusion elsewhere that the "Philip Roth" of the novel "finally breaks free of his indecision and puts his future on the line" for Israel, a validation of the state as the "sacral center" of the American Jew ("Homelands of the Heart" 292). Such a reading is undermined in the hastily contrived conclusion, where "Roth" does not so much surrender to the state as symbolically demonstrate, by implicating himself, how easily Jewish Americans are duped, for the sake of "identity," into supporting Israel's breaches of Jewish ethics. The three venomous epics that followed, *Sabbath's Theater, American Pastoral*, and *The Human Stain*, demonstrate further the tragic consequences of the thoughtlessness of that vacant identity.

Chapter Six

"A Stranger in the House"

Assimilation, Madness, and Passing in Roth's

Figure of the Pariah Jew in Sabbath's Theater

(1995), American Pastoral *(1997), and*

The Human Stain *(2000)*

To become a new being. To bifurcate. The drama that underlies America's story, the high drama that is upping and leaving—and the energy and
cruelty that rapturous drive demands. —Philip Roth, *The Human Stain*

Sometime after writing *Operation Shylock*, Roth must have concluded that if
the logic of his own arguments, whether voiced by Zuckerman, "Roth," or
Moishe Pipik, had any merit—if America truly *was* Zion, then the same kind
of struggle he had waged against the anti-Jewish spirit of modern Zionism
must necessarily be brought back to bear on Jewish American complacency.
For Roth, the latter has led to fatal forms of forgetfulness and the annihilation
of Jewish (or any other form of) selfhood. For a very long time, it seemed that
Roth would remain perpetually buoyant, his novels energized by the sheer
variety of ways they skewered pristine notions of essential definitions and
identities. But lately, he seems to be preparing to write the epitaph for the
dialectic between the Jewish and the American that has for so long provoked
him. After exploring the complexities of Jewish life in Israel, Roth has returned to the Diaspora with a vengeance, demonstrating, in the bleakest
novels of his career, an apparently fierce affinity for a Diaspora informed by
positive values—just as the possibilities of its preservation are rapidly fading.
These late novels constitute Roth's threnody for a Jewishness that cannot
survive complacency.

As a student of literature I have long been excited by the notion that Roth's gloom owes a debt to the skeptical visions of early antecedents, such as the immigrant and tenement narratives of Anzia Yezierska and Ludwig Lewisohn. For instance, like Roth, Yezierska (thoroughly radical and political before her coreligionists were ready to accept that in a woman writer) had a singularly abrasive relationship with American Jewry—resented by newly arrived immigrants for her critical attitude toward their language, manners, and traditions and by Americanized "allrightniks" for her condemnation of their betrayal of the past. Following her spectacular rise to prominence from tenements and sweatshops to Hollywood, Yezierska retreated from the fame and fortune commercial success brought her. Art imitating life, the Yezierska heroine, after years of struggle, typically achieves material success but fails to overcome her sense of alienation from mainstream culture. The talmudic saying adapted as an epigraph to her last work—"Poverty becomes a poor man like a red ribbon on a white horse"—chides those who bought into the myth of the American dream and turned their backs on ethnic community. For Yezierska, the Jew was so adapted to exile, homelessness, and struggle that s/he could never be fulfilled by the consolations of assimilation and material well-being. In Yezierska's short story, "Dreams and Dollars," Rebecca is persuaded to leave the Upper East Side tenement to join her sister and prosperous brother-in-law in the magical world of Los Angeles. But still longing for the sweatshop poet of her dreams, she is sickened by the materialism and vacuous culture of the "allrightniks":

"It would kill me to stay here another day. Your fine food, your fresh air, your velvet limousine smothers me. . . . It's all a desert of emptiness painted over with money. Nothing is real. The sky is too blue. The grass is too green. The beauty is all false paint, hiding dry rot. . . ." Rebecca towered over her sister like the living spirit of struggle revolting against the deadening inertia of ease. "What is this chance that you are giving your children? Will that feed their hungry young hearts? Fire their spirits for higher things? *Children's hands reach out for struggle. Their youth is hungry for hardships, for danger, for the rough fight with life even more than their bodies are hungry for bread.*" (*How I Found America* 230, emphasis mine)

In similar terms of loss and frustration, the tormented writer Ludwig Lewisohn later described the breakdown of communal identity that lay at the end of Jewish struggle, in a 1939 polemic, *The Answer*:

Escape, escape, anything on any irrelevant periphery. Anything but the center, the heart, the blood. Virgin Spain. The Soviet Fatherland. Anything but the real, the attainable, the given, that for which real work can be done in a world of reality and real sacrifices made and real tears shed and real blood; anything but that to which one is called by nature and unperverted instinct and tradition and where one is wanted and needed and where . . . one can give one's whole heart. Any place but home. Any people except one's own. Any God except the God of one's fathers. . . . Utopia is the opiate of great sections of the Jewish people. (121–122)

The novelist's discomfiting candor here pre-echoes the stark utterances of Roth's recent protagonists. I offer Yezierska and Lewisohn as visionary foremother and forefather of Roth, whose midcentury ruminations in *Goodbye Columbus* would bear witness to the moment that the individual Jew not only abandoned the quixotic ideologies of the past but faced the manifest evidence of his/her arrival and material successes in white America. In arguing for a far more traditional and bound Roth than was once assumed, this relational dynamic between the novelist and his forebears' ways of representing the end of material struggle suggests a possible source for his uneasy vacillation between representing the Jewish American experience as a creatively vital struggle and disparaging the hollowed-out failure of Jewish American life.

The recently intensified preoccupation with the shattering of his characters' sexual, political, and material hopes that marks his recent novels conforms to the logic of the novelist's entire oeuvre. Roth's America has long been a site of darkly comic humiliations, but lately the comedy is noticeably on the wane, as his novels increasingly form a landscape of dislocation that prevents any form of arrival or fulfillment. For years, his protagonists had been locked in acrimonious conflict with their families, with Jewish Others, with themselves over questions of just what constituted "authentic" Jewishness. In Roth's post-Israel fiction, the protagonist takes on America itself, always with devastating consequences for Jewish identity.

A sharp and as yet irreversible shift came into Roth's oeuvre during the composition of *Sabbath's Theater*. It is difficult to determine precisely when —or precisely why—Roth concluded that the displacement of ethnic particularism by an ethic of bland universalism was dangerous not only for the Jews, but for America itself. But this is the dark prospect that emerges from this novel. This dark novel aroused a more hostile response among the critics than any novel since *Portnoy*. Indeed, Ruth Wisse, sounding a great deal like Syrkin at the beginning of Roth's career, condemned the protagonist for "snatching peanuts from a crowd that is still amused enough to watch him suffer, but whose moral attention he cannot command" ("Sex, Love and

Death" 65). To say that *Sabbath's Theater* is Roth's most explicitly sexual novel is saying a great deal, considering the fact that his oeuvre is filled with descriptions of erotic fantasies and nearly every sexual act imaginable. Perhaps for that very reason, it is also his most seriously moralizing novel to date. To assess the distance that Sabbath has traveled, we should take a backward glance at the intoxicated observations of Alexander Portnoy: "How do they get so gorgeous, so healthy, so *blond*? Their fathers are men with white hair and deep voices who never use double negatives, and their mothers the ladies with the kindly smiles and the wonderful manners. . . . [T]hese blond-haired Christians are the legitimate owners of this place" (*Portnoy's Complaint* 163–65). In Roth's earliest works, the "Shiksa" was always the blue-blooded American ("O America! America! it may have been gold in the streets to my grandparents . . . but to me . . . America is a *shikse* nestling under your arm whispering love love love love love!" [*Portnoy's Complaint* 165]); she is still an embodied fantasy of Otherness, but now it is the Jew who is privileged to take his Americanness for granted. Early in the novel, on the occasion of the death of Drenka, Mickey Sabbath's great love (his "Serbo-Croatian Catholic Shiksa lover"), Roth's protagonist encounters a startling premise, though we don't actually hear what is revealed until the novel's last pages. Two hours before the pulmonary embolus that will suddenly kill her, Sabbath's mistress whispers to him in heavily accented English, "My secret American boyfriend. . . . To have a lover of the country . . . I was thinking this all day, to tell you, Mickey. To have a lover of the country which one . . . it gave me the feeling of having the opening of the door" (417). This is all we need to solve the mystery of Sabbath's inexplicably bad behavior, the secret of his peculiarly radical failure to thrive. The moment the Jew is merely mistaken for an "American" is a fatal one for Roth.

In his eloquent disillusionment, Sabbath is the most radical disturber of order in Jewish American literature. He harbors a secret, dangerous knowledge about America itself: "Many Americans hated their homes. The number of homeless in America couldn't touch the number of Americans who had homes and families and hated the whole thing" (100). A sexual addict, the havoc Sabbath inflicts on domesticated others stems not from a chain of tragic events or misunderstandings but from his very nature. Sabbath's eventual madness and self-destructive tendencies are even prophesied by his late Yiddishe mama ("You should have had a family. You should have had a profession. Puppets!"), confronting him as a ghost: "Even as a tiny child you were a little stranger in the house . . . always a little stranger, making everything into a farce. . . . Look now. Making death itself into a farce. Is there anything more serious than dying? No . . . even killing yourself you won't do with dignity" (160).

For Roth, Sabbath may represent the transition from conscious Jew to mindless pagan "goy." Possibly Roth portrays Sabbath as a *shtetl Ostjude* who, having "moved beyond the pale," finds himself in tragic conflict with his surroundings, an ordeal that takes him down a ladder, from social shame to alienation to mental illness. The most transgressive of Roth's characters, Sabbath's drives lead him to be cruelly exploitative of those who have been most supportive of him. For Sabbath, there is nothing in life as meaningful as the desires of the moment. Readers will not be surprised to note that Sabbath repeatedly insists that the nihilistic self, slave to desire, is merely a performance. In *The Counterlife*, Nathan Zuckerman also asserted that "I am a theater and nothing more than a theater" (321). But the earlier novel's playful staging of subjectivity, with its endless parade of speculations, dissolves here into a less ambiguous nihilism.

In *Sabbath's Theater*, the "theater" connotes the performative Jewish self bereft of any other meaning. In terms tellingly evocative of Roth's own fictions, the "atmosphere" of the theatrical space that surrounds Sabbath is described as "insinuatingly anti-moral, vaguely menacing, and at the same time, rascally fun" (97). Like most of Roth's later work, the novel raises important questions about the nature of impersonation and linguistic selfhood. This is consistent with Roth's earlier insistence that the meaning of Jewish culture could be explained by language and argument. For instance, not long after the breaking of Zuckerman's jaw in *The Anatomy Lesson* (1983), Roth felt compelled to spell out just why this was such a tragedy: "I knew what I was doing when I broke Zuckerman's jaw. For a Jew a broken jaw is a terrible tragedy. It was to avoid this that so many of us went into teaching rather than prizefighting." Admitting that the most important Jewish quality of his novels "doesn't really reside in their subject matter," Roth has asserted that their "Jewishness" owed instead to "the nervousness, the excitability, the arguing, the dramatizing, the indignation, the obsessiveness . . . above all the *talking*. The talking and the shouting. . . . It isn't what it's talking *about* that makes a book Jewish—it's that the book won't shut up" (Searles 181). But this dictum no longer seems to have satisfied the novelist of the 1995 novel, for the central metaphor of *Sabbath's Theater* poses the nagging question about just what "essence" undergirds the performativity of ethnic difference with far greater urgency than we are accustomed to: Who really is Mickey Sabbath?

In his best days, Sabbath was the "one-time puppet master of the Indecent Theater of Manhattan" (12), an avant-garde street performer. But even in his artistic heyday, there was a dark undercurrent to his puppetry. Apparently his manipulative control of his environment extended to both his wives, who are forced to conform to the amoral subject-object paradigm that rules Sabbath and his creative and personal fiefdom. As Debra Shostak argues: "Nikki, the 'malleable' actress to Sabbath's 'willful director' serves as 'his instrument, his implement, the self-immolating register of his ready-made world,' . . . Nikki, whose name echoes Mickey's to suggest a doubling of him, a sameness with a difference, leaves a tangible absence where there was always an ontological absence" ("Roth/CounterRoth" 123). But the real import of Sabbath's objectification of others resides in its ironic unraveling of his own selfhood. Sabbath's "performance art" substitutes phallic power—what he acknowledges as a "hell-bent-for-disaster erotomania" (156)—for authentic selfhood. Sabbath relies on his penis, and the theatrical surrogate of his manipulative hands, to constitute the only subjectivity he trusts. His earliest street performance involves his own undisguised fingers on a puppet stage where they coax young women to join him in creating representations of transgressive desire. After a number of these performances, it is clear that Roth is inviting us to interrogate the reality of a self that substitutes throwing his voice onto others, or insatiable desire for sexual penetration, for a sense of responsible agency.

The celebration of a physical self works fine for Sabbath in his early life, particularly when in his late adolescence he joins the merchant marines, which exposes him to the delights of prostitutes in international ports. As the narrator remarks about Sabbath's inexorable and thoughtless journey, "His life was one long flight from what?" (125). Later, it becomes obvious that Sabbath's audacious verbal and sexual performances are a frantic attempt to compensate for two unbearable losses. The first of these is Nikki's inexplicable disappearance in New York City. Then, in the days following Drenka's demise, Sabbath spends a good deal of time in the rural pre-Revolutionary graveyard (a setting that underscores the Jew's encroachment on America's hallowed grounds), where perhaps because he senses himself to be "as invisible as any of those buried around him," he masturbates, exulting in cherished erotic memories of his beloved. The language with which Sabbath grieves for Nikki's mysterious absence reveals more about the madness that gradually overtakes him than about her actual fate: "apart from the world . . . with no church, no clan to help her through, not even a simple folk formality around which her response to a dear one's death could mercifully cohere" (110). Earlier, the death of Sabbath's older brother, Morty, a pilot downed in World War II, leads to the rapid deterioration of his mother as well as to seventeen-year-old Mickey Sabbath's decision to go off to sea. "Mort" is linked to Sabbath's own death wish; he keeps time with his brother's Army Benrus, returned to the family two years before they received his body. The watch is key to Sabbath's own private sense of keeping Jewish time: "He had been winding the watch every morning since it became his in 1945. His grandfathers had laid tefillin every morning and thought of God; he wound Morty's watch every morning and thought of Morty" (147).

Sabbath's lifelong embrace of the transgressively erotic is an attempt to compensate for the losses he has never come to terms with, including Morty's, his mother's, Nikki's, and finally, Drenka's. At last, Sabbath flees the ultimate loss, the prospect of his own bodily decay and his impending absence. In his old age, Sabbath seems set on ending his life as an Old World Jew, a transformation curiously reminiscent of Zuckerman's encounters in Jerusalem or the radical "conversion" of the title character in "Eli the Fanatic." Like an itinerant peddlar wandering the countryside, he is given shelter in the bourgeois Upper East Side home of an old friend. Norman, his host, is not entirely pleased to see Sabbath, who appears "like a visitor from Dogpatch, either like a bearded character in a comic strip or somebody at your doorstep in 1900, a wastrel uncle from the Russian pale who is to sleep in the cellar next to the coal bin for the rest of his American life" (141). In spite of his scandalous nature and utter lack of religiosity, Sabbath embodies the inerradicable essence of the shtetl Jew. But he also shares the perverse gift of many of Roth's memorable protagonists, in "making people uncomfortable, comfortable people especially" (141). Confronting Norman's "bright, brown, benevolent eyes" and youthful, athletic body proves too much for Sabbath, who, exhausted by "war, lunacy, perversity, sickness, imbecility," and the recent suicide of an old friend, suffers a complete breakdown.

Waking the next morning, Sabbath seethes with hate for his genteel surroundings. Norman's sunlit kitchen with its "robust" greenhouse atmosphere and "terra-cotta floor" earns his special disgust. Like the unruly, coarse "id" Freud sought to help assimilate in the bourgeois-Christian West, Sabbath's "yid" emerges to uncannily resemble what James A. Sleeper calls "the *pintele yid*, that ineradicable . . . Jewishness which surfaces at least occasionally to create havoc with carefully calculated loyalties and elaborately reasoned postures" (122). In a caustic passage strikingly reminiscent of Neil Klugman's encounter with the Patimkin's bulging refrigerator, Sabbath is inexplicably enraged by the "obscene" display of cereals, breads, and

eight jars of preserves, more or less the band of colors you get by passing sunlight through a prism: Black Cherry, Strawberry, Little Scarlet . . . all the way to Greengage Plum and Lemon Marmalade, a spectral yellow. There was half a grapefruit (segmented) under a taut sheet of Saran Wrap, a small basket of nippled oranges of a suggestive variety he'd not come across before, an assortment of tea bags in a dish beside his place setting. The breakfast crockery was that heavy yellow French stuff decorated with childlike renderings of peasants and windmills. (158)

It is immediately after his stirring encounter with the repulsive good life that Sabbath rifles through the underwear drawers of Norman's absent daughter. Caught in the act by the family's maid, Sabbath collapses after a ridiculous attempt to seduce her. The manifest failure of labido is interwoven with melancholic recollections of his dead brother and the dead past, compelling him to reconcile himself with "The-desire-not-to-be-alive-any-longer" (191). Like Zuckerman, the inevitable aging of his body forces Sabbath to confront the sterile artifice of his own bodily existence. Suffering from chronic pain caused by a crippling, disfiguring arthritis, he loses the ability to perform, sexually and otherwise. But this barren episode merely echoes the encounter which has led to his present plight, in which he cynically subjects Kathy Goolsbee, a young student, to the sterile degradation of phone sex. Both encounters form a sharp contrast with the youthful exuberance and spontaneity with which he performed in his puppet theater. Unlike the subjects of Sabbath's early street performances, in which he successfully seduced countless good-humored young women, Goolsbee eludes Sabbath's mastery and "accidentally" allows the taped recordings of their phone sex to surface as a scandal that dooms his marriage and career.

Yet in the beginning, it was good. As Sabbath recalls it, America was, for a brief time, utopian potentiality, a boundless place of

sand and ocean, horizon and sky, daytime and nighttime—the light, the dark, the tide, the stars, the boats, the sun, the mists, the gulls. There were the jetties, the piers, the boardwalk, the booming, silent, limitless sea. . . . You could touch with your toes where America began. They lived in a stucco bungalow two short streets from the edge of America. The house. The porch. The screens. The icebox. The tub. The linoleum. The broom. The pantry. The ants. The sofa. The radio. The garage. . . . In summer, the salty sea breeze and the dazzling light; in September, the hurricanes; in January, the storms. They had January, February, March, April, May, June, July, August, September, October, November, December. And then January. And then again January, no end to the stockpile of Januaries, of Mays, of Marches. August, December, April—name a month, and they had it in spades. They'd had endlessness. He'd grown up on endlessness. (30–31)

But the ailing Sabbath of bittersweet memory who conjures up the Whitmanian catalogue of a lyrical childhood has been "exiled for nearly thirty years" to a place where "he could name hardly anything." By the time that Sabbath returns to childhood's beginnings, many pages later, the site of "endlessness" shrinks to a place of reduced hopes and withered dreams. Encountering the loss of the past in the present moment, Sabbath renounces "this always-beginning, never-ending present. It's inexhastibility, he finds repugnant" (204). He has been out of touch with America for more decades even than "Rip Van Winkle," to whom he compares himself. But whereas the former missed only the Revolution, Sabbath descends from his nostalgic reverie in the mountains to a New York that is "utterly antagonistic to sanity and civil life": "A showcase for degradation, overflowing with the overflow of the slums, prisons, and mental hospitals of at least two hemispheres, tyrannized by criminals, maniacs, and bands of kids who'd overturn the world for a pair of sneakers" (189–90). After experiencing the lovelessness of the "city gone completely wrong," Sabbath seems more determined than ever to submit to the degeneration and decay, the great undertow of sadness engulfing his being.

Toward the end of the last of five satiric obituaries he composes for himself, Sabbath imagines leaving the world with the following legacy:

He is survived by the ghost of his mother, Yetta, of Beth Something-or-other Cemetery, Neptune, New Jersey, who haunted him unceasingly during the last year of his life. His brother, Lieutenant Morton Sabbath, was shot down over the Philippines during the Second World War. Yetta Sabbath never got over it. It is from his mother that Mr. Sabbath inherited his own ability never to get over anything.

Also surviving is his wife, Roseanna, of Madamaska Falls, with whom he was shacked up on the night that Miss Kantarakis disappeared or was murdered by him and her body disposed of. Mr. Sabbath is believed by Countess du Plissitas to have coerced Mrs. Sabbath, the former Roseanna Cavanaugh, into being an accomplice to the crime, thus initiating her plunge into alcoholism.

Mr. Sabbath did nothing for Israel. (194–95)

Of course it is the last, sardonic indictment, slyly appended as if a mere afterthought, that parodies the communitarian measure with which *all* Jews are finally judged in such obituaries. In a vain attempt to overcome the glaring fact of his loss of Zion, eros, and self, Sabbath attempts to return to his origins, like his author revisiting the past with an increasingly urgent nostalgia. Embodying the pariah Jew without roots or ties to the past, Sabbath is constantly depicted in various states of physical and existential instability and exhaustion: "[Sabbath] clutched the edge of a street vendor's stand. . . . Thoughts went on independently of him, scenes summoning themselves up while he seemed to wobble perilously on a slight rise between where he was and where he wasn't. He was trapped in a process of self-division that was not at all merciful" (201).

For Roth, Sabbath is a surrogate for the postassimilationist Jew who experiences his loss of the past as an annihilating force beyond his control. Disengagement is a violent, wrenching process, which Sabbath experiences as a "pale analog to what must have happened to Morty when his plane was torn apart by flak: living your life backward while spinning out of control" (201). Visiting his old neighborhood, he finds himself on the doorstep of his ancient cousin Fish, a man he assumed was long dead. For Sabbath, the one-hundred-year-old Fish perversely embodies "[t]he incapacity to die . . . *the perverse senselessness of just remaining*" (384). Sabbath knows that he himself is just around the corner from Fish, a deaf and senile old man with urine stains on his pants. Where Sabbath had hoped to rediscover the vitality of the past and perhaps the potential for renewal of his own selfhood, he finds only further confirmation of loss and decay.

The true significance in Sabbath's encounter with the forces of thanatos—death, impotence, loss—relates to Roth's mythic representation of the annihilation of the Jewish subject. Failing to get what he desperately needs from Fish—memory, community, identity—Sabbath resorts to what he knows best, namely the exploitation of others (that is the essential nature of the pariah) by stealing from his decrepit cousin the box containing his dead brother's personal effects, which besides Morty's track letter, photos, purple heart, and dog tags, include a Bible, yarmulke, and American flag. Like his encounter with the failing Fish, the relief in discovering the artifacts that bear witness to his dead brother's existence proves all too transient a consolation, for "they transformed nothing, abated nothing, neither merged him with what was gone nor separated him from what was here" (413). There is not a more succinct nor abject description of the failure of Jewish continuity in all of Roth's oeuvre.

In spite of the manifest impermanence and inhospitable nature of the past, Sabbath fetishistically places his brother's red, white, and blue yarmulke on his head, cloaking himself in the American flag that shrouded Morty's body as though in substitution for a Jewish prayer shawl, "determined never again to dress otherwise."[1] Knowing fully what his greenhorn parents were forced to learn (and conjuring up the foundational, greenhorn narratives of Cahan and Yezierska), he struggles futilely to reverse the cultural consequences of their performance: "A man of mirth must always dress in the priestly garb of his sect. Clothes are a masquerade anyway. When you go outside and see everyone in clothes, then you know for sure that nobody has a clue as to why he was born and that, aware of it or not, people are perpetually performing in a dream" (413). Like Zuckerman, Sabbath's sterility represents Roth's repudiation of the traditional Jewish notion of holy sparks leaping across the gap between generations. Instead of the weight of tradition, Sabbath witlessly bears a scrap of cloth that conceals an uncertain message.

Sabbath's quest began with the death of his beloved Drenka, and so he returns to her at the novel's end. It is Drenka's death, more than any of the numerous losses narrated, that convinces Sabbath of his own manifest decline and hollowness. Though once rejecting the disembodied presence of his dead mother ("There are no ghosts"), he can no longer resist the eerily seductive logic of her final words: "'Wrong. There are only ghosts'" (162). At the end of it all, eros and thanatos again mingle as Sabbath (fondly recalling the "golden showers" the lovers once shared) urinates on his lover's grave: "[t]o drill a hole in her grave! To drive through the coffin's lid to Drenka's mouth! . . . He was to urine what a wet nurse is to milk. Drenchèd Drenka, bubbling spring, mother of moisture and overflow, surging, streaming Drenka, drinker of the juices of the human vine—sweetheart, rise up before you turn to dust, come back and be revived, oozing all your secretions!" But at the end, Sabbath confronts the enormity of failure, the lasting legacy of his sterility: "even by watering all spring and summer . . . he could not bring her back, either Drenka or anyone else" (445).

Underscoring his cultural sterility, Sabbath's penis (like Pipik's) no longer "performs," reduced to "a spout without menace or significance of any kind, intermittently dripping as though in need of repair" (445). Nor is he able to complete even this pathetically symbolic gesture toward fecundity, for he is interrupted by the arrival of Drenka's son, flashing the lights of his police car: "Stop what you are doing, sir! *Stop now!*" . . . You are pissing on my mother's grave!" (445). Like the righteous Naomi who punishes Alexander Portnoy, Matthew Balich descends on the unzipped performer, whose traces of oozing physicality are all that remain of the once-vital puppeteer and ventriloquist: "You desecrate my mother's grave. You desecrate the American flag. You desecrate your own people. With your stupid fucking prick out, wearing the skullcap of your own religion! . . . Wrapped in the flag"(446). At this terrible moment of confrontation with the athletic young cop, Sabbath's (the "anti-illusionist") inner voice confesses that "[h]e had not realized how very long he'd been longing to be put to death. He hadn't committed suicide, because he was waiting to be murdered" (445, 450).

Like a taunting Jewish comic on stage, Sabbath is "fixed in the spotlight as though he were alone among the tombstones to perform a one-man show, Sabbath star of the cemetery, vaudevillian to the ghosts, front-line entertainer to the troops of the dead," until he is taken briefly into custody. But after a brief exchange, the cop, virile goy that he is, merely ejects the Jew from the police car in disgust. Still intent on provoking the cop into an act of redemptive violence, a suicidal Sabbath desperately spells out his pariah status: "I'm a ghoul! I'm a ghoul! After causing all this pain, the ghoul is running free! *Matthew!*" (451). But the cruiser drives off, and Sabbath perversely pulls back from the brink of destruction: "he couldn't do it. He could not fucking die. How could he leave? How could he go? Everything he hated was here" (451). Fleeing both death and American domesticity, Sabbath ends as wanderer and loser, a discarded clown who cannot give up on his circular journey of skeptical destructiveness. Defeated and yet unconquerable, Sabbath is the Jewish luftmensch sublime, and the narrative that he outlives is as devastating a subversion of Jewish utopianism as are Roth's critiques of Hebrews in Zion.

Though others have offered readings of the *Counterlife* and *Operation Shylock* as celebrations of the inventiveness and indeterminacy of the Jewish subject, *Sabbath's Theater* represents an exponentially darker phase in Roth's examination of the post-assimilationist Jewish self that is notably less supportive of such readings. That the novel may actually constitute an extended allegory that passes self-judgement on the writer's own career becomes eerily apparent in a telling comment Roth made years earlier. Indeed, the tormented trickster Sabbath is foreshadowed in the very terms with which Roth describes the writer's art: "Think of the ventriloquist. He speaks so that his voice appears to proceed from someone at a distance from himself. . . . His art consists of being present *and* absent; he's most himself by simultaneously being someone else, neither of whom he 'is' once the curtain is down" (Searles 167).

◆

Over the years, Roth's more attentive critics have noted ways in which each successive novel may be read as a riposte to the previous. Thus the outrageous protagonist of *Sabbath's Theater* is followed by a somber meditation on the losses incurred in becoming the "Swede," a Jew so bland that he has even shed Jewish irony as if that exigent quality of diasporic self-consciousness was a vestigial trace of something whose function he no longer requires or even recalls. *American Pastoral* is, by far, Roth's most claustrophobic novel. Unlike earlier narratives in which his characters exuberantly pursue the option of lighting out for the open spaces of America or even the Middle

East, most of its intense emotions are acted out within the setting of a single family, most of which is contained within the elaborately deconstructed space of a disastrous dinner party. It concerns the fate of Swede Levov, a post-ethnic, post-assimilation businessman who has successfully left behind the industrial, urban culture of his Jewish immigrant parents for a life in which he can dabble in such pastoral pleasures as cattle-breeding and enjoy the rewards of his marriage to an Irish American beauty queen and a house made of stones assembled from Revolutionary War campsites.

His life is an assimilationist fantasy come true, exponentially more ambitious than Neil Klugman's desire to leave poor Newark for the fleshpots of Short Hills and Brenda Patimkin's (still recognizably Jewish) upper-middle-class family, and like *Portnoy*, its bleak outcome is ensured. In his audacious forgetting, Swede resembles classical figures such as Job, or even the tormented conformist Willy Loman in Arthur Miller's *Death of a Salesman*. But the singular disaster that overtakes Swede, who has completely bought into America's mythic vision of itself, has uniquely Rothian proportions. The well-ordered world of rationality, good manners, and good taste will be abysmally desecrated by Merry, the Swede's own terrorist daughter, described as "a pariah exiled in the very country where her family had triumphantly rooted itself in every possible way."

In the mid-nineties, soon after the novel appeared, at a time when Roth's power to arouse true controversy seemed to have been long extinguished, he was suddenly once again the subject of a charge that he was insufficiently sensitive to—even outright against—those who most needed his support. But this time the attack came from an unexpected quarter, the Jewish Left. In a (1997) article, Michael Lerner, publisher and editor of *Tikkun*, accused Roth not only of a willful distortion of 1960s radical culture but of having failed to get with the program: "Philip Roth never joined us in taking the next step: imagining an alternative and trying to build it. Trapped in the isolating individualism of the 1950s mind-set . . . Roth shared its individualist and anti-communitarian assumptions" ("The Jews and the 60s" 13). For Lerner, Roth was woefully "tone-deaf" to the higher vision of "us," which means that unlike Lerner he failed to sign on to the struggle of the Children of Light against the Children of Darkness: "emotionally most of us were intuitively in tune with the Weathermen's insistence that we had an absolute moral obligation to fight this war with every fibre of our moral sensibilities" (15). Hence, Lerner is dismayed that the novel offers no redeeming portrayals of the radical left. Indeed, the only sixties activist to appear in the novel is poor Merry herself. Since she is an even more pathetically dysfunctional and grotesque creature than Portnoy or Sabbath, Lerner's offended literary piety is as heart-felt as was Syrkin's: "for those who saw Roth as the writer who was on the side of the kids, the guy we believed could 'see through hypocrisy' and expose its ludicrous underbelly, this book will force a serious re-evaluation. Many will question how much Roth ever really understood about what was happening around him" (15). The failures of a Judaism tainted by American materialism and selfishness are Roth's failures as well: "This cynicism makes him unable to understand the soul of people who actually are moved by prin-ciples" (16). But Lerner's essay seems to have been written about a work that he wishes Roth had written rather than about *American Pastoral*. Hasty to defend the Weatherman politics of the sixties ("most of the violence emanat-ing from the antiwar movement was not the product of the movement but of paid police agents"), Lerner forgets that, just as in *The Counterlife* (a novel he purports to admire, for what he takes as its "progressive politics"), Roth takes great pains to create a political dialectic, or actually a plurality of voices rang-ing from Johnsonian democrats to Merry herself, an impassioned protester. In the end, Lerner's Roth, "having given up on the hopes for social transfor-mation" (16), is the real disappointment of Weequahic, a villain indistin-guishable from the novelist's fictional oeuvre of masturbators and selfish seekers of fame and money. What Lerner fails to understand is that Roth's novel is actually less about the wider world of the sixties counterculture than it is yet another allegorical rephrasing of his old struggle with the losses incurred in feeling at home. For *American Pastoral* is about the sixties in the sense that *Sabbath's Theater* is about street art. Like most of Roth's later work, it is chiefly an elaborate allegory about Jewish assimilation and amnesia.

Like *Sabbath's Theater*, *American Pastoral* is about a lost Zion, not Pales-tine but Weequahic, writ large as a mythic site of scarcity, struggle, and Jew-ish dreaming. This was the circumscribed ethnic and ethical world of the industrious father, and what Roth says of his father in the autobiographical *The Facts* uncannily resembles his fictional oeuvre to date: "Narrative is the form that his knowledge takes, and his repertoire has never been large: fam-ily, family, family, Newark, Newark, Newark, Jew, Jew, Jew." In this new, arguably more autobiographical, phase of his career, Roth's characters are no longer in exile from Zion but rather from the past. As Louis Menand argues, Levov's fatal flaw is that he "can't go back, because the little world he came from has been closed down, vandalized, destroyed. All the little worlds of prewar America are closed down. He is in exodus from the diaspora" (94).

In order to grapple with the inner contradictions and paradoxes of the novel's opaque protagonist, Roth resurrects Nathan Zuckerman, but not in an easily recognizable form; he is a much more subdued Zuckerman than the restless and sardonic writer we last saw in *Counterlife*. The effects of prostate surgery have left him impotent, incontinent, and morosely reflective, causing Lorrie Moore to conclude (perhaps rushing to associate him with his creator) that "Zuckerman has become a melancholic poet of twilight and chagrin" ("The Wrath of Athena" 7). He seems to be on board mostly to narrate or fabricate the story of *American Pastoral*'s Job-like hero, Seymour "Swede" Levov. Zuckerman knew the "Swede" when the latter was a high-school sports star, celebrated as a symbol of hope by his entire hometown of slum-reared Jews during wartime—"a boy as close to a goy as we were going to get" (10). The eerily Aryan-looking athlete vigorously fulfills this collective assimilationist yearning by serving in the Marines, marrying his college sweetheart, Miss New Jersey of 1949, taking over his father's prosperous business, and moving out to the country where he buys a hundred-and-seventy-year-old stone farmhouse, in rural "Old Rimrock." The monumental ordinariness that he has achieved marks the end of the Jewish diaspora, which is precisely why he earns his Job-like fate. In the psychic economy of the novel, Seymour's "Hellenic" pursuit of the beauty queen is an idolatrous impulse.

Obsessed as always with Jewish libidinal urges and excess, Roth is now intent on locating the demonic underside of post-ethnic *normality*. For Levov is everything that Zuckerman, Sabbath, and Portnoy are not: irony-free, sexually well adjusted, and utterly at home. In his golden days of athletic glory, Levov's seeming aloofness and passivity "made him appear, if not divine, a distinguished cut above the more primordial humanity of just about everybody else at school" (5). Perhaps the most remarkable aspect of his achievement, and what disturbs Zuckerman the most, is Swede's apparent innocence of Jewish self-consciousness: "wit or irony is like a hitch in his swing for a kid like the Swede, irony being a human consolation and beside the point if you're getting your way as a god. Either there was a whole side to his personality that he was suppressing or that was as yet asleep or, more likely, there wasn't" (5). That absence alone is a monstrous omen for the aged Zuckerman, a precursor of a Job-like doom that awaits his childhood idol as his narrative unfolds. But what seems of equal importance is the Swede's uncanny "normality," causing Zuckerman to wonder,

Where was the Jew in him? . . . Where was the irrationality in him? . . . Where were the wayward temptations? No guile. No artifice. No mischief. All that he had eliminated to achieve his perfection. No striving, no ambivalence, no doubleness. . . .

[W]hat did he do for subjectivity? There had to be a substratum, but its composition was unimaginable. (20)

Years later, Zuckerman still wonders at the Swede's "unconscious oneness with America," which was precisely the tantalizing promise that captivates the wartime neighborhood: "The Jewishness that he wore so lightly as one of the tall, blond athletic winners must have spoken to us too—in our idolizing the Swede and his unconscious oneness with America, I suppose there was a tinge of shame and self-rejection" (20). In short, America fits the Swede just like one of the gloves his Weequahic family manufactures. But of course only a self that is barely Jewish can be fully at ease with the paradigmatic American mold.

Even as a youngster, Nathan Zuckerman was dazzled by the ease with which the ironically named Seymour (Roth's blindest protagonist to date) projected a sense of at-homeness. The Swede embodies the fondest assimilationist fantasies of the first immigrant generation of Jewish dreamers:

Conflicting Jewish desires awakened by the sight of him were simultaneously becalmed by him; the contradiction in Jews who want to fit in and want to stand out, who insist they are different and insist they are no different, resolved itself in the triumphant spectacle of this Swede who was actually only another of our neighborhood Seymours whose forbears had been Solomons and Sauls and who would themselves beget Stephens who would in turn beget Shawns. (20)

But incredibly, that process somehow transforms his daughter, Merry, a precocious and idealistic teenager, into an enraged terrorist inspired to "bring the war home." What Merry hopes to make visible to her blinkered father is that in fact it is his decent hope to sustain ordinariness that is monstrously unreasonable. A chronic stutterer, Merry's iconoclasm evokes Moses, Judaism's archetypal disabled speaker, though ironically, she would lead the Israelites out of the Promised Land back into the wilderness. As Merry sees it, the United States has destroyed the rural life of South Vietnam through genocidal policies. And so it follows that her parents are members of a morally obtuse middle class so engaged in adding to their material well-being in "Zion" that they cannot see the suffering of the Vietnamese. But the Swede, for whom the glove metaphor is a lived reality, cannot even begin to comprehend his aberrant offspring: "Hate America? Why he lived in America the way he lived inside his own skin. All the pleasures of his younger years were American pleasures, all that success and happiness had been American and he need no longer keep his mouth shut about it just to defuse her ignorant hatred" (157). Nevertheless, in 1968 the profoundly unhappy sixteen-year-old progeny of the mixed marriage sets off a bomb in the Old Rimrock post office, killing a beloved local doctor.

Seymour and Dawn ultimately divorce, the idyllic home is sold, and the family glove business transported to Puerto Rico after failing to adjust to the demographic shifts and violence of the inner city where it originated. Merry disappears in the murky Vietnam-era underground where she remains hidden from the Swede until the summer of 1973, when Seymour discovers that she is living a solitary existence in a hellish downtown Newark building. Roth seems unwilling to offer much in the way of explanation of just why the assimilation of his characters necessarily produces such monstrous creatures as Merry or Sabbath, whose bodily decay and vermin-like qualities fulfill antisemitic myths no less than Kafka's Gregor Samsa. In any case, the descendants of those who would deny their peoplehood face invariably bleak outcomes in Roth's latest phase as a commentator on the Jewish American scene. When Seymour finds her in a "piss-soaked" hovel that is "worse than her greenhorn great-grandparents . . . fresh from steerage" had endured, Merry is unwashed, criminally insane, and he cannot comprehend the unraveling of his life: "Three generations. All of them growing. The working. The saving. The success. Three generations in raptures over America. Three generations of becoming one with a people. And now with a fourth it had all come to nothing. The total vandalization of their world" (237). The abrupt, stacatto sentences are the futile utterances of a man whose life has spun irrevocably out of control: "You're not my daughter. You are not Merry," he informs his only progeny, as the chaotic enormity of displacement begins to shatter his precious myth of rootedness.[2] Now a practicing Jain, ironically veiled so as not to inadvertently do harm to microscopic organisms, and living under five strict vows of renunciation, which, though not the 613 commandments of *Halacha*, are oddly reminiscent of the inconvenience and discomfort that Jewish Orthodoxy imposes, Merry signifies a grotesque "caricature": "They wanted to kill him off with the story of a pariah exiled in the very country where her family had triumphantly rooted itself in every possible way, and so he refused to be convinced by anything she had said" (263). Reeling as much from the manifest physical decay and degradation of his daughter and her inane rhetoric as from her confession to four murders, in a frenzied state of denial and grief, Seymour transgresses the Jewish taboo against violence. Forcing her mouth open as if to summon forth the demon that possesses her, he is shattered by self-recognition brought about as "at last the *true* smell of her reached him (265, emphasis added): "Her foulness had reached him. She is disgusting. . . . Her smell is the smell of everything organic breaking down. It is the smell of no coherence" (265). As his vomit spews forth from him, the radical decomposition of Seymour and Merry are one and the same, embodying the fate of the hopes, lives, and investment in ordinariness of "three generations" of Jewish Americans.

American Pastoral is a novel caught between the sheer potentiality of Jewish life and "no coherence"—a pessimistic outlook that hints that, in escaping from the small Jewish world of struggling Weequahic's neighborhood and working-class families, the Swede has fatally compromised himself. Roth, who at a crucial phase in his career was highly cognizant of the tradition of monstrous and humiliating transformations and transferences of identity that occur in the family dramas of other Jewish writers, such as Bruno Schulz and Franz Kafka, has little trouble in conjuring up his own horrific nightmare of assimilation. Terrified by his monster-daughter, Levov turns to his brother Jerry, who seems to have been waiting for years for the opportunity to expose his brother's assimilationist utopianism as an inane fallacy:

You wanted Miss America? Well, you've got her, with a vengeance—she's your daughter! You wanted to be a real American jock, a real American marine, a real American hotshot with a beautiful Gentile babe on your arm? You longed to belong like everybody else to the United States of America? Well, you do now, big boy, thanks to your daughter. The reality of this place is right up in your kisser now. With the help of your daughter you're as deep in the shit as a man can get, the real American crazy shit. America amok! America amuck! (277)

This is a story about colossal misjudgments and maladjustments, but of all it is a matter of *tone*. First there is the disconsolate distraction of Zuckerman's muted narration—incontinent and unhappy in his premature old age and isolation, he seems too exhausted to live, except perhaps to serve as a witness to the Swede's staggering demise. But what is really doomed here is the Newark Jews' collective dream, in which Zuckerman (in an address he imagines giving at his forty-fifth high school reunion), implicates himself as well, even at the height of his nostalgia: "The place was bright with industriousness. There was a big belief in life and we were steered relentlessly in the direction of success: a better existence was going to be ours. The goal was to have goals, the aim to have aims" (41). At first Zuckerman notably fails to understand what has gone wrong with the Swede's life; his ignorance parallels the Swede's (if not the reader's) own delusion over the costs incurred by the American dream. In spite of his resolve "to respect everything one is supposed to respect, to protest nothing; never to be inconvenienced by self-distrust; never to be enmeshed in obsession, tortured by incapacity, poisoned by resentment, driven by anger," everything unravels to a degree as spectacularly and unfairly punitive as the cruelties visited upon Job.

If Zuckerman is Roth's surrogate, it may be that old Lou Levov, Seymour's father, the retired glove manufacturer, is a ghostly echo of Roth's father, ranting (as the latter often does in *Patrimony*) about lost values and community. At a dinner party, Lou amuses the indulgent WASP-ish gentry with an explosive tirade directed against their decadent upbringing of their children. The dinner party, occupying fully one-third of the novel's four-hundred-odd pages, exposes the inner decay of Seymour's entire generation, causing the Swede, who has struggled manfully to serve as a buffer between his father and the latter's liberal persecutors, to experience a sudden revelation: "His daughter was an insane murderer hiding on the floor of a room in Newark, his wife had a lover who dry-humped her over the sink in their family kitchen, his ex-mistress had knowingly brought disaster upon his house, and he was trying to propitiate his father with the on-the-one-hand-this and on-the-other-hand-that" (358). Relenting, at the end of a life that has utterly unraveled, he is clearing a social space for his father's outrage to at last penetrate: "degrading things should *not* be taken in their stride! I say *lock* them in their rooms if they take this in their stride! I remember when kids used to be at home doing their homework and not out seeing movies like this. This is the morality of a country that we're talking about" (358). Lou Levov's splenetic outburst in the bourgeois interior of Waspish America has interesting effects. Not only does it erupt like a prophetic jeremiad through an otherwise restrained and modulated, almost Jamesian novel. He effectively "outs" himself—and his son—as undomesticated Jews. Like Zuckerman's uncivil performance in England, like Sabbath's desecrations, Roth is eager for Levov to rebel against the shallow decorum demanded by his Gentile hosts. As John Murray Cuddihy (always a wise companion to read alongside Roth) notes: "Intensity, fanaticism, inwardness—too much of *anything*, in fact—is unseemly and bids fair to destroy the fragile solidarity of the surface we call civility" (13–14). Roth's Jews have always rebelled against Emancipation's "gentling," exposing themselves, but if the diaspora liberalism of the Swede has any meaning, it is that there is no longer a viable subculture to expose. Ironically, his father's "bad form" at the decorous social gathering is reminiscent of Sabbath's desecration of his old friend and business associate's placid haven of civility and good taste, though of course the old man's disturbance of order is based on moral outrage.

Still, if for the most part *American Pastoral* appears hostile to the Swede's pursuit of the Catholic Miss New Jersey, money, and status, there is actually a strong undercurrent of admiration for Jewish ambition. Portnoy would certainly have embraced the essential terms of this emancipatory "desire to go the limit in America with your rights, forming yourself as an ideal person who gets rid of the traditional Jewish habits and attitudes, who frees himself of the pre-America insecurities and the old, constraining obsessions so as to live unapologetically as an equal among equals" (41). In part it is the quintessential American rhetoric in which these sentiments are grounded that makes the downfall of the Swede so terrible to behold, as blandness, self-satisfaction, and happiness prove deadly in his WASP-ish success story.

Perhaps because of this, Roth's novel succeeds on a more macro scale than anything he has previously attempted. Documenting the hopes and fears of an entire class, it has great cultural insights into the experience of generations of Jewish Americans. But this novel also achieves a great deal on a different level, suggesting that Roth's concerns are not primarily with the epic political and social dimensions of Jewish American life, but rather with the spiritual condition of his characters' inner lives. And precisely because Roth's vision is so tightly focused on what befalls a single assimilated individual—struck by "a sliver off the comet of the American chaos"—*American Pastoral* does rise to a "universalist" tone that has been the hallmark of Jewish literary parochialism, from Kafka to Arthur Miller and Bernard Malamud:

He was really living it out, his vision of paradise. This is how successful people live. They're good citizens. They feel lucky. They feel grateful. God is smiling down on them. There are problems, they adjust. And then everything changes and it becomes impossible. Nothing is smiling down on anybody. And who can adjust then? . . . Who is set up for tragedy and the incomprehensibility of suffering? Nobody. The tragedy of the man not set up for tragedy—that is every man's tragedy. (81)

"Lost himself to his own people": Self-Liberation and Revelation in *The Human Stain*

For Roth, as for Reznikoff, Jewish tradition enacts a restless questioning, but in Israel and America, his questing Jewish subject discovers that this paradigm is forgotten by communities that increasingly share little else besides complacent self-satisfaction. Roth's elegiac novels about woeful characters may one day be judged as an appropriate coda for an age witnessing the twilight of Jewish cultural impact. His career constitutes the most wide-ranging acknowledgment of the disappearance of Jewish neighborhoods as well as of the obsolescence of ghetto and Zionist nostalgia alike. But thus far he has been unable or unwilling to speculate on alternative forms of Jewish identification. In the end—and the rich irony is inescapable—no other writer has taken with the same seriousness Syrkin's insistence that in the American Diaspora the forces of acculturation and secularism would utterly erode the claims of piety and peoplehood. There are recent signs that Roth has begun to think about this problem across ethnic lines as a profoundly American tragedy.

In *Goodbye Columbus*, Neil is torn between his ambition and his empathy for Carlota, the Patimkins' black maid, and a little black boy who visits the public library where he works. Each quietly suggests a core of "authenticity," a racial identity that, unlike that of the suburban Jews, *can't* be compromised or made invisible. In the novel's racialized construction of authenticity the former seemingly *can't* assimilate. But in *The Human Stain* (2000), Roth conjures up an African-American character whose light-colored skin and his ambitions enable him to overcome the fatal trap of race. Perhaps not since the Harlem Renaissance writer Nella Larsen, in *Quicksand* (1928) and *Passing* (1929), brilliantly limned the psychic conflict of the subject caught between black and white worlds has an American novelist so provocatively placed the individual's spectres of guilty betrayal, inner rage, and quest for authenticity in the context of examining an America obsessed with the seductions and dangers of reinventing oneself. In other words, *The Human Stain* (2000) is much more than the novel that completes the philosophic and cultural trilogy begun powerfully with *American Pastoral* (followed by the tepid installment of *I Married a Communist* [1998]); it is a tour de force that sums up of all of Roth's previous treatments of the equivocating, rebellious, diasporic self adrift from the anchorage of identity and collective life—and ultimately transcends these themes to expose the most troubling shadows in contemporary American life. After a lifetime of laying bare his protagonists' startling self-inventions, Roth seems to have wanted to outpace his readers' expectations by conjuring up this tale of an aging "white" classics professor who has buried his blackness in the most audacious act of presumptuous transformation the novelist has conceived of yet.

This is a far-ranging work indeed—with its angry linkages between Hawthorne's indictment of American puritanism in *The Scarlet Letter* and the Clinton and Lewinsky scandal (America's "ecstasy of scandal") and its numerous subplots—featuring a variegated cast of characters ranging from a Vietnam War veteran to a breathtakingly imbecilic French literary theorist, various forms of cultural idiocy that presumably enrage the novelist. Rich with intertextual layers (besides Hawthorne, there are clear allusions to the mysterious ethnic origins of Fitzgerald's Gatsby), Roth's novel takes its place among other great American classics of double-consciousness by writers such as W. E. B. Du Bois, James Weldon Johnson, and Jessie Fauset. Not only does it audaciously resurrect their ways of framing the fate of the tragic mulatto, but it creates a richly imagined protagonist whose utilitarian betrayals of the claims of family and peoplehood at once sustain and richly complicate the central concerns of his career. Though ostensibly *The Human Stain* may be the least "Jewish" of Roth's latest novels, coming to terms with the plight of its tormented hybrid hero is a fitting way for us to take our leave of the novelist's recent career. In imagining a character who could "color himself just as he chose" (109), Roth sets the stage for the most combative staging of the war between the self and the collective to date.

The central plot concerns Coleman Silk, an elderly professor of classics who has resigned from his post at a New England college to which he had devoted his life. Accused of using hurtful language in his classroom, the distinguished ex-dean, who single-handedly transformed Athena College from its modest origins into a reputable institution, is forced to resign amidst other rites of purification that have overtaken America at the close of the century. But the real story is that Coleman Silk is a black man who decided to pass himself off as a white Jew, "the first and only Jew ever to serve at Athena as dean of faculty." Ever since his early days, hurting his father by dedicating his adolescence to boxing, Silk has been going it alone, testing his ever-expanding potential for self-liberation.

Though a number of critics have seized on the notion that Coleman Silk's duplicitous act of "passing" may have been inspired by Henry Louis Gates Jr.'s representation of the life of Anatole Broyard, a *New York Times* critic who died in 1990, in the former's *13 Ways of Looking at a Black Man* (1997), Roth tells it differently. Apparently, the consequences of self-transformation, self-invention, and the alternative destiny have been haunting his thought since his days as a graduate student at the University of Chicago, where he had a brief interracial relationship:

I don't think I'd understood before then that a black middle class of any size existed, and her family came as news to me. . . . Anyway, we began to go out, and I met the family, who were very pale Negroes, decidedly so on her mother's side. And I never forgot her mother saying that there were relatives of hers who'd been lost to all their people. That was the phrase she used—"lost to all their people." The girl explained

to me later what her mother was talking about—that these relatives, who could physically pull it off, had given up identifying themselves as Negro, had moved away and
had joined the white world, never to return. And that I never forgot . . . both the story
and the people made a lasting impression. Self-transformation. Self-invention. The
alternative destiny. Repudiating the past. (Interview with Charles McGrath 8)

Interestingly, the phrase "lost to all their people" is hauntingly echoed by
Coleman Silk's sister in an exchange with Zuckerman toward the end of the
novel: "'Mother went to her grave wondering why Coleman did it. 'Lost himself to his own people.' That's how she put it'" (324).

　　Undoubtedly, as much as it planted the seed for Roth's resonant portrayal
of the light-complexioned Coleman's self-liberating exile, Roth's early encounter with the discontinuities of blackness in America strengthened his resolve to explore the shadowy subjectivities of unmoored Jews. For as always,
the greatest irony of the stories told throughout this thematic trilogy remains
to be filled in by the observant reader who notices the acute parallel between
the story told and that of its ironic witness and narrator—Zuckerman's own
rebellion and exile from his New Jersey family. Where Nathan produces a
scandalous book, the precocious Coleman emerges from a stint in the Navy,
moves to New York where people often assume he is Jewish, and jettisons
"the whole ramified Negro thing." In freeing themselves from other people's
definitions and expectations, both men cast themselves adrift. For his part,
Silk spends the following four decades as an academic committed to "serious
things," relieved from his blackness.

　　Ironically, Zuckerman has taken Silk for one of just a handful of Jews who
penetrated the English and classics departments of academia in Zuckerman's
own generation—Roth's sly wink perhaps back toward Irving Howe and
Lionel Trilling. In a haunting juxtaposition of black Jewish identities, Zuckerman and Silk fox-trot together on the latter's porch: "'Come. Let's dance.'
'But you mustn't sing into my ear.' . . . He led, and, as best I could, I followed" (25). Mindful of his own impotence after cancer surgery ("a harmless
eunuch") the once-dionysiac Zuckerman eagerly responds to "this still vital,
potent participant in the frenzy" of life:

I gave him my hand and let him place his arm around my back and push me dream-
ily around that old bluestone floor. . . . On we danced. There was nothing overtly carnal in it, but because Coleman was wearing only his denim shorts and my hand
rested easily on his warm back as if it were the back of a dog or a horse, it wasn't
entirely a mocking act. There was a semi-serious sincerity in his guiding me about on
the stone floor, not to mention a thoughtless delight in just being alive. (37)

This black and Jewish dance may be the most magical and fulfilled moment in all of Roth's recent fiction, clarifying what some readers may have long suspected; Roth's attitudes toward the erotic life and ethnic difference are remarkably congruent. At least in the moment when Zuckerman, bemused by the homoerotic overtone of dancing with Silk to the strains of "Bewitched, Bothered, and Bewildered," contemplates the "contaminant of sex, the redeeming corruption that de-idealizes the species and keeps us everlastingly mindful of the matter we are" (37). For no less than the frailty of the flesh, "Blackness" and "Jewishness" (whatever these might mean) are part of the "human stain"—by which Roth intends not its stigma but its redolent life. And Zuckerman is not so blind as to deny the ironic mirroring of his and Silk's combative identities: "The dance that sealed our friendship was also what made his disaster my subject. And made his disguise my subject" (45). For of course "disguise" has always been Zuckerman's special province. In this sense, each man seems to be an agent of revelation for the other. But alas, this is to be one of the last encounters between the two men: "I did no more than find a friend, and all the world's malice came rushing in" (45). For, in an ironic turn that is all too consistent with Silk's classical training, the man who has lived as a Jew earns a Jew's death, brought on by his lover's antisemitic ex-husband whose experiences in Vietnam transformed into a vicious psychotic. In the wake of Silk's tragic demise, Zuckerman is left to struggle futilely to redeem another's tragedy through narrative justice, all the more poignant because Nathan's "commentary" is, as always, two-thirds an act of his own imagination.

Coleman's father, whose love for Shakespeare leads him to bestow his son with the fraught middle name of "Brutus" from *Julius Ceasar*—"the most educational study of treason ever written" (92)—seems to set in motion Silk's fate, as betrayer of his father's ideals. Soon, his father not long in the grave, Silk joins the navy as a white man, an act of hubris that culminates in "the worst night of his life"—a degrading incident at a famous white whorehouse in Norfolk from which bouncers hurl him violently onto the street, which leads to an alcoholic binge to deaden the pain of the injuries inflicted on him. His uniform bespattered from his own blood and vomit, Silk experiences one of his few moments of self-knowledge:

This was what came of failing to fulfill his father's ideals, of flouting his father's commands, of deserting his dead father altogether. . . . If he kept this up, his life would amount to nothing. How did Coleman know that? Because his father was speaking back to him—the old admonishing authority rumbling up once again from his father's

chest. Look at where he was now. . . . Why? Because of his credo, because of his inso-
lent, arrogant "I am not one of you, I can't bear you, I am not part of your Negro we"
credo. The great heroic struggle against their we—and look at what he now looked
like! The passionate struggle for precious singularity, his revolt of one against the
Negro fate—and just look where the defiant great one had ended up! The tragic,
reckless thing that you've done! (182–83)

Decades later he is still secretly haunted by this humiliating setback to his
ambition, which curiously foreshadows his later degradation by academia.
But apart from this occasion, with its near-Shakespearean epiphany, Coleman Brutus Silk never again questions his relentless course toward self-
actualization.

Of all the illuminating ironies that enrich this eventful novel, the most
revealing may be the linguistic trap that has caused Professor's Silk's disgrace
and exile—his choice of the word "spooks" in class upon looking up from his
roll sheet to inquire about the whereabouts of two students who have failed
to show up by the sixth week of class: "Does anyone know these people? Do
they exist or are they spooks?" obviously employing the word in its primary
dictionary definition of "ghosts or specters." But when it is discovered that
the two missing students are black the innocent remark is mistaken for an
archaic racial slur; when an infuriated Silk refuses to apologize, his "resigna-
tion" is inevitable. But as ridiculous as the academic community's condem-
natory political correctness might be, there is nonetheless something about
Silk's jocular choice of language that is disturbing in another sense. For what
is Silk's choice of the awkward idiom but a rupture of the uncanny, Roth's
notion of "identity" rushing in to lay claim to the being who has tried to
smother it?

Not much time passes after this episode when Professor Silk, disgusted
with his well-meaning but condescending lawyer (who has no notion of his
client's actual origins), angrily dismisses him with the strange remark: "I
never again want to hear that self-admiring voice of yours or see your smug
fucking lily-white face" (81). Strange that is, until the reader stumbles across
the last angry words spoken to Coleman by his brother after learning of
Coleman's treatment of their mother: "*Never*. Don't you dare ever show your
lily-white face around that house again!" (145). At this point it seems evident
that—tormented as he is by the linguistic echoes and utterances that seemingly burst forth from him of their own accord—Coleman Silk is haunted by
nothing more nor less than the ghost within him, of his own repressed past.

"Spooks" and now "lily-white" . . . as witness and chronicler of his friend's rapid downfall, Zuckerman is befuddled by the latter's use of "faintly anti-quated locutions" and perhaps alarmed by the deeper meanings encrypted in the utterances that come "flying from his mouth" (84). Perhaps this can be explained in part by briefly drawing from the "relief theory" that has been argued from Freud onward, namely that laughter is the result of energy discharge. On this account, when we laugh, we do so because a quantum of otherwise unneeded nervous energy has gained release. Instead of the more conventional notion that laughter is a demonstration of domination and tri-umph, laughter for Freud acts much like a release valve that allows for the expression of otherwise forbidden impulses (*Jokes and Their Relation to the Unconscious* 290). The origins of Silk's manipulation of identity may lie in what the psychoanalytic community identifies as "play," with all its duplici-tous forms of humor. Since a child, Silk has continually tinkered with family ties and identity as if they were things devoid of meaning. Hence, Silk's "innocent" classroom jest has all the surface appearance of joking but actu-ally harbors a traumatized psyche's deeper purposes. The linguistic release of a joke circumvents the psychological inhibitions that have been erected in us, and in so doing liberates psychic energy. Silk's joking remark is "tenden-tious" in Freud's sense, deriving from the tapping of deep, repressed forces that can ultimately be traced back to the id instincts of life and death. And for Silk, insofar as the "joke" of his repressed identity has arguably contributed to the demise of his mother, and later, his wife's fatal heart-attack, "life and death" are indeed the high stakes of his deception.

It is of the utmost importance to note that the narrative never suggests that Silk's eventual willingness to be taken for a Jew, by his colleagues, his wife, and later his children, embodies any spiritual or philosophical affinity for Judaism. For Silk has no more desire to embrace the collective "we" than any other of Roth's secular heroes. On the contrary, the novel's ingenious prem-ise is that Silk's cunning choice is no more or less than a disguise in the flight from his own "we." The son of a New Jersey optician, Coleman Silk discov-ers in his early twenties that he can easily pass for white—and in that "pass-ing" abandon his family and origins. In his Zuckerman-like logic, such seem-ingly modern constructs as "Afrocentrism" and "black consciousness" are merely the regrettable shackles of idolatry: "Ancestor worship—that's how Coleman put it. Honoring the past was one thing—the idolatry that is ances-tor worship was something else. The hell with that imprisonment" (144). Silk is Roth's most persuasive apologist ever for the American Dream. For as a young boxer (a vocation that his father struggles in vain to halt) in the forties he is taken on a tour of white colleges by a sympathetic Jewish trainer, where he first encounters the hypnotic allure of invisibility. Soon after this revelation, Silk leaves home determined to leave behind the contemptuous, energy-draining "Ur of we" to savor the intoxicating pleasures of the manifestly diasporic "I." When all is said and done, what is most compelling about the ever-spontaneous Coleman Silk (as with Roth's Jewish heroes) is the sheer *reasonableness* of his position. It is difficult to see in his quest for fulfillment a betrayal. "He was Coleman, the greatest of the great *pioneers* of the I. . . . You can't let the big they impose its bigotry on you any more than you can let the little they become a we and impose its ethics on you. . . . Never for him the tyranny of the we that is dying to suck you in, the coercive, inclusive, historical, inescapable moral *we* with its insidious *E pluribus unum*" (108). Like Portnoy and the other Jewish sons who long to escape their stifling origins, Silk yearns to let out "the raw I with all its agility. *Self*-discovery—*that* was the punch to the labonz. Singularity. The passionate struggle for singularity. The singular animal" (108). Even after his life has unraveled Coleman refuses to allow guilt to taint his sense of his liberation as anything less than a lofty, principled achievement that fulfills the nation's highest ideals of the fulfillment of individual promise. He was neither "radical, revolutionary, embittered anarchist, nor madman"—"unless it is revolutionary to believe that disregarding prescriptive society's most restrictive demarcations and asserting independently a free personal choice that is well within the law was something other than a basic human right—unless it is revolutionary, when you've come of age, to refuse to accept automatically the contract drawn up for your signature at birth" (155). But in imagining that by simply marrying a Jewish woman whose kinky hair will prevent any awkward questions about the texture of his children's hair, Silk sets in motion the inevitable resentments of his progeny (not to mention the family he lives behind), who inevitably await the Rothian deceiver, like the denouement of a Greek tragedy.

Besides being a fitting doppelganger for Zuckerman, there is a little bit of Mickey Sabbath in Silk too, for in the wake of the racist scandal and his new status as a pariah, he finds himself, at age 71, liberated by Viagra and throwing himself into an affair with Faunia Farley, an emotionally and physically battered woman whose illiteracy liberates her intellectual lover from "the ridiculous quest for significance." By the end of the novel, Silk is both "pariah and renegade" (332), the punitive markers by which Roth's independent heroes are inevitably known as a natural condition of their quest for existential freedom. But of all Roth's Jewish heroes to whom he might be compared, Silk most resembles the Swede of *American Pastoral*, his self-confidence and optimism reminiscent of the latter's intrinsic boyishness: "the quickness, the urge to action that we used to call pep." And he shares the latter's eventual "weariness and spiritual depletion" (15). But in crossing racial lines, it is evident that Roth was gesturing to a tragedy that is at once as profoundly American as it is parochial.

As laden with a sense of a classical tragedy unfolding as is Silk's own tense narrative, the quiet presence of Zuckerman as the receiver and interpreter of these events may be its most compelling feature. For instance, we cannot fail to be struck that, in his advanced years, Zuckerman is thinking about how the most intrinsic feature of any act of "passing" or self-transformation is its *cruelty*: "To become a new being. To bifurcate. The drama that underlies America's story, the high drama that is upping and leaving—and the energy and cruelty that rapturous drive demands" (342). In response to Silk's Machiavellian transformation, Zuckerman finds himself musing in wonder, "did he get, from his decision, the adventure he was after, or was the decision in itself the adventure? . . . Was he merely being another American and, in the great frontier tradition, accepting the democratic invitation to throw your origins overboard if to do so contributes to the pursuit of happiness?" (334). These eerily resemble the questions Nathan had asked years earlier of Henry after the latter's reinvention of himself as a zealous West Bank settler. But more to the point, this is the question that Roth has been asking about the choices made in the wake of American affluence all along.

From the moment that Neil Klugman begins to lust to exchange his sweltering and claustrophobic Newark origins for the cool pastoral heights of Short Hills, Roth has been interrogating the spiritual losses incurred in the material choices the grandchildren of Jewish immigrants who arrived in the holds of steamers have made, seemingly against their better natures. But as *The Human Stain* makes abundantly clear, the charge of carnal materialism that once made his Jewish audience squirm, is now unambiguously targeted at America's hardened individualism, which ultimately devours all. After Silk confronts his mother with his decision, she instantly seizes on the far-reaching effects of her son's "exhilarating notion of freedom":

"I'm never going to know my grandchildren. . . . You're never going to let them see me," she said. "You're never going to let them know who I am. 'Mom,' you'll tell me, 'Ma, you come to the railroad station in New York, and you sit in the bench in the waiting room, and at eleven twenty-five A.M., I'll walk by with my kids in their Sunday best.' That'll be my birthday present five years from now. 'Sit there, Mom, say nothing, and I'll just walk them slowly by.' And you know very well that I will be there. The railroad station. The zoo. Central Park. Whatever you say of course I'll do it. (137)

Though this melodramatic device is perhaps a tad too reminiscent of those old jokes about Jewish mothers being left to sit in the dark, in the novel's mythic universe of betrayal and abandonment (and Zuckerman's role as narrator) it is a development that makes chilling sense. In his sister's pointed contrast between Silk's radical individualism and that of Walt, a brother who has struggled for his people, Coleman—a figure Roth has taken great pains to make immensely sympathetic to the reader—exits the novel with feet of clay:

Her point was that Coleman was *not* one of those ex-GIs fighting for integration and equality and civil rights; in Walt's opinion, he was never fighting for anything other than himself. Silky Silk. That's who he fought as, who he fought for, and that's why Walt could never stand Coleman, even when Coleman was a boy. In it for himself, Walt used to say. In it always for Coleman alone. All he ever wanted was out. (324)

But ultimately it is not only Coleman and Zuckerman who are implicated here. In unexpected moments the old sting of Syrkin's and Podhoretz's reproaches break through this work. In Coleman's embittered rejection of what he refers to variously as "the persecuting spirit" and "the *tyranny* of propriety" the reader stumbles onto what seems to be the palimpsest of Roth's earliest struggles with the smothering, inhibiting coercions of group piety: "As a force, propriety is protean, a dominatrix in a thousand disguises, infiltrating, if need be, as civic responsibility, WASP dignity, women's rights, black pride, ethnic allegiance, or emotion-laden Jewish ethical sensitivity." For Coleman Silk, those in the community whose puritan instincts have been agitated by his relationship with Faunia Farley, are those for whom "not even that most basic level of imaginative thought had been admitted into consciousness to cause the slightest disturbance" (153). One of the novel's most penetrating moments is ironically voiced by the battered, illiterate Faunia. Contemplating the plight of a black crow whose exposure to humans has left him unfit to rejoin the tribe of birds, she remarks on the fatal consequences of "the human stain" in ways that at once illuminate the idiocies behind the Clinton scandal and the kind of essentialist identification that her lover, Silk, has struggled to liberate himself from: "all the cleansing is a joke. A barbaric joke at that. The fantasy of purity is appalling. It's insane. What is the quest to purify, if not *more* impurity?" (242).

◆

In his Israel-situated fiction, Roth interrogates the validity of the very concept of America's civic Judaism, by which Jews demonstrate their passionate support for Israel without risking any of the burdensome trappings of communal life or religion. In England and Israel, Zuckerman can make stirring speeches against antisemites and Jewish Zealots alike, in defense of diasporic liberalism. But he will not join the Jerusalem minyan; and, back "home" in America, neither Zuckerman nor any other of Roth's protagonists ever actually succeeds in locating a viable Judaism to sustain them. This is the intertextual weave that links Roth's unsettling Jewish dream of his father's disappointed corpse to the profound abjection of his characters. Like the corpse Roth dresses for eternity, there is little but thin cloth with which Sabbath can shield himself against the manifest evidence of spiritual and cultural debility.

Virtually all of Roth's recent would-be Jewish visionaries and ideologues engage in sincere quests for the "authentic," but each meets a similarly humiliating fate, whether we are speaking of the explosively fanatic Merry Levov in *American Pastoral*, the idealistic fall of Marxist Iron Rinn (born Ira Ringold) in *I Married a Communist*, or the academic community's betrayal of Professor Silk in *The Human Stain*. It is as if, at the end of the twentieth century, Roth imposes on his Jewish characters a return to the original predicament of the Emancipation. With the dissolution of the sustaining sacral center of Jewish life, nothing remains but the restraint of the modernization process. As Cuddihy remarks:

The ideology of Diaspora liberalism was essentially a decision and a utopian dream: it was the decision to remain in the West (neither emigrating nor revolting); it was the dream that, by dint of *nudzhing* and *kvetching*, litigation and voting, education and modernization, a neutral society might awake from the nightmare of history, offering neutral spaces and public places where Jew and Gentile might mingle. (230)

All well and good. But what vexes Roth's narratives is the question of what remains after this genial contract. There was a time when it seemed possible, without overreaching, for critics to read the multiplicity, open-endedness, and simultaneity of Roth's narratives as if they bore an affirmative relation to the Jewish textual tradition, where many opinions and ideologies literally coexist on a single page of Talmud.

His device of the "counterlife"—a shaping presence within his dialectical works long before its explicit articulation in *The Counterlife*—may indeed bear a family resemblance to the discursive role of the rabbinic commentaries. As Michael A. Fishbane argues, these "demonstrate the simultaneity of diverse interpretations in the lifetime of the Jew." Centuries before the supposed advent of "postmodernism," this "often polyvalent voice of tradition was . . . an ever-present reality for the Jew . . . in both the synagogue and the study house" (74). Rather than reject the viability of inherited tradition, it seemed that the post-*Portnoy* Roth secularized it, claiming it as an intrinsic feature of the assimilated Jews' existential reality. For a time it seemed as if it stood as one of the most traditional aspects of his relation to the past. But the remorselessly elegiac tone of each of the novels that has succeeded *Counter-life* has made it difficult to sustain such a reading for much longer. For where Roth is arguably *enabling*, he also insinuates a form of stagnation. In Rezni-koff's rendition of Diaspora, Jews pay the consequences of their identity, but for Roth, America is simply a site of radical irresponsibility, where Jews, like the slippery author himself, merely have the privilege of disappearing into any number of roles and guises. That Roth hasn't (or isn't quite able)—to explore other versions of Diaspora—suggests what a monumental a challenge lies ahead for future generations of Jewish American writers.

Like the canine subject of Kafka's "Investigation of a Dog," the Swede and Coleman Silk are content to live in the illusory security of forgetfulness. This is the source of Roth's comedy and also his horror. Reversing the ethos of immigration that has been so intrinsic to literary diasporism, Roth recasts the topos and telos of the Jewish journey so that the blessings of mobility are replaced by the cursed wanderings of mad daughters and old men, lost in America. Even Zuckerman is resigned to his fate as an impotent recluse, a witness to the stories of others rather than the explicator of his own. What makes it so difficult to read these late novels is that their outcomes are so pessimistically foreclosed. There is little surprise that the heretic Sabbath ends up unhappily on the edge of America, pathetically clutching his brother's shroud, or that the prosperous postassimilation, postethnic but nevertheless Job-like "Swede" sees his pastoral dream destroyed. And this produces a certain degree of incoherence. For instance, though the Swede's claim to the American pastoral via the abandonment of his Judaism presumably leads to his downfall, Roth does not presume to speculate on what the alternative to a Seymour Levov might look like. In the end, Roth, no less than Syrkin in *Gleanings*, willfully represents the landscape of Diaspora as a site of sterility. In the absence of affliction, Roth peoples his narratives with pariahs so that unruly, coarse Jews erupt from beneath the skin of the "passing" Jew of American culture and the placid New England countryside. Hence Zucker-man in *Counterlife*, along with Sabbath and Merry Levov, shares the destiny of the "proud pariahs" Cuddihy points to, who "experience Western civilization as an incognito or secularized form of Christianity, and . . . openly resist it *as* such" (231). But is it possible for Roth to imagine an alternative

Diaspora, one in which a vigorous Jewish culture endures in spite of full Gentile acceptance? Or one that espouses an identity based on a more substantive platform than its resistance to Christianity?

The perverse possibility remains that Roth's deranged characters are in fact positive models of an "authentic" inassimilable Jewishness, rather than the unconscious adherents of bourgeois civility that Cuddihy describes. Jewish "madness" becomes linked to Jewish *difference* and thus to Jewish continuity. Of a sort. Or perhaps Roth's vigorously pessimistic outlook of late is the logical consequence of a cultural imagination that in the end has not as its concern the epic of Jewishness, in or out of Israel, but rather takes as its enduringly ephemeral touchstone the memory of one ethnic Newark neighborhood.[3] In Roth's oeuvre, memory and the myths of a personal history replace collective memory and peoplehood. Like Mickey Sabbath, Roth has lately struggled to impersonate his former potent self by recovering the past, through what Debra Shostak describes as "peopling the stage with memories and ventriloquizing others who might attest to a historically present self" ("Roth/CounterRoth" 130). Roth's characters journey to old countries and old neighborhoods, but they fail to find themselves at home. Moreover, the creation of anachronistic pariah figures like Mickey Sabbath suggests the disintegration of the Jewish present into return, introspection, and loss. Sabbath's and Roth's other intuitive pariahs are not beings of higher sanity; rather, they embody highly skeptical, but ultimately helpless, even destructive, gestures toward the empowered Jewish community.

At the beginning of Philip Roth's career, the historian Isaac Deutscher described the essence of Jewish intellectual life in the pages of *Partisan Review*. While seemingly accounting for the riches of the Jewish intellectual tradition in Europe, Deutscher's model actually seemed more appropriate for a Jewish American audience than for the remnant of Jews that still remained in Europe:

Have [Spinoza, Heine, Marx, Luxemburg, Trotsky, and Freud] anything in common with each other? . . . They had in themselves something of the quintessence of Jewish life and of the Jewish intellect. They were a priori exceptional in that as Jews they dwelt on the boundaries of various civilizations, religions, and national cultures. They were born and brought up on the borderlines of various epochs. Their minds matured where the most diverse cultural influences crossed and fertilized each other. They lived on the margins or in the nooks and crannies of their respective nations . . . of it, and yet not of it. It was this that enabled them to rise in thought above their societies, above their nations, above their times and generations, and to strike out mentally into wide new horizons and far into the future. (556)

For decades since, Jewish American writing has depended on the vital myth that marginal existence engendered extraordinary creative powers. Whether in the lachrymose historiography that portrayed Jewish diasporic history as unrelenting tragedy, stimulating Lazarus's return to Jewish identity, or in the more nuanced perspective that filled the pages of *The Menorah Journal*, the creative visions of earlier generations of Jewish American writers responded to a sense that Jewish identity would remain an eternally embattled one. This paradigm valorized the writer who remained poised forever on the margins of the Jewish and Gentile worlds. Now that the verisimilitude of this marginality is coming into question, and the cultural imperative of affliction is losing relevance, writers like Roth find themselves in an unenviable position. The problem Susser and Liebman delineate—"no really adequate alternative to the view of Jewish existence as precarious, disempowered, and embattled has evolved" (27)—poses a significant challenge to the future of Jewish writing.

Writing in an age in which even greater numbers of Americans (Jewish and otherwise) feel less responsibility toward the abstract collectivities of nation and peoplehood, Roth's great topic has become the fatal detachment of the individual from the collective. Ironically, the novelist who seemingly began his career with a dionysiac celebration of the unfettered individual has lavished his creative energies in his last three novels on foreboding portrayals of detached Jewish characters who, released from the social collective, pursue self-directed lives that end disastrously. Few writers have more forcefully accepted the implicit summons of Cuddihy's imperative that "No Jew is free as long as telling the truth is *eo ipso* to become an informer to the *goyim*" (230). Yet today, Roth's novels—his antiheroic pariahs—evade the possibility of an unapologetically diasporic identity, a Judaism (not "Jewishness") in the absence of antisemitism, in an open and inviting society. Having buried Herman Roth in a shroud that will permanently mark him for eternity, Roth seems to have belatedly retreated to the once-certain demarcations of tribalism. Whether or not he will extricate himself from the mythological place where he is currently grounded, from his present binary signifiers of diasporic identity, to produce a Jewish subject that might transcend the equally negating polarities of a monolithic separative self and an anomalous collective being, depends on his response to this challenge. But regardless of the outcome, the success of the Jewish writer's struggle must be understood in relation to a greater cultural problem affecting the Diaspora as a whole, one that it has still barely begun to confront.

Conclusion

Jewish Dreaming, Jewish Geography

in a Transitional Age

> You have two worlds, but neither one
> brings you joy.
> Here, nothing good is meant for you
> There, you are not worthy of anything good.
> Relief from your worries
> the two worlds will never give you
> Not the heavens, not the earth
> Poor man, you are to be pitied.
> —Mordechai Gebirtig, "Two Worlds"

Arnold Eisen once argued that "Jewish culture for Jews in Israel remains virtually *inescapable*. Try as one might, one cannot successfully leave it behind" ("In the Wilderness" 35). There was a time when I was grateful to accept the simple logic of this imperative. Hence, as I milked cows and harvested date trees in a desert kibbutz in the pre-Intifada Israel of 1975, it was always with a presumption of adding to that "culture." As a full-fledged citizen-soldier it didn't really matter *what* I did. But not many years later I discovered it was precisely this moral complacency that Roth skewered so artfully in *Counterlife* and *Operation Shylock*, inspiring like-minded readers and myself to reconsider the inviolability of American Jewry's vicarious anchors as well as our own "Israeli" identity.

The Jewish American literary journey that I've traced in rough outline from the end of the nineteenth century until the present pivots on the writer's acceptance or rejection of the notion of Return. Whether propelled by a fundamental skepticism or by a radically utopian transformation of what had once been messianic time into the political, the imaginative catalyst for the four writers featured in my study has been the tension between Zion and Diaspora. This struggle began in Emma Lazarus's attempts to reimagine Judaism's quasi-mythological navigation of its geography within America's material "republic of letters," where the Jewish American poet's rescue and redemption narratives mark a passionate effort to replace the merely circular wanderings of the Jewish journey with a triumphal linear itinerary crowned by arrival. In her utopian imagination, nationality and peoplehood would be effortlessly synthesized once the Jews proved themselves as virile as other peoples. Lazarus translated the Jews for a post-emancipation era of nationalist identities. Face to face with the precariousness of her own "native" standing, she made a monumental adjustment, forging powerful linkages between Hebraic and American identities. Lazarus's call for the Jew to transcend the unmanly humiliations of exile to become farmers, artisans, and soldiers has been met—and exceeded. The descendants of the Maccabees she celebrated in her verse have created a formidable military strength—and a labyrinth of moral dilemmas—she could not have dreamt of.

At the same time, "Jewishness"—as the living substratum of a religion and culture—is diminished in her poems, as if anticipating the bewildering paradoxes of both the modern state of Israel and the ultra-assimilated Jewish American. In the very period that Lazarus's prose campaigns for settlement in Palestine (to wean the immigrants away from their atavistic tendencies) and her lyrics romanticize Jewish antiquity, she is notably silent on the possibilities of Jewish continuity in the American milieu. The decidedly ambiguous strains of her poetry anticipate all the confusions that were to follow in Jewish American efforts to articulate the logic of a homegrown Zionism. Lazarus's life and poetry illuminate the potential for alienation as well as an energetic resourcefulness in the writer's response to the predicament of marginality. The difference between freedom and selfhood and the burden of communal insularity haunt Lazarus's own literary subjectivity just as she resurrects Hebraic might in a time of Jewish self-doubt. The "translation" of identity, like that of a text, always entails gains as well as losses. Hence, in claiming one Jewish history Lazarus remained a stranger to other ways of seeing the past. She repudiated the religion of living Jews and yet she thought that the act of claiming an ancient racial lineage—what she called "nourishing the sacred fires of ancient memory" (by which she meant a link to a sacred and distant landscape)—would somehow hold the key to belonging to the American future (*Selections* 15). The contradictions between modern identity and ancient lineage that animate Lazarus's late body of proto-Zionist poetry and polemics are largely *reactive*. So disturbed was Lazarus by the Jews' sudden visibility that she devoted enormous energy to creating narratives in which the ugly particularities of the present are submerged in a romanticized past of biblical heroism and a future of Zionist rebirth.

Of course, since Lazarus's disparagements of shtetl culture, Jews in the Diaspora have come to regret the way in which Zionism loathed their values and history. Daniel and Jonathan Boyarin, Paul Breines, Sidra Ezrahi, and many others cited throughout this study have come to wonder whether there might not be an unspoken relation between the negative qualities Lazarus and European Zionists identified (various forms of "neurosis," "passivity," and "repression") and the gentleness, world-citizenship, and exuberant creativity of post-Enlightenment Jewry in the Diaspora.

But as we have seen, subsequent writers have also confronted (and arguably contributed to) the shattering of the communal, religious, and ideological forms that had once validated life outside the Holy Land. Whereas Reznikoff has a nostalgic affinity for the resilience of the (masculine) diasporic individual cut off from the sanctity of community, Syrkin tends toward an empowering, if defensive, politics of communal life. Yet for all the differences that we distinguished between them, their poetry shares an adversity-centered worldview, a perception of unending Gentile hostility that both tested and shored up Jewish resistance. Though Reznikoff did not share Syrkin's faith in a separate political solution, his lyrics—written under the historical shadow of the Holocaust and other catastrophes—suggest that even when the Jew becomes integrated in America, communal apprehension and historical consciousness would naturally and aptly remain as latent residual forces. Translated into an enduring textual culture, they would preserve the Jewish collective. Reznikoff exposes the world as a place of violent, unpredictable dispersal but also reveals the ethical potential of that condition. He constructed a unique variant of what Sidra Ezrahi calls textual repatriation, or "alternative sovereignty" (*Booking Passage* 10). But this lofty vision must be weighed against the question of whether or not the privatized-individualist style of Jewish American life has proven effective in creating a sense of communal cohesiveness or is capable of interpreting the Jewish heritage in deeply meaningful intellectual or spiritual ways. This is the question that preoccupied Syrkin.

Measured in the bluntly statistical terms that were intrinsic to Syrkin's ideology, the Jewish population is indeed shrinking throughout the Diaspora. In *Vanishing Diaspora* (1996), Bernard Wasserstein concludes that the

Jews of Europe will not survive: "[We are] witnessing the disappearance of the European Diaspora as a population group, as a cultural entity and as a significant force in European society and in the Jewish world. Slowly but surely, they are fading away. Soon nothing will be left but a disembodied memory" (289–90). Syrkin would hardly have been surprised by Wasserstein's pessimistic prognosis for the European remnant, just as the disproportionate material successes of their American coreligionists afforded her little hope that they would overcome a terminal demographic decline. Indeed, the sociologist substantiates Syrkin's fears of the Diaspora's utter dissolution by assimilation by drawing a haunting lesson from the Jews who settled and thrived in Kai-feng, China, in the twelfth century. After eight centuries of continuity, having encountered little or no hostility from their Chinese neighbors, they eventually absorbed the culture and practices of Confucian society. In the nineteenth century they reportedly sold their holy scrolls, which they were no longer able to read (290). It is not difficult to imagine the lesson Syrkin would have gleaned from the monumental loss.

In contrast, Reznikoff knew that survival *at any price* was never a part of the Jewish bargain. Reading Reznikoff in this time of terrible violence has made me acutely aware of the historic irony that the very ideology that sought to "normalize" Jewish life engendered a garrison state still struggling to define its borders and identity, leaving behind a Diaspora equally unsure of its role in influencing that state's precipitous policies—and unsure of its own identity. His poetry is informed by Deuteronomy's vision of "Justice, justice shalt thou pursue, that thou mayest live" (16:20), a call that makes the tug of war between ethnic hegemony and ethical survival all the more complicated in the context of a modern state. Reznikoff's lyrical formulation of Jewish life—namely, choosing Torah over terrain—may prepare us to confront an age in which Jews are forced to encounter the entanglements of hybridity in unprecedented ways. Alongside the haunting lesson of the Chinese Jewish community, it is imperative to recall how, in the late twentieth century, the Falashas, or Jews of Ethiopa (who believe they are descended from Hebrews who returned to Africa with the Queen of Sheba, after her visit to King Solomon) imposed themselves on global Jewish consciousness, and more recently, the Lemba, an ethnic group from Southern Africa, have been shown to be genetically similar to most other Jews. Their recent ingathering by the Jewish state does not overshadow the fact that such discoveries demonstrate that Judaism, even in antiquity, was always a more *scattered* and diverse phenomenon than has been assumed. This places ancient Jewish culture in a position analogous to the one it occupied at the dawn of modernity, embodying a trend that is increasingly being seen as the destiny of the world's peoples. If, today, most of us inhabit one form of diaspora or another, as Reznikoff envisioned, our Jewish children must prepare to inherit the world of cultural hybridization that these intermingling and converging diasporas are engendering.

This would imply an endless process of renewal, of translation. John Felstiner, the authoritative translator of poet Paul Celan, sees the need for a deeper understanding of the fact that, "Jewishly, exile implies the need for translation. 'Trans-late': 'Carry-across.' The word 'Hebrew' itself denotes a 'crossing-over' people: Abraham out of Ur to Canaan, Moses through the Red Sea to Sinai, Joshua across the Jordan into the Promised Land, the Israelites back from Babylon to Zion, Spain's Jews fleeing the Inquisition, Europe's seeking America" (338). Reznikoff would concur. For Reznikoff, the problem of translation required reimagining the relevance of Jewish history for a multiethnic age in which religious and ethnic identity was based on individuals rather than collectives. Finding the tensions that might separate his Jewish and American identities to be creative, even his historical poetry resists bringing to light the "essence" of Jewish culture; instead of fixed boundaries, his vision is that of a dynamic, flowing, interactive, and often highly conflictual process of cultural formation, a scattering that shares the fate of all beings. Even the enormity of the Holocaust failed to diminish his sense of responsibility to the narratives concerning the massacres of American Indians and slavery. Though much of Reznikoff's poetry transmits a strong Jewish identity dependent on the paradigm of adversity, he always intimated that even secular Jews should follow the Orthodox posture of a critical attitude toward the surrounding culture.

Unlike Reznikoff, Roth's narratives presuppose that there is no longer a truly Jewish exilic experience relevant to the circumstances of American Jewry, a loss he construes as a form of blurring of identities or a fatal closure that revokes a certain Jewish literary privilege. Roth confronts the demise of the vulnerability and historical consciousness that earlier literary visions depended on, and his cultural anxiety seems to me not entirely ungrounded. An astute historian and vigilant observer of the contemporary Jewish American scene, Stephen Whitfield, warns that

The associational patterns, the bonds of intimacy in workplace and neighborhood, the direct links to the Old World—all were strong enough to honor the claims of ethnicity, in the absence of religion. For the first few generations, Jewish identity was secure enough to keep intact a community from which a culture could emerge. By the end of the century, however, that identity has destabilized, so that the boundaries between Jews and others have mostly been obliterated. Jews have become so indistinct . . . the task of describing [Jewish culture] may become insurmountable. (224)

In Roth's works, the sovereign authority for the Jewish American is the Self, an ascendancy that marks a departure from what was once an inescapable framework of identity—familial, communal, traditional, even the Jewish neighborhood—inherited at birth. Ironically, in view of the charges leveled against him throughout his career, the cumulative impact of his last several novels seems nothing less than a confirmation of the dark predicament described by Marie Syrkin. Ultimately, the tension over alternative identities, Diaspora versus Zionism, masks an indelible feature of each of Roth's narratives, the problem of a lost wholeness irrecoverable in contemporary Jewish life.

Using the past only to define the mournful self in the present, the novels considered here exhibit the novelist's alarming tendency to take the past and turn it singularly inward, rather than to reflect outward the way a genuine diasporist, such as Reznikoff, would try to do. Specifically, this marks the difference between fiction that mirrors only the self, and a Jewish writing that resonates beyond the decline of a particular generation. For all his arch denials, there may well be an autobiographical resonance here. Seymour Levov's exodus from ethnic, urban Newark for the American pastoral parallels Roth's sojourn with Claire Bloom in a converted farmhouse in rural Conneticut, a relationship that led to mental dissolution and marital breakup.[1] In Roth's turning away from the polyphony and playfulness that are the prerogative of the diasporic text toward the pessimistic teleology we examined, we witness the writer's hardening toward something that resembles the linearity of the Zionist journey.

But Roth's fictions also bring us to the brink of confronting the true crisis of postmodern Jewish life in America, a moment in which, as Susser and Liebman argue, "Jewish singularity and the justifications for Jewish survival" will no longer be able to "draw from the fortress mentality of the besieged." Except perhaps for the settlement Jews of Roth's Agor, the ideology of affliction has deteriorated into "a mental construct independent of its empirical referent" (25). Roth fully knows that this accounts for why Jewish Americans secretly preferred a beleaguered Israel threatened by terrorism and war for the identity and purpose with which it endowed them. But in the end, like Syrkin, Roth fails to contribute to an authentic reckoning with the continuity of Jewishness in America. The Jewish writer, along with the rest of us, will have to create new paradigms: "Rather than Jews being defined in contrast to others, more self-referring categories [will] need to be worked out" (33). The very tradition that once ensured survival has different implications in the welcoming environment of America. Under the benign conditions of the latter, the "ideology of affliction" merely "simulates Jewish substance when it is, in fact, lacking. It artificially resuscitates a moribund ethno-religious consciousness although it cannot tell those who are affected by this historical reflex why they ought to survive as Jews" (34).

One need not look far to realize that the grim vision of creative decline Roth presents is far from the whole story. Though there are still critics who echo Irving Howe's argument in the introduction to his 1977 anthology that Jewish American fiction had "probably moved past its high point" (leaving little to say following the well-trod terrain of immigration, acculturation, and assimilation), there are plenty of signs of revitalization (*Jewish-American Stories* 17). Much of the vigor in this new period seems to be coming from women writers. Unlike Roth's portrayal of an acute *absence* or endgame, there is evidence of a generation eager to point to the practices and customs that signify, and maintain, a vital, if not uncompromised, Judaism. Younger writers like Anne Roiphe, Tova Reich, Rebecca Goldstein, and Nessa Rapoport are demonstrating the seemingly endless possibility of dialogue between sacred Jewish sources, traditional Judaism, and the present, in ways that are not anchored solely in the Holocaust or Israel. At the time of this writing, Grace Paley and Cynthia Ozick are still contributing fresh visions of Jewish culture. Indeed, the current Jewish American literary scene is dominated by women such as Lilian Nattel (*The River Midnight*) and Allegra Goodman (*Kaaterskill Falls*), whose novels cross generations to mediate the urgent themes of gender, family, the community, and other intrinsic features of the Jewish substratum.

Unlike the secular subjects of my study, such writers, as Ted Solotaroff observes, are often "anchored in the present-day observant Jewish community . . . drawn to the intense and growing dialogue between Jewish [culture] and modernity under the impact of feminism, the sexual revolution and the Holocaust" (64). Perhaps what most divides these attempts from Roth, Bellow, and Malamud's fictions is a sobering up from that generation's peculiar blend of nostalgia, irreverence, and cynicism, and a shift toward reimagining diasporic continuity. Rather than the painful schisms that cause the downfall of Roth's narrators, there is an increased sense of confidence in taking possession of the materials of the past. For instance, Nomi Eve, author of *The Family Orchard* (2000), a critically acclaimed novel that chronicles six generations, recently told an interviewer that it makes perfect sense to me that I should be able to write the book I have written at this point in the history of our times. I am the granddaughter of bakers and farmers. One set of my grandparents were orchardmen and women, *pardessanim*, who participated in and suffered terribly and celebrated through the birth of the Jewish state. The other set of my grandparents are bakers. My American grandparents were child-immigrants to the U.S. from Russia. My grandparents tilled the land and fought the war; my parents recovered from their parents' hard histories, and I have been given the gifts of time, material comfort and security. From this relatively placid and precious vantage, I can write what couldn't really be written before in my family. Couldn't be written because it was being lived through. (Krug 10)

Precisely because they show a mature ability to come to terms with the material well-being and cultural security that Roth's protagonists flee, this new literary Eve and her generation not only resist the old story of decline and loss, but feel well situated to represent the Diaspora as an intergenerational journey still very much unfolding.

Of late, Jewish American writers have begun to rouse themselves to re-assess the place to which the heady days of Zionist heroics have brought them. As the novelist Anne Roiphe points out, Jewish Americans, though at first reluctant, are awakening to the stark realization that Jewish money sent to Israel is no longer needed to enable the cause of Zionist redemption:

Our money no longer provides the rungs of the ladder that lead to the future. Israelis who come visiting discuss their stock portfolios; the greening of the desert has less to do with drip irrigation than capitalization, expansion, and management skills. So American money sent to Israel is an expression of our wish to pretend to be needed. (63)

Clearly Roiphe is representative of a generation of writers for whom active questioning of either the vicarious forms of Jewish American identity or the policies and actions of the state of Israel is no longer considered tantamount to a self-destructive nihilism. But the critical question remains, what will replace Israel as an energizing source for Jewish identity and continuity?

When it was forced on us we thought of our precarious place as a tragedy, but now that it is chosen, continues out of free will, we can contribute to the Jewish experience by continuing to absorb the world around us, to bring to Judaism customs, thoughts from the outside. We will continue to serve Jewish history outside the Land of Israel. We have to think of ourselves as contributors of ideas and culture. Our Americanness is not a handicap for the Jewish people. In our communities in the

United States we are in the process of creating a particular blend of pluralistic Judaism, American to the core but Jewish in heart and form. If we adapt, if we don't disappear, we will grow to respect this American-Jewish culture that we are building. (63)

Roiphe reassures Jewish Americans that if they can learn to "accept ourselves as a stream leading into the river of Jewish life," they may ultimately enrich Israel, offering "a unique influx into the Jewish story of outside cultures, myths, customs." For their part, Israelis may come to recognize the need to import a diasporic ethos into Israel.

Uneasy in Zion

Even in Israel the Jew is a nomad, that is to say, his wanderings are part of his thought. The Jews—even when they were dispersed throughout the world, and wherever they are now—have always been in exile in relation to the place they were in before. What are the dreams of the Israelis? One of them dreams about Morocco, another about Poland, another about Germany. Even the youngsters don't actually lose that. There is a kind of melancholia, a nostalgia which finally is the world. The Jew is the world.
—Edmond Jabès, talking with Bracha Ettinger Lichtenberg

The Shoah and the birth of Israel, the two epic events of the Jewish experience in the twentieth century, both have their origins in the nation-state. The latter greatly intensified the problem of the "Jewish Question" as well as the Jewish answer—the modern state of Israel. Yet in our time there are intriguing indicators suggesting that the new century, with the consolidation of worldwide communication and multinational corporations, will be a place in which individual identities will no longer be defined by the nation-state. Without succumbing to utopianism—war and drought will continue to be factors as much as the global market—it hardly seems a stretch to suggest that in the not-too-distant future, identities will be at once more local and more transnational, based on community as well as international communication. And this of course is precisely the paradigm of which the Jews have been history's most consistent exemplars—a global people expressed as vital local communities. It is impossible to imagine that the Israel-Diaspora nexus itself won't be utterly transformed as the greater world comes to participate in this distinctive condition.[2]

The fictional narratives and poetry that I've described in this study follow two trajectories that illuminate the problem of identity in Israel and the Jewish world as a whole: the numbed, defensive approach that clings to a nonnegotiable self or territory in the wake of extermination, and the dynamic paradigm that approaches Jewish history and subjectivity as an ongoing process of renegotiation. If Lazarus wrote for an age transfixed by the logic of racialized geographies and cultural essences, the literary descendants of the Zionist settlers she envisioned have begun to confront the haunting uncertainties of Judaism's role in a world of cultural hybridization. In our own time, we can see how the impact of global developments, mass migrations, displacements, and the unprecedentedly rapid mixing of once homogeneous populations is leading to an exciting, unknown future of global syncretism. Strong evidence of the post-Zionist writer's enduring identification with the notion of Diaspora was exemplified by a recent global conference, sponsored by the National Foundation for Jewish Culture. This event was the first such international gathering of significant proportions in ten years. The previous event, "The Writer in the Jewish Community: An Israeli–North American Dialogue," delivered no more or less than the tensely polarized debates that its title promised. Held in the early days of the first Intifada, its Israeli and American participants engaged in a highly acrimonious debate, though perhaps not exactly in the way that one might assume. According to a journalist present at the scene, "Ruth Wisse and Cynthia Ozick, rallying to the defense of the policies of the Israeli government at the time, accused the Israeli writers of hand-wringing and disloyalty to Zionism, while the Israelis, in particular Amos Elon and Anton Shammas, blasted their accusers for what they characterized as a kind of literary fascism" (Kessler 10).[3] But ten years later, the conference I attended in the San Francisco Bay Area had an agenda with even broader implications. Instead of repeating the rigid binary representation of Jewish identity that dogged the first event, this conference was distinguished by its apparent interrogation of a much earlier view of Jewish culture as a cosmopolitan, transnational realm. These days it is rare for such a variety of Jewish literary personalities to gather in one venue. From Europe came novelists, poets, and critics—Anthony Rudolf, Emanuel Moses, George Konrad, Gila Lustiger, and Norman Manea; from Israel, novelists Aharon Appelfeld, Orly Castel-Bloom, Nava Semel, and the playwright Joshua Sobol; from Latin America, writers Moacyr Scliar, Ilan Stevens, and Victor Perera; from North America, Allegra Goodman, Grace Paley, Tillie Olson, Chaim Potok, Jonathan Rosen, Mordechai Richler, and John Hollander. Many of these writers described their sense of hybridity or biculturalism. Feminist poet Irena Klepfisz pleased everyone by remarking that, having been born in Warsaw and lived briefly in Sweden before moving to the Bronx, she determined over the years to make her English lyrics "more Judaized and less transparent and universal." But there were enough uncomfortable moments, in which the bitter debate waged a decade earlier seemed to burst through, to suggest that the problem I have been exploring in these pages will continue to shape the Jewish literary visions of the future.

After days of listening to writers and critics describe their indebtedness to Joyce and other cosmopolitan influences, the journalist and essayist Hillel Halkin protested: "I am not nostalgic for Jewish marginality and alienation. Having only recently gained a majoritarian culture of our own in Israel we may be losing it without fully reaping its benefits."[4] Interestingly, the sharpest responses to Halkin's complaint—that the writers he had heard too often engaged in fatal forms of nostalgia for heterogeneous worlds—came from two other Israelis. The playwright Yoshua Sobol arose to praise the virtues of what he called Judaism's "erotic" tendencies:

Our mission as Jews is to open ourselves up and develop a dialogue with other cultures. Cultures, like people, oscillate between the erotic and the neurotic. Erotic cultures are interested in intercourse and exchange, in living metabolically, in the exchange of the spiritual and the material. . . . The quintessence of Jewish culture is eroticism—a lively contact with others. (Sobol, audiotape)

Sobol concluded his remarks with a revealing epigraph, which he credited to a chasidic tale: "Never celebrate the truth in the place that you've found it because it is no longer there." Thinking about Sobol's remark caused me to recall my understanding of Reznikoff's response to Hebrew's return to a majoritarian culture—and its flight from interpenetration. I have speculated that whereas Syrkin admired the fact that Zionism had produced a greater number of Hebrew speakers, writers, and books than had ever existed before, Reznikoff knew that such independence had diminished the genius of what had traditionally been a minority discourse in foreign and hostile empires. As Aberbach argues, "*Hebrew* creativity in the diaspora has virtually died out in the process of being violently transplanted into the land of its birth" (27). And yet it must be remembered that ancient Hebrew writing developed under imperial rule. Besides producing the social conscience of the prophets (who struggled against the rule of force), it engendered the creative tension between talmudic law and aggadic narratives; the willingness to face the worst inhumanity and imagine the best. More than ever, the Hebrew writer must invent new ways to pull his language free from the centrifugal pull of the ethno-sectarian conflict that seems to be the murderous legacy of all twentieth-century claims to "Homeland," whether in the Balkans or the Middle East.

Another participant in the 1998 "Writing the Jewish Future" conference visibly startled a number of people when she announced that, "I do not feel at home when I am at home [in Israel]. . . . I don't agree with this struggle to preserve a traditional identity" (Castel-Bloom, audiotape). In her Hebrew fiction, Orly Castel-Bloom, born in Tel-Aviv in 1960, rejects the role of cultural imperialist, desiring to welcome and mingle with other groups present on her native land's soil. Alluding to the suffocatingly collective "oneness" that is imposed on young Israelis, she declared,

With great anticipation I am looking at the foreign workers who enter Israel legally and illegally every time I have to fetch a member of my family from the airport. "Do stay, for a long time," I plead with them with all my heart. "Do mingle in our society, you and your descendants. Show that there is this, this, and this." This pluralism should be part of our daily life and culture. Israel should be heaven and haven to all refugees. Accept and welcome the foreigner; it is an investment . . . for one day he will surely write good Hebrew literature. Let them in and let us play a little bit more with our DNA.

As Castel-Bloom hinted, Israel is rapidly becoming, like Europe and the United States, a multiracial, multiethnic, and multireligious society—a development for which it is not even remotely prepared. In this light it may well be that the Jewish tradition of erotic contact will continue to thrive in its linguistic homeland precisely because of the gross conditions of injustice in modern Israel. If the contributions of Sobol and Castel-Bloom (representing writing from entirely different generations) are any indication, Hebrew literature may still possess an ethically revolutionary potential. Unfortunately, at this moment in time, there seems little for the Hebrew writer to say beyond bearing witness to the manifest failure of Zionism to reconcile Judaism with the state.

◆

Looking back on the Jewish American experience in the twentieth century, it now appears that "assimilation" outside the Jewish Homeland may be a more spirited and resistant process than the darkest literary visions explored in this study would suggest, a creative way for Jews to draw from and revision the various aspects of kinship, religion, and culture that make up the enigma of Judaism. But at the same time, it increasingly appears that for many of

Israel's Jews, now as in antiquity, Zion may cease to feel like a welcome home-land. With the waning of ideology (the counterpart to the Diaspora's "ideol-ogy of affliction"), it has become less taboo for individual Israelis to recog-nize and indulge the interests of the self rather than the collective. Since the 1980s there has been a growing exodus from Israel, particularly among native-born Ashkenazi Jews, a change accompanied by a dramatic decrease in Western immigration. Fewer Jews in Israel and the West, save for the ultra-Orthodox, are content to be swallowed up in the tidal shift from ideological democracy to territorial theocracy. Besides the ever-tempting desire to mimic the materialism of America, many Israelis, touched by the violence of two Intifadas, are increasingly dismayed by the moral image the nation projects to the rest of the world. Hence, we may very well face a startling transformation of Jewish Diaspora, in which, as William Freedman ironically notes,

> Israel itself may be the new diaspora, another seat of it at any rate; and this is indeed a matter of exile—exile not from his land, for the Jew is in his land; not from his peo-ple, for nominally he is among his people—but exile from the concept most early Zionists spoke and wrote and dreamed of, exile in the land of the Jews from the values and ethos he may identify with Jewishness, exile from what for most of the past two centuries has in large measure defined the Jewishness he identifies with, admires, and would cling to. (240–41)

Throughout the twentieth century, waves of Jews have escaped hostile envi-ronments to settle in Israel—first from a genocidal Europe, then from Arab countries in the 1950s, Ethiopia in the 1970s, Russia from the 1980s until the present. But by the 1980s more Jews were emigrating from Israel annually than were immigrating to it. The fourth largest Israeli city in population is Los Angeles. Incongruous as it may seem, increasing numbers of Israelis, sabras and immigrants alike, realize that dwelling in Israel without a commit-ment to prophetic social values (of the nature that made Reznikoff's King David refuse to drink the water brought from his home village because the gift risked human life) amounts to little more than a transference of Exile to the State of Israel. In her old age, even Marie Syrkin, witnessing the shift of political power from socialist Labour to the right-wing Likud, recognized this fragility of Zionism's promise. Hence, it is little wonder that Israel is increasingly filled with "diasporic" Jews, pariah figures whose attentiveness to the moral claims of Palestinians, Lebanese civilians, and Israeli Arab citi-zens has increasingly earned them the role of disaffected outsider, clinging hopefully to the anachronistic values of Western liberal tradition that Halkin says are not essential to a Jewish civilization.

Though it is difficult for a culture to embrace change while under fire, there were intriguing signs of a new consciousness that emerged between the two Intifadas. In subterranean ways not yet fully understood, the political struggle to come to terms with the Palestinian refugees may very well play an important role in this creative process. Perhaps the most visible signs of this phenomenon are the sudden popularity of "oriental song," which originated in the Arab countries of origin of Sephardic Jews, and the recent trend of Ashkenazic Jews traveling from Israel to the Jewish homelands overtaken by the Holocaust. I am thinking as well of a 1990s exhibit at the Israel Museum, entitled "Routes of Wandering," where artists demonstrated that Hebrew could not inoculate itself against the "infection" of the topos of Jewish wandering outside the regimen of the state. The artists employed choice images, from vehicles of transportation to suitcases and maps, to settings such as vacated buildings or actual nomadic sites, all of which embody mobility and transience. In this and subsequent venues, Israeli artists have begun to look more closely at the desert and the fragile Bedouin culture that seems to reveal unsettling traces of the ancient Jewish past of nomadism. Indeed, myths such as the command given to Abraham, *Lech Lacha* ("Get you gone from your country and from your birthplace and from your father's house"), the story of Cain, the expulsion of Ishmael into the desert, and the narrative of Ruth the Moabite offer a richly circuitous terrain, repetitions of wandering that haunt the certainties of the present. Indeed, it may be that the primordial essence of Hebrew monotheism, often vilified as the source of global violence, will yet offer the richest countertraditions to rebuke those who would root themselves in blood-drenched soil. Monotheism, after all, evolved as a strategy for being-at-home wherever one was. One midrashic tradition that interprets the rock under Jacob's head as metonymy for the entire Land of Israel is answered by Rabbi Shimeon, who suggested that God folded the rock like a scroll or ledger before placing it under Jacob's head. Who knows whether the divine gift kindled dreams—or nightmares—of Jewish wandering that night? But Shimeon's wonderful suggestion that "Eretz Israel" was a portable text richly delineates the eternal challenge that sustains Judaism as a civilization in exile.

But such manifestations of the subversive potential of unofficial art or even the midrashic imagination, however attractive, do not have the same immediate consequences for a country's self-mirroring as its official, dogmatic institutions. So on a recent visit to Bet Hatefutsoth, Israel's Diaspora Museum, I was startled to see signs of an ideological transformation. I first experienced the museum in the 1970s, as a new Israeli citizen, when one could view models of European and North American synagogues immaculately preserved under glass. A path winding through the humiliating history of Exile culminated in a sloping ramp (intended to subject the visitor to a not-too-subtle sensation of aliya [ascent]) leading to the implied spiritual redemption that, in the modern state, is the result of immigration. The message then was that real Jewish life occurred in Israel, not in the archaic museum cultures that one had ascended from. In the new gallery, the museum's governing board hopes to offer changes that would no longer polarize Exile and Home, offering instead an opportunity for the individual to make his or her own way through the difficult questions of continuity, identity, and pluralism. Rather than clinging to the anachronism of the early Zionists' dire warnings of an enervated *Galut*, the new exhibition aspires to reimagine the Diaspora-Israel nexus as a spirited partnership.

Not long after the 1982 invasion of Lebanon, Rabbi Alexander Schindler, then leader of Reform Jewry, warned that Jewish Americans had "slipped into the sloppy equation which says that Judaism equals Zionism equals Israel. We do ourselves irreparable harm when we make Israel our surrogate synagogue, when we permit our Jewishness to consist almost entirely of a vicarious participation in the life of the state."[5] Twenty years later it seems truer than ever that decline in the continuity of Jewish Americans and Israelis alike may threaten most when the members of these communities can no longer forge ethical narratives to account for their role in the world. Even more so for the Jewish writer. Long before Edward Said (who in turn took his cue from Theodor Adorno) advanced the notion that Diaspora creates a critical distance from certainty, there was Reznikoff, whose poetry richly delineates the notion that it is a moral imperative not to be too much at home in one's home, that a people's creative and moral energy can best be marshaled in the face of such uncertainty. Whether in Israel or America, the challenge will remain much as Reznikoff once perceived it: either to apprehend Judaism's prophetic message about the plight of the stranger, or to submit to the state in all its inept and destructive cynicism. Inscribing themselves in a tradition that survived centuries of persecution without power, Jewish writers and readers in Israel and America alike must imagine what it will take for the Jewish people everywhere to do more than either accept the erasure of full assimilation or acquiesce to the violence of the state. Because we were strangers in Egypt.

Notes

Introduction

1. See, for example, the recent "Diaspora and Immigration" issue of *South Atlantic Quarterly* 98.1/2 (Winter/Spring 1999), which offers comparative readings of South Asian, Hispanic, Irish, African, Muslim, and Jewish diasporic space.
2. Quoted in Jonathan Sacks, "Love, Hate, and Jewish Identity." Quotation appears on page 27.
3. For a discussion of Zionist utopias as a literary genre, see Sidra Ezrahi, *Booking Passage: Exile and Homecoming in the Modern Jewish Imagination*, 73–82.
4. Generations prior to the Boyarins' radical critique of Zionist literalism, the Diaspora historian Simon Dubnow proposed a cultural/spiritual Jewish nationalism that transcends the territorial/political. Dubnow's work will be described in more detail in subsequent chapters.
5. Henceforth, I will describe the works under discussion as *Jewish American* in conscious homage to Arthur Fiedler's taxonomy in his essay on Isaac Bashevis Singer, where he also predicted that the Jewish American literary subgenre was breathing its last gasp. See Leslie A. Fiedler, "I. B. Singer, or, the American-ness of the American-Jewish Writer," 73.
6. For example, in preparing the theoretical grounds for this study, I have learned a great deal from Said's cogent observation that

   Seeing "the entire world as a foreign land" makes possible originality of vision. Most people are principally aware of one culture, one setting, one home; exiles are aware of at least two, and this plurality of vision gives rise to an awareness of simultaneous dimensions, an awareness that—to borrow a phrase from music—is contrapuntal . . . for an exile, habits of life, expression or activity in the new environment inevitably occur against the memory of these things in another environment.

   Edward Said, "Reflections of Exile," *Granta* 13, 159–72. Quotation appears on pp. 171–72.

1. Emma Lazarus, Zion, and Jewish Modernity in the 1880s

1. Lazarus's poems and prose cited in this chapter are from *The Poems of Emma Lazarus*, 2 vols. (Boston: Houghton Mifflin Company, 1888); *Emma Lazarus: Selections from Her Poetry and Prose*, ed. Morris U. Schappes (New York: Emma Lazarus Federation of Jewish Women's Clubs, 1967). Cited parenthetically in the text as *Poems* and *Selections*, respectively. Two of Emma's sisters, Mary and

Annie, published *The Poems of Emma Lazarus* (1888) after her death. Volume I contains an illuminating biographical sketch by her sister Josephine, which also appeared the same year in the *Century*. Volume II contains her final work, "By the Waters of Babylon, Little Poems in Prose," and numerous translations from the "Hebrew poets of medieval Spain," including Solomon Ben Judah Gabirol, Abul Hassan Judah Ben Ha-Levi, and Moses Ben Ezra. The most sophisticated critical treatments of Emma Lazarus include Dan Vogel, *Emma Lazarus*, and Diane Lichtenstein, *Writing Their Nations: The Tradition of Nineteenth-Century American Jewish Women Writers*, ch. III. See also Lichtenstein's "Words and Worlds: Emma Lazarus's Conflicting Citizenships," and Carole S. Kessner, "Matrilineal Dissent: Emma Lazarus, Marie Syrkin and Cynthia Ozick." I am especially indebted to Bette Roth Young's *Emma Lazarus in Her World: Life and Letters*, especially for information on Lazarus's reputation among the critics. References to Young's work will be cited parenthetically in the text as *Life and Letters*.

2. Though she had numerous American admirers, at one time her reputation overseas was even higher. Turgenev thought her only novel, *Alide*, an exceptional work. British critics thought her "Admetus" superior to Browning's *Belaustion's Adventure* and her "Tannhäuser" better than William Morris's "The Hill of Venus."

3. Translator of Jewish classics and founder of the Jewish Publication Society (1888), Szold saw Lazarus as "a golden promise of that future when the old Jewish spirit—women of culture and refinement not disdaining to foster it tenderly—shall once more flame up with all the brilliancy of the Spanish period she so devotedly studied" (D. Vogel 24). In demonstrating that a reborn Israel might teach the world to bridge the "Orient and the Occident," antiquity and modernity, Lazarus directly inspired Henrietta Szold and thus the Zionist fantasies of generations of Americans who would not dream of uprooting themselves. Szold founded Hadassah, the Women's Zionist Organization of America in 1912, which eventually established numerous hospitals, clinics, and laboratories in Palestine. In 1933 she became director of Youth Aliya, an international rescue operation that brought young Holocaust victims to Palestine for rehabilitation.

4. A recent example is Howard M. Sachar's monumental *A History of Israel from the Rise of Zionism to Our Time* where Lazarus is not mentioned in over a thousand pages of text. Likewise, she is all but excluded from Gerald Sorin's highly praised *A Time for Building: The Third Migration, 1880–1920*.

"Proto-Zionism" seems the appropriate term for Lazarus's views because, though she had a vision of political restoration, the term "Zionism" only began to appear in the press in the 1890s. In 1896, an article in *Harper's Weekly* described the "Zionite Movement" as a "collection of movements" that shared consensus only on the necessary return to Israel. See Milton Plesur, "The American Press and Jewish Restoration during the Nineteenth Century."

5. For a brief but perceptive account of Lazarus's "surprisingly modern form and technique" see Steven Rubin, "Poets of the Promised Land," 199–204.

6. Gitenstein notes the peculiar "aptness" of America's great champion of the melting pot theory being "inspired to admit her Jewishness by a Christian novel." See *Apocalyptic Messianism and Contemporary Jewish-American Poetry*, 4–5.

7. Lazarus's ancestors, maternal as well as paternal, were active members of this synagogue. Samuel Lazarus, her great grandfather, was clerk of the synagogue from 1788 to 1795 and Jacob Hart, her father's maternal grandfather, was a noted benefactor. Eleazar Lazarus, her grandfather, coauthored the first Hebrew-English Sephardic prayerbook in this country and was president of the synagogue from 1846 to 1849. On her mother's side, a great-great grandfather, Isaac Seixas, also served as president of Shearith Israel, as did a number of uncles. One of these, the Rev. J. J. Lyons, was cantor for thirty-eight years. See David deSola Pool and Tamar deSola Pool, *An Old Faith in a New World: Portrait of Shearith Israel, 1654–1954*, 502–3.

8. Lazarus's renderings of Heine were soon followed by translations of Goethe, Petrarch, and Leopardi. Eventually her romantic prose and poetry appeared in some of America's most influential magazines, including the *Critic* and *Century*, each of which had thousands of Christian readers. At the time, *Century* was the most powerful arbiter of literary taste in America.

9. Josephine Lazarus, "Emma Lazarus," *Century* 36 (October 1888), 875–84; quoted in Young, 13. Lazarus biographers and scholars have usually accepted the version of the poet that is presented in Josephine's essay for *Century*, which appeared the year after her death. In this somewhat one-dimensional portrait, Emma is a Jewish priestess whose "somber streak" inevitably rose out of her belonging to a "race born to suffer." Young is perhaps too harsh when she claims that Josephine's essay "imprisoned her sister in an identity Emma would not have recognized." Interestingly, this revisionist account seems uncritically to echo the concerns of Emma's younger sister, Annie, who wrote a letter to Bernard G. Richards in February 1926, denying his request for the rights to publish Emma's "Jewish poems": "There has been a tendency on the part of her public," Annie Lazarus writes, "to overemphasize the Hebraic strain of her work, giving it this quality of sectarian propaganda, which I greatly deplore, called forth by righteous indignation at the tragic happenings of those days. . . . [U]nfortunately, owing to her untimely death, this was destined to be her final word" ("Annie Lazarus to Bernard G. Richards, February 25, 1926, Papers of Bernard G. Richards, Jewish Theological Seminary Library).

This matter is complicated by the fact that Emma was Annie's older sister by nearly a decade. It is true that Annie possessed far more material than Josephine because of her travels with Emma in Europe. But the "divided stream" of Jewish life that Emma spoke of represented an actual division in her family: whereas one sister carried on her activist tradition, Annie Lazarus renounced the strug-

gle, married a Catholic, and converted. And Emma once issued a barbed indictment of converts: "We should prove to Christian missionaries that 'converted
Jews' are probably not only the most expensive of all marketable commodities
but also the most worthless after they are purchased" (Jacob 208). Thus we
might understand Annie's edict from her home in Italy forbidding the printing
of "anything Jewish" in a new edition of Emma's works as an act of intellectual
revenge, or at the least an expression of her own enduring cultural anxiety.

10. Edmund Clarence Stedman (1833–1908) was an influential poet and critic. John
Burroughs (1837–1921) was a highly regarded popular nature writer and close
friend of naturalists such as John Muir and Theodore Roosevelt. Their attempts
to intervene in her cultural identity are oddly similar to the early-twentieth-
century "conversion" of the Jewish American social scientist Horace M. Kallen
by his Boston Brahmin professor, Barrett Wendell, whose teaching at Harvard
emphasized the profound influence of what he called "Hebraism" on the American character. This parallel speaks volumes about the uncertainty of early Jewish American intellectual identities.

11. Emerson, who had guided her early works and facilitated their publication in
Century and *Scribner's*, was disturbed by her "abstract distance," which may be
a euphemistic reference to her occasional preoccupation with her coreligionists;
what he took to be her failure to engage fully with "American" subjects. For
instance, in November 1868, he was thrilled by her "Admetus" ("a noble poem
which I cannot enough praise"), but a few months later wrote her again, firmly
counseling that, "though you can throw yourself so heartily into the old world of
Memory," still, "high success must ever be to penetrate into and show the celestial element in the despised present" (Ralph L. Rusk, ed., *Letters to Emma
Lazarus*, 9). The complete correspondence between Lazarus and Emerson may
be found in *The Letters of Ralph Waldo Emerson*, ed. Ralph Rusk, vol 6.

12. The friendship must have recovered to some extent; years later Lazarus visited
Emerson and his family in Concord at his invitation, "to correct our village narrowness." Ralph Waldo Emerson, Letter to Emma Lazarus (July 22, 1876),
Rusk, 16. She met the Concord circle, including Bronson Alcott and William
Ellery Channing, who gave her a copy of his book on Thoreau as well as the latter's compass. Though Lazarus apparently "forgave" Emerson and later established a warm epistolary relationship with his daughter, Ellen, she ceased to
idolize him and in "Emerson's Personality" (1882) wrote: "Let me not be understood as implying that his literary judgment was infallible . . . in defiance of
all canons, very inferior as well as obscure writers might be exalted by him to
a dizzying eminence, almost lifted into immortality, by one of his golden sentences. . . ." Lazarus was no doubt still infuriated that Emerson had canonized
mediocre poets such as Tom Taylor and Mrs. C. F. Alexander while refusing to
introduce her as an American poet of merit. See "Emerson's Personality," *Century* 24 (1882), 454–66.

13. Her utter exclusion from the American canon subsequent to Emerson's snub was first rectified by the *Cambridge History of American Literature* in 1920. In spite of her family's immersion in American culture, contemporary readers invariably associated her with a condition of "otherness." Many of her admirers wrote to her, detailing the problems of identity and nationhood that troubled their own lives. In 1883, James Russell Lowell (American minister to England), who had met Emma Lazarus during a London visit earlier that year, wrote to her, complaining bitterly that he had been forced to resign from his elected post as Lord Rector of the University of St. Andrews because of his "extraterritoriality." Lowell and many others seem to have anticipated sympathy from Lazarus, presumably because of her own insider/outsider position in society. See Rusk, 73.

14. There seems to have been at least a small group of (non-Jewish) European political dreamers who were unaware of how negligible was the actual influence of Lazarus's lyrics and personality upon both American political policy and her utterly indifferent American coreligionists. The mystic Laurence Oliphant (1829–1888), who wrote several travel books and a novel, encouraged her to rally American Jewry to pressure Turkey to allow Jewish immigration. The possible break-up of the Ottoman Empire excited his hopes for immediate national redemption. After living with the "lunatic" American prophet Thomas Lake Harris in the utopian community of the Brotherhood of New Life on the shores of Lake Erie, Oliphant traveled to Palestine where he settled. His support of Jewish colonization may be linked to his interest in land speculation in Palestine. Lazarus read his essay for *The Nineteenth Century*, "The Jew and the Eastern Question" (1883), and quoted it frequently in her "Epistle to the Hebrews" series. Interestingly, Oliphant's Jewish secretary in Palestine was Naphtali Herz Imber (1856–1909), the author of the Israeli national anthem, "Hatikvah." See Arthur Zeiger, "Emma Lazarus and Pre-Herzlian Zionism," 81. See also Rusk, 53–54.

15. Editorial, *The Reform Advocate* (July 22, 1893), 441–42. Quoted in Barbara Kirshenblatt-Gimblett, "A Place in the World: Jews and the Holy Land at World's Fairs," 64. Emphasis mine.

16. Some years later Madame Ragozin achieved greater fame as a collaborator on the first American edition of "The Protocols of the Elders of Zion."

17. "Russian Jews and Gentiles," *Century Magazine* 23 (1882), 919. Also excerpted in *Selections*, 70–74.

18. My reading of Lazarus's martial lyricism is indebted to Sander Gilman's studies of representations of the male Jew in the culture of the West. Gilman demonstrates that by the nineteenth century the relationship between the image of the Jew and that of the devil of the middle ages is no longer found in a religious (superstitious) but rather in a secularized, scientific context. For example, the Jew's foot is no longer the cloven-foot of the devil but is transformed into "the

pathognomonic foot of the 'bad' citizen of the new national state." See Sander Gilman, *The Jew's Body*, 39–40.

19. In David Biale's close reading of the Germanic origins of the Zionist youth movement, he notes the historical irony that, influenced by the values of the German *Wandervogel* (the neoromantic youth movement that was also anti-semitic), the Zionists uncritically echoed the latter's call for a new body and psyche to be built up by a new relation with the land. As an early-twentieth-century popular song in Palestine rejoices, "We came to the land to build it and be built by it," just as early postcards "typically featured virile young farmers in Palestine contrasted with old frail Orthodox Jews in the Diaspora." See *Eros and the Jews*, 179, 185.

20. The coffee house symbolizes the rootless decadence of the city; accordingly coffeehouse Jews had lost their nerve and their beauty. See George L. Mosse, *Confronting the Nation: Jewish and Western Nationalism*, 127.

21. Even before the appearance of this sonnet, Lazarus was committed to a variety of educational projects that seemed to offer potential for changing the image (and perhaps the essence) of the Jews as usurers and shopkeepers. She contributed to ill-fated projects such as the agricultural settlements founded by groups of young Jews from southern Russia calling themselves *Am Olam* (Eternal People). These were established in New Jersey, Louisiana, Oregon, and the Dakotas, but all failed by 1885. Lazarus was especially interested in the colony of Vineland, New Jersey, which she suggested should be renamed after George Eliot.

22. This anxiety over Jewish otherworldliness has since become ingrained in Jewish American identity. At the very moment that Jewish American identification with Israel has begun to wane, a fascination with another variety of toughness— "Jewish crime" suddenly emerges. Richard Cohen's *Tough Jews* (1998) is a crassly nostalgic paean to thugs such as Arnold Rothstein and Meyer Lansky. For Cohen, these gangsters were quasi-Zionists, liberating the Jew from the stifling constraints of Jewish exceptionalism. Just as Lazarus's virile tropes replaced the Jewish shame of powerlessness in the pogroms, Cohen rejects "books and prayers, mourning and wailing," and invokes violent Jewish masculinity to exorcise the spectre of the Shoah.

23. I define "territorialism," here and in the chapters that follow, as both territorial sovereignty and, in its absence, a people's will to normalize itself through land possession backed up by defensive means.

24. African American slave narratives exhibit a similar double bind, as their authors were fully aware of both the arbitrary way in which white middle-class standards of behavior were applied to blacks and also of how the environment in which most blacks lived prevented the full development of those very capacities that white readers appeared to value so highly. Because of this, ethnic writers in the nineteenth century were often forced to adapt narrative stances that partially acceded to the very racist ideologies they sought to undermine.

25. This principle was articulated by liberal philosophers such as John Toland in England and Gotthold Ephraim Lessing in Germany. The phrase "the essential oneness of all human nature" occurs throughout Jacob Katz, "The Term 'Jewish Emancipation': Its Origin and Historical Impact."

26. Particularly in the aftermath of the Holocaust, Christ would be seen as the ironic symbol of contemporary Jewry, suffering and yet rising. David G. Roskies describes the post-Enlightenment interest of Jewish writers and artists, from Sholem Asch to Marc Chagall, in a dechristianized Jesus as a mythic archetype, often as a suffering Jew martyred by gentile society in *Against the Apocalypse: Responses to Catastrophe in Modern Jewish Culture*, 264–81, 284–89.

27. See Hans Kohn, *Prophets and Peoples: Studies in Nineteenth Century Nationalism* (New York: Collier Books, 1969); Boyd Shafer, *Nationalism: Interpreters and Interpretations* (New York: Macmillan, 1963); Eric Hobsbawn, *Nations and Nationalism since 1780: Programme, Myth, Reality* (Cambridge, Cambridge UP, 1992).

28. Abram S. Isaacs, "Will the Jews Return to Palestine?" *Century* 26 (1883), 156–67.

29. Like the Yiddish Bund in later years, Isaacs thought that even the most persecuted east-European populations should "remain where they are. . . . [I]t is the duty of their leaders and spokesmen to champion their rights, even as the German Israelites have finally acquired their political emancipation" (Zeiger 95). Isaacs's opposition was soon joined by the defensive rhetoric of American Reform's leadership. For example, in early 1883, Rabbi Isaac M. Wise complained that, "If Miss Emma Lazarus and others who handle a pen would lay aside their romantic notions of race, nation, Holy Land, Restoration . . . they could render good service to their co-religionists and to the cause of humanity, which is disgraced by the blind prejudices of those narrow-minded individuals who see in the Jew a stranger, an indefinable scarecrow of their bewildered imagination" (Zeiger 89). Wise's articulation of diasporism strongly suggests that Lazarus's territorialism was seen as a threat to the possibility of conceiving of immigrant Jews as competent American citizens. See "A Problematic Champion," *Jewish Messenger* LII (January 26, 1883), 4. Quoted in Zeiger, 94.

30. Samuel S. Cox, *Orient Sunbeams, or From the Porte to the Pyramids, By Way of Palestine*. Quoted in Moshe Davis, *America and the Holy Land*, 31.

31. In the mid-century, Mordechai Manuel Noah, whose *Discourse on the Restoration of the Jews* (1843) presented the author's anti-assimilative argument, explicitly called for the purchase of land in Palestine in preparation for Israel's redemption. Opposing the increasing efforts to proselytize the Jew, and voicing a Jewish messianism centered on Palestine, Noah's Zionism countered the prevailing ideology of his age much as Kallen's Zionism would be set in opposition to American nativism in the 1920s. Even as early as 1825, contriving to establish an autonomous Jewish polity under the name of Ararat in the United States, Noah asserted the primacy of Palestine for future Jewish Americans: "In calling

the Jews together under the protection of the American constitution and laws and governed by our happy and salutary institutions, it is proper for me to state that this asylum is temporary and provisionary. The Jews never should and never will relinquish the just hope of regaining possession of their ancient heritage" (Silberschlag 7). There is no direct evidence to suggest that Lazarus had heard of her predecessor, but Noah's liberal interfaith exposition of the role that the United States should perform, by virtue of its traditions, in the restoration of the Jew (even foreseeing Jewish agriculture and commerce in the valley of the Jordan), was strikingly similar to Lazarus's proto-Zionist rhetoric.

32. In 1879 there was an early attempt to establish an American Kollel (community) in Jerusalem in collaboration with the American consul, intended for Jews from the United States as well as from lands where they had never been granted citizenship and were thus totally disenfranchised. See Moshe Davis, *America and the Holy Land*, 24.

33. The Holy Land would remain a central feature of national identity, inspiring the rhetoric of the Constitution and countless place names across America. Thus, by the time Jews arrived in the United States, with their own religious yearning for Zion still intact, they struggled to assimilate into a culture that they discovered had already formed its own links to their sacred space. American places of biblical origin soon included Eden, Rehoboth, Sharon, Bethel, Hebron, Mt. Tabor, Shiloh, Tekoa, and numerous others. There is a Zion in at least fifteen states. See Moshe Davis, "The Holy Land Idea in American Spiritual History."

34. As the nineteenth-century archeologist Edward Robinson notes, the world of an American child was formed by a sense of an indelible connection to the biblical past:

> As in the case of most of my countrymen, especially in New England, the scenes of the Bible had made a deep impression upon my mind from the earliest childhood.... [I]n no country are the Scriptures better known, or more highly prized. From his earliest years the child is there accustomed not only to read the Bible for himself; but he also reads or listens to it in the morning and evening devotions of the family, in the daily village-school, in the Sunday-school and Bible-class, and in the weekly ministrations of the sanctuary. Hence, as he grows up, the names of Sinai, Jerusalem, Bethlehem, the Promised Land, become associated with his earliest recollections and holiest feelings.

> Edward Robinson, *Biblical Researches in Palestine, Mount Sinai and Arab Petraea*, I, 46.

35. Michael Ragussis traces this nineteenth-century binary tendency to a moment as early as Coleridge's remark: "The two images farthest removed from each other which can be comprehended under one term, are, I think, Isaiah—'Give ear O Earth' and Levi of Holywell Street—'Old clothes!'—both of them *Jews!*" (Ragussis 329).

36. Their Holy-Land works included Stephens's *Incidents of Travel in Egypt, Arabia Petrea, and the Holy Land* (New York: Harper, 1838); Curtis's *The Howadji in Syria* (New York: Harper, 1852); Taylor's *The Lands of the Saracen* (New York: Putnam, 1856); Bryant's *Letters from the East* (New York: Putnam, 1869); Browne's *Yusef; or, The Journey of the Frangi, a Crusade in the East* (New York: Harper, 1853); Melville's *Clarel: A Poem and Pilgramage in the Holy Land*, ed. W. E. Bezanson (New York: Hendricks House, 1960), and Twain's *The Innocents Abroad*. All these contributed heavily to American interest in a *past*-oriented Holy Land, as did General Lew Wallace's enormously popular novel *Ben Hur* (1880). A confident, expanding America, through the imaginations of its authors, began to explore the Holy Land just as it began to sense the limits of its own wilderness. American Presidents, including Ulysses S. Grant and Theodore Roosevelt, also visited and Abraham Lincoln was said to have considered a journey before his assassination. See Lester I. Vogel, *To See a Promised Land*, 42, 61–65.

37. Edwin R. A. Seligman taught at Columbia as a lecturer on economics from 1885 until 1931, when he became professor emeritus in residence. He founded the *Political Science Quarterly* in 1886 and is credited with helping Cuba to reorganize its economy in 1932.

38. The Seligman-Hilton affair was covered extensively in the *New York Times*, June 19–24, 1877, including a front-page interview with Hilton, who explained that the Seligman Jew

    is of low origin, and his instincts are all of the gutter—his principles small—they smell of decayed goods, or of decayed principles. But he has extracted cash out of the gutter, his rags, his principles, and he shoves his person upon respectability. He is too obtuse or too mean to see his vulgarity, or to go where it may not be on public exhibition. He is shoddy, false, squeezing—unmanly; but financially he is successful. . . . And the very fact that the Seligman "Jew" makes such a fuss because people don't want his society, and makes such a noise to force himself where he is unwelcome, instead of going elsewhere, proves him to be just what I described him. (*New York Times*, June 20, 1877, 1)

    See John Higham, *Send These To Me*, 149–51.

39. By the year of her death, Lazarus's zeal was rewarded by sudden momentum within the world of Christian millennial politics. In 1888, the Chicago minister William E. Blackstone returned from a Holy Land visit determined to resettle Jews in Palestine. A letter to President Harrison was eventually drafted and signed by 413 prominent Americans, including Speaker of the House "Czar" Reed, J. P. Morgan, and J. D. Rockefeller, to the effect that he should give serious consideration to the "condition of the Israelites and their claims to Palestine as their ancient home" and that he use the influence of the presidency to achieve that goal (*Zion in America* 199).

40. In ways that evoke my reading of Lazarus, Brian Swann argues that Eliot's Deronda is a "cultural fusion," a "Protestant Jew, the realization of the Evangelical dream of conversion raised to universal meaning." See "George Eliot's Ecunemical Jew, or, the Novel as Outdoor Temple," 41.

41. For the most recent instance of a Jewish critic's unqualified enthusiasm for the novel's representation of Jewish nationalism, see Ruth Wisse, *The Modern Jewish Canon*, 239–44.

42. Eliot's nature-derived trope would reappear as an essential feature of Josephine Lazarus's account of Zionism's logic: "According to Webster's Dictionary, Nation is derived . . . from the Hebrew word 'Noutz,' which signifies a 'sprout,' originally denoting a family or race of men descending from a common progenitor. Under [this] primary heading they [the Jews] must certainly be included as a Nation, however strenuously the opponents of Zionism would like to forswear or deny it" ("Zionism and Americanism" 265).

43. That same year Lazarus wrote to Rose Hawthorne Lathrop, crowing that she has "gone through a course of George Eliot lately & have been rereading most of her novels this summer—what a mine they are!" And three years later, she praised Eliot's "intellectual and moral greatness," as if in the Englishwoman she had found a new source of cultural authority to supplant Emerson, her now fallen idol. Lathrop (1851–1926) was the daughter of Nathaniel Hawthorne. See Young, Emma Lazarus to Rose Hawthorne Lathrop (September 9, 1882), Letter 6RHL, and Emma Lazarus to Helena de Kay Gilder (1885), Letter 35HdeKG.

44. Though Lazarus, like Emerson and Arnold, consistently drew from the pseudo-anthropology that constituted nineteenth-century *racialism*, it must be understood that this was still a far cry from *racism*. Whereas racialists posit that individual ethnic groups are always identifiable by innate characteristics, racists contend that races are not only "different" but ranks them according to superior and inferior features.

45. This cultural demarcation is often visible in early British and American Jewish literature. David Quixano, the hero of Israel Zangwill's assimilationist play *The Melting Pot* (1908), a Russian Jew whose entire family was killed in the Kishinev pogrom, is given a Sephardic pedigree because the Sephardim had already earned a reputation as an assimilable, almost invisible, Jewish aristocracy— unlike the uncouth *Ostjuden* (eastern European Jews).

46. Interestingly, when Lazarus was first commissioned to write for the Bartholdi Statue Fund, it was immediately suggested that she "[t]hink of that Goddess standing on her pedestal down yonder in the bay . . . holding her torch out to those Russian refugees of yours you are so fond of visiting at Ward's Island." This strongly suggests the possibility that, for the poet, the sonnet's ostensibly "universal" appeal was already linked to the plight of a particular wave of immigrants. From a sketch entitled "She Gave an Impulse to Higher Things," *The American Hebrew* (December 9, 1887), 5.

47. In Walt Whitman's 1871 "Song of the Exposition," the Muse is summoned to "migrate from Greece and Ionia." See *Leaves of Grass: Comprehensive Reader's Edition*, 709.

48. See Franz Kafka, *Amerika*, in *The Penguin Complete Novels of Franz Kafka*, trans. Willa and Edwin Muir (Penguin, 1983); and Henry Roth, *Call It Sleep* (Noonday Press, 1991).

49. Interestingly, the most important twentieth-century Zionist in American literature, Ludwig Lewisohn (1882–1955), who also struggled with feelings of alienation in Christian America, would see the problem of Heine's conversion in precisely the same terms: "He has been called a renegade because of his baptism. This is absurd. Judaism is not a religion, it is a race. The faith which that race happens to hold, meant as little to Heine as any other faith. He was no whit less a Jew for being a Lutheran." Quoted in Ralph Melnick, *The Life and Work of Ludwig Lewisohn*, I, 73.

50. It is of the utmost significance that Lazarus's first literary activity after withdrawing from Emerson was to return to her beloved Heine.

51. Hence, ironically, even those whom she might have embraced as allies were alienated by her unorthodoxy. The Reform Jews, composed of German Jews who had migrated to the United States in the first half of the nineteenth century, had been deeply patriotic in Germany, even when their position was fragile. Arriving in the United States, they brought their post-Enlightenment notion of patriotism with them and proclaimed their fierce allegiance to this country, removing all prayers addressing the traditional return to Zion. They thoroughly Americanized their religion, which Lazarus applauded, and would remain determined anti-Zionists until after the Holocaust.

52. Lazarus's outspoken Jewish critics also included Cyrus Sulzberger, prestigious coeditor of *American Hebrew*; the Philadelphia rabbi Sabato Morais, who denounced her as a false messiah; and Dr. Abraham Isaacs, editor of the *Jewish Messenger*, who even drew comparisons between her scheme and the racism of Adolph Stoecker and the activities of the anti-Semitic Congress held in Dresden in 1883. After fifteen years of publishing her poetry, the journal *Jewish Messenger* ran an editorial (January 26, 1883) denouncing her intrusions into politics, warning darkly that her nationalism would reveal Jews to be "strangers and aliens in Europe and America; patriots only in Palestine." Dr. Isaacs seems to have been one of the first observers to note the simultaneous emergence of Jewish and German nationalisms. See *Jewish Messenger* 53 (January 28, 1883), 4.

53. Her acute sense of timing and her awareness of the artist's political responsibilities also connect her to these two figures, who saw their vocation as Jewish poets linked especially to times of crisis.

54. See Mark A. Raider's discussion of this rhetoric in *The Emergence of American Zionism*, 72.

2. Marie Syrkin and the Post-Holocaust Politics of Jewish American Identity

1. As Mark Raider notes, Zionism had broad appeal to a variety of ethnic nationalist groups. Such "endorsement of the Jewish national home illustrates, at least implicitly, Labor Zionism's attempt to strengthen relations with important American political power brokers. It was assumed . . . that such support would benefit segments of American society beyond the reach of Zionist movement [*sic*], including other nationally minded American ethnic groups, like the Irish and Poles, associated with organized labor" (*Emergence of American Zionism* 204).

2. George W. Seymour's article is quoted in Arthur Aryeh Goren, "'Anu banu artza' in America: The Americanization of the *Halutz* Ideal," 89.

3. Labor Zionism must be considered in the context of other turn-of-the-century labor movements and radical reform movements, whose growth was a response to the failure of classical liberalism to guarantee the emancipation and enfranchisement of both individuals and marginalized groups. Like all the other bourgeois reform movements, Zionism had ideological pretensions to solve a host of social problems with a single solution.

4. Kallen, who was less rooted in the East European milieu, evolved a Zionist philosophy suited to the existential reality of Jewish Americans by consistently affirming the strong contributions of Jews to their Diaspora lands just as it expressed enthusiasm for the socialist Zionist enterprise.

5. The poems of *Gleanings* represent the lived experience of seven decades, but for unknown reasons the last lyrics are placed first.

6. Zionism by no means constitutes the sole output of her public energies: *Your School, Your Children: A Teacher Looks at What's Wrong with Our Schools* (1944) was a highly praised critique of the New York City High School system based on her years of teaching experience. Shorter works of social criticism on subjects such as the merit system also appeared in venues such as *The New York Times Magazine*.

7. Interestingly, both Meir and Syrkin outlived their husbands by many years and in their married lives often went their separate ways in spite of staying legally married, because of their jobs and frequent travel. Syrkin's son David Bodansky says that his mother never once voiced criticism of Golda, whom she knew years before the latter became prime minister: "My mother remained a life-long defender of the Labor Party's policies. I remember a dinner party in Israel in 1970 in which my mother sat stunned as a leftist railed against Meir's policies toward the Palestinians. We thought it was sacrilegious!" Personal communication, February 11, 1998.

8. Even a cursory examination of the most popular Jewish American periodicals of

the period, *The Menorah Journal, New Palestine, Jewish Frontier,* and *Jewish Spectator,* reveals extensive Zionist contributions by those writers.

9. For instance, as a young woman, she attended meetings of the pan-collegiate International Zionist Association but soon grew disenchanted by its less than fervent policies. In her acerbic critique it is evident that the high-minded ideal-ism of the I.Z.A. students fell woefully short of the material commitment of authentic political Zionism: "A Jewish student of a certain type went to the I.Z.A. meeting to sing the *Hatikvah* when he remembered Zion. To remember Zion in a vague ineffable way, was the chief function of the Zionist student groups. . . . A too platonic love for Zion, rather than a sense of living alliance with a concrete Palestine was [their] unsubstantial basis." Quoted in Kessner, "Marie Syrkin: An Exemplary Life," 56.

10. Rabbi Herbert Bronstein, personal interview, July 3, 1996.

11. See Marie Syrkin, *Nachman Syrkin, Socialist Zionist: A Biographical Memoir and Selected Essays,* 239, an important work for understanding Marie Syrkin's complicated relationship to Jewish culture; surviving friends and members of her immediate family feel that it reveals as much about the daughter as the father.

12. "Our Stand," *Jewish Frontier* (December 1934), 5.

13. Revisionism was a militaristic form of Zionism associated with the charismatic Vladimir Jabotinsky, a movement opposed both to Jewish socialism and to efforts to reconcile Arab and Jewish land rights in Palestine.

14. Marie Syrkin, "The Essence of Revisionism: An Analysis of a Fascist Tendency in Jewry," 6-10. See also Hayim Greenberg, "The Irresponsible Revisionists," 6-8.

15. Volume 8 of Toynbee's *A Study of History* appeared in 1954. Syrkin's response to Toynbee's conception of the Jews as a fossilized relic, "Toynbee and the Jews," as well as the record of a public exchange of letters between Toynbee and Syrkin, is reprinted in *The State of the Jews,* 171-83.

16. Besides her numerous translations, Syrkin herself was anthologized. Two of her poems appear in *The New York Times Book of Verse,* edited by Thomas Lask, which contained the "best" poetry published in the *Times* between 1920 and 1970. Her authoritative translations of Yiddish and Hebrew verse were included in collections such as Mark Van Doren's *Anthology of World Poetry* (Harcourt, 1928), Hubert Creekmore's *Little Treasury of World Poetry* (Decker Press, 1952) as well as Greenberg and Howe's *A Treasury of Yiddish Poetry* (Schocken Press, 1969).

17. Carole Kessner, though varying in emphasis, confirms my sense that there are important differences between the two:

> Charles' Jewishness, though secular, was more "spiritual" than Marie's. His was not at all political, though he was very interested in Jewish his-tory. Hers was almost completely political and ethical. It would be correct to say that both had a very strong sense of their Jewish identities, but

Charles was, let us say, more abstract. I would say that both had a deep sense of belonging and commitment to the Jewish people. Charles' was expressed primarily in his poetry; Marie's was expressed primarily in her journalism. . . . [T]he poetry was secondary, though I have argued that if push came to shove she would have said that she would rather been a poet than anything else. Letter, Carole Kessner to Ranen Omer, June 11, 1996

18. Marie's correspondence with her father is informed by her passion for Jewish poetry, an inclination that impressed her father. A 1923 letter accompanying the gift of three volumes of poetry (two in Yiddish, one in Russian) instructs her to write more translations and critical articles on Yehoash, Rosenfeld, and Mani Leib: "Splendid stuff for at least ten articles." Letter to Marie Syrkin December 13, 1923, American Jewish Archives.

19. Though it is not common knowledge, Anita Norich demonstrates that the Yiddish press in America offered even earlier reports of atrocities (March 1940). See "'Harbe sugyes/Puzzling Questions' in Yiddish and English Culture in America During the Holocaust," 91–110.

20. Editorial, "Under the Axis," *Jewish Frontier* (November 1942), 3.

21. Marie Syrkin, *Jewish Frontier* (July 1944), 6–8.

22. There is something disturbing about Syrkin's emphasis in this period. Like Lazarus, she sought out Jewish fighters as if there was still a need to prove the Jews' "worth" by proving that they had engaged in combat and shed their blood heroically. There is a terrible irony inherent in Syrkin's apparent conviction that Jews had to base their struggle for national rights on the same German ideal of sacrifice to the state that the Nazis had exploited.

23. Syrkin's *Blessed is the Match* (1946) is also the title of her powerful presentation of interviews with survivors of the death camps, the first book of its kind.

24. Syrkin reported on the trials for the *Jewish Frontier*. Her son, David Bodansky, told me that of all the controversies Syrkin committed herself to, she was particularly proud of her role in revealing the true nature of Soviet rule: "There was an amazing credulity on the part of the liberal left that she responded to"—"their dangerously stubborn unwillingness to believe that Communism was capable of such atrocities. And she was right of course. She was rightly proud of her judgment during this period." Personal communication, February 11, 1998. See "The Moscow Trials," 15–16.

25. In the aftermath of Syrkin's analysis of the Soviet regime, Syrkin and other Labor Zionist sympathizers were subject to fierce counterattacks by the Jewish American radical left, including such groups as the American Bundists, the Young People's Socialist League, and anti-Zionists within the Jewish Labor Committee. See Raider, 176–77.

26. Arendt covered the Eichmann trial for the *New Yorker*, in a five-part series during 1962–63, well in advance of the publication in book form as *Eichmann in Jerusalem: A Report on the Banality of Evil* (New York: Penguin, 1980 [1963]).

For Syrkin's nuanced critique, see "Miss Arendt Surveys the Holocaust," in *The State of the Jews*, 184–97.

27. Bodansky agrees that "the lack of Hebrew was a distinct loss to her." Personal Interview, February 11, 1998.

28. From the beginning of Syrkin's career, she left little doubt that she aligned herself to her father's political legacy. In a 1935 note to Hurwitz she requests that her articles for *The Menorah* be accompanied by the information that "the writer is the daughter of Dr. Nahum Syrkin, founder of the Socialist-Zionist movement." When her articles appeared she arranged for copies to be sent to Ben Gurion and other Labor Zionists. Marie Syrkin, Letter to Henry Hurwitz, March 10, 1935, Henry Hurwitz Memorial Collection, American Jewish Archives.

29. A decade after the novel first appeared, Syrkin discussed it in "Jewish Awareness in American Literature" (1964). For a recent, more patently offensive instance of the JAP (Jewish American Princess) and other Jewish stereotypes in American literature, see chapter 7 of William Styron's novel *Sophie's Choice* (1979). Her most recent incarnation may be found in the American media's coarse representations of Monica Lewinsky.

30. Interestingly, *The Lionhearted*, Reznikoff's novel about the struggle of medieval Jews in the time of Richard Coeur de Lion (the title ironically transfers the flattering epitaph to the English King's persecuted Jewish subjects), appeared in 1944. In this temporal context, it is difficult to see how Syrkin's terms might constitute anything other than an implicit repudiation of Reznikoff's choices in representation.

31. For commentary on this, and similar rabbinic strategies for negotiating with the realities imposed by the non-Jewish world, see Arnold M. Eisen, *Galut: Modern Jewish Reflection on Homelessness and Homecoming*, 35–42.

32. Quoted in Ze'ev Levy, "Zionism," in *History of Jewish Philosophy*, ed. Daniel H. Frank and Oliver Leaman, 776–85.

33. Besides Arendt's controversial argument that Eichmann was merely a banal cog, one of her recurrent themes was the complicity of the European communal leadership, which Arendt insisted must share responsibility for the extermination of the Jews. Writers like Podhoretz and Kazin were particularly outraged by Arendt's notion of Eichmann's "banality," dismissing her as a prisoner of German philosophy, which trivialized evil. But Syrkin herself immediately focused on the charge of Jewish collaboration, protesting that "[t]here are limits to which polemical vulgarity should not descend, particularly when trailing moralistic clouds. . . . The overwhelming effect of [Arendt's] report is of a blinding animus and of a vast ignorance." She goes on to argue that:

> Opponents of Zionism may attack it for any number of reasons which seem good to them—as illusory, narrowly parochial, contrary to the long-range interests of the Jews—but the persistent parallel between Eichmann's dream of a Devil's Island and Herzl's vision of a Jewish state, of

the Nazi expulsions and concentrations of their captives for their destruction with the hope, even if mistaken, of Jewish revival, is out of the realm of decent argument. The smearing of a concept by repeatedly confounding it with something admittedly evil is a technique with which the student of Nazi practices is not unacquainted. It is hard to believe that Arendt does not know what she is doing.

See "Miss Arendt Surveys the Holocaust," 250–67.

34. In *Foregone Conclusions: Against Apocalyptic History*, Michael André Bernstein describes the discursive ways in which backshadowing, literary and otherwise, has often condemned the Jews who died in the Shoah for failing to pursue the obvious "correct" course.

35. This disturbing post-Holocaust trope of nonidentity has also been memorably invoked by two survivors of the Holocaust, most famously in Paul Celan's "Psalm" and "There was earth inside them," both found in his 1963 volume significantly entitled *Die Niemandsrose*. I am grateful to Krzysztof Ziarek for this reference. Leslie Morris, who has translated and explicated the poetry of Rosa Auslaender, informs me that the "Niemand," as well as "Niemandsland," also "comes up in a number of Auslaender poems." "Niemand" appears in Auslander's 1974 volume of essays, *Ohne Visum*. Like Celan, Auslaender plays with "Niemand" as both a name ("Ich bin Koenig Niemand") and a pseudonym in her poetry. But it remains unclear whether or not Celan and Auslaender were familiar with the Sudeten narrative that provoked Syrkin.

36. Marie Syrkin, "The Crack in the Gilded Ghetto," 13–16. Whereas Nahman Syrkin's thought represents the first systematic attempt to formulate messianic tradition within a socialist context (ethical and utopian rather than Marxist), Borochov's major study, *The National Question and the Class Struggle* (Transaction, 1905), integrated Jewish nationalism with orthodox Marxist analysis. See also Gideon Shimoni, *The Zionist Ideology*.

37. This son was lost in infancy sometime in the early 1920s during her brief marriage to the biochemist Aaron Bodansky.

38. These terms are translated as: Jewish immigration to Israel, also denoting ascent; emigration from Israel, also denoting descent; the biblical name for Israel, denoting the Land and out of the Land, or "there." See Yerah Gover's analysis in "Diasporic Representations in Israeli Literature," 189.

39. 1988 was a highly charged year that put many Zionists on the defensive. Among other events, the PLO's Madison Avenue branch contrived a scheme to send its intellectuals as well as its deported guerrilla leaders to Israel on a ship that would echo the voyage of the *Exodus*, the 1947 voyage that carried Jewish survivors of Nazi death camps. See Avishai Margalit, "The Kitsch of Israel"; Marie Syrkin, "'Phony Israel': An Exercise in Nastiness," 265–71.

40. But she continued to vacillate, resigning for ideological reasons from the board of the leftist magazine *Tikkun*, soon after its first issue. David Bodansky says that

Syrkin was stung by *Tikkun*'s sharp criticism of the Labor Party's hawkish policies vis-à-vis the Palestinians. Personal communication, February 11, 1998.

41. Personal communication, February 17, 1998.

42. With their origins in the pre-state period of Emma Lazarus, these various discourses greatly enlivened Jewish cultural and literary discourse. They included the defensive (Orthodox) charge that a secular Jewish state in the biblical homeland opposes traditional religious teachings; the nineteenth-century Reform idea that statehood represents a betrayal of the universalist "mission" of the Jews; the socialist notion that Zionism was a regressive expression of bourgeois nationalism; and the assimilationist charge that support for a Jewish state raised the problem of dual loyalty and endangered Diaspora communities.

3. *Convivencia*, Hybridity, and the Jewish Urban Modernist

1. The term "diaspora" first appears in the Septuagint, the Egyptian Jewish translation of the Hebrew Bible into Greek in 250 B.C.E. The literal translation, "to be scattered" (like seeds), derives from the Hebrew of Deuteronomy 28:64, *v'hefitzcha* ("you will be scattered").

2. See David Biale, Michael Galchinsky, and Susan Heschel, eds., *Insider/Outsider: American Jews and Multiculturalism*.

3. Whereas Syrkin's previous marriage to Maurice Samuel had been disastrously short-lived, forcibly annulled by her father, the second marriage in 1919 to Bodansky, an instructor of biochemistry, was a failure apparently because the latter had no wish to see Syrkin pursue a separate career of her own. The tumultuous decade that followed brought a series of wrenching losses and gains from which the poet drew many of the private subjects treated in *Gleanings*: the death of her first son, the birth of another, the death of her father, divorce, and eventually marriage to Reznikoff, who respected her autonomy.

4. Years later, the mysterious posthumous surfacing of the manuscript for the novel *The Manner Music* caused Syrkin anguish for its caustic portrayal of the unsympathetic wife of the central character, a musician who is clearly a surrogate for the poet. The wife in Reznikoff's novel is a Zionist—as if to imply that the true artist and Jewish nationalist are natural antagonists. Though this might seem harsh, and undoubtedly it did to Syrkin, it could be said that she gives as good as she gets in the autobiographical lyrics of *Gleanings*.

5. The *Jewish Frontier* was founded in 1934 and served as the official organ of the Labor Zionist Organization of America, but soon steered away from socialism in favor of its Zionist message. Of all the Jewish journals in this pre-state period, the *Frontier* was by far the most uncompromisingly political and explicitly ideological, hardly a congenial setting for Reznikoff. Thus it is regrettable that critics such as Louis Harap distort the poet's lifelong resistence to ideology by reduc-

tively claiming that he "was a Labor-Zionist," merely on the basis of Reznikoff's reluctant association with the *Frontier*. See *Dramatic Encounters: The Jewish Presence in Twentieth-Century American Drama, Poetry, and Humor and the Black-Jewish Literary Relationship* (New York: Greenwood Press, 1987), 58. Carole Kessner confirms my sense that one shouldn't be misled by Reznikoff's presence at the pro-Zionist journal: "He got this job because Marie wangled it for him. He was a notoriously bad bread winner." Letter, Carole Kessner to Ranen Omer, June 11, 1996.

6. See Jacques Kornberg, *Theodore Herzl: From Assimilation to Zionism* (Bloomington: Indiana UP, 1993), 21, 66, 154, 162.

7. See also Ranen Omer, "The Stranger in the Metropolis: Urban Identities in the Poetry of Charles Reznikoff." My own reading of Reznikoff is indebted to numerous conversations with Stephen Fredman whose *Menorah for Athena: Charles Reznikoff and the Jewish Dilemmas of Objectivist Poetry* has alerted me to some of the most important features of Reznikoff's diasporism. Fredman demonstrates how, for Reznikoff, the linked concepts of race, homeland, and state fundamentally undermine the ethical possibility of open dialogue and even poetry itself.

8. In a similar spirit he has Benjamin Sheftall, a Jew who immigrated to the colonies in 1733, remark hopefully that "Georgia lay in the same latitude as Palestine, which God had chosen for His people." In "Jews in Georgia," November 1942, ts., Henry Hurwitz Memorial Collection, American Jewish Archives, Box 46, Folder 11: p. 9.

9. In Reznikoff's poetry, a lack of rootedness often takes the form of *mutual* exile in which the poet wanderer shares the condition of those he observes. Exile has a particular value in Reznikoff's poetry. To fully comprehend this it is important to note that Reznikoff not only read Hannah Arendt's *Menorah* review of Gershom Scholem's *Major Trends in Jewish Mysticism* but also borrowed her copy via Henry Hurwitz. In Scholem's work, "exile" is never a condition of passive suffering but rather a restless activity that can hasten the coming of a messianic age. Though a Zionist, Scholem points out that a startling range of recent historical Jewish trends, from Hasidism to early Reform Judaism (in both Germany and America), share an acceptance of *Galut* existence as the unalterable destiny of the Jewish people and, therefore, a diminishing concern with the restoration of Zion.

10. Rather than claim that Judaism survives in spite of such proximity, Roth lays out a case in a *Menorah* essay for a Judaism that actually *required* the presence of other cultures for the sake of its own coherence and in order to ensure transmissibility from one generation to the next: "It was an age when Hebraic culture was in utter decadence. The last word in human knowledge seemed at this time to have been expressed in the current Greek philosophy, with which Hebraism had to be reconciled if it were to retain any permanent value." Cecil Roth, "Paradoxes of Jewish History," 18.

11. Many decades later, Hook recalled that Cohen's polemic had "made a great difference to us." See Norman Podhoretz's interview with Sidney Hook, "On Being a Jew," 31.

12. Howard M. Sachar argues that it was a sweeping pro-Zionist orientation that provoked the rise of America's first militantly anti-Zionist group from within the ranks of the Reform Central Conference of American Rabbis: "The issue was first joined at the annual CCAR convention in June 1941, when the assembled rabbis endorsed a resolution favoring a Palestinian Jewish army brigade. The resolution passed, but only after heated debate. The anti-Zionists were furious. While fully sharing their colleagues' concern for the unfolding Jewish tragedy in Europe, in their hearts they feared the militant Zionist response to that tragedy." Nine months later a group of the anti-Zionist rabbis gathered to found the American Council for Judaism. See *A History of the Jews in America*, 565.

13. Henry Hurwitz served as the unofficial "chancellor" of the Menorah movement, which originated at Harvard in 1906 and eventually spread to colleges throughout the United States and Canada. He was the editor of *The Menorah Journal* from 1915 until his death in 1961.

14. Frequently accused of being "assimilationists," the *Menorah* intellectuals would have appreciated Ha-Am's nuanced distinction between *hitbolelut* ("assimilation") and *hikkuy shel hitharut* ("competitive assimilation"). Whereas the former obliterated Jewish identity, the latter represented a healthy and vigorous inroad into the host culture without withdrawing from Judaism.

15. Henry Hurwitz, Letter to Rabbi Louis I. Newman, President Intercollegiate Menorah Association, November 18, 1918 (37/14), Henry Hurwitz Menorah Association Memorial Collection, American Jewish Archives, Cincinnati, Ohio.

16. Henry Hurwitz, Letter to Louis D. Brandeis, February 10, 1930 (6.16), Henry Hurwitz Menorah Association Memorial Collection, American Jewish Archives, Cincinnati, Ohio.

17. Henry Hurwitz, Letter to Carl Alpert, June 24, 1941 (1/8), Henry Hurwitz Menorah Association Memorial Collection. At the time, Alpert was editor of *The New Palestine*.

18. In opposing "the effort to establish a national state in Palestine . . . as a philosophy of defeatism," the American Council for Judaism was severely censured and repudiated by such groups as the Zionist Organization of America and the Central Conference of American Rabbis. See Thomas A. Kolsky, *Jews against Zionism: The American Council for Judaism, 1942–1948*, 74–76.

19. "I must tell you how much I relished the review by Hannah Arendt in the last issue. If she can do others as well, I hope to read her often in *The Menorah*." See Charles Reznikoff, Letter to Henry Hurwitz, February 29, 1944, *Selected Letters*, 318. Significantly, Reznikoff's editorial remarks to Hurwitz refer to Hannah Arendt's essay on the writer Stefan Zweig's autobiography, *The World of Yesterday*, a work that firmly rejects the notion that the Jews should ever become a

nation again. Zweig's response to World War I was to embrace humanism and pacifism and to renounce all exacerbated forms of nationalism, including political Zionism.

20. Charles Reznikoff, Letter to Elliot Cohen, December 1, 1929. In Fredman's analysis of a similar statement made by Reznikoff many years later in a review of *The Menorah Treasury* (1964), he informs me that "Reznikoff presents the *Menorah Journal* as a Land of In-Between, where Jews with any or no relationship to Judaism could meet in an American context; from this position they could argue for their belonging to the cultural elite of America and of the world." Personal communication. See also *A Menorah for Athena: Charles Reznikoff and the Jewish Dilemmas of Objectivist Poetry* (Chicago: Chicago UP, 2001).

21. In a letter to Henry Hurwitz, Reznikoff calls the report "good, straightforward, unpretentious." See Charles Reznikoff, Letter to Henry Hurwitz, August 2, 1932, *Selected Letters*, 187.

22. Zachary Lockman's recent analysis of Labor Zionism's exclusionary practices in the twenties and thirties supports Shuster's report: "Labor Zionism's relative success in excluding Arab workers from the Jewish sector and constructing as self-sufficient a Jewish enclave as possible in the four decades before 1948—a strategy bound up with the articulation of certain visions of itself and of Arabs—was a key factor in making partition and Jewish statehood in most of Palestine possible." See Zachary Lockman, "Exclusion and Solidarity: Labor Zionism and Arab Workers in Palestine, 1897–1929." Quotations appear on pages 236, 237.

23. Charles Reznikoff, "A Jewish Treasury" (Mandeville Department of Special Collections, University of California, San Diego), 3–7.

24. The first booklength history of the DPs, by Herbert Agar, was titled *The Saving Remnant* (London: Rupert Hart-Davis, 1960), and its title-page quotes Chaim Weizmann's remark in 1933: "If, before I die, there are a half-million Jews in Palestine, I shall be content, because I know that this 'Saving Remnant' will survive." Rather than the popular term "survivor," many Holocaust survivors have embraced the same trope that Reznikoff found so morally compelling: "That term ["survivors and children of survivors"] may be fine for external consumption, but for understanding ourselves and the sources of our parents' motivation, *sheris ha'pleyte* tells us more. Perhaps we can even get America to use the term 'saving remnant.'" See Samuel Norich, "Choosing Life," *Forward* (January 21, 2000), 1, 3.

25. By the forties, other Jewish American poets had begun to voice this theme of historical endurance, often linking the tropes of "alienation" and "indestructibility." Delmore Schwartz, in "Vocation of the Poet," writes that "the Jew is at once alienated and indestructible; he is an exile from his own country and an exile even from himself, yet he survives the annihilating fury of history. In the unpredictable and fearful future that awaits civilization, the poet must be pre-

pared to be alienated." See Donald A. Dike and David H. Zucker, eds. *Selected Essays of Delmore Schwartz*, 23.

26. There is a certain sense in which Dubnow and Reznikoff might be said to share with the Zionists a common utopian mentality. Whether one believes in the permanence of Diaspora or the return of all Jews from Exile, one may still be harboring unreasonable hope.

27. Charles Reznikoff, "Introductory Note for 'Pharisee,'" June 1944 ts., Henry Hurwitz Memorial Collection, American Jewish Archives.

28. Its most prominent recent occurrence is probably in Edward Said's *Orientalism*, where the entire passage is quoted enthusiastically: "The man who finds his homeland sweet is still a tender beginner; he to whom every soil is as his native one is already strong; but he is perfect to whom the entire world is as a foreign land" (259).

29. The significance of Dubnow's formulation for what I have been calling Reznikoff's diasporist poetics lies in the former's capacity to illuminate the *Galut* as the key symbol of Jewish culture. History was more than a scorecard of persecutions—it was also a succession of intellectual and cultural triumphs:

> The first part of Jewish history, the biblical part, is a source from which, for many centuries, millions of human beings belonging to the most diverse denominations have derived instruction, solace, and inspiration. It is read with devotion by Christians in both hemispheres, in their houses and their temples. Its heroes have long ago become types, incarnations of great ideas. The events it relates serve as living ethical formulas. But a time will come—perhaps it is not very far off—when the second half of Jewish history, the record of the two thousand years of the Jewish people's life after the biblical period, will be accorded the same treatment. This latter part of Jewish history is not yet known, and many, in the thrall of prejudice, do not wish to know it. But ere long it will be known and appreciated [. . .] It is our firm conviction that the time is approaching in which the second half of Jewish history will be to the noblest part of *thinking* humanity what its first half has long been to *believing* humanity, a source of sublime moral truths. ("Diaspora" 258–59)

Dubnow's conception of Jewish identity is one that lives in the present, contributing to world culture. He argues that Jews must somehow preserve their apartness and yet also perform a kind of mission to "the rest of the nations" (259) and this too has a crucial, if sometimes oblique, role in Reznikoff's poetry.

30. See Daniel Boyarin, "Épater L'embourgeoisement: Freud, Gender, and the (De)Colonized Psyche." Quotations appear on pages 33, 39. See also Daniel Boyarin and Jonathan Boyarin, "Diaspora: Generational Ground of Jewish Identity." Emphasis mine.

31. Nachman Syrkin, "Min hachutzah ha'ohelah," 263–72. Horace M. Kallen, *The Book of Job as a Greek Tragedy*, 10, 11. More recently, Gerson D. Cohen has

argued that rabbinic Judaism succeeded in drawing "so many thousands of souls to its ethical monotheism . . . precisely because rabbinic Judaism was able to interpret the Bible and to reformulate it in Hellenistic terms." *Jewish History and Jewish Destiny*, 153.

32. Cynthia Ozick has represented the tensions of such boundary crossing in her short story "The Pagan Rabbi" in which a brilliant scholar, obsessed with transcending his "corporeality," attempts to join his soul with the spirit of Nature, which, he hallucinates, is embodied in a sapling in a deserted urban park. The story ends tragically when, after attempting copulation with the spirit, the young rabbi realizes the enormity of his idolatrous error and hangs himself from a limb of his sylvan mistress, leaving behind friends and family in bitter destitution.

33. George Steiner eloquently describes the essence of Hegel's reductive construction of the Jew's ontological "foreignness": "The sensibility of the Jew is, *par excellence*, the medium of the bitter struggle between life and thought, between spontaneous immediacy and analytic reflection, between man's unison with his body and environment and man's estrangement from them." In "Our Homeland, the Text," 6.

34. A few years later, Reznikoff (who, if his letters covering nearly sixty years are any indication, rarely refused a literary commission, particularly when it offered him an opportunity to indulge his passion for the Jewish past) uncharacteristically refused an offer that had reached him through the offices of *The Menorah*. The offer was to create propagandistic "stories for the Zionist Organization." Charles Reznikoff, Letter to Henry Hurwitz, May 1, 1945, *Selected Letters*, 320.

35. I am thinking particularly of this verse: "For in Your sight a thousand years are like yesterday that has passed, like a watch of the night." *Tanakh: A New Translation of the Holy Scriptures According to the Traditional Hebrew Text* (Jewish Publication Society: Philadelphia, 1985), 1216.

36. Spinoza is a particularly significant figure to Reznikoff and perhaps not merely for the symbolic weight of his iconoclasm. In Spinoza's view of the world, the Exile of the Jews was not truly an exile because Jerusalem no longer served as the center of Jewish geography. Much of his thought was devoted to a rigorous demystification of the centrality of the Land of Israel to Jewish identity. As Arnold M. Eisen observes in his analysis of the *Tractatus*: "Spinoza left the matter of Jewish homecoming to the realm of fantasy and 'superstition' where, apparently, he felt it belonged. Instead he focused—though he of course did not use the word—on Jewish life in exile . . . because exile and not Zion would henceforth be the site of all the redemption which Jews (or anyone else) could hope to achieve." In an important sense, Reznikoff's conflicts with ideology parallel that of Spinoza. In his own search to universalize the Jewish diasporic experience, Reznikoff also engages in a demystification of the past. It doesn't seem unreasonable to suppose that in his own modest project Reznikoff might have hoped to contribute to Spinoza's intention to strip away "the many-layered

dress of imagery and significance in which the Land had been draped for centuries." See Arnold M. Eisen, *Galut: Modern Jewish Reflection on Homelessness and Homecoming*, 61–62.

4. Diasporism in Charles Reznikoff's *Nine Plays* and Beyond

1. Charles Reznikoff, Letter to Albert Lewin, September 16, 1922, *Selected Letters*, 27. *The Menorah Journal* published the verse drama two years later and Reznikoff privately printed and published the entire collection as *Nine Plays* (1927).
2. Charles Reznikoff, "The Black Death," in *Nine Plays*, 74–84. Quotation appears on page 75. Hereafter cited parenthetically by page number.
3. As Linda Simon points out, Reznikoff "allows time and place to fade, so that in the final scene, 'Years later' intrudes into our own time." See Linda Simon, "Reznikoff: The Poet As Witness," in *Man and Poet*, 233–50. Quotation appears on page 247.
4. A few originals, as well as copies of these manuscripts, can be found in the American Jewish Archives, Cincinnati, Ohio.
5. Interview, "Charles Reznikoff and Reinhold Schiffer: The Poet in His Milieu," *Man and Poet*, 109–26. Quotation appears on page 120.
6. Reznikoff first exhibited a compassionate interest in other minorities as a precocious freshman at the School of Journalism in Missouri. According to Reznikoff his first "human interest" story for a local newspaper originated when "I was taking a walk and I passed the town's Negro cemetery. I noticed there were no headstones on the graves—instead there were toys, dolls, and other ornaments. These poor people, I realized, could not afford headstones, so they used their ingenuity instead." What we notice at once about this recollection is not only Reznikoff's sympathy for a materially impoverished population but his interest in "their ingenuity," the creative and adaptive remedies that a strong people learns to apply to exigency. It seems particularly revealing that sixty-five years later, in what would be his last, unfinished project, Reznikoff's energetic sympathies were still stimulated by the historical oppression of African Americans. Ten days before his death he told an interviewer that he had uncovered the memoirs of a former slave and was beginning to transform this account into poetry. See Ruth Rovner, "Charles Reznikoff—A Profile." In a similar vein, "Coral," perhaps the most fully realized drama of his *Nine Plays* (1927), is a sympathetic reconstruction of Nat Turner and the Abolitionist movement. In fellow Objectivist Louis Zukofsky's contemporary interpretation of what Reznikoff meant by the enigmatic title of this play, he concluded that it suggested that America could not escape its past in the slave trade and that it cast "doubt on whether man, like coral, can build upon each others' skeletons to create a new land." See Tom Sharp, "Reznikoff's Nine Plays," *Man and Poet*, 271. And in her

own essay-memoir, Syrkin recalls that he "would get involved in an act of simple helpfulness that would expand beyond the original intent. . . . Something about Charles provoked demands beyond the call of duty. . . . Sometimes he initiated these episodes. Once on a bus he noticed a young black who had been injured and was bleeding. Charles ended up by taking him by taxi to a hospital in Harlem where he was commended by the receptionist for his kind heart." See Marie Syrkin, "Charles: A Memoir," in *Man and Poet*, 37–67. Quotation appears on pages 58–59. In these days of deteriorating black-Jewish relations it is worth noting that on the whole, the *Menorah* Jews frequently and insistently invoked the plight of blacks, including the problem of lynchings in the South and their unfair treatment in the labor market in the urban North, many years before most Jews had entered the American middle class. Kallen had appeared at a Pan-African conference in 1919, and his speech, "Africa and World Democracy" was widely circulated as an NAACP pamphlet. See Hasia R. Diner, *In the Almost Promised Land: American Jews and Blacks, 1915–1935*, 137.

7. If anything, this experience of struggle can be traced to the late-nineteenth-century Yiddish-speaking milieu of Reznikoff and his Russian parents: "Poverty was one of the absolutes in Jewish life, a fact reflected in the language and literature of eastern European Jews. Yiddish . . . developed innumerable words for *poverty*. A Yiddish thesaurus needs nineteen columns of fine print for all the synonyms for *misfortune*; *good fortune* needs only five." See Gerald Sorin, *A Time for Building: The Third Migration, 1880–1920*, 14.

8. The role of Hebrew as the "authentic" voice of Jewish self-preservation and renewal in moments of crisis is evocatively preserved in a prewar joke recalled by David Aberbach, in which an "elegant Parisian woman [is] about to give birth while trying to hide her east European origins. She does not realize that her doctor is also Jewish and knows her secret. As long as she groans in French, the doctor advises his assistant to wait. Finally, she shrieks, '*Ribbono shel olam!*' [Master of the Universe]. '*Maintenant*,' the doctor says, '*le temps est arrivé.*'" See *Revolutionary Hebrew, Empire and Crisis: Four Peaks in Hebrew Literature and Jewish Survival*, 12.

9. Charles Reznikoff, "A Jewish Treasury," Mandeville Department of Special Collections, University of California, San Diego, 3.

10. He goes on to say that the *Menorah*'s editors "were always proud of the fact that they had never belonged to what they called the Jewish Establishment in America and their freedom from party, sect, or institution [provided] both a variety of perspectives on a given problem and the perspective of variety on the subjects which they regarded as Jewish." Robert Alter, "Epitaph for a Jewish Magazine," 51–55. Frequent contributors included Mordechai Kaplan (who first articulated his dream of a Reconstructionist Judaism in its pages), Lionel Trilling, Maurice Samuel, Ludwig Lewisohn, Horace Kallen, Clifton Fadiman, and Cecil Roth. Even disaffected Jews such as Hannah Arendt were attracted to the *Menorah*'s

intellectual and cultural independence. Non-Jewish social thinkers, including Randolph Bourne and John Dewey, also contributed to its cultural debates. Reznikoff's earliest books were reviewed in the *Menorah*, he published a staggering number of his poems, plays, historical sketches, and reviews in its pages, and was a contributing editor for over two decades.

11. As yet unpublished but quoted in Shirley Kaufman's "Charles Reznikoff, 1894–1976: An Appreciation," 51–56.

12. There is always the possibility that, in spite of the risk of wasted meanderings, the exilic imagination conceives a greater whole, as Paul Auster discovered after a long afternoon's encounter with Reznikoff in his West End Avenue apartment: "What at first seemed to be an endless series of digressions, a kind of aimless wandering, turned out to be the elaborate and systematic construction of a circle." See Paul Auster, "The Decisive Moment," *Man and Poet*, 163.

13. Charles Reznikoff, "An Introductory Note to Genesis" ts., N.D., Charles Reznikoff Correspondence. Henry Hurwitz Memorial Collection, American Jewish Archives.

14. Bourne later claimed to have borrowed the term from Jewish intellectuals. Randolph Bourne, "Trans-National America," 249, 255. See also "The Jew and Trans-National America."

15. Syrkin's numerous essays in this period appeared in *The Jewish Frontier*, *Commentary* and *The New Republic*. Of these, "In the DP Camps," "The DP Schools," "Mass Graves and Mass Synagogues" are reprinted in *The State of the Jews*. For her critique of the Wandering Jew trope in Western culture see "How Israel Affects American Jews," *The State of the Jews*, 287.

16. Recently, Salo Baron's student, Arthur Hertzberg, the historian of modern Zionism, has suggested ways in which the doctrine of the saving remnant may prove highly relevant to Jewish continuity in a postnationalist, multiethnic world. He argues that "Zionism . . . was the necessary response to an age of human history that is ending." Hertzberg's view suggests to me that in the near future Reznikoff's poetic representations of varied and adaptive Jewish life may find an increasingly receptive Jewish audience no longer persuaded that the Jews are destined to achieve a quiet perfection in their own land, insulated within their own culture: "Contrary to the prevailing cliché . . . those Jews who remain will not consist primarily of Lubavitcher Hasidim waiting for the rebbe to reappear as the Messiah. Our future will not be situated in B'nei Brak or Borough Park. In age after age, the lasting energy of that saving remnant has expressed itself in a variety of forms and beliefs. Those who survived the expulsion from Spain in 1492 did not lock themselves up in some new ghetto. On the contrary, they were a varied and creative group of people who made signal contributions to mercantilism, to philosophy, to literature, to poetry, indeed, to all the fields of human endeavor." Arthur Hertzberg, "Zionism in a Multiethnic World," 52–53, 92–94.

17. To see how much other literary children of immigrants (notably Saul Bellow in *Augie March*, 1953) begin to take up this theme of movement in the mid-forties and early fifties, see Sidra Dekoven Ezrahi's "State and Real Estate: Territoriality and the Modern Jewish Imagination," 428–48.

18. Letter to Henry Hurwitz, June 30, 1929, *Selected Letters*, 67. Here Reznikoff ostensibly joined in on an increasingly popular disparagement of the American rabbi, yet in doing so I think he was probably more interested in laying claim to a vital role for Jewish intellectuals and poets in Judaism's evolution as a living stream of ideas than in simply rejecting religion.

19. See for example, "Jeremiah in the Stocks" (*Poems* I, 123–26), "The Lion of Judah" (*Poems* I, 127), and "The Shield of David" (*Poems* I, 127–28). It is noteworthy that Reznikoff concludes this narrative sequence of the prophetic experience with meditations on two secular "prophets" of modernism in "Spinoza" and "Karl Marx."

20. Uriel Simon's interesting characterization of the prophet's naked humanity as "evidence of the existential gulf between the sender and the messenger" is found in his preface to *Reading Prophetic Narratives*.

21. Heschel, "Yisrael: Am, Eretz, Medinah: Ideological Evaluation of Israel and the Diaspora," quoted in Edward K. Kaplan, *Holiness in Words: Abraham Joshua Heschel's Poetics of Piety*, 112.

22. Comparing these two we might feel that, as Reznikoff never visited Europe and the DP camps as Syrkin did, he lacked her proximity to catastrophe. If his pristine vision escapes relatively unscathed, it owes primarily to the blessings of a false innocence. But it is crucial to acknowledge that for many years he pored over the trial transcripts of atrocity, sharing with Syrkin the burden of serving as a witness for the witnesses, to create finally the devastating effects of his late work *Holocaust*.

23. Hasia Diner's remarkable study, *In the Almost Promised Land: American Jews and Blacks, 1915–1935*, documents numerous instances of the Russian Jews' early identification with blacks, rather than with mainstream culture: "The black migration from the South was compared to the exodus from Egypt as well as to the Jewish mass migration from eastern European oppression. . . . The anthem sung at Garvey's conventions was called [by the Yiddish Press] 'The Negro Hatikvah'—the Hatikvah being the Zionist anthem." In 1917 a writer in the Yiddish *Forward* considered the predicament of both groups: "The Negro diaspora, the special laws, the decrees, the pogroms and also the Negro complaints, the Negro hopes are very similar to those which we Jews . . . lived through" (76). Because of such "similarities," many Russian Jews seemed to think of themselves as appropriate advocates for racial understanding: "Many of us were oppressed in Old Russia as the Negroes in free America. We can understand them better and therefore we sound their appeal wide and quickly" (71). Reznikoff was very much a part of this population of Jewish immigrants and

their children, who saw themselves as cultural bridges between the white and black worlds "because they understood both." Interestingly, Diner claims that this warm relationship, though far more complicated than what I have indicated here, drastically deteriorated only after knowledge of the Holocaust gradually began to have its searing impact on Jewish American consciousness:

> In the pre-Holocaust years [Jews] sided with blacks partly out of a reticence to tackle anti-Semitism. After the war a strident and aggressive search to expose and ferret out anti-Semitism, no matter how minor, wherever and whenever it raised its head, replaced the timidity. Before American Jews learned about Dachau, and the Warsaw Ghetto, and the crematoria and gas chambers, they went to great lengths to prove that they were not self-serving; that their motives for involvement in black affairs stemmed only from the historic bonds of empathy and commiseration. After the destruction of European Jewry and the birth of Israel, Jewish leaders openly and unabashedly talked about self-interest: how would participation in black causes "help" Jews? Was donating time, money and emotion to CORE or SNCC or the NAACP "good" for Jews? When it became less than obvious that such behavior was worthwhile from a Jewish standpoint, American Jews, with a certain degree of sadness and with memories of the past, backed off and began to look elsewhere to satisfy their quest for security and survival. (242–43)

Marie Syrkin's own response to the Shoah seems altogether representative of the shifting paradigm Diner describes.

5. Philip Roth's Lamentations for Diaspora

1. Far from both Hana Wirth-Nesher, who interprets Zuckerman's adventures in Eastern Europe as evidence of "a literature of retrieval," and Andrew Furman, who optimistically extols "Mickey Sabbath's journey of retrieval in *Sabbath's Theater*" (*Contemporary Jewish American Writers* 35), the novelist can be read primarily as a mourner of the desiccated American present.
2. Recently, Philip Roth called this character, who has lived with him—and us—for decades, his "alter-brain." See "Interview with Charles McGrath," 8.
3. Marie Syrkin, "The Fun of Self-Abuse," 64–68; reprinted in *The State of the Jews*, 331–37. Years later, Roth's antagonistic relation with Syrkin would be reworked in the guise of the stern and sanctimonious Judge Wapter who interrogates a hapless Nathan Zuckerman in the *Ghost Writer* (1979), the inaugural appearance of Roth's younger alter-ego (who has just written a story that seems to evoke Roth's "Epstein" in *Counterlife*): "Can you honestly say that there is anything in your short story that would not warm the heart of a Julius Streicher or a Joseph Goebbels?" (103–4).

4. Interestingly, the trope of the impotent Jew in Zion can be traced back to Josef Haim Brenner's *Shekol vekishalon* (*Breakdown and Bereavement*), a 1924 Hebrew novel in which the protagonist, newly arrived from Russia to join an agricultural commune, suffers an injury to his groin. As Ruth Wisse observes, "the theme of impotence is thus introduced as both a private and public matter. . . . [T]he Jew-in-Palestine's inability to . . . surmount his weakness augurs badly for the collectivity of which he forms a part." See *The Modern Jewish Canon*, 90.

5. Naomi's vigorous response must be understood in its organic relation to what would evolve as Roth's dialectical aesthetic, a consistent feature of his art that assumes its most explicit form in the counterlives exhibited in *The Counterlife* and *Operation Shylock*. Already we find the essential qualities of a counterlife (provoked by the tension between subjectivity and the collective) embedded in the "dictionary definition" of *Portnoy's Complaint* that precedes the title page, which reads in part: "A disorder in which strongly-felt ethical and altruistic impulses are perpetually warring with extreme sexual longings, often of a perverse nature."

6. Marie Syrkin, Letter to the Editor, *Commentary* 55.3 (March 1973), 8–9.

7. From such passages, the persuasiveness of Louis Menand's reading seems compelling:

> Roth didn't think that Portnoy represented liberation. He thought that *representing* Portnoy represented liberation—liberation from what he regarded as the id-less stereotypes of Jewish characters in contemporary fiction, and from middlebrow notions of stylistic decorum. Roth didn't think he was escaping from Newark. He thought he was escaping from Leon Uris. (Menand 94)

8. Scholem's two articles originally appeared in the Israeli newspaper *Haaretz*. They later were translated and published as a single piece, as Gershom Scholem, *Portnoy's Complaint*.

9. Recently, Roth claimed only to have learned about Scholem's attack years later from a Tel Aviv University professor. Upon hearing the latter imply that Scholem's judgment that Roth had irreparably endangered the Jews of *Galut* was just, the novelist replied that "history had obviously proved Scholem wrong: more than fifteen years had passed since the publication of *Portnoy's Complaint* and not a single Jew had paid anything for the book, other than the few dollars it cost in the bookstore." According to Roth, the Israeli professor huffed "not yet, but the Gentiles will make use of it when the time is right" (Searles 246).

10. In part, my consideration of Roth's codification of the pariah figure constitutes a response to Sandra Gustafson's provocative response to an earlier version of this essay—that perhaps Roth harnesses the assimilated Jewish subject primarily as a critique of the conventions and norms of the American middle class. To be sure, many of Roth's protagonists do share a dread of any unifying, centralizing, or hierarchizing world order. There are moments when such allegori-

cal "Judaism" devolves into a rationalization that masks the subject's egoistic strategies for resisting all forms of cooperation and responsibility. Hence, Zuckerman's "tribal" embrace of circumcision, at the close of *The Counterlife*, remains a deeply mysterious, nearly indecipherable act that will form the overarching basis of my efforts to interrogate Roth's attitude to Judaism.

11. Roth once thanked the Jewish board who had bestowed on him the *Present Tense* Joel H. Cavior Literary Award by suggesting that his entire career owed to Jews who had contradicted his "sense of the contradictions of Jewish life," as if there would have been no novels without the successive waves of acrimony. Alan Cooper, *Philip Roth and the Jews*, 227.

12. Ian Hamilton, "A Confusion of Realms: Interview with Philip Roth," *The Nation* (June 1, 1985), 679–81. Reprinted in Searles, 195.

13. In *Zuckerman Unbound* he briefly revived his old notoriety and struggles with the Jewish literary establishment by inventing Alvin Pepler, a parodic version of Roth, who authors an attempt to vindicate his reputation decades after he played an ambiguous role in the infamous quiz show scandals (which occurred at about the same time as Roth's earliest fiction). Just as Sheldon Grossbart had whined to his superior officer Nathan Marx in "Defender of the Faith," the nebbishy Pepler now whines for Jewish solidarity and tribal loyalty to his cause:

    "If I have to say so myself, I don't think it did the Jewish people any harm having a Marine veteran of two wars representing them on prime-time national television for three consecutive weeks. I made no bones about my religion. I said it right out. I wanted the country to know that a Jew in the Marine Corps could write a publishable book. . . . Whoever innocent I harmed and left besmirched, all the millions I let down, Jews particularly—well, they would finally understand the truth of what happened. They would forgive me." (146–47)

14. See two essays by Riv-Ellen Prell: "Rage and Representation: Jewish Gender Stereotypes in American Culture" and "Cinderellas Who (Almost) Never Become Princesses: Subversive Representations of Jewish Women in Postwar Popular Novels."

15. In her comparison of Roth's Portnoy to Bellow's Herzog, Syrkin had seemed to suggest that Roth's impiety had no precedent in Jewish American letters: "Whereas Portnoy, despite his high IQ appears to exist in a vacuum, Herzog's moral intensity is conveyed as vividly as his erotic misadventures. And where Bellow has rich humor, Roth must make do with farce" (334–35).

16. While Roth later qualifies his remarks—"in our unprecedented Western freedom there may well be a subject for imaginative scrutiny of no less gravity"— it is also true that, since the 1988 interview, his subsequent novels are increasingly about political crisis and severely alienated individuals, suggesting that his youthful hunger for the "revolutionary sense of seriousness" embodied in his literary heroes (Kafka, Beckett, Joyce) is increasingly unsatisfied by merely

contesting the sunny, frequently domestic, story of Jewish American success that had been his special focus. In the years since, Roth has approached this problem by writing a new style of novel that has been called "fiction as self-accusation." David Brauner coined this term to explain the strategies behind Roth's various self-impalements in novels such as *The Ghost Writer* and *The Professor of Desire*. See "Fiction as Self-Accusation: Philip Roth and the Jewish Other."

17. Roth's foray into "the Other Europe" taught him a great deal about narration and reality in those years. His interest in presenting himself as the protagonist of *Operation Shylock* seems to have its origins in his reading of Tadeusz Konwicki, an author published in his Penguin series. Commenting in 1984, Roth remarked on how Konwicki's strategy "strengthens the illusion that the novel is true—and not to be discounted as fiction—by impersonating himself" (Searles 168).

18. Hillel Halkin, *Letters to an American Jewish Friend: A Zionist's Polemic*, 87. Marie Syrkin and Robert Alter's reviews are quoted on the cover of the paperback version.

19. See for example, Robert M. Greenberg, "Transgression in the Fiction of Philip Roth."

20. Paul Breines, *Tough Jews: Political Fantasies and the Moral Dilemma of American Jewry*, 22–23. Breines's own position on Zionism and violence is somewhat more complex than what I am presenting here. For example, he claims that Zionism hasn't usurped Jewish identity, so much as restored a much-needed balance, liberating

> the heritage of gentleness from its Jewish constraints, opening it to *everyone*. By creating a state of their own in the only way a state can be created—through armed conquest—Zionists brought to an end both the history of Jews as unresisting victims of anti-Jewish brutality and the image of the Jew as the defenseless, peace-loving conscience of a violent, non-Jewish world. That in turn generated both the opportunity and the need for anyone and everyone to embody the violent world's defenseless, peace-loving conscience. (49–50)

21. "I don't know if I am moving up or down the cultural ladder, or simply sideways, when I recall that there has been the song "Exodus," preceded by the movie *Exodus*, preceded by the novel *Exodus*. However you slice it, there does not seem to be any doubt that the image of Jew as patriot, warrior, and battle-scarred belligerent is rather satisfying to a larger segment of the American public." From a 1961 speech delivered at Loyola University for a symposium on "The Needs and Images of Man," reprinted in *Reading Myself and Others* as "Some New Jewish Stereotypes," 137–47. Quotation appears on p. 138.

22. Roth has imagined an uncanny encounter between an assimilated Jew and his roots before. In "Eli, the Fanatic," the mere sight of a pious Other is enough to

induce an unsettling sense of Jewish vertigo in the member of a prosperous, largely Protestant, suburban community:

When he was close enough to call out, he didn't. He was stopped by the sight of the black coat that fell down below the man's knees, and the hands which held each other in his lap. By the round-topped, wide-brimmed Talmudic hat, pushed onto the back of his head. And by the beard, which hid his neck and was so soft and thin it fluttered away and back again with each heavy breath he took. . . . His face was no older than Eli's. (*Goodbye Columbus* 253)

And when Eli next confronts the "greenie" (newcomer), now wearing the clothes Eli has given him, his own identity is shattered:

The recognition took some time. He looked at what Eli wore. Up close, Eli looked at what he wore. And then Eli had the strange notion that he was two people. Or that he was one person wearing two suits. The greenie looked to be suffering from a similar confusion. They stared long at one another. Eli's heart shivered, and his brain was momentarily in such a mixed-up condition that his hands went out to button down the collar of his shirt that somebody else was wearing. What a mess! (289–90)

23. Indeed, in essence, the Zuckerman novels are about the act of writing itself, more than any surrounding reality. Most of *The Ghost Writer* (1979), the first of the Zuckerman novels, is set in the home of the lonely writer E. I. Lonoff and explores various forms of literary malfeasance. *Zuckerman Unbound* (1981) examines Zuckerman's success after writing his shocking bestseller, the *Portnoy*-like novel *Carnovsky*.

24. For a brilliant parody, with enduring timeliness, on the impact of Jewish American fundamentalism on Israeli politics, see Tova Reich's darkly comic novel *The Jewish War* (1995).

25. This skeptical resistance toward embracing the pastoral, or natural realm, as a forbidden territory somehow *treyf* for the Jewish subject has had a surprisingly weighty endurance in Jewish American fiction. Witness Saul Bellow's negative dismissal of the edenic Ludeyville in *Herzog* (1964) as a "remote green hole" and Cynthia Ozick's "The Pagan Rabbi" (1966) wherein a gifted young rabbi loses his soul and life in worship of a seductive wood nymph, not to mention Reznikoff's struggle between the "Hebraic" and "Hellenic" views of Nature.

26. For a fastidious WASP like John Updike, the novel's willingness to give all its fervent characters a fair hearing proves too much of a good thing: "[Roth's] characters seem to be on speed, up at all hours and talking until their mouths bleed. There are too many of them; they keep dropping out of sight and when they reappear they don't talk the same." John Updike, "Recruiting Raw Nerves," 298.

6. Assimilation, Madness, and Passing

1. This episode is peculiarly consistent with ways in which American Jewry has chosen to commemorate the triumphal consonance of Jewish/American identities. In the Skirball Cultural Center of Los Angeles, there is a red-white-and-blue " 'V' for Victory" flag stemming from the Second World War, invoking prayers for the nation and for President Roosevelt, written in English, Hebrew, and Yiddish," among similar artifacts. See Stephen J. Whitfield, *In Search of American Jewish Culture*, 226.

2. There is a startling correlation between Roth's latest fiction and the angst articulated in the earliest Jewish American fiction of the century. For instance, in Isidor Schneider's *From the Kingdom of Necessity* (1935), a story that narrates the transition from shtetl to America, a character laments the cost of Americanization: "All children go mad in America, and lose their respect. A dollar in their hands makes them kings who rule their parents. It is a lunatic country. May it burn up." Madness—as the affliction of Jewish children of assimilated parents—is a theme that has preoccupied Roth throughout his career, from Eli the Fanatic and Portnoy to Sabbath and Merry Levov, where it reaches its apparent nadir.

3. In *The Prague Orgy* (1985), Zuckerman ruefully distinguishes his "Zion" as the "Jewish Atlantis of an American childhood dream" (64).

Conclusion

1. See Claire Bloom, *Leaving a Doll's House: A Memoir*.

2. For an illuminating discussion of the limitations of contemporary Israeli representations of otherness, see Yerah Gover, "Diasporic Representations in Israeli Literature."

3. See E. J. Kessler, "Eros in the Rain."

4. As one journalist later observed, Halkin's bombast was "as muscularly nationalist a statement as was made in three days."

5. *New York Times*, December 5, 1982.

Works Cited

Aberbach, David. *Revolutionary Hebrew, Empire and Crisis: Four Peaks in Hebrew Literature and Jewish Survival*. New York: New York UP, 1998.

Alter, Robert. "Epitaph for a Jewish Magazine." *Commentary*. May 1965.

———. "Poet of Exile." *Commentary*. February 1977.

Anderson, Amanda. "George Eliot and the Jewish Question." *The Yale Journal of Criticism* 10.1. 1997: 39–61.

Anderson, Benedict. *Imagined Communities*. London: Verso, 1991.

Antler, Joyce. *The Journey Home: Jewish Women and the American Century*. New York: Simon and Schuster, 1997.

Ardolino, Frank. "The Americanization of the Gods: Onomastics, Myth, and History in Philip Roth's *The Great American Novel*." *Arete* 3. 1. Fall 1985.

Arendt, Hannah. *Eichmann in Jerusalem: A Report on the Banality of Evil*. New York: Penguin, 1980 [1963].

———. *The Jew as a Pariah: Jewish Identity and Politics in the Modern Age*. Ed. Ron Feldman. New York: Grove Press, 1978.

———. "Zionism Reconsidered." *Menorah Journal* 33.2. Autumn 1945. Reprinted in *Zionism Reconsidered: The Rejection of Jewish Normalcy*, ed. Michael Selzer. London: The Macmillan Company, 1970.

Asch, Sholem. *Children of Abraham: The Short Stories of Sholem Asch*. New York: Irvington Publishers, 1982.

Avishai, Bernard. "The State of Zionism." *Social Praxis* 4. 1976/77.

Bach, Gerhard, and Blaine Hall. *Conversations with Grace Paley*. Jackson: UP of Mississippi, 1997.

Barack-Fishman, Sylvia. "Homelands of the Heart: Israel and Jewish Identity in American Jewish Fiction." In *Envisioning Israel: The Changing Ideals and Images of North American Jews*, ed. Allon Gal. Jerusalem: The Hebrew UP, 1996.

———. "Success in Circuit Lies: Philip Roth's Recent Explorations of American Jewish Identity." *Jewish Social Studies: History, Culture, and Society* 3. 1997, 111–31.

Baum, Charlotte, Paula Hyman, and Sonya Michel Baum. *The Jewish Woman in America*. New York: New American Library, 1977.

Ben-Arieh, Yehoshua. *The Rediscovery of the Holy Land in the Nineteenth Century*. Jerusalem and Detroit: Magnes Press and Wayne State UP, 1979.

Ben-Yehuda, Eliezer. "She'elah nekhbadah" (A Weighty Question) 1879. In *Hachalom veshivro: Mivchar ketavim be'inyanei lashon* (The Dream and its Fulfillment: Selected Writings), ed. with an introduction and notes by Reuven Sivan. 2nd edition, Tel Aviv: Bar Ilan University Press, 1986.

Bercovitch, Sacvan. *The American Puritan Imagination: Essays in Revaluation*. London: Cambridge UP, 1974.

Berkowitz, Michael. *Western Jewry and the Zionist Project: 1914–1933*. Cambridge: Cambridge UP, 1997.

Berkson, Isaac B. *Theories of Americanization: A Critical Study, with Special Reference to the Jewish Group*. New York: Columbia UP, 1920.

Bernstein, Charles. "Reznikoff's Nearness." *Sulfur* 13.1. Spring 1993.

Bernstein, Michael André. *Foregone Conclusions: Against Apocalyptic History*. Berkeley: U of California P, 1994.

Biale, David. *Eros and the Jews*. New York: Basic Books, 1992.

———. *Gershom Scholem: Kabbalah and Counter-History*. Cambridge, Mass.: Harvard UP, 1979.

———. *Power and Powerlessness in Jewish History*. New York: Schocken Books, 1986.

———, Michael Galchinsky, and Susan Heschel, eds. *Insider/Outsider: American Jews and Multiculturalism*. Berkeley, U of California P, 1998.

Birnbaum, Pierre, and Ira Katznelson, eds. *Paths of Emancipation: Jews, States, and Citizenship*. Princeton: Princeton UP, 1995.

Bleich, David. "Learning, Learning, Learning: Jewish Poetry in America." Pp. 179–93 in Jonathan N. Barron and Eric Murphy Selinger, *Jewish American Poetry: Poems, Commentary and Reflections*. Hanover, N.H.: Brandeis UP, 2000.

Bloom, Claire. *Leaving a Doll's House: A Memoir*. Boston: Little, Brown, 1996.

Bloom, Harold. *Agon: Towards a Theory of Revision*. New York: Oxford UP, 1982.

Booth, Alison. *Greatness Engendered: George Eliot and Virginia Woolf*. Ithaca, N.Y.: Cornell UP, 1992.

Bourne, Randolph S. "The Jew and Trans-national America." *Menorah Journal* 2. December 1916.

———. *The Radical Will: Selected Writings, 1911–1918*. New York: Urizen Books, 1977.

Boyarin, Daniel. "Èpater L'embourgeoisement: Freud, Gender, and the (De)Colonized Psyche." *Diacritics* 24. 1994.

———. "Masada or Yavneh? Gender and the Arts of Jewish Resistance." In *Jews and Other Differences: The New Jewish Cultural Studies*, ed. Daniel Boyarin and Jonathan Boyarin. Minneapolis: U of Minnesota P, 1997.

———. "Purim and the Cultural Poetics of Judaism—Theorizing Diaspora." Poetics Today 15.1. Spring 1994: 1–8.

———. *Unheroic Conduct: The Rise of Heterosexuality and the Invention of the Jewish Man*. Berkeley: U of California P, 1997.

Boyarin, Daniel, and Jonathan Boyarin. "Diaspora: Generational Ground of Jewish Identity." *Critical Inquiry* 19.4. 1993: 693–725.

Boyarin, Jonathan. *Storm from Paradise: The Politics of Jewish Memory*. Minneapolis: U of Minnesota P, 1992.

———. *Thinking In Jewish*. Chicago: U of Chicago P, 1996.

Brauner, David. "Fiction as Self-Accusation: Philip Roth and the Jewish Other." *Studies in American Jewish Literature* 17. 1998: 8–16.

Breines, Paul. *Tough Jews: Political Fantasies and the Moral Dilemma of American Jewry*. New York: Basic Books, 1990.

Brenner, Josef Haim. *Breakdown and Bereavement*. Philadelphia: Jewish Publication Society, 1971.

Burrell, David B. "Philosophical Reflections on Religious Claims and Religious Intransigence in Relation to the Conflict." In *Philosophical Perspectives on the Israeli-Palestinian Conflict*, ed. Tomis Kapitan. London: M. E. Sharpe, 1997.

Castel-Bloom, Orly. Address, "Reflections on Literature and Identity." Writing the Jewish Future Conference. National Foundation for Jewish Culture. San Francisco, Feb. 2, 1998.

Cheyette, Bryan. *Between 'Race' and Culture: Representations of 'the Jew' in English and American Literature*. Stanford: Stanford UP, 1996.

Clifford, James. "Diasporas." *Cultural Anthropology* 9.3. 1994: 302–38.

———. *Routes: Travel and Translation in the Late Twentieth Century*. Cambridge: Harvard UP, 1997.

Cohen, Gerson D. *Jewish History and Jewish Destiny*. New York: Jewish Theological Seminary of America, 1997.

Cohen, Hermann. *Religion of Reason*. 1918. Trans. Simon Kaplan. New York: Frederick Unger, 1972.

Cohen, Morris Raphael. "Zionism: Tribalism or Liberalism?" *The New Republic*. March 8, 1919.

Cohen, Richard. *Tough Jews*. New York: Simon and Schuster, 1998.

Cohen, Yoel. "The Jewish Diaspora News Media and the 1982 Lebanon War." In *Israel and Diaspora Jewry: Ideological and Political Perspectives*. Jerusalem: Bar Ilan UP, 1991.

Cooper, Alan. *Philip Roth and the Jews*. New York: State U of New York P, 1996.

Cowen, Philip. *Memories of an American Jew*. New York: International Press, 1932.

Cox, Samuel S. *Orient Sunbeams, or From the Porte to the Pyramids, by Way of Palestine*. New York: G. P. Putnam's Sons, 1882.

Cuddihy, John Murray. *The Ordeal of Civility: Freud, Marx, Lévi-Strauss and the Jewish Struggle with Modernity*. New York: Basic Books, 1974.

Davidson, Michael. *Ghostlier Demarcations: Modern Poetry and the Material Word*. Berkeley: U of California P, 1997.

Davies, W. D. *Jewish and Pauline Studies*. Philadelphia: Fortress Press, 1984.

———. *The Territorial Dimension of Judaism*. Berkeley: U of California P, 1982.

Davis, Moshe. *America and the Holy Land*. London: Praeger, 1995.

———. "The Holy Land Idea in American Spiritual History." Pp. 3–33 in *With Eyes Toward Zion: Scholars Colloquium on America–Holy Land Studies*, ed. Moshe Davis. New York: Arno Press, 1977.

Dawidowicz, Lucy S. *What Is the Use of Jewish History?* Ed. Neal Kozodoy. New York: Schocken Books, 1992.

de Sola Pool, David and Tamar. *An Old Faith in a New World: Portrait of Shearith Israel, 1654–1954*. New York: Columbia UP, 1955.

Deutscher, Isaac. "The Wandering Jew as Thinker and Revolutionary." *Partisan Review* 25. 4. Fall 1958: 556.

Dike, Donald A., and David H. Zucker, eds. Selected Essays of Delmore Schwartz. Chicago: U of Chicago P, 1970.

Diner, Hasia R. *In the Almost Promised Land: American Jews and Blacks, 1915–1935*. London: Greenwood Press, 1977.

Dubnow, Simon. "Diaspora." in *Encyclopedia of the Social Sciences*. New York: Macmillan, 1931.

———. "An Essay in the Philosophy of History." *Ideas of Jewish History*, ed. Michael A. Meyer. Detroit: Wayne State UP, 1987.

———. *History of the Jews*. Vol. 5. Trans. Moshe Spiegel. South Brunswick, N.J.: T. Yoselof, 1973.

———. *Nationalism and History: Essays in Old and New Judaism*. Philadelphia: Jewish Publication Society of America, 1958.

Edelheit, Hershel, and Abraham J. Edelheit. *A World in Turmoil: An Integrated Chronology of the Holocaust and World War II*. New York: Greenwood Press, 1991.

Eisen, Arnold M. *Galut: Modern Jewish Reflection on Homelessness and Homecoming*. Bloomington: Indiana UP, 1986.

———. "In the Wilderness: Reflections on American Jewish Culture." *Jewish Social Studies*. 5.1/2. Fall 1998/Winter 1999: 25–39.

Eliot, George. *Daniel Deronda*. Ed. Graham Handley. Oxford: Clarendon Press, 1984.

———. *The Impressions of Theophrastus Such*. London: Everyman, 1995.

Emerson, Ralph Waldo. *The Collected Works of Ralph Waldo Emerson*. Ed. Alfred R. Ferguson et al. 5 volumes to date. Cambridge, Mass.: Belknap Press of Harvard University Press, 1971.

———. *Representative Men: Seven Lectures*. Ed. Douglas Emory Wilson. Cambridge: Belknap Press, 1996.

Endelman, Todd M. "The Legitimization of the Diaspora Experience in Recent Jewish Historiography." *Modern Judaism* 11.1. February 1991: 195–209.

Ezrahi, Sidra Dekoven. *Booking Passage: Exile and Homecoming in the Modern Jewish Imagination* (Los Angeles: U of California P, 2000).

———. "Israel and Jewish Writing." *Religion and Literature*. Spring 1999: 9–21.

———. "State and Real Estate: Territoriality and the Modern Jewish Imagination." In *Terms of Survival: The Jewish World Since 1945*, ed. Robert S. Wistrich. New York: Routledge, 1995.

Ezrahi, Yaron. *Rubber Bullets: Power and Conscience in Modern Israel*. New York: Farrar, Straus and Giroux, 1997.

Falk, Avner. *A Psychoanalytic History of the Jews*. London: Associated University Presses, 1996.

Fein, Leonard. *Smashing Idols and Other Prescriptions for Jewish Continuity*. New York: The Nathan Cummings Foundation, 1994.

——, ed. *Jewish Possibilities: The Best of Moment Magazine*. London: Jason Aronson, 1987.

Feingold, Henry L. *Lest Memory Cease: Finding Meaning in the American Jewish Past*. New York: Syracuse UP, 1996.

——. *Zion in America: The Jewish Experience from Colonial Times to the Present*. New York: Hippocrene, 1974.

Felstiner, John. "Jews Translating Jews." Pp. 337–44 in *Jewish American Poetry: Poems, Commentary, and Reflections*, ed. Jonathan N. Barron and Eric Murphy Selinger. Hanover, N.H.: Brandeis UP, 2000.

Feuerlicht, Roberta Strauss. *The Fate of the Jews: A People Torn Between Israeli Power and Jewish Ethics*. New York: Times Books, 1983.

Fiedler, Leslie A. "I. B. Singer, or, the American-ness of the American-Jewish Writer." *Fiedler on the Roof*. Boston: D. R. Godine, 1991.

Finkelstein, Norman. "Tradition and Modernity, Judaism and Objectivism: The Poetry of Charles Reznikoff" (unpublished manuscript).

Fisch, Harold. "Reading and Carnival: On the Semiotics of Purim." *Poetics Today* 15:1. Spring 1994.

Fishbane, Michael A. *Judaism: Revelation and Traditions*. New York: HarperCollins, 1987.

Frank, Daniel H., and Oliver Leaman, eds. *History of Jewish Philosophy*. New York: Routledge, 1997.

Frankel, Jonathan. *Prophecy and Politics: Socialism, Nationalism and the Russian Jews, 1862–1917* (Cambridge: Cambridge UP, 1981.

——. "The 'Yizkor' Book of 1911—A Note on National Myths in the Second Aliya." In *Religion, Ideology and Nationalism in Europe and America: Essays Presented in Honor of Yehoshua Arieli*. Jerusalem: The Historical Society of Israel, 1986.

Fredman, Stephen. *A Menorah for Athena: Charles Reznikoff and the Jewish Dilemmas of Objectivist Poetry*. Chicago: U of Chicago P, 2001.

Freedman, William. "Israel: The New Diaspora." In *Diaspora: Exile and the Jewish Condition*, ed. Ètan Levine. New York: Jason Aronson, 1983.

Freud, Sigmund. *Jokes and their Relation to the Unconscious*. Trans. James Strachey. New York: W. W. Norton, 1972.

Friedlander, Israel. "The Problem of Judaism in America." *Past and Present: Selected Essays*. New York: The Burning Bush Press, 1961.

Friedman, Saul S. "Emma Lazarus: American Poet and Zionist." Pp. 220–46 in *Women in History, Literature and the Arts: A Festschrift for Hildegard Schnuttgen in Honor of Her Thirty Years of Outstanding Service at Youngstown State University*. Youngstown, Ohio: Youngstown State UP, 1989.

Furman, Andrew. *Contemporary Jewish American Writers and the Multicultural Dilemma: Return of the Exiled.* Syracuse, New York: Syracuse UP, 2000.

———. *Israel Through the Jewish-American Imagination: A Survey of Jewish-American Literature on Israel, 1928–1995.* Albany: State University of New York, 1997.

Gal, Allon. *Envisioning Israel: The Changing Ideals and Images of North American Jews.* Jerusalem: The Magnes Press, 1996.

Galchinsky, Michael. "Scattered Seeds: A Dialogue of Diasporas." In *Insider/Outsider: American Jews and Multiculturalism*, ed. David Biale, Michael Galchinsky, and Susan Heschel. Berkeley: U of California P, 1998.

Gans, Herbert. "Symbolic Ethnicity." *Ethnic and Racial Studies* 2. 1979.

Gilman, Sander. *Jewish Self-Hatred: Anti-Semitism and the Hidden Language of the Jews.* Baltimore: Johns Hopkins UP, 1986.

———. *The Jew's Body.* New York: Routledge, 1991.

Gitenstein, Barbara R. *Apocalyptic Messianism and Contemporary Jewish-American Poetry.* Albany: State U of New York P, 1986.

Glanz, Rudolf. *The Jew in Early American Wit and Graphic Humor.* New York: Ktav Publishing, 1973.

Glazer, Nathan. "Jewish Intellectuals." *Partisan Review: The Fiftieth Anniversary Issue*, ed. William Phillips. New York: Dimensions, 1985.

Goldstein, Sidney, and Alice Goldstein. *Jews on the Move: Implications for Jewish Identity.* Albany: State U of New York P, 1996.

Goren, Arthur A. "'Anu banu artza' in America: The Americanization of the Halutz Ideal." In *Envisioning Israel: The Changing Ideals and Images of North American Jews*, ed. Allon Gal. Jerusalem: Magnes Press, 1996.

———. "Celebrating Zion in America," In *Encounters with the 'Holy Land': Place, Past and Future in American Jewish Culture*, ed. Jeffrey Shandler and Beth Wenger. Philadelphia: National Museum of American Jewish History, 1997.

Gottheil, Richard. *Zionism.* Philadelphia: The Jewish Publication Society of America, 1914.

Gover, Yerah. "Diasporic Representations in Israeli Literature." *Response: A Contemporary Jewish Review* 68. Fall 97/Winter 98: 185–96.

Graetz, Heinrich. *The History of the Jews.* 5 vols. Philadelphia: Jewish Publication Society, 1967.

Greenberg, Hayim. "The Irresponsible Revisionists," *Jewish Frontier.* November 1943.

Greenberg, Robert M. "Transgression in the Fiction of Philip Roth." *Twentieth Century Literature* 43. 1997: 487–506.

Gruen, Erich S. *Heritage and Hellenism: The Reinvention of Jewish Tradition.* Berkeley: U of California P, 1998.

Grumet, Elinor Joan. *The Menorah Idea and the Apprenticeship of Lionel Trilling.* Ph.D. dissertation, University of Iowa, 1979.

Gustafson, Sandra. "Nations of Israelites: Prophecy and Cultural Autonomy in the Writings of William Apess." *Religion and Literature* 26.1. Spring 1994.

Guttmann, Allen. *The Jewish Writer in America: Assimilation and the Crisis of Identity.* New York: Oxford UP, 1971.

Haam, Ahad. *kol kitve Ahad Haam.* Tel Aviv: Devir, 1947.

Halkin, Hillel. "After Zionism: Reflections on Israel and the Diaspora." *Commentary.* June 1997.

———. "Israel's Civil War within the Ranks of the Left." *The Chronicle of Higher Education.* March 13, 1998.

———. *Letters to an American Jewish Friend: A Zionist's Polemic.* Philadelphia: The Jewish Publication Society of America, 1977.

Halpern, Ben. "The Americanization of Zionism, 1880–1930." In *Essential Papers on Zionism*, ed. Jehuda Reinharz and Anita Shapira. New York: New York UP, 1996.

———. *The Idea of the Jewish State.* Cambridge: Harvard UP, 1969.

———. *Jews and Blacks: The Classic American Minorities.* New York: Herder and Herder, 1971.

———. "Soliloquies on a Colloquium: II and III." *Jewish Frontier.* March 1967.

Hamilton, Ian. "A Confusion of Realms: Interview with Philip Roth." *The Nation.* June 1, 1985: 679–81.

Harap, Louis. *The Image of the Jew in American Literature: From Early Republic to Mass Immigration.* Philadelphia: The Jewish Publication Society of America, 1974.

Harshav, Benjamin. *Language in Time of Revolution.* Berkeley: U of California P, 1993.

Heine, Heinrich. *Poems and Ballads.* Trans. Emma Lazarus. New York: Hartsdale House, 1947.

Heinze, Andrew R. *Adapting to Abundance: Jewish Immigrants, Mass Consumption, and the Search for American Identity.* New York: Columbia UP, 1990.

Heller, Deborah. "George Eliot's Jewish Feminist." *Atlantis: A Women's Studies Journal.* 8. 1983: 37–43.

Herford, R. Travers, ed. and trans. *The Ethics of the Talmud: Sayings of the Fathers.* New York: Schocken Books, 1945.

Hertzberg, Arthur. "Zionism in a Multiethnic World." *Moment.* February 1998.

———, ed. *The Zionist Idea: A Historical Analysis and Reader.* New York: Harper & Row, 1959.

Herzl, Theodor. *The Jews' State: A Critical English Translation*, trans. Henk Overberg. New York: Jason Aronson, 1997.

Heschel, Abraham Joshua. *The Earth Is the Lord's and the Sabbath.* New York: Harper Torchbooks, 1966.

———. *The Sabbath: Its Meaning for Modern Man.* New York: Farrar, Straus and Giroux, 1951.

Heschel, Susannah. "Jewish Feminism and Women's Identity." In *Seen but Not Heard: Jewish Women in Therapy*, ed. Rachel Siegel and Ellen Cole. New York: Harrington Park Press, 1991.

———. *On Being a Jewish Feminist: A Reader*. New York: Schocken Books, 1983.

Heymann, Michael. "The State of the Zionist Movement on the Eve of the Sixth Congress." In *Essential Papers on Zionism*, ed. Jehuda Reinharz and Anita Shapira. New York: New York UP, 1996.

Higham, John. *Send These to Me: Jews and Other Immigrants in Urban America*. New York: Atheneum, 1975.

———. *Strangers in the Land*. New York: Atheneum, 1959.

Hindus, Maurice. *A Traveler in Two Worlds*. New York: Doubleday, 1971.

Hindus, Milton. "Charles Reznikoff." In *The "Other" New York Jewish Intellectuals*, ed. Carole S. Kessner. New York: New York UP. 1004.

———. *Charles Reznikoff: A Critical Essay*. Santa Barbara: Black Sparrow Press, 1977.

———, ed. *Charles Reznikoff: Man and Poet*. Orono, Maine: National Poetry Foundation, 1984.

Howe, Irving. *Jewish-American Stories*. New York: New American Library, 1977.

———. *World of Our Fathers: The Journey of the East European Jews to America and the Life They Found and Made*. New York: Harcourt Brace Jovanovich, 1976.

———. *A Margin of Hope: An Intellectual Autobiography*. San Diego: Harcourt Brace Jovanovich, 1982.

Hoyt, Charles Alva. "The New Romanticism." In *Bernard Malamud and the Critics*, ed. Leslie and Joyce Field. New York: New York UP, 1970.

Hurwitz, Solomon. "George Eliot's Jewish Characters." *Jewish Forum* 5. 1922.

Hurwood, David Lynn. "Israel: First Pilgrimage." *The Yale Review*. Spring 1970.

Hyman, Paula E. *Gender and Assimilation in Modern Jewish History: The Roles and Representations of Women*. Seattle: U of Washington P, 1995.

———, and Deborah Dash Moore, eds. *Jewish Women in America: An Historical Encyclopedia*. 2 vols. New York: Routledge, 1997.

Israel, Richard J. "Can Israel Contribute to an American Jewish Ideology?" *Jewish Frontier*. March 1967.

Jacob, H. E. *The World of Emma Lazarus*. New York: Schocken Books, 1949.

Jacobson, Matthew Frye. *Whiteness of a Different Color: European Immigrants and the Alchemy of Race*. Cambridge, Mass.: Harvard UP, 1998.

Kakutani, Michiko. "Confronting the Failures of a Professor Who Passes." *New York Times*. May 2, 2000.

———. "Sabbath's Theater." *New York Times*. August 22, 1995.

Kallen, Horace. *The Book of Job as a Greek Tragedy*. New York: Moffat, Yard and Company, 1959.

———. *The Struggle for Jewish Unity*. New York: American Jewish Congress, 1933.

———. *Zionism and World Politics*. 1921. Reprinted Westport, Connecticut: Greenwood Press, 1975.

Kamenetz, Rodger. *Stalking Elijah: Adventures with Today's Jewish Mystical Masters*. San Francisco: HarperCollins, 1997.

Kaplan, Edward K. *Holiness in Words: Abraham Joshua Heschel's Poetics of Piety*. Albany: State U of New York P, 1996.

Kaplan, Mordechai. *Judaism as a Civilization*. New York: Macmillan, 1934.

———. "The Next Step in Zionism," in *Forum for the Problems of Zionism, World Jewry, and the State of Israel*. 4. Spring 1959.

Katz, Jacob. *From Prejudice to Destruction: Anti-Semitism, 1700–1933*. Cambridge: Cambridge UP, 1980.

———. "The Term 'Jewish Emancipation': Its Origin and Historical Impact." In *Studies in Nineteenth-Century Jewish Intellectual History*. Cambridge, Mass.: Harvard UP, 1964.

Katznelson, Ira. "Between Separation and Disappearance: Jews on the Margins of American Liberalism." Pp. 157–205 in *Paths of Emancipation: Jews, States, and Citizenship*, ed. Pierre Birnbaum and Ira Katznelson. Princeton: Princeton UP, 1995.

Kaufman, Shirley. "Charles Reznikoff, 1894–1976: An Appreciation." *Midstream*. August/September, 1976.

Kazin, Alfred. *On Native Grounds: An Interpretation of Modern American Prose Literature*. New York: Reynal and Hitchcock, 1942.

Kern, Stephen. *The Culture of Time and Space: 1880–1918*. Cambridge, Mass.: Harvard UP, 1983.

Kessler, Clive S. "The Politics of Jewish Identity: Arendt and Zionism." *Hannah Arendt: Thinking, Judging, Freedom*, ed. Gisela T. Kaplan and Clive S. Kessler. London: Allen and Unwin, 1989.

Kessler, E. J. "Eros in the Rain." *Forward*. February 13, 1998: 1, 10.

Kessner, Carole S. "Behind the Polemics: A Woman." *Reconstructionist* 45. July 1979.

———. "Marie Syrkin: An Exemplary Life." In *The "Other" New York Jewish Intellectuals*, ed. Carole S. Kessner. New York: New York UP, 1994.

———. "Matrilineal Dissent: Emma Lazarus, Marie Syrkin and Cynthia Ozick." Pp. 197–215 in *Women of the Word: Jewish Women and Jewish Writing*, ed. Judith R. Baskin. Detroit: Wayne State UP, 1994.

———. "On Behalf of the Jewish People: Marie Syrkin at Ninety." *Jewish Book Annual* 46 (1988–1989). New York: Jewish Book Council, 1988.

Kirshenblatt-Gimblett, Barbara. "A Place in the World: Jews and the Holy Land at World's Fairs." Pp. 60–82 in *Encounters with the "Holy Land": Place, Past and Future in American Jewish Culture*, ed. Jeffrey Shandler and Beth S. Wenger. Hanover, N.H.: UP of New England, 1997.

Kitaj, R. B. *First Diasporist Manifesto*. New York: Thames and Hudson, 1989.

Klein, Marcus. *Foreigners: The Making of American Literature, 1900–1940*. Chicago: U of Chicago P, 1981.

Klingenstein, Susanne. *Enlarging America: The Cultural Work of Jewish Literary Scholars, 1930–1990*. Syracuse, N.Y.: Syracuse UP, 1998.

———. *Jews in the American Academy, 1900–1940: The Dynamics of Intellectual Assimilation*. New Haven, Conn.: Yale UP, 1991.

Kolsky, Thomas A. *Jews against Zionism: The American Council for Judaism, 1942–1948*. Philadelphia: Temple UP, 1990.

Kraut, Benny. *From Reform Judaism to Ethical Culture: The Religious Evolution of Felix Adler*. Cincinnati: Hebrew Union College Press, 1979.

Krow-Lucal, Martha G. "Marginalizing History: Observations on *The Origins of the Inquisition in Fifteenth-Century Spain* by B. Netanyahu." *Judaism* 46. Winter 1997.

Krug, Nora Berkley. "How Jewish Women Novelists are Reinventing the Past." *Forward*. February 4, 2000: 10–11.

Lainoff, Seymour. *Ludwig Lewisohn*. Boston: Twayne Publishers, 1982.

Lazarus, Emma. *Admetus and Other Poems*. New York: Hurd and Houghton, 1871.

———. "The Eleventh Hour." *Scribner's* 16. June 1878: 242–56.

———. *Emma Lazarus in Her World: Life and Letters*. Ed. Beth Roth Young. Jerusalem: Jewish Publication Society, 1995.

———. "Emerson's Personality." *Century* 24 (1882).

———. *Emma Lazarus: Selections from Her Poetry and Prose*. Ed., with introduction and notes, Morris U. Schappes. New York: Emma Lazarus Federation of Jewish Women's Clubs, 1967.

———. *Letters of Emma Lazarus*. Ed. Morris U. Schappes. New York: New York Public Library, 1949.

———. *The Poems of Emma Lazarus*. 2 vols. Boston: Houghton Mifflin, 1888.

Lazarus, Josephine. "Biographical Sketch of Emma Lazarus." In *Poems of Emma Lazarus*. 2 vols. Boston: Houghton Mifflin, 1888.

———. "Zionism and Americanism." *Menorah: Monthly Magazine for the Jewish Home*. May 1905: 262–68.

Leibowitz, Yeshayu. *Judaism, Human Values, and the Jewish State*. Ed. Eliezer Goldman. Cambridge, Mass.: Harvard UP, 1992.

Lerner, Michael. *Jewish Renewal*. New York: Grosset/Putnam, 1994.

———. "The Jews and the 60s: Philip Roth Still Doesn't Get It." *Tikkun*. May/June 1997: 13–16.

Lester, Julius. "The Outsiders." *Transition* 68. Winter 1995.

Levias, Caspar. "The Justification of Zionism." *Central Conference of American Rabbis*. *Yearbook* 9. 1899.

Levinas, Emmanuel. *Difficult Freedom: Essays on Judaism*. Trans. Sean Hand. Baltimore: Johns Hopkins UP, 1997.

Levine, Etan, ed. *Diaspora: Exile and the Jewish Condition*. New York: Jason Aronson, 1983.

Levine, Samuel H. "Palestine in the Literature of the United States to 1867." In *Early*

History of Zionism in America, ed. Isidore S. Meyer. New York: American Jewish Historical Society, 1958.

Levy, Ze'ev. "Tradition, Heritage and Autonomy in Modern Jewish Thought." Pp. 41–56 in *Autonomy and Judaism: The Individual and the Community in Jewish Philosophical Thought*, ed. Daniel H. Frank. Albany: State U of New York P, 1992.

———. "Zionism." In *History of Jewish Philosophy*, ed. Daniel H. Frank and Oliver Leaman. New York: Routledge, 1997.

Lewisohn, Ludwig. *The Answer: The Jew and the World, Past, Present and Future.* New York: Liveright Publishing, 1939.

Lichtenberg, Bracha Ettinger. "'This is the desert. Nothing strikes root here': A Talk with Edmond Jabès." Pp. 246–56 in *Routes of Wandering: Nomadism, Voyages and Transitions in Contemporary Israeli Art*, ed. Yigal Zalmona. Jerusalem: Israel Museum, 1991.

Lichtenstein, Diane. "Words and Worlds: Emma Lazarus's Conflicting Citizenships." *Tulsa Studies in Women's Literature* 6.2. Fall 1987: 247–63.

———. *Writing Their Nations: The Tradition of Nineteenth-Century American Jewish Women Writers.* Bloomington: Indiana UP, 1992.

Lipset, Seymour Martin. "The American Jewish Community in a Comparative Context." In *The Ghetto and Beyond: Essays in Jewish Life in America*, ed. Peter I. Rose. New York: Random House, 1969.

Liptzin, Solomon. *Generation of Decision: Jewish Rejuvenation in America.* New York: Bloch Publishing Company, 1958.

Lockman, Zachary. "Exclusion and Solidarity: Labor Zionism and Arab Workers in Palestine, 1897–1929." In *After Colonialism: Imperial Histories and Postcolonial Displacements*, ed. Gyan Prakash. Princeton: Princeton UP, 1995.

Longfellow, Henry Wadsworth. *The Complete Writings of Henry Wadsworth Longfellow.* 11 vols. Boston: Houghton Mifflin, 1904.

Lott, Eric. "The New Cosmopolitanism." *Transition* 72. Winter 1996.

Lyons, Joseph. "In Two Divided Streams." *Midstream.* Autumn 1961: 78–85.

Malin, Irving, ed. *Contemporary American-Jewish Literature: Critical Essays.* Bloomington: Indiana UP, 1973.

Mann, Vivian B., Thomas F. Glick, and Jerilynn D. Dodds, eds. *Convivencia: Jews, Muslims, and Christians in Medieval Spain.* New York: George Braziller, 1992.

Marcus, Jacob Rader. "Zionism and the American Jew." *The American Scholar* 2. May 1933.

Margalit, Avishai. "The Kitsch of Israel." *The New York Review of Books.* November 24, 1988.

Marmari, Hanoch. "Life After Zionism." *The Jerusalem Report.* February 8, 1976.

Martin, Biddy, and Chandra Talpade Mohanty. "Feminist Politics: What's Home Got to Do with It?" In *Feminist Studies/Critical Studies*, ed. Teresa de Lauretis. Bloomington: Indiana UP, 1986.

Martone, John. "On Charles Reznikoff and 'Talking Hebrew in Every Language Under the Sun.'" *Sagetrieb* 7. Fall 1988.

Matza, Diane. "Heritage as Detail and Design in Sephardi American Poetry." Pp. 306–319 in *Jewish American Poetry: Poems, Commentary, and Reflections*, ed. Jonathan N. Barron and Eric Murphy Selinger. Hanover, N.H.: Brandeis UP, 2000.

Melnick, Ralph. *The Life and Work of Ludwig Lewisohn.* Vol. 1. Detroit: Wayne State UP, 1998.

Meltzer, Milton. *A History of Jewish Life from Eastern Europe to America.* London: Jason Aronson, Inc., 1996.

Menand, Louis. "The Irony and the Ecstasy." *The New Yorker.* May 19, 1997: 88–94.

Merriam, Eve. *Emma Lazarus: Woman with a Torch.* New York: Citadel Press, 1956.

Meyer, Michael A. *Jewish Identity in the Modern World.* Seattle: U of Washington P, 1990.

Meyer, Susan. "'Safely to their Own Borders': Proto-Zionism, Feminism, and Nationalism in *Daniel Deronda. ELH* 60. 1993: 733–58.

Michaels, Walter Benn. *Our America: Nativism, Modernism, and Pluralism.* Durham: Duke UP, 1995.

Milbauer, Asher Z., and Donald G. Watson. *Reading Philip Roth.* London: Macmillan, 1988.

Miron, Dan. *The Images of Shtetl and Other Studies of Modern Jewish Literary Imagination.* Syracuse, N.Y.: Syracuse UP, 2000.

Modder, Montagu Frank. *The Jew in the Literature of England.* Philadelphia: The Jewish Publication Society of America, 1939.

Moore, Lorrie. "The Wrath of Athena." *The New York Times Book Review.* May 7, 2000: 7.

Mosse, George L. *Confronting the Nation: Jewish and Western Nationalism.* Hanover, N.H.: Brandeis UP, 1993.

Neusner, Jacob. *The Jewish War Against the Jews: Reflections on Golah, Shoah, and Torah.* New York: Ktav Publishing, 1984.

———. *The Way of Torah: An Introduction to Judaism.* 4th ed. Belmont, Calif.: Wadsworth Publishing, 1988.

Noah, Mordechai. *The Selected Writings of Mordechai Noah.* Ed. Michael Schuldiner and Daniel J. Kleinfeld. Westport, Conn.: Greenwood Press, 1999.

Norich, Anita. "'*Harbe sugyes*/Puzzling Questions' in Yiddish and English Culture in America during the Holocaust." *Jewish Social Studies* 5.1/2. Fall 1998/Winter 1999.

Nyburg, Sidney L. *The Chosen People.* Philadephia: J. B. Lippincott Company, 1917.

Olan, Levi A. *Felix Adler: Critic of Judaism and Founder of a Movement.* New York: Union of American Hebrew Congregations, 1951.

Oliphant, Laurence. *The Land of Gilead: With Excursions in the Lebanon.* New York: n.p., 1880.

Omer, Ranen. "The Stranger in the Metropolis: Urban Identities in the Poetry of Charles Reznikoff." *Shofar: An Interdisciplinary Journal of Jewish Studies.* Fall 1997.

Ozick, Cynthia. *Art and Ardor.* New York: Knopf, 1983.

Paley, Grace. *The Little Disturbances of Man.* New York: Viking Press, 1959.

Pauli, Hertha. "The Statue of Liberty Finds Its Poet." *Commentary.* November 1945.

Peel, J. D. Y. *Herbert Spencer on Social Evolution.* Chicago: U of Chicago P, 1972.

Pessen, Edward. *Riches, Class, and Power Before the Civil War.* Lexington: Basic Books, 1973.

Plesur, Milton. "The American Press and Jewish Restoration during the Nineteenth Century." Pp. 55–76 in *Early History of Zionism in America,* ed. Isidore S. Meyer. New York: Arno Press, 1977.

Podhoretz, Norman. "Hannah Arendt on Eichmann: A Study in the Perversity of Brilliance." *Commentary* 36.3. September 1963.

——. "On Being a Jew." *Commentary.* October 1989.

Prell, Riv-Ellen. "Cinderellas Who (Almost) Never Become Princesses: Subversive Representations of Jewish Women in Postwar Popular Novels." Pp. 123–38 in *Talking Back: Images of Jewish Women in American Popular Culture,* ed. Joyce Antler. Hanover, N.H.: UP of New England, 1998.

——. "Rage and Representation: Jewish Gender Stereotypes in American Culture." Pp. 248–68 in *Uncertain Terms: Negotiating Gender in American Culture,* ed. Faye Ginsburg and Anna Lowenhaupt Tsing. Boston: Beacon, 1990.

Quartermain, Peter. *Disjunctive Poetics: From Gertrude Stein and Louis Zukofsky to Susan Howe.* Cambridge: Cambridge UP, 1992.

Radhakrishnan, R. "Ethnicity In An Age of Diaspora." *Transition* 54. Winter 1991.

Ragussis, Michael. *Figures of Conversion: "The Jewish Question" and English National Identity.* Durham: Duke UP, 1995.

Raider, Mark. *The Emergence of American Zionism.* New York: New York UP, 1998.

Ram, Uri. "Zionist Historiography and the Invention of Modern Jewish Nationhood: The Case of Ben Zion Dinur." *History and Memory* 7.1. Spring/Summer 1995.

Reinharz, Jehuda, and Anita Shapira, eds. *Essential Papers on Zionism.* New York: New York UP, 1996.

Reznikoff, Charles. *By the Waters of Manhattan.* New York: Charles Boni, 1930.

——. *Family Chronicle.* Princeton, N.J.: Markus Weiner Publishers, 1988.

——. *Holocaust.* Santa Barbara: Black Sparrow Press, 1976.

——. "Inteview with Reinhold Schiffer: The Poet in His Milieu." In *Charles Reznikoff: Man and Poet,* ed. Milton Hindus. Orono, Maine: National Poetry Foundation, 1984.

——. *The Lionhearted.* Philadelphia: The Jewish Publication Society of America, 1944.

——. *Nine Plays.* Privately printed: 1927.

——. *Poems 1918–1975: The Complete Poems of Charles Reznikoff.* Ed. Seamus Cooney. 2 vols. Santa Rosa: Black Sparrow Press, 1977.

——. *Selected Letters of Charles Reznikoff 1917–1976.* Ed. Milton Hindus. Santa Rosa: Black Sparrow Press, 1997.

——. *Testimony: The United States 1885–1915.* Santa Barbara, Calif.: Black Sparrow Press, 1979.

Robinson, Edward. *Biblical Researches in Palestine, Mount Sinai and Arab Petraea.* Vol. I. Boston: Crocker and Brewster, 1841.

Roiphe, Anne. "Love without a Checkbook." *The Jerusalem Report.* October 16, 1997: 63.

Rorty, Richard. *Contingency, Irony and Solidarity.* Cambridge: Cambridge UP, 1989.

Rosenzweig, Franz. *The Star of Redemption.* Trans. William H. Hallo. Notre Dame: Notre Dame UP, 1985.

Roskies, David. *Against the Apocalypse: Responses to Catastrophe in Modern Jewish Culture.* Cambridge, Mass.: Harvard UP, 1984.

Rossel, Seymour. *The Holocaust: The World and the Jews, 1933–1945.* West Orange, N.J.: Behrman House, 1992.

Rotenstreich, Nathan. "Gershom Scholem's Conception of Jewish Nationalism." In *Gershom Scholem: The Man and His Work,* ed. Paul Mendes-Flohr. Albany: State U of New York P, 1994.

Roth, Cecil. "Paradoxes of Jewish History." *Menorah Journal.* October 1930: 17–26. Originally delivered as the Inaugural Lecture of the Menorah Summer School on July 7, 1930.

Roth, Henry. *Call It Sleep.* New York: Avon Books, 1965.

Roth, Philip. *American Pastoral.* Boston: Houghton Mifflin Company, 1997.

——. *The Anatomy Lesson.* New York: Vintage Books, 1996.

——. *The Counterlife.* New York: Farrar, Straus & Giroux, 1987.

——. *The Facts: A Novelist's Autobiography.* New York: Vintage International, 1988.

——. *The Ghost Writer.* New York: Vintage Books, 1995.

——. *Goodbye Columbus.* Boston: Houghton Mifflin Company, 1959.

——. "Goodbye, Nathan Zuckerman." *Time.* November 7, 1983: 89.

——. *The Human Stain.* Boston: Houghton Mifflin Company, 2000.

——. Interview with Charles McGrath. *The New York Times Book Review.* May 7, 2000: 8.

——. "The Jewish Intellectual and American Jewish Identity." In *Great Jewish Speeches Throughout History.* Ed. Steve Israel. Northvale, N.J.: Jason Aronson, 1994.

——. "A Bit of Jewish Mischief." *The New York Times Book Review.* March 7, 1993: 1, 20.

——. "Jewishness and the Younger Intellectuals: A Symposium." *Commentary* 31. April 1961: 306–59.

——. *Operation Shylock.* New York: Vintage Books, 1993.

———. *Patrimony: A True Story*. New York: Simon and Schuster, 1991.

———. *Portnoy's Complaint*. New York: Random House, 1969.

———. *The Prague Orgy*. New York: Vintage Books, 1996.

———. *Reading Myself and Others*. New York: Farrar, Straus and Giroux, 1975.

———. *Sabbath's Theater*. Boston: Houghton Mifflin Company, 1995.

Rothenberg, Jerome. "Commentary on 'Nokh Aushvitz' (After Aushwitz)." In *Jewish American Poetry: Poems, Commentary, and Reflections*, ed. Jonathan N. Barron and Eric Murphy Selinger. Hanover, N.H.: Brandeis UP, 2000.

Rovner, Ruth. "Charles Reznikoff—A Profile." *Jewish Frontier*. April 1976.

Rubin, Barry. *Assimilation and Its Discontents*. New York: Times Books, 1995.

Rubin, Daniel, ed. *Anti-Semitism and Zionism: Selected Marxist Writings*. New York: International Publishers, 1987.

Rubin, Steven, J. "Poets of the Promised Land: 1880–1920." In *Jewish American Poetry: Poems, Commentary, and Reflections*, ed. Jonathan N. Barron and Eric Murphy Selinger. Hanover, N.H.: Brandeis UP, 2000.

Rusk, Ralph. *Letters to Emma Lazarus in the Columbia University Library*. New York: Columbia UP, 1939.

Sachar, Howard M. *A History of Israel from the Rise of Zionism to Our Time*. Rev. ed. New York: Knopf, 1996.

———. *A History of the Jews in America*. New York: Alfred A. Knopf, 1992.

Sacks, Jonathan. "Love, Hate, and Jewish Identity." *First Things* 77. November 1997: 26–31.

Said, Edward. *Orientalism*. New York: Pantheon Books, 1978.

———. "Reflections of Exile." *Granta* 13.

Samuel, Maurice. "The Tribune of the Golus." *Jewish Book Annual* 25. 1967–68.

Sarna, Jonathan D. "The Israel of American Jews." *Sh'ma*. September 30, 1994.

Satlof, Claire R. "History, Fiction and the Tradition: Creating a Jewish Feminist Poetic." In *On Being a Jewish Feminist: A Reader*, ed. Susannah Heschel. New York: Schocken Books, 1983.

Schappes, Morris, ed. *Letters of Emma Lazarus*. New York: New York Public Library, 1949.

Schneider, Gertrude. *Mordechai Gebirtig: His Poetic and Musical Legacy*. London: Praeger, 2000.

Scholem, Gershom. "Portnoy's Complaint." Trans. E. E. Siskin. *CCAR* (Central Conference of American Rabbis). June 1970: 56–58.

Searles, George J. *Conversations with Philip Roth*. Jackson: UP of Mississippi, 1992.

Segev, Tom. *The Seventh Million: The Israelis and the Holocaust*. Trans. Haim Watzman. New York: Hill and Wang, 1933.

Seidman, Naomi. *A Marriage Made in Heaven: The Sexual Politics of Hebrew and Yiddish*. Berkeley: U of California P, 1997.

Selzer, Michael, ed. *Zionism Reconsidered: The Rejection of Jewish Normalcy*. London: Macmillan, 1970.

Shandler, Jeffrey, and Beth S. Wenger. "'The Site of Paradise': The Holy Land in American Jewish Imagination." Pp. 10–40 in *Encounters with the Holy Land: Place, Past and Future in American Jewish Culture*, ed. Jeffrey Shandler and Beth S. Wenger. Hanover, N.H.: Brandeis UP, 1997.

Shapiro, Alan. "Commentary." Pp. 152–54 in *Jewish American Poetry: Poems, Commentary and Reflections*, ed. Jonathan N. Barron and Eric Murphy Selinger. Hanover, N.H.: Brandeis UP, 2000.

Shavit, Yaacov. *Athens in Jerusalem: Classical Antiquity and Hellenism in the Making of the Modern Secular Jew*. Trans. Chaya Naor and Niki Werner. London: Vallentine Mitchell and Co., 1997.

Shechner, Mark. "Dear Mr Einstein: Jewish Comedy and the Contradictions of Culture." Pp. 141–58 in *Jewish Wry: Essays on Jewish Humor*, ed. Sarah Blacher Cohen. Bloomington: Indiana UP, 1987.

Shimoni, Gideon. *The Zionist Ideology*. Hanover, N.H.: UP of New England, 1995.

Shostak, Debra. "Roth/CounterRoth: Postmodernism, the Masculine Subject, and *Sabbath's Theater*." *Arizona Quarterly* 54.3. Autumn 1998: 119–140.

——. "'This Obsessive Reinvention of the Real': Speculative Narrative in Philip Roth's *The Counterlife*." *Modern Fiction Studies* 37.2. Summer 1991: 197–215.

Shreiber, Maeera. "The End of Exile: Jewish Identity and Its Diasporic Poetics." *PMLA* 113.2. March 1998.

——. "'Jewish Trouble' and the Trouble With Poetry." Unpublished essay, 1998.

Shuster, Zacharia. "Letters from Abroad: Tel-Aviv: Progress and Problems in Palestine." *The Menorah Journal* 20.2. Summer 1932.

Silberschlag, Eisig. "Zionism and Hebraism in America." In *Early History of Zionism in America*, ed. Isidore S. Meyer. New York: American Jewish Historical Society, 1958.

Silberstein, Laurence J. *The Postzionism Debates: Knowledge and Power in Israeli Culture*. Routledge: New York, 1999.

Simon, Uriel. *Reading Prophetic Narratives*. Trans. Lenn J. Schramm. Bloomington: Indiana UP, 1997.

Sleeper, James A. "Authenticity and Responsiveness in Jewish Education." In *The New Jews*, ed. James A. Sleeper and Alan L. Mintz. New York: Vintage Books, 1971.

Smith, George Adam. *The Historical Geography of the Holy Land*. London: Hodder and Stoughton, 1894.

Sobol, Yehoshua, and Orly Castel-Bloom. "Writing the Jewish Future." Public lecture given at the National Foundation for Jewish Culture Conference, San Francisco, February 2, 1998.

Solotaroff, Ted. "Marginality Revisited." In *The Writer in the Jewish Community: An Israeli–North American Dialogue*, ed. Richard Siegel and Tamar Sofer. London: Associated UP, 1993.

Sorin, Gerald. *A Time for Building: The Third Migration, 1880–1920.* Baltimore: Johns Hopkins UP, 1992.

Starr, Joyce R. *Kissing through Glass: The Invisible Shield Between Americans and Israelis.* Chicago: Contemporary Books, 1990.

Stein, Leonard. *The Balfour Declaration.* New York: Simon and Schuster, 1961.

Steiner, George. "Our Homeland, the Text." *Salmagundi* 66. Winter/Spring 1985.

Stevenson, Anne. "Charles Reznikoff in His Tradition." *Charles Reznikoff: Man and Poet*, ed. Milton Hindus. Orono, Maine: National Poetry Foundation, 1984.

Stollman, Aryeh Lev. *The Far Euphrates.* New York: Riverhead Books, 1997.

Susser, Bernard, and Charles S. Liebman. *Choosing Survival: Strategies for a Jewish Future.* New York: Oxford UP, 1999.

Swann, Brian. "George Eliot's Ecumenical Jew, or, the Novel as Outdoor Temple." *Novel.* Fall 1974.

Syrkin, Marie. "American Jews and Israel: A Symposium." *Commentary* 85.2. February 1988.

———. *Blessed Is the Match.* Philadelphia: Jewish Publication Society, 1947.

———. "Charles: A Memoir." In *Charles Reznikoff: Man and Poet*, ed. Milton Hindus. Orono, Maine: National Poetry Foundation, 1984: 37–67.

———. "The Crack in the Gilded Ghetto." *Jewish Frontier.* January 1972.

———. "The Cultural Scene: Literary Expression." In *The American Jew: A Composite Portrait*, ed. Oscar Janowsky. New York: Harper, 1942.

———. "The Essence of Revisionism: An Analysis of a Fascist Tendency in Jewry." *Jewish Frontier.* April 1940.

———. "The Fun of Self-Abuse." *Midstream.* April 1969: 64–68.

———. *Golda Meir: Israel's Leader.* Philadelphia: Jewish Publication Society, 1969.

———. *Gleanings: A Diary in Verse.* Santa Barbara: Rhythms Press, 1979.

———. "How Not to Solve 'The Jewish Problem.'" *Common-Ground* 2.2. Autumn 1941.

———. "Jewish Awareness in American Literature." In *The American Jew: A Reappraisal*, ed. Oscar I. Janowsky. Philadelphia: The Jewish Publication Society of America, 1964.

———. "Marie Syrkin and Trude Weiss-Rosmarin: A *Moment* Interview." *Moment.* September 1983. Reprinted in Leonard Fine, ed., *Jewish Possibilities: The Best of Moment Magazine.* Northvale, N.J.: Jason Aronson, 1987.

———. "Miss Arendt Surveys the Holocaust." *Jewish Frontier.* May 1963. Reprinted in *Jewish Frontier Anthology 1945–1967.* New York: Jewish Frontier Association, 1967.

———. "The Moscow Trials," *Jewish Frontier.* May 1937.

———. *Nachman Syrkin: Socialist Zionist, A Biographical Memoir and Selected Essays.* New York: Herzl Press, 1961.

———. "'Phony Israel': An Exercise in Nastiness." In *With Friends Like These: The Jewish Critics of Israel*, ed. Edward Alexander. New York: Shapolsky, 1993.

———. *The State of the Jews*. Washington, D.C.: New Republic Books, 1980.

———, ed. *Hayim Greenberg Anthology*. Detroit: Wayne State UP, 1968.

———, ed. *A Land of Our Own: An Oral Autobiography by Golda Meir*. New York: G. P. Putnam's Sons, 1973.

Syrkin, Nachman. "The Jewish Problem and the Socialist-Jewish State." In Arthur Hertzberg, *The Zionist Idea: A Historical Analysis and Reader*. New York: Atheneum, 1973.

———. "Min hachutzah ha'ohelah" (From the Outside into the Tent). In *Kitvei N. Syrkin* (N. Syrkin's Writings), ed. B. Katznelson and I. Kaufman. Tel Aviv: Ben Zui Institute, 1939.

Taylor, H. O. *The Medieval Mind: A History of the Development of Thought and Emotions in the Middle Ages*. Cambridge, Mass.: Harvard UP, 1959.

Teller, Judd L. "America's Two Zionist Traditions." *Commentary* 20.4. October 1955: 343–52.

Toynbee, Arnold Joseph. *A Study of History: Abridgement of Volumes VII–X*. Oxford, UK: Oxford UP, 1987.

Tuchman, Barbara. *Bible and Sword*. New York: New York UP, 1956.

Twain, Mark. *The Innocents Abroad*. 2 vols. Hartford, Conn.: American Publishing, 1869.

Updike, John. "Recruiting Raw Nerves." In John Updike, *More Matter: Essays and Criticism*. New York: Alfred A. Knopf, 1999.

Umansky, Ellen M., and Dianne Ashton, eds. *Four Centuries of Jewish Women's Spirituality: A Sourcebook*. Boston: Beacon Press, 1992.

Urofsky, Melvin. *We Are One*. Garden City, N.Y.: Anchor, 1978.

Vaughan, Leslie J. "Cosmopolitanism, Ethnicity and American Identity: Randolph Bourne's 'Trans-National America.'" *Journal of American Studies* 25.3. 1991.

Veblen, Thorstein. "The Intellectual Pre-eminence of Jews in Modern Europe." *Political Science Quarterly* 34.1. 1919. Reprinted in Max Lerner, ed., *The Portable Veblen*. New York: Viking Press, 1948.

Vidal-Naquet, Pierre. *The Jews: History, Memory, and the Present*. Trans. David Ames Curtis. New York: Columbia UP, 1996.

Vogel, Dan. *Emma Lazarus*. Boston: Twayne Publishers, 1980.

Vogel, Lester I. *To See a Promised Land: Americans and the Holy Land in the Nineteenth Century*. Pennsylvania: Pennsylvania State UP, 1993.

Wagenknecht, Edward. *Daughers of the Covenant: Portraits of Six Jewish Women*. Amherst: U of Massachusetts P, 1983.

Walzer, Michael. *Exodus and Revolution*. New York: Basic Books, 1985.

Wasserstein, Bernard. *Vanishing Diaspora: The Jews in Europe since 1945*. Cambridge, Mass.: Harvard UP, 1996.

Weinberger, Eliot. "Another Memory of Charles Reznikoff." Pp. 105–6 in *Charles*

Reznikoff: Man and Poet, ed. Milton Hindus. Orono, Maine: National Poetry Foundation, 1984.

Weingartner, Fannia, ed. *Felix Adler and Ethical Culture: Memories and Studies*. New York: Columbia UP, 1981.

Weinreich, Max. "The Reality of Jewishness versus the Ghetto Myth: The Sociolinguistic Roots of Yiddish." In *To Honor Roman Jakobson*. Vol. 3. The Hague: Mouton, 1967.

Weisman, Ze'ev. *Political Satire in the Bible*. Atlanta: Scholar's Press, 1998.

Weiss, Richard. *The American Myth of Success: From Horatio Alger to Norman Vincent Peale*. New York: Basic Books, 1969.

Wheatcroft, Geoffrey. *The Controversy of Zion: Jewish Nationalism, the Jewish State, and the Unresolved Jewish Dilemma*. New York: Addison-Wesley, 1996.

Whitfield, Stephen J. *In Search of American Jewish Culture*. Hanover, N.H.: Brandeis UP, 1999.

Whitman, Walt. *Leaves of Grass: Comprehensive Reader's Edition*. Ed. Harold W. Blodgett and Sculley Bradley. New York: New York UP, 1965.

Wieseltier, Leon. "When a Sage Dies, All Are His Kin." *The New Republic*. December 1, 1997.

Wirth-Nesher, Hana. "From Newark to Prague: Roth's Place in the American Jewish Literary Tradition." Pp. 216–29 in *What is Jewish Literature*, ed. Hana Wirth-Nesher. Philadelphia: The Jewish Publication Society of America, 1994.

Wisse, Ruth R. *If I Am Not for Myself: The Liberal Betrayal of the Jews*. New York: Free Press, 1992.

———. "The Jewish Writer and the Problem of Evil." In *Terms of Survival: The Jewish World Since 1945*, ed. Robert S. Wistrich. New York: Routledge, 1995.

———. *The Modern Jewish Canon: A Journey Through Language and Culture*. New York: Free Press, 2000.

———. *The Schlemiel as Modern Hero*. Chicago: U of Chicago P, 1971.

———. "Sex, Love and Death." *Commentary*. December 1995: 65.

Witenko, Barbara. *Feminist Ritual as a Proccess of Social Transformation*. Ph.D. dissertation, New York University, 1992.

Wolosky, Shira. "An American-Jewish Typology: Emma Lazarus and the Figure of Christ." *Prooftexts* 16.1. January 1996.

Wouk, Herman. *Marjorie Morningstar*. Boston: Little, Brown, 1955.

Yaffe, James. *The American Jews: Portrait of a Split Personality*. New York: Random House, 1968.

Yerushalmi, Yosef Hayim. *Zakhor: Jewish History and Jewish Memory*. Seattle: U of Washington P, 1982.

Yezierska, Anzia. *How I Found America: Collected Stories of Anzia Yezierska*. New York: Persea Books, 1991.

Young, Bette Roth. *Emma Lazarus in Her World: Life and Letters*. Jerusalem: Jewish Publication Society, 1995.

Zeiger, Arthur. "Emma Lazarus and Pre-Herzlian Zionism." Pp. 77–109 in *Early History of Zionism in America*, ed. Isidore S. Meyer. New York: American Jewish Historical Society, 1958.

Zerubavel, Yael. *Recovered Roots: Collective Memory and the Making of Israeli National Tradition*. Chicago: U of Chicago P, 1995.

Zierler, Wendy. "The Making and Re-making of Jewish-American Literary History." Unpublished essay, 1998.

Index